REGULATION AND COMPETITION IN AIR TRANSPORTATION

REGULATION and COMPETITION in AIR TRANSPORTATION

by SAMUEL B. RICHMOND

New York and London

COLUMBIA UNIVERSITY PRESS 1961

To Evelyn

LIBRARY OF CONGRESS CATALOG CARD NUMBER: 61-10981
MANUFACTURED IN THE UNITED STATES OF AMERICA

Preface

. . . economic regulation alone cannot be relied on to take the place of the stimulus which competition provides . . . in air transportation. . . . Further development of the industry demands the encouragement of free initiative and enterprise subject only to the condition that the competitive services shall not be wasteful. Civil Aeronautics Board, *Colonial Air, et al., Atlantic Seaboard Op.* 4 CAB 552, 555.

Thus spoke the Civil Aeronautics Board in 1944. Competition in air transportation is desirable, but, on the other hand, there should not be too much.

This brief quotation poses the basic problem which inspired this study and which has concerned the air transportation industry since the passage of the Civil Aeronautics Act in 1938, and for the preceding decade and a half—ever since man realized that the airplane offered possibilities for commerce as well as for adventure. How should this proper amount of competition be ascertained and realized?

We speak of competition, but what is competition? What is the proper amount of competition? Which should be the competing carriers? Can competition and regulatory policing be substituted for one another? How can regulation and competition be blended? And in what proportions? What control mechanisms or courses of action are available to the Civil Aeronautics Board for its regulation of competition? What has the Board tried to do? Has it accomplished its ends? These are some of the problems which have been considered in this study and on which, hopefully, at least some light has been shed.

This study started in the Autumn of 1956 as a one-year project. The project grew and its time schedule was continually revised as each of the problems it considered expanded under analysis. This volume should be regarded as Volume I of a continuing study.

An earlier publication ("Creating Competition," *Journal of Air Law and Commerce,* Autumn, 1957) introduced and described some of the statistical considerations, The present volume covers in detail much of the legal, economic, and historical analysis involved in treating these questions.

The next efforts will be directed toward an analysis of the decision problem of the Civil Aeronautics Board. Our purpose will be to assess and combine as many as possible of the goals of the Civil Aeronautics Act (now the Federal Aviation Act) into an analytical system, or model, based on rational and objective criteria. This may well be beyond our abilities, but hope springs eternal, and work on it has already begun.

In this volume, readers may note that several ideas and, indeed, some of the quotations may be found at more than one place in the book. There are two reasons for this. First, many of the Civil Aeronautics Board's statements find relevance with respect to more than one of the concepts which are treated separately here, and therefore they require repetition. Second, and more important, I considered a certain amount of repetition desirable in order to make each chapter self-sufficient, or nearly so, and to make each suitable for readers with varying degrees of familiarity with the background materials.

This study was started under and financed by a grant from the Faculty Research Fund of the Graduate School of Business, Columbia University. For their generosity, consideration, and patience, I thank Dean Courtney C. Brown, Associate Dean Clarence C. Walton and Professor Roger F. Murray. The latter two gentlemen, as successive Associate Deans during the period of this study, had, in turn, the responsibility, under Dean Brown, for the administration of the study grant.

I owe a large debt to Mr. James C. Buckley who first brought me into this exciting area of economics of air transportation. I am indebted also to Mr. Edward A. MacNeal and the late Dr. Wilfred Carsel for the intellectual stimulation and analytical skills which they brought to our common efforts in air transportation analyses.

The computations, tabulations, and other machine operations

were performed primarily at the Watson Scientific Computing Laboratory at Columbia University. During the Sabbatical year, which I spent in the Operations Research Group at Case Institute of Technology, I was given the use of the facilities of the Case Computing Center. My indebtedness to both of these organizations is great.

Throughout the study I had the good fortune to have as research assistant and later, as consultant, my friend, Mr. William A. Jordan. His creative thinking, high standards, and untiring devotion were important sources of support at every stage of the study.

It am deeply indebted to Examiner Paul N. Pfeiffer of the Civil Aeronautics Board, who was ever patient with my endless requests for data and more data, and who, in the late stages of the study, read the entire manuscript and made valuable suggestions. His discerning insights and long experience were most helpful and reassuring.

Many persons contributed at various stages of the project. Mr. Leonard Rubin, as research assistant, spent many hours in conscientious application of his keen analytical and legal abilities. There were several charming airline reservation agents, who, under Mr. Jordan's direction, performed much of the tedious schedule analysis. I am indebted to my daughter Phyllis for her assistance in proof reading. Most important, for her support and assistance throughout the entire project, I owe boundless gratitude to Evelyn, my wife.

Others, too numerous to name, have assisted in various capacities and my gratiude to them is no less for having omitted listing them by name.

All of the data in the book have been checked and rechecked in order to reduce the probability of errors in the final result. However, for whatever shortcomings remain, the responsibility is solely mine.

S.B.R.

Englewood, New Jersey
April, 1961

Contents

CHAPTER I

Introduction and Early History

INTRODUCTION

The airline industry in the United States, although consisting of a group of independent business enterprises financed by private capital and managed by private businessmen, has throughout its entire history been intimately influenced by the federal government. In the economic sphere, the government has, via its support of the air carriers in their infancy and later via direct actions, regulated the rate of growth and the pattern of development of the industry. The economic history of the development of the airline industry in the United States is in one sense the history of pioneering adventurers and intrepid entrepreneurs; but, in another sense, it is the history of a series of actions of the government of the United States. These actions have been those of both the Congress as the original source of power and of the various agencies, such as the Post Office and the Civil Aeronautics Board, acting under powers delegated to them by the Congress.

The government of the United States, as many of the governments of the world, has seen fit to encourage and bolster the development of the air transportation industry by providing appropriate legislation, by offering needed services to that industry, and by outright financial subsidy. On the other hand, in contrast with the situation in many other nations, the airline industry in the United States is not government owned, nor does it enjoy monopoly status; rather, it consists of privately owned—often competing—firms. However, it is a regulated industry, subject to various sorts of economic regulation intended to protect and to serve the public interest. Although many American industries are similarly regulated, the airline industry has its own peculiar characteristics which differentiate it from the other regulated transportation and public utility industries. These characteristics, both economic and noneconomic, influence the specific forms and objectives of its economic regulation.

The Civil Aeronautics Act of 1938, as incorporated in the Federal Aviation Act of 1958, the law under which the industry is at present operating, states that the Civil Aeronautics Board (formerly called the Civil Aeronautics Authority), which is the regulatory body created by the Act in order to carry out its policies,

> . . . shall consider the following, among other things, as being in the public interest and in accordance with the public convenience and necessity— . . . .
>
> Competition to the extent necessary to assure the sound development of an air-transportation system properly adapted to the needs of the foreign and domestic commerce of the United States, of the Postal Service, and of the national defense.[1]

Thus, the framers of the Act perceived in competition a mechanism whereby these three sometimes conflicting objectives—commerce, the postal service, and the national defense—might be served. Conversely, it is because of the close relationship and possible conflicts between the development of a privately owned air transportation system and these noneconomic factors, which might be referred to collectively as representing the "national interest," that many of the nations of the world have not permitted competition to exist among airlines, but have preferred to foster the growth of a single air carrier system. The domestic air transportation system of the United States, because of the national tradition of private enterprise and because of the personal characteristics of the framers of the 1938 Act, has progressed in its unique way. The system which has emerged, and which is still developing under the Act, is one of "regulated competition," under which, in continental United States (excluding Alaska), a dozen "trunk" airlines, a comparable number of "local" airlines, three helicopter and two all cargo carriers [2] serve specific routes, many of which are assigned to more than one airline so that competition for traffic and profits may exist among the air carriers involved. Indeed, in the United States, both in the Act and in fact, competition has been regarded as a supplement to and as a tool of regulation.

The Civil Aeronautics Board, in the performance of its regulatory functions, has always been faced with the problem of determining just what does constitute the "competition" envisioned by the Act, and further, of defining the amount of competition which constitutes the "extent necessary" referred to in the Act. This creation and regulation of competition has been a continuing process, requiring a large amount of time and effort on the part of the Board and its staff as the industry has developed. As traffic increased and routes prospered, the individual airlines sought to expand their routes, both by serving new, previously unserved routes and by entering as competitors into the heavily travelled routes of other carriers. At the same time the original airline or airlines on those routes sought to prevent the entrance of competitors. It has been a common spectacle at Civil Aeronautics Board proceedings to see two airlines, each trying to enter the other's lucrative markets, yet each jealously seeking to maintain the monopoly of its own routes by keeping the other out. In such route proceedings, in which large areas and heavily travelled routes are discussed, a major portion of the industry may become involved, in company with federal agencies, state and local governments, and local organizations such as Chambers of Commerce. These proceedings typically become complex and costly, and they may require as long as two or more years before the emergence of a final decision. In any event, such proceedings have often resulted in a decision by the Board to increase the route systems of at least some of the carriers involved, and selected carriers have been authorized to operate over routes already served by other carriers. It it with the competitive aspects and problems of the routes granted domestic trunk airlines that this study is primarily concerned.

Before considering these problems in detail we shall briefly examine airline competition and regulation before the passage of the Civil Aeronautics Act in 1938 and, in Chapter II, we shall investigate the characteristics and processes of the regulatory system which has developed since 1938.

AIRLINE ECONOMIC REGULATION BEFORE 1938

Such governmental economic regulation, influence, and support as existed in the early history of commercial air transportation in the United States was exercised via the several Air Mail Acts of 1925 through 1935. While these laws served their primary function of making air service available to the Post Office, they evoked certain unexpected and undesirable responses on the part of the various enterprises which were trying to establish themselves in this new industry. Among these responses were: "cutthroat" competition, cartel building, and governmental collusion.[3]

The Kelly Act (Air Mail Act of 1925) in effect inaugurated commercial air transportation in the United States.[4] At that time, because of the high cost of service and the relative scarcity of passengers, regular passenger air service had not yet become economically feasible. The Army had been carrying the mail since 1918 when the first airmail service was started. The Kelly Act, which was designed to transfer this airmail operation to private firms, authorized the Post Office Department to contract for the carriage of mail by air. Since the nonmail traffic could not, in these early days, support private air carriers, the postal service, in order to have available to it any transport of mail by private air carriers, had to provide the income necessary to sustain these carriers. Thus the postal service, by its policies and procedures with respect to the letting of airmail contracts, to a great extent controlled the growth of, and, in effect, "regulated" the commercial air carriers.

The Kelly Act provided for short term contracts, assigned by competitive bidding, and it limited payments to carriers to 80 percent of the revenues of airmail postage sales. A disappointingly small carrier response led to the amendment of the Act one year later. This change authorized four-year contracts, assigned by competitive bidding, and it greatly increased the permissible amount of airmail payments, thereby subsidizing the carriers.

The postal service was, thus, the first major customer of the air carriers, and it has remained an important source of their revenue. Although, at the present time, the trunk carriers are not directly subsidized, in that the revenues received for carriage of airmail are determined on the basis of an estimate of the costs incurred in providing the airmail service, this is a relatively recent development. In the earlier days, airmail revenues constituted the mechanism whereby the commercial air carriers were enabled to come into being and to continue to exist economically. For the year 1959,

United States mail revenues constituted only 2.5 percent of the total revenue of the domestic trunk airlines.[5]

By 1927, all airmail routes were being flown by commercial rather than military aircraft. However, important problems stemmed from the fact that, since routes might be withdrawn after four years in favor of a lower bidder, it was still difficult for carriers to procure capital for expansion or even for consolidation of what had already been gained.

Under the McNary-Waters Act of 1930, rates, although still the result of competitive bidding, could be based on the space-mileage flown, rather than on the amount of mail carried over the route. This was of considerable promotional importance to the passenger transportation aspects of the industry since it made possible the use of larger aircraft with passenger capacity.

In the spring of 1930, the Postmaster General called a conference, the purpose of which was to coordinate old routes and form two new transcontinental routes between New York City and Los Angeles. At this and a subsequent series of meetings of the carriers held at the request of the Postmaster General, the carriers were told to decide among themselves which of them should get the various individual segments along the new routes. These so-called "spoils conferences" were clearly not consistent with a program of competitive bidding for routes.

By 1934, after a period in which the government found its mail costs rising for lack of bidders, and while the quality of service was not materially improved, the Special Senate Committee on Investigation of Air Mail and Ocean Mail Contracts found that three large combines or cartels were receiving 90 percent of all airmail payments. The United Aircraft and Transport Corporation (19 subsidiaries in all phases of aviation) received about one-third of all payments, the General Motors-North American complex controlled many aviation and nonaviation subsidiaries and received one-third of all payments, and the Aviation Corporation of Delaware and its 80 subsidiaries received about one-fourth of all payments.[6]

In February, 1934, because of their collusive and illegal aspects, all airmail contracts were cancelled by President Roosevelt. However, by this time, passenger and express revenues were sufficient to enable operations to continue, but at great loss to the airlines. The Army, although quite unprepared for this kind of operation, was assigned the task of flying the mail. The result of this precipitous action was a series of fatal crashes which led, in June, to the enactment of the Air Mail Act of 1934.

The Act of 1934 required that certain standards of conduct be complied with before an airmail contract could be granted. Airline independence was to be assured by the prohibiting of certain financial, corporate, and personal relationships among firms in the aviation field. Also, all persons involved in the earlier collusive proceedings were barred from managerial positions in bidding airlines. The Interstate Commerce Commission was empowered to fix rates and make contracts. Competitive bidding was retained and short term contracts were reinstituted.

The Air Mail Act of 1934 still allowed routes to be established freely by nonsubsidized airlines, since only those with mail contracts were regulated. If such a nonsubsidized carrier established a competitive route, this lowered the passenger and express revenues of the subsidized carrier and consequently damaged its financial position. Also, some of the subsidized airlines established off-line, uneconomical and supposedly unsubsidized routes. Since *anyone* could fly any route, these problems were widespread.

The Air Mail Act of 1935 prohibited off-line routes to any subsidized carrier if established in the territory of another subsidized carrier. The act also disallowed losses incurred on nonmail schedules and routes. Since it was difficult to maintain service without mail payments, this act deterred most airlines from expanding beyond their assigned routes.

This, then, was the situation which existed during the years 1935 to 1938. The airlines, still suspect for their past management practices, found it particularly difficult, in this depression period, to raise long term capital for the purchase of new aircraft and the construction of new facilities. Competition by the unsubsidized carriers continued to present a problem, and it was still possible to institute service on new routes without government approval.

The mail carriers were apprehensive of this potential competition, and, as a consequence, then, as now, they favored governmental control of entry into new routes. In the Congressional hearings in 1937, the head of the Air Transport Association referred to this freedom of entry as threatening

> unbridled and disastrous competition if we do not take heed. It leaves the small lines in a very precarious position. It requires some orderly procedure, preferably, I personally believe, the procedure of certificates of convenience and necessity already embodied in our Federal legislation as to railroads and interstate motor carriers.[7]

In 1956, after almost two decades under the Act of 1938, an executive of the Air Transport Association again indicated that the scheduled airline industry still viewed with alarm the kind of competition which was permitted before 1938 under the Air Mail Acts. Referring to the Civil Aeronautics Act of 1938, he said:

> Prior to the act, you had more mergers than you have ever had since the act was passed. Prior to the act you had insolvency and bankruptcy in the industry. As I recall, about half of the total investment in air transportation had gone down the drain—about $60 million of the $120 million which had been invested in the business.
>
> And the purpose of the act was to stop the unbridled competition which had been taking place up to that point, to regulate competition, to do it on the basis of certificates of public convenience and necessity.[8]

Two former chairmen of the Civil Aeronautics Board, Oswald Ryan and Ross Rizley, have also described the situation in 1938 as "chaotic" and have referred to the undesirable implications with respect to both economics and safety.

> At the time we took over in 1938 the airline industry was in a state which was characterized by the committees of Congress as chaotic. There was no security for airline investment. Almost all of the airlines were either on the edge or moving toward bankruptcy when we were sworn in in 1939. If you will read the reports of the committees to the Congress recommending the bill which became the Civil Aeronautics Act of 1938, you will see the reasons why the Congress took the action it did in adopting this act. They looked out upon this industry, saw this chaotic economic condition, and they said it was due in large part to excessive competition. And that was true, because at that time anybody could start an airline who could collect a few airplanes and personnel, and put that airline right in parallel competition with an existing airline on which capital and effort had been spent in order to establish it. There was no protection against such destructive competition on

routes that could not support it. The result was a number of crashes that took place, one killing a United States Senator, a man very much loved in the Senate at the time. That started an investigation. In the investigation they discovered that the safety in airline operation depended upon the carrier being in a sound economic condition; and when they recommended a bill to the Congress, they took those facts into consideration.[9]

Prior to the enactment of the Civil Aeronautics Act of 1938 conditions in the air transport industry could only be described as chaotic and the financial conditions of the companies engaging in air transportation as precarious.[10]

To be sure, there is some disagreement as to the actual conditions prevalent in the industry at that time. Senator O'Mahoney of Wyoming, in a memorandum submitted to the Senate Select Committee on Small Business,[11] in 1953, stated flatly,

> Although the Board in support of its restrictive policies has repeatedly relied on allegedly chaotic conditions in the industry at the time in seeking justification for the policies it has adopted, the record fails to disclose that such conditions existed.[12]

He developed this position at some length.[13]

In any event, the House Committee on Interstate and Foreign Commerce in its 1937 report recommending enactment of a Civil Aeronautics Act, stated that,

> The present air-transportation system has been developed at great expense both to the Government and private industry, to say nothing of the lives taken during this development. It is now seriously threatened by the initiation of unregulated airlines, unhampered by any duty to perform the governmental service of carrying mails and not covered by the present law. The Government cannot allow unrestrained competition by unregulated air carriers to capitalize on and jeopardize the investment which the Government has made during the past 10 years in the air-transport industry through the mail service and which was planned to permit and at present is permitting the Government to carry on its airmail service at constantly decreasing costs per unit.[14]

With respect to the regulation of the industry before the Civil Aeronautics Act of 1938, the Celler Committee in 1957 concluded that,

> From the administrative standpoint, the status of carrier control and regulation did not appear to be any more satisfactory. At least three Government agencies had responsibilities in civil aeronautics and there

was no provision for centralized authority. The Interstate Commerce Commission, to whom aviation was a totally new phenomenon was charged with fixing reasonable rates. The Department of Commerce, under the Air Commerce Act of 1926, still had control of the civil airways and the safety functions of the Government. Routes, to the extent they were subject to control through mail contracts, were the primary responsibility of the Postmaster General under the Airmail Act of 1934.[15]

These were the conditions which the Civil Aeronautics Act of 1938 sought to correct.

CHAPTER II

Regulation of the Domestic Airlines

THE NATURE OF REGULATION

The airline industry in the United States is a regulated industry in the "public utility" sense, and, in common with the other similarly regulated industries, is subject to regulation by an independent commission. In the case of the airlines industry, that commission is, of course, the Civil Aeronautics Board.

The regulatory commissions in the United States are appointive bodies charged with the administration of the law under which their respective regulated industry or industries operate. These commissions, which are created by the legislature, act as arms of the legislature and are authorized to exercise a wide range of discretion in their administration of the law. Their function is

> to interpret the general principles of the statute in the light of the requirements of the particular utility and community, to exercise continuing supervision over the operations of the companies subject to its jurisdiction, and to report to the legislature on the effectiveness of the existing controls and on the possibilities of improvement.[1]

Charged as it is with the administration of the airlines industry, the Civil Aeronautics Board, because of the unique characteristics of that industry and of the statute under which the Board and the industry operate, is faced with many problems which it does not share with other regulatory bodies operating in other regulated industries. On the other hand, the existance of a common form of regulation suggests that this industry must have certain general features in common with at least some of the other regulated industries.

The "regulated industries" are those industries to which the Congress of the United States or the individual state legislatures, or both, have decided to apply certain kinds of regulation. In the case of the states, this regulation has generally been based on the contention that the industry is "affected with a public interest," and that the regulation is the exercise of the police power of the government in protection of the public interest. In the case of the federal government, these activities are based on the congressional power to regulate interstate and international commerce. The regulated industries include the private gas, electric, sewage, and water services, the public transportation and other communications industries, insurance companies, banks, warehouses, slaughterhouses, and many others.

The wide variety of industries thus regulated has always challenged students of regulation to ascertain just what are the common characteristics which have caused these industries to become subject to the kind of governmental control they share. In the past, much reliance has been placed on the term "affected with a public interest," but this has not been fruitful since, although these industries are clearly of extreme importance to the public, there are many other industries which are of great public importance, but which are not regulated. Irston R. Barnes has suggested that,

> there [is] no essential or inherent difference between the public interest attaching to businesses subject to public utility regulation and the public interest attaching to other enterprises. The fundamental differences lie in the measures necessary to protect that public interest. . . . [P]ublic control of business is justified whenever the public interest is clearly discernable and the means of protecting that public interest are available.[2]

The purpose of the regulation, then, is to protect the public interest. Its purpose is not to protect the life or the earnings of specific firms in the regulated industry unless that protection be in the public interest. It is this distinction between the public interest and the interests of the regulated firms that has been the source of most of the criticism of regulatory bodies and, indeed, of the very system of regulation by independent commission. The charge is often made that the commissioners, because of their close professional and social relationship with the regulated industry, may become identified with the industry and become its defenders rather than its regulators.[3] The Celler Committee Report maintained that,

> Inasmuch as Federal regulatory legislation in general has developed to prevent unfair, abusive, and discriminatory practices in natural monopoly situations or from the atmosphere of desperation surrounding a general economic crisis in the competitive system, it is not surprising that the role of competition within the regulatory framework has been subordinated. The basic techniques of regulatory bodies are anti-competitive in nature. Once regulation has been imposed upon a given sector of the economy, freedom of entry is henceforth severely restricted, expansion restrained, consolidations encouraged, and anticompetitive agreements sanctioned by enforcement officials.[4]

On the other hand, it has been maintained that in the air transportation industry, because of the control (and, thus, limitation) of merger, regulation makes for more competition than would prevail in the absence of regulation. Mr. Warren Lee Pierson, Chairman of the Board of TWA, in testimony before a Senate committee in 1953, upheld this view, saying:

> I believe that there is more competition in the air-transportation system today than if it were completely unregulated.
>
> We have all observed the tendency toward centralization in major unregulated industries to the point where a handful of units dominate the entire field, and I am sure that in a completely unbridled competitive atmosphere, the air-transportation system would have undergone the same evolution. As a matter of fact, it has been stated by those who have made studies that the air-transport industry is one of the most intensely competitive in the United States today.[5]

The experience of the airlines of Alaska has often been cited in support of this position that regulation does in fact preserve competition, by preventing the devouring or destruction of the weak by the strong.

Through the subsequent years after 1946 the fares and rates of the nonscheduled carriers became competitive within themselves as they gradually sought to undercut one another. During this period such companies, known as Yakima Sky Chief, Lavery Air Service, Arctic Pacific, Trans Alaskan, Northern Airlines, Arnold Air Service, Pacific Alaska,

Golden Northern Airways, Arctic Frontier, and others, provided a nonscheduled service; but today, with the exception of a few, they are nonexistent in the States-Alaska market—not because of CAB orders to cease and desist but because of the uneconomic condition they found themselves in as a result of their own rate wars.[6]

The original nonscheduleds are largely out of that picture today. The ones who are in there are people with a better organization and better equipment, and who have been able to survive in the very rough struggle, which includes all nonscheduleds during those years.[7]

The argument reduces itself to a question which is easy to identify but difficult to answer. If unregulated competition does result in the emergence of only a few carriers—too few to offer the benefits of competition to the public—then what is the net long run effect of a regulatory mechanism which serves to lessen the force of this competition and which limits the competition to a level of intensity which may permit the survival of enough carriers to assure that at least some of the manifestations of competition will continue to exist in individual air transportation markets? It seems clear that, under these conditions, while in its early stages, the industry may be less competitive or less intensively competitive than it might be without regulation; the regulation, by thus limiting competition, assures the continued existence and the preservation of such competition as it does permit, or indeed, create.

THE RATIONALE FOR REGULATION OF THE AIRLINES

The specific rationale for regulation varies from one industry to another. One commonly cited reason is that a particular industry is a "natural monopoly"; that is, the industry should, in the public interest, be monopolistic, and then the purpose of the regulation would be to protect against the evils otherwise inherent in monopoly. A classic illustration of this is the telephone industry. Competition in the telephone industry would involve expensive duplication of poles, wires, switching equipment, and, possibly, the necessity for customers to subscribe to more than one noninterconnected telephone system in order to communicate with all telephone subscribers.

Industries which may thus be characterized as natural monopolies are few indeed. The transportation industries typically are not in this sense natural monopolies, except possibly for local transit companies on specific routes. Certainly it is not the case in the airlines industry.

What then is the economic basis for regulation and the associated restriction of competition as found in the airlines industry? Perhaps the general answer is that it is subject to control because it is feared that the operation or lack of operation of the unregulated competitive market forces may have adverse consequences for the public at large. The history of regulation in the airlines industry, and particularly the conditions in that industry in the years prior to the Civil Aeronautics Act, has indicated that economic regulation of some sort is desirable; and that the regulation must be designed to suit the specific needs and problems of the industry.

An interesting summary of some of these distinctive characteristics of the airlines industry is given in the Celler Committee Report.

> In many significant ways, however, the airlines industry and regulation of the industry is different from the normal public utility. In the first place the typical public utility statute does not have developmental and promotional objectives nor does it usually affirmatively recognize competition as being an element in determining the public interest. Further, the airlines industry does not have the physical limitations of a natural monopoly. Unlike the situations where the requirements of efficiency permit only one operating factor, as in dam sites, railroads or pipeline rights-of-way, or municipal power distribution systems, in air transportation many competitors can utilize the same airport facilities and operate over the same airlanes. In the typical public utility, relatively large investments are required to purchase the equipment and construct the facilities necessary to go into business. The air transport industry is substantially different. There is an absence of large fixed investments. There are no rights-of-way to buy nor are the operators required to bear the expense of installing and maintaining ground connections between the various facilities. There are no rails or roads to be built between stations involving the expense of surveys through remote districts or tunneling through mountains. On the contrary, the flexibility of aircraft permits a maximum ability to connect widely separated markets with a relatively small initial expenditure.[8]

For the purposes of this study it is the promotional nature of the Civil Aeronautics Act as embodied in its affirmative recognition of competition as an element in the public interest that constitutes the most important distinctive characteristic of airline regulation.

THE CIVIL AERONAUTICS ACT OF 1938

The Civil Aeronautics Act of 1938 created the Civil Aeronautics Board, but its functions and even its name were somewhat different from those of the present. The word "Board" is not used in the original form of the Act, rather, various duties under the Act were assigned to the *Civil Aeronautics Authority,* the *Civil Aeronautics Administrator,* and the *Air Safety Board.* In 1940, administrative changes were made whereby the *Civil Aeronautics Board* was established as an independent agency to perform certain of the functions of the Civil Aeronautics Authority and the Air Safety Board. The Air Safety Board was eliminated, and the Administrator of Civil Aeronautics was transferred to the Department of Commerce. The original functions of the various offices were rearranged with the result that, broadly speaking, the Civil Aeronautics Board (CAB) was charged with the economic regulation and control of the air transportation industry and with the rule-making and accident investigatory functions of the Air Safety Board. The Civil Aeronautics Administration (CAA) of the Department of Commerce and the Administrator of Civil Aeronautics were to develop and operate air navigation facilities, publish aeronautical maps and charts, license flight personnel and aircraft, register aircraft, and enforce safety rules.[9] Under the Federal Aviation Act passed in 1958, the Civil Aeronautics Administration and some of the air safety functions of the Civil Aeronautics Board were combined with the office of the newly created Federal Aviation Agency. However, the economic functions of the Civil Aeronautics Board were not changed. Since this study is concerned essentially with the economic regulation of the airlines industry, the functions of the FAA and the CAA are not of further interest here.

THE CIVIL AERONAUTICS BOARD

The Civil Aeronautics Board is composed of five members appointed by the President of the United States, with the advice and consent of the Senate, for a term of six years, with the proviso that no more than three shall be from the same political party. The President designates annually one of the members of the Board as chairman and one of the members as vice-chairman. Board members are not permitted to engage in any other business, vocation, or employment, and they may have no pecuniary interest in or own the securities of any civil aeronautics enterprise. The major activities of the Board are:

The regulation of fares and rates for carriage of persons and property;
The fixing of subsidy and service mail rates;
The guarantee of loans to certain classes of carriers for purchase of flight equipment;
The enforcement of the economic provisions of the Federal Aviation Act of 1958;
The approval or disapproval of mergers and control and interlocking relationships, and of intercarrier agreements affecting air transportation;
The regulation of air carrier accounting practices and the development of air carrier reporting systems;
The maintenance of public records of tariffs, schedules, and other material required to be filed by air carriers;
The licensing of domestic air routes and, with approval of the President, of international air routes operated by U.S. and foreign air carriers;
Participation in the negotiation of air agreements between the United States and other governments covering the exchange of air rights;
Authorization of the navigation of foreign civil aircraft in the United States;
Assuring protection of the public by (1) requiring the performance of safe and adequate air carrier service, and (2) eliminating rate discriminations and unfair competition or unfair and deceptive practices in air transportation;
Investigation and determination of probable cause of civil aircraft accidents; and
Adjudication of appeals from safety enforcement decision of the Administrator of the Federal Aviation Agency, and participation in safety rulemaking proceedings of the Administrator as appropriate.[10]

One very important power of the Board is that it is authorized to exempt many operations from antitrust actions; that is, the

Civil Aeronautics Act provides that any person affected by an order made under certain sections of the Act shall be relieved of the operations of the "antitrust laws" insofar as may be necessary to enable such person to do anything authorized, approved, or required by such order.

THE REGULATION OF AIR ROUTES

For the purposes of this study, the most important of the powers of the Board is the exclusive power to grant "certificates of public convenience and necessity," without which no regularly scheduled air route may be flown. The 1938 Act reads:

> Sec. 401. [*52 Stat. 987, as amended by 56 Stat. 265, 61 Stat. 449, 49 U.S.C. 481*] (a) No air carrier shall engage in any air transportation unless there is in force a certificate issued by the Authority [Board] authorizing such air carrier to engage in such transportation: *Provided,* That if an air carrier is engaged in such transportation on the date of the enactment of this Act, such air carrier may continue so to engage between the same terminal and intermediate points for one hundred and twenty days after said date, and thereafter until such time as the Authority [Board] shall pass upon an application for a certificate for such transportation if within said one hundred and twenty days such air carrier files such application as provided herein.

Those routes, referred to in the proviso, and in operation at the time of the Act in 1938, are the so-called "grandfather routes" which the Board inherited and which are the basis for today's various route structures.

Through this regulatory power the Board fulfills its promotional mandate. As Gellman has pointed out,

> While the issuance of a certificate of public convenience and necessity is itself not considered to be promotional in character in other fields of transportation, it must be so construed in the air transportation field because such a certificate usually carries with it the authority to transport mail, the payment for which constitutes the second promotional device employed by the Board.[11]

In the issuance of its certificates of public convenience and necessity, the Civil Aeronautics Board has been always faced with the choice between new carriers and existing carriers. That is, when the Board has decided that a particular route requires new or additional service authorization, the Board may issue the necessary certificate to an existing carrier thereby expanding its routes; or, the Board may certificate a new carrier enterprise which could, upon receipt of the certificate, enter the airline industry. The Board has not chosen the latter path in the domestic trunkline industry. There have been no new domestic trunkline carriers certificated under the Act. Indeed, the Board has certificated new local carriers and new all-cargo carriers and, in 1959, issued certificates with limited authority to the so-called "supplemental" carriers. However, with respect to the trunkline system, it has preferred to promote competition among the trunkline carriers by granting parallel routes via the expansion of the routes of existing carriers. Recently, however, the Board has granted trunkline-type competitive authorizations to certain of the local carriers over specific routes, thus, in these few cases, making competitors of carriers which did not exist at the time of the Act, but which had existed for a decade at the time of the decisions conferring this new authority.

The Board's policy was clearly stated in 1941 in the *Delta Air Corporation Case*.

> The number of air carriers now operating appears sufficient to insure against monopoly in respect to the average new route case, and we believe that the present domestic air-transportation system can by proper supervision be integrated and expanded in a manner that will in general afford the competition necessary for the development of that system in the manner contemplated by the Act. In the absence of particular circumstances presenting an affirmative reason for a new carrier there appears to be no inherent desirability of increasing the present number of carriers merely for the purpose of numerically enlarging the industry.[12]

The Board has been both criticised and praised for this policy, the development, execution, and effects of which constitute an important part of the subject of this study.

However, at the outset, it must be emphasized that the many policies of the Board have not been unchanging over the two decades of its existence. On the contrary, the changing Board membership causes wide swings in the attitude of the Board with respect to various long-range policies and programs. In 1956, the then Civil Aeronautics Board Chairman, Ross Rizley, emphasized this fact before the Celler Committee.

You know, we keep talking about philosophy. We keep talking about the philosophy of the Board. Well, the philosophy of the Civil Aeronautics Board changes from day to day. It depends on who is on the Board as to what the philosophy is. You just cannot say that the Board as a whole ever has a fixed philosophy for any very fixed period of time because as the members come and go, and they do come and go pretty fast down there.[13]

The general policy framework specified by the Congress, and under which the Board operates is stated clearly in Section 2 of the Civil Aeronautics Act of 1938, although, as indicated in the statement cited above by the former chairman, and by the history of regulation under the Act, it is subject to considerable latitude in interpretation. That policy statement of the Act is of extreme importance to this study in that it contains the often cited reference to the desirability of competition.

Sec. 2. [*25 Stat. 980, 49 U.S.C. 402*] In the exercise and performance of its powers and duties under this Act, the Authority [Board] shall consider the following, among other things, as being in the public interest, and in accordance with the public convenience and necessity—

(a) The encouragement and development of an air-transportation system properly adapted to the present and future needs of the foreign and domestic commerce of the United States, of the Postal Service, and of the national defense;

(b) The regulation of air transportation in such manner as to recognize and preserve the inherent advantages of, assure the highest degree of safety in, and foster sound economic conditions in, such transportation, and to improve the relations between, and coordinate transportation by, air carriers;

(c) The promotion of adequate, economical, and efficient service by air carriers at reasonable charges, without unjust discriminations, undue preferences or advantages, or unfair or destructive competitive practices;

(d) Competition to the extent necessary to assure the sound development of an air-transportation system properly adapted to the needs of the foreign and domestic commerce of the United States, of the Postal Service, and of the national defense;

(e) The regulation of air commerce in such manner as to best promote its development and safety; and

(f) The encouragement and development of civil aeronautics.[14]

Given this mandate of paragraph (d) with respect to competition, it remained for the Board, through its decisions in route proceedings, to implement its interpretation of the statute with respect to the kinds and amount of competition which it finds to be in accord with the public convenience and necessity.

While this policy statement of Section 2 is of primary importance in influencing the actions of the Board with respect to competition, it must not be assumed that this statement supporting competition stands alone in the Act. On the contrary, there are, in other sections of the Act, various other provisions which are designed to safeguard competition in the industry. Section 408, which restricts consolidations, mergers, and acquisitions of control by requiring Board approval of such actions, states that the Board

> shall not approve any consolidation, merger, purchase, lease, operating contract, or acquisition of control which would result in creating a monopoly or monopolies and thereby restrain competition or jeopardize another air carrier not a party to the consolidation, merger, purchase, lease, operating contract, or acquisition of control: *Provided further,* That, if the applicant is a carrier other than an air carrier . . . the [Board] shall not enter such an order of approval unless it finds that the transaction proposed will promote the public interest by enabling such carrier other than an air carrier to use aircraft to public advantage in its operation and will not restrain competition.[15]

Similarly, Section 409, which deals with interlocking relationships, prohibits a wide range of such possible restrictions on the free operation of competition. Section 411 of the Act provides the mechanism whereby the Board may eliminate "unfair or deceptive practices or unfair methods of competition in air transportation or the sale thereof." Indeed, the very power to prescribe rates and practices is part of the mechanism for safeguarding competition in the industry. By way of illustration, Section 1002 (e) provides that in rate making the Board shall consider

> (5) The need of each carrier for revenue sufficient to enable such carrier, under honest, economical, and efficient management, to provide adequate and efficient air carrier service.

Thus, Congress clearly expressed its determination that competition—to some unspecified degree, and in various unspecified forms—shall prevail in air transportation.

CHAPTER III

The Concept of Competition

THE GENERAL DEFINITION

The word "competition" means many things to many people. Webster defines competition as implying a struggle or contest between two or more persons for the same object, or, in its commercial usage as "The effort of two or more parties, acting independently, to secure the custom of a third party by offering most favorable terms." This definition, of course, conforms to the common nontechnical interpretation of the word. It is *vying for economic advantage.*

Economists, on the other hand, have used the word more technically, and have defined a hierarchy of possible competitive situations, varying from "perfect" competition, at one extreme, to monopoly, or the absence of competition, at the other, with various modifications of competition, such as "imperfect" or "monopolistic" or "oligopolistic," lying between the two extremes. Perfect competition is represented by the situation in which there are very many firms all producing an identical product and where each firm produces a small share of the total output of the industry, so that no single seller may exercise control over the market price. This is a rare situation found only with respect to some securities and to certain agricultural commodities which are traded on organized exchanges.

At the other extreme, perfect monopoly is just as rare. In that case, the seller has no competitors. His control over the price of the commodity is limited only by fear of governmental action, adverse public opinion, or decreased sales as customers cease using his product, usually by moving toward a substitute product which, for ideal monopoly, should not be a close substitute.

In our world of differentiated products, especially in the consumer field, almost every seller may be said to be a "monopolist" with respect to his own peculiar combination of goods, services, patents, and brand names. On the other hand, almost all of these are, in another sense, competitors because of the ability to substitute other available goods or services. This condition of "imperfect" or "monopolistic" competition indeed describes most of our modern business activity. Each seller does have some control over the price at which he sells because he does offer a product which is differentiated to some extent, either because of location or reputation or quality or color or shape of the product or even the personality of the seller. However, in most cases the available substitutes are sufficiently close so that the seller's price discretion is closely limited by the market forces themselves.

In our economy we do find some situations which approach perfect competition and, at the other extreme, we find some monopolistic firms. Typically the latter are the regulated utilities such as telephones, electricity, and gas. Between these two extremes we find all conceivable intermediate degrees of competition and monopoly, with the situation changing over time even within the same industry. Thus we have a mixed economy, one in which the basic decisions about what shall be produced by the economy, how much of it shall be produced, who shall purchase the output of the economy, what the prices shall be, etc., are decided, in some instances, by the forces of the market, in other cases by business management, and in yet other cases by the government. Sometimes, because of our peculiar institutional framework and economic regimen, the decision is made by two or even all three of these agents.

Competition, in any of its economic senses, exists only where the decisions are made or controlled in some degree by competitive market forces, and when there are two or more independently acting sellers of reasonably close substitute commodities. Then, the changes in prices, product characteristics, or quantities produced, are, although made by the seller, made to some degree in his response to the market forces as he sees them and as he understands their implications for the goals he seeks to achieve.

THE TRADITION OF PRESERVATION OF COMPETITION

The historical tradition of the United States with respect to competition is that competition should be fostered and preserved. The actions of our legislatures, our executive agencies, and our courts for many decades have made this an integral part of our heritage. With respect to air transportation, competition is stipulated, as we have noted, in the Civil Aeronautics Act itself. Historically, the Government of the United States not only takes the position that competition should be preserved, but also actively participates in many kinds of positive actions calculated to preserve competition. These are, of course, primarily the so-called "antitrust" activities.

Clearly, no matter what the government might seek to accomplish, it cannot feasibly create the atomistic conditions of the economists' ideal of perfect competition in most of the industries of the nation. Thus, the economic benefits that may be derived from that ideal state are only of academic interest. Does the impossibility of attaining this ideal state of perfect competition mean the cause is lost? Or that there is little or nothing to be gained from seeking to preserve competition in such modified forms as might be attainable? The answer is, clearly, negative. Competition should be preserved, and the competition which is, by tradition, to be preserved in the United States is well worth preserving although it may be quite different from the economic ideal. In the words of Corwin D. Edwards who has dealt extensively with this problem,

> The competitive system which, it is presumed, the government should try to preserve is not that perfect and universal competition that exists only in the writings of certain economists. Rather, it is the competitive element of a mixed economic society that has long contained, and, if competition is preserved, will still contain, large amounts of governmental control, wide differences in the power of business units, substantial obstacles hindering access to markets, monopolized activities under public sanction, and various types of agreed action. A considerable body of economic literature defines the idealized regime of perfect

competition. But there is no similar consensus as to the scope and significance of the competitive elements of a mixed economy.[1]

The competitive process which it is the purpose of a competitive policy to preserve is simpler, cruder, and less comprehensively beneficial than the perfect competition of classical economics.[2]

The competitive policy presupposes that unchecked private power will ordinarily be used to bring about exploitation and restriction of output; but in striking at extreme departures from competition it does not necessarily aim at an atomized competition such as was envisaged in the older economic theory.[3]

The "competition" that we seek to preserve is that "vying for economic advantage," which, in terms of sellers of goods or services, is the competitive pursuit of customers. This means, as a minimum, that there must be two or more sellers, with no collusion among them about certain policies and practices, particularly those defining the price-product package which they individually offer to the public.

COMPETITIVE BEHAVIOR

Competition in business is "vying for economic advantage" among two or more sellers (or buyers) of a commodity. From the sales side it is the striving of a seller to earn maximum benefit—usually measured by some function of profits—via the sales of his product despite the existence and actions of one or more competing sellers. These profits may be maximized by selling more of the product, by selling it at a higher price, by producing it more economically, or by some combination of these.

A seller may, in most business situations, increase the sales of his product by decreasing the price, and if the characteristics of the demand for his product and the costs of production are such that the decreased price causes a large enough increase in sales, then the price cut may indeed increase the profitability of the business. If, however, the increase in sales represents merely diversion of customers from competitors whose prices have not been cut, it may be anticipated that the competitors' prices will soon be similarly reduced. After that has taken place, the market share of the first price cutter may return to its original level, and the only benefit which may remain to him is his share of such increase in the total size of the market as may have resulted from the general price decrease in the industry. In this way however, prices tend ideally to be reduced to the lowest economical level for the least efficient surviving competitor.

The other way for a competitor to seek an increase in his sales is to try to make his product be or seem to be more attractive. This is usually done by modification of the product or by some form of sales promotion (advertising, publicity, public relations) or both. Of course, if this product modification or product advantage, either real or imagined, is sufficiently great, then it may be possible for the seller to increase his profitability, not only by selling more of the product, but by selling it at a higher price.

The third method by which a seller may vie for economic advantage is by obtaining or producing his product at the lowest possible cost. This is a very important aspect of competition; and its operation, when transmitted to the public via its effect on prices, represents one of the most important potential benefits of competition.

Competitive behavior on the part of competing firms ideally benefits the customers who thereby are able to obtain more and better goods and services for their money. However, to the extent that competition departs from the economic ideal, and to the extent that the techniques of competition are therefore limited or their range narrowed, obviously the potential benefit to the consumer from the competitive behavior is similarly limited in type and scope. The optimum balance of product and price is not likely to be reached if, for example, in their competitive behavior, the competitors rely primarily on sales promotion related to minor product characteristics and underemphasize prices and basic product design. As the ways in which competitors compete become limited, those that remain naturally become controlling and, although there may still be active competition in that the sellers do vigorously strive competitively for customer patronage, the potential public benefit from the competition is decreased.

HOMOGENEOUS OLIGOPOLY

When the number of sellers is small, the resulting competitive situation is referred to as "oligopoly"; and when, in addition, the product sold is the same for all of the sellers, the situation is referred to as "homogeneous oligopoly." It will be seen that the forces at work in this kind of situation tend to lead to certain familiar kinds of action on the part of the competing sellers. If the scope of the market is sufficiently small so that all of the customers, as well as the various sellers themselves, are aware of the prices charged by each of the sellers, then, if the prices of all of the sellers are not identical, the business will all tend to flow to the low-price seller, subject, of course, to his capacity limitations. Thus, if one of the sellers cuts prices, the others must follow or lose all or most of their business, under the assumption that the products of all sellers are identical, or sufficiently so to cause customers to shift from one seller to another in response to price changes. In this kind of situation (homogeneous products and high cross-elasticities of demand), retaliatory price cuts can cause an initial small price reduction to lead quickly to a disastrous price war. The history of transportation in this country is replete with illustrations of such price wars. Particularly, the four competing trunk railroads between New York and Chicago were subject to this kind of competitive phenomenon before the creation of the Interstate Commerce Commission. Probably the most generally familiar examples of this kind of price war occur in the gasoline service station industry.

These price wars can have tragic consequences for the sellers, and, for that reason, once a price is set and operating in a situation of homogeneous oligopoly, there is great reluctance to tamper with it. As a result, in most industries which have these characteristics, a *modus vivendi* becomes established, whereby the various sellers can operate, change their prices as they feel necessary, and even compete vigorously without the danger of destructive price wars. The two phenomena which frequently emerge are "price leadership" and "product differentiation." Under price leadership, if one of the firms changes its price, the others follow. The initiating firm knows that the others will not construe a price reduction as a predatory action, and that, in the case of a price rise, the others will follow the rise rather than bask in the patronage of the price leader's customers. This may be because of implied tacit agreement, or it may result from the fact that the price leader is so strong in the market, that his actions necessarily dominate. That is, if the price leader is so large that the others could not handle his customers if they did not follow a price rise, they will not find it to their advantage to hesitate, and, on the other hand, in the case of a price cut, they are forced to follow or lose their business to the leader. In this kind of situation, the identity of the price leader is clear and unchanging. However, in some situations of homogeneous oligopoly, where no one firm is clearly dominant, the mantle of price leadership may move from one firm to the other, as the various firms react to price changes in such a way as to avoid price wars. In these cases, the identity of the price leader may not be predictable from one price change to the other. In any situation, it may be that particular firm which happens to be the largest, strongest, most aggressive, newest, or oldest, or which may merely have, by tacit consent, accepted the role of price leader.

Such a "price leadership" situation does not necessarily imply the existence of a dishonest, illegal, or unethical conspiracy to thwart the competitive forces and to avoid the unpleasant effects of price competition. This kind of price behavior may develop quietly and unperceptibly as each of the small number of well-known and easily identifiable competitors keeps watch on the market behavior of the others. Further, there are industrial, professional, technical, and social associations which provide opportunity for exchange of information and views with respect to the likely response to any price changes.

Thus, an important consequence of the inherent price instability, characteristic of such oligopolistic situations, is that *price competition* tends to be avoided. Conversely, the various oligopolists are indeed "competitors" in that they are rivals in selling their goods. Their avoidance of price competition stems obviously from their fear of the consequences rather than from any desire to shelter their competitors. They gravitate therefore toward the non-price methods of competition, such as product characteristics, service, public relations, and advertising. Retaliation to these forms of competition is neither so swift nor so effective in cancelling the initial advantage as in the case of price changes. Prices are suceptible of precise measurement and comparison among the sellers, and the implications of price differentials are readily understood by the customer. For most forms of nonprice competition, the effect on customers is not so clear.

In a homogeneous oligopolistic situation, competitive actions tend to be directed toward "product differentiation"; that is, each of the individual sellers tries to make the oligopoly less homogeneous by making his product distinctively different from the others. This serves two purposes. First, it hopefully causes customers to prefer his product and to select it even though the prices are identical, and, second, it seeks to lessen the effect of price changes, thereby escaping from the necessity for selecting between the Scylla and Charybdis of "follow-the-leadership" or price-wars.

When competition is thus oriented toward the product and away from price, the potential benefit to the public is limited to improvements in the product and, further, to only certain aspects of the product. For example, in the airlines industry, if the competitive factors were to be solely the quality of the meals, the attractiveness of the stewardesses, and the amount of advertising, the competition might still be intense, but the only benefits the consumer could obtain from this would be better meals, more attractive stewardesses and, hopefully, more information. Although these factors may be of considerable importance to some passengers, the traveling public does not, by virtue of this kind of competition, enjoy lowered prices, more frequent or more convenient schedules, or superior aircraft. For the public to reap competitive gains with respect to prices, schedules, or aircraft, competition must take those forms. It is not the intensity or violence of the competition *per se* that benefits the consumer, it is the resulting balance between product and price which yields and measures that benefit. In our tradition, competition is considered to be an important mechanism for helping to achieve an optimum balance. However, the mere existence of competition, as defined above, in terms of "vying for patronage," does not insure the automatic achievement of that goal. That optimum is inevitable only when the competitive framework is the virtually nonexistent economic ideal.

REGULATION AS A SUBSTITUTE FOR COMPETITION

In those regulated industries which have been referred to as "natural monopolies" and in certain other industries such as some of the railroads, where it was felt that parallel competition would be unduly wasteful, or that, at most, it should be limited to a very few competitors, one of the purposes, if not the main purpose, of the regulation is to act, in one sense, as a substitute for the market forces of competition. That is, it sought to secure for the public a reasonable balance of product and price. The commission was supposed to be

> . . . an expert body to require what competition otherwise would do—that is, compel the monopolistic operator to render adequate service at a price no higher than reasonable.[4]

On the other hand, in those regulated industries which are not natural monopolies, regulation may seek, among other things, to protect against possible undesirable consequences of unregulated competition. However, even in this kind of industry, when regulation is applied, it may be possible and desirable to use controlled competition as an adjunct to regulation, so that, at least to some extent, the market forces would provide the familiar benefits of competition. This clearly was in the mind of the Congress in the enactment of the Civil Aeronautics Act, wherein appears the familiar direction to the regulatory body to

> . . . consider the following, among other things, as being in the public interest, and in accordance with the public convenience and necessity . . . (d) Competition to the extent necessary to assure the sound development of an air transportation system properly adapted to the needs of the foreign and domestic commerce of the United States, of the Postal Service, and of the national defense. . . .[5]

Thus the purpose of the Act was to promote air transportation through regulated competition. The Act prescribed a blend of competition and regulation, and the regulatory agency was empowered to determine the proportion of each in the blend.

However, the importance of this statement in the Act goes far beyond the purely economic sphere. It indicates that the purposes and goals of regulation and of such competition as is considered to be in the public interest shall not be exclusively economic. The noneconomic purposes to be served by the regulatory body and regulated competition are clearly spelled out, although the relative weight of each of these goals is not. Clearly this lack of specificity is the essence of the discretionary framework within which a regulatory commission operates. The Board must judge, in each case, how the various objectives must be weighted and balanced. This is, of course, one of the important reasons for some of the seeming inconsistencies when successive Board decisions are examined and analyzed from the point of view of only one of the objectives.

It is the consistent seeking for the public interest which is the proper object of the Board. If consistency with respect to all named goals, definitively weighted, were the only objective, the regulatory body could be replaced by a set of operating rules embodied in an all-inclusive manual. This unwillingness of the Congress to try to specify the exact role of and amount of competition in achieving the various purposes of the Act properly leaves much to the discretion of the individual Board members. This, coupled with the changing membership of the Board, accounts for the varying positions of the Board with respect to competition. It could hardly be otherwise. The result is that the airline industry and its regulation are characterized by an ever-changing mixture of competition as a substitute for regulation and regulation as a substitute for competition.

In an early interpretation of this aspect of the Civil Aeronautics Act, the Board stated:

> Two fundamental policies are established by the act: one directed to the achievement of regulatory control over those who render the public service of air transportation; the other seeking the maximum of sound development of the industry in the public interest. The first protects the public in its use of air transportation services and an example of such protection is found in the provisions of the Act which require air carriers to furnish adequate service. The second involves a promotional rather than a regulatory function, and undertakes to foster and encourage the maximum development of air transportation. In some instances this calls for something more than mere attainment of adequate service under protective regulation; it demands improvement and achievement through developmental pioneering. The full development and technological improvement of air transportation cannot be gained by regulation alone; to achieve improvement an incentive is necessary and under the Act that incentive should flow in part from competition between air carriers.[6]

In the usual unregulated competitive situation, where there is free entry, large or excessive profits act to draw new competitors into the field. The certification of new competitive carriers into specified markets by the Civil Aeronautics Board is intended to have this same effect, and, to the extent that the Board uses traffic or revenue criteria as the basis for its judgement of the need for a competitive carrier, the regulatory body is performing that "competitive" action. However, it acts conservatively in that, normally, only one or two additional carriers are added to a market at one time. In this way, the Board seeks to provide the benefits of competition, and, at the same time, to protect the air transportation system from excessive competition. Thus, under the current competition-regulation blend, the entry situation with respect to individual air transportation markets is, as traffic levels become high, that new carriers do come into the market, but the decision to bring another carrier into a given market is very carefully made. The number of carriers brought into a market seldom exceeds one or two, and the new carriers are selected from among the air carriers already in existence.

AIRLINE COMPETITION

In the air transportation industry, competition may exist when two or more carriers are authorized to perform essentially the same service. Of course, it is not possible for the services offered by the two air carriers even over the same route to be identical as in the "perfect" competition identical-product sense, because each carrier has its own distinctive schedule pattern, history, experience, safety record, passenger services, equipment, and other aspects of its product package which tend to differentiate it from that of the other carriers.

It is this product differentiation which makes possible "active competing," a conception which is impossible under and inconsistent with the definition of perfect competition, where products are identical. This is because by "active competition," we mean the pursuing, on the part of a business firm, of policies and practices designed to emphasize and perhaps increase the distinctiveness and the effectiveness of its own combination of product and price. The purpose of this is an attempt to induce potential customers, given a free choice between its product and that of its competitors, to select its product because of the real or imagined superiority of its product-price package. Further, with identical or nearly identical prices, the selection among the carriers must be made on the basis of this product differentiation; namely, the customer's impressions about the various aspects of the service offering: reputation, schedule pattern, type of equipment, customer services, etc.

Of course, there are many other forms which competition among air carriers can take besides competition for customers. That is, two carriers, even though they may operate in different areas of the country, may nevertheless be active competitors for equipment from the same manufacturers or suppliers, but that form of competition will not be of interest here. Also, another—more indirect—form of competition which may occur in regulated or semiregulated industries may be competition among firms in seeking favorable action on the part of the regulatory body, the legislature, or other governmental agencies. This varies from the retention of expensive counsel and the preparation of elaborate presentations for commission proceedings, to lobbying activities and even the less ethical favor-seeking activities which, on occasion, become exposed with considerable publicity in the press. In these and other ways, competing firms may be "vying for economic advantage." This, however, is not "competition" in the sense in which that word will be used here. As used here, competition refers to vying for economic advantage by seeking to do more business or more profitable business by actions designed to influence those with whom the firm does business, particularly, in this case, the customers.

Thus, "competition" refers only to the competition for air travelers between two or more carriers both authorized to provide essentially the same basic service, i.e., to carry passengers between the same two geographical locations. Then, active competition between the air carriers may take the form of price competition, advertising competition, or product competition.

WHEN DOES COMPETITION EXIST?

Competition in air transportation may exist on several different and distinct levels. In the first instance, air transportation is, to a greater or lesser extent, competitive with the various modes of surface transportation. Further, competition may exist between certificated airlines and other air operators such as charter services and supplemental air carriers as well as between public carriers and private or executive aircraft. Finally, and of primary interest here, is competition among certificated air carriers.

In this last and most important case—competition among certificated air carriers—the determination of when competition may be said to exist is not always easy. Clearly, when two airlines are both authorized to fly unrestricted nonstop "turnaround" service between two points, and when they both offer a full complement of flight schedules between those two points, and when they both compete actively and with comparable success for passengers, then competition may be said to exist between those two points. However, there are many city pairs such that the decision as to whether or not air competition exists between them is not clear. For example, in many cases there is a restriction on the operating authority of one or more of the carriers involved. This restriction may take the form of one or more required intermediate stops, or it may be a restriction on the "turnaround" authority, such that the carrier may be required to originate or terminate all flights serving the two cities at a point or points beyond the two cities in question. Restrictions such as these affect the ability of the restricted carrier to offer services tailored to the needs of the travelers between the two cities in question. This does not necessarily mean that a carrier, thus restricted, may never operate enough schedules at convenient hours to capture a significant portion of the market even against a competing unrestricted carrier. However, typically, these restrictions do constitute a serious obstacle to effective active competition.

On the other hand, the existence of equivalent authorization does not invariably produce active and effective competition. Such competition exists only when both the *authorization* and *willingness* to compete exist. Perhaps we might add a third essential ingredient, the *ability*. By this is meant the availability of financial, personnel, and equipment resources adequate to permit the offering of a competitive air service pattern. For example, for a considerable period of time after Continental Airlines was authorized to compete with United Airlines between Denver and Chicago and after Northeast Airlines was authorized to compete with Eastern

Airlines and National Airlines between New York and Miami and after Trans World Airlines was authorized to compete with United Airlines between Denver and New York, such competing services were not offered because of the unavailability of competitive equipment in adequate numbers, although the authority and desire on the part of the respective carriers seemed to be present.

The existence or absence of competition may be ascertained on the basis of many different definitional criteria. For example, competition may exist when two carriers are authorized to offer any service between two points, or when they are authorized to offer the same best service between two points; or, regardless of whether they are authorized to or do in fact offer the same service between two points, competition may exist when two or more carriers each carry a certain fixed minimum share of the traffic. This last criterion, which has been widely used to define the existence of competition or "effective competition" in terms of the success, as measured by the market share, of the less successful competitor(s), will be discussed in a later section.

In seeking to select among these various criteria for adjudging the existence of competition, one must be guided by the purpose which the dichotomy; competitive vs. noncompetitive, is to serve. If it is intended—as in this study—to serve as a tool for analysis of the actions of the Civil Aeronautics Board, then the criterion must be based on the legal authorizations of the carriers. Thus, for our purposes, a city pair is "competitive" if more than one carrier is authorized to serve that pair. The criterion, in this case, might be restrictive and define competition as existing only when more than one carrier is authorized to offer the best service which any of the carriers is authorized to offer between the pair. For example, if one of the carriers can offer nonstop turnaround service, at least one other carrier should be able to offer that same service if it so desires. On the other hand, the definition may be less limiting and define competition as existing when more than one carrier is authorized to offer *single-plane service* (i.e., where the passengers are not required to change airplanes at some intermediate point) between the pair even though there may be differing amounts or kinds of restrictions on the operating authorities of the various carriers. The previously-cited criterion, which is based on traffic and which defines competition as existing when two or more carriers each carry some specified minimum proportion of the passengers between the pair, does not inquire at all into the operating authority of the carriers, but may indeed identify as a competitive pair, one such that only one of the carriers (or, possibly, none) is authorized to provide single-plane service at all. This definition, which finds considerable usefulness elsewhere, as will be noted below, is not useful for the purpose of this study.

COMPETITIVE CITY PAIRS

In this study which deals with the decisions of the Civil Aeronautics Board, a competitive criterion based on Board action is used. The existence of competitive authorizations for single-plane service creates what will be referred to as "competitive city pairs." A competitive city pair is a pair of cities such that *more than one carrier is certificated to offer single-plane transportation to passengers between those two cities.* The carriers are *competitive carriers;* and *competition* may be said to exist in that travel market.

This criterion is based solely on the characteristics of the certificates of public convenience and necessity under which the carriers operate, and it therefore depends solely on the actions taken by the Civil Aeronautics Board. It is independent of whether the carriers are *active competitors* who are offering service and striving for business, and it does not require that the authorizations be for *equivalent best service.* That is, there is no need that the carriers be equally restricted or free from restrictions. Finally, it is quite different from the definition for *effective competition* as given by former CAB Chairman, Mr. Ross Rizley: "In terms of individual markets, effective competition may be said to exist where two or more carriers actively contend for access to available traffic on approximately even terms." [7]

Our definition, depending as it does on the actions of the CAB as given in the certificate of public convenience and necessity, is independent of the actions taken by the various carriers in response to the certificate provisions. Therefore, its use permits analysis of the actions and of the traffic of the carriers, both newly certificated and previously certificated, which developed in response to the competitive certifications. That is, the response of the carriers as measured by their schedule offerings, and the response of the public to the schedule offerings as measured by the traffic carried can be analyzed as a function of the kinds of competitive authorizations issued and as a function of the intentions and purposes of the CAB in issuing the various certificates.

Another matter of considerable interest is the existence, between certain city pairs, of multiple carrier competition, that is, three or more competing carriers. New or additional multiple carrier competition comes about in two ways. First, in many cases three or more competitive carriers have been authorized in order to create the multiple carrier competition which the Board has decided was warranted in the public interest. Second, it may come about as a consequence of route extensions made for other purposes. In some cases, notably New York–Washington and various pairs of cities on the routes between these two cities (New York–Philadelphia, Baltimore–Washington, etc.), many carriers have been authorized to serve these city pairs simply as a consequence of their authorizations to offer service between these cities and the other cities on their routes branching in directions going south and west from Washington. The authorization to Braniff, for example, to serve both Washington and New York on its flights from Dallas and other southwest points, permitted the service of local New York–Washington passengers, although the Board's primary purpose was to create additional service between these eastern cities and the southwest. This kind of extension of a route to include, for example, the New York–Washington segment on a route that otherwise would have served these two cities as the unconnected ends of two branches separating at, say, Atlanta, is sometimes referred to as "entry mileage." In this way, the number of competitive carriers authorized to serve New York–Washington has grown to ten, including one local service carrier. Clearly, the purpose of the Board in certificating the most recently added competitors was not necessarily related to any conclusion on the part of the Board that the public interest required more competitors between New York and Washington.

In any event, multiple-carrier competition does exist between many city pairs, and the question naturally arises whether the intensity or the benefits of competition are functions of the number of competitors. This question may well merit later investigation.

EFFECTIVE COMPETITION—THE 10 PERCENT CRITERION

In some empirical studies,[8] competition or *effective competition* has been defined as existing between two cities if there are two or more carriers each carrying more than 10 percent of the traffic between the two cities. By this criterion, regardless of any operating restrictions which may attach to the certificate of either of the two carriers, ". . . monopoly pairs are those between which 90 percent or more of the traffic was transported by a single carrier while competitive pairs are all pairs other than monopoly" [9] Gill and Bates defined "an effective competitive routing . . . as one which carried 10 percent or more of the passengers moving via the most heavily traveled routing." [10]

> This 10% rule, while admittedly arbitrary, was adopted by the authors after extensive discussion with leading airline traffic and sales officials. A 10% participation by a competitor was felt to be the minimum participation necessary to constitute effective competition from the standpoint of influencing a competitor's service or rates under normal conditions.[11]

In using this traffic participation criterion, the sources cited above have not related it to the nature of the authorizations. A pair was considered to have effectively competitive service if the division of traffic among the competitors met the requirements of the definition, regardless of whether or not the competitors were authorized to offer equivalent best service. This traffic share criterion has a distinct computational advantage, in that, for statistical studies, it is susceptible of automatic analysis by data processing equipment or by statistical clerks without the necessity for consultation of any data except the traffic data themselves. Under this scheme, the selection of city pairs which have "competitive" air service is a purely automatic operation.

On the other hand, this scheme does have very serious conceptual shortcomings. For example, the operating authority of one of the carriers may be so restricted that the typical passenger does not have anything approaching an equivalent choice between the carriers. In fact, one of the carriers may not be permitted to offer single-plane service between these two points,[12] but may still be able, by careful scheduling, to offer two-plane connecting service which does in fact, possibly because of unwise scheduling or simply because of lack of concern on the part of the other carrier, capture 10 percent of the market. Although this situation might meet the 10 percent criterion for effective competition, neither the restricted carrier described above nor the unrestricted nonstop turnaround 90 percent carrier would consider this a competitive situation.

This objection is not limited to those city pairs which have only one carrier certificated for single-plane service. In many cases where there have been two or more carriers so certificated, but where the operating rights of the competing carriers were not equivalent, the restricted carriers have applied for removal of restrictions to permit them to compete more effectively in markets where they do, in spite of their present restrictions, nevertheless carry 10 percent or more of the traffic. The managements of these airlines would hardly concede that, under the restrictions, they were in a position to offer "effective competition."

Another factor disturbing the relationship between the intensity or effectiveness of the competition and the distribution of passengers among the competitors is historical participation. In some cases the historical participation of a particular carrier in a market may be such that, although a new carrier is certificated to offer equivalent service, and although the new carrier does attempt to compete actively, the traditional association between the original carrier and the route is such that, in the face of the active competition of the original carrier, the new carrier may have difficulty in capturing a significant share of the market. In these cases, there is active competition, although the second carrier may not be carrying a particular specified minimum share of the traffic. The benefit to the public results from the efforts of the original carrier to maintain his dominant position in the market. In cases such as this, if both competitors are actively vying for market share, there may be no change in market share over time in spite of the intensity of the competition.

A further difficulty with this definition is that, if one of the competing carriers is, for one reason or other, so successful a competitor that he captures more than 90 percent of the market, then, by definition, competition has ceased to exist. If this happens because one carrier withdraws all or most of his flights, then the remaining carrier obviously will carry more of the traffic than it would carry if the other had continued to offer comparable schedules. A competitor may prefer not to compete because he has a better route structure, and he concentrates on his other more profitable segments. In that case has competition ceased to exist? It may be that the second competitor is ready to return to the market as soon as there is any reason to suspect that he can compete more favorably. This may continue to afford the stimulus to optimum service and efficiency on the part of the remaining competitor, so that there is indeed the effect of competition in that the public continues to gain the benefits of the competitive price-product package. In that case, there is no need for a fixed minimum market share for the smaller competitor in order for certain benefits of competition to be realized.

Indeed, it is not the case that the benefits of competition become available to air travelers over a particular route segment only when both carriers have captured a specified minimum share of the market. Nor is it the case that, when they have captured that share of the market, the benefits of competition have been realized. As illustrations of competitive benefits without changes in market share, one need only cite the many examples of service improvement on the part of the first carrier at the time that a second carrier was certificated. Also, those routes where the original carrier improved his service upon the initiation or announcement of a CAB proceeding which might conceivably result in a competitive certification.

Thus, the decision on the part of the Board to create competition, and the ensuing certification of a competitive carrier, may or may not create competitive service. On the one hand, the mere existence of unexercised rights may produce the desirable benefits of competition in view of the impending threat to the operations of the still sole operator. On the other hand, the actual inauguration of service by the second carrier, and, perhaps, even the capturing of a significant share of the market, may still leave the total service offering to the consumer something short of that which might be considered adequate by the Board or possibly even less than that previously offered by the original monopoly carrier.

For the purposes of this study, where one of the objects of the analysis is to measure the extent to which new competitive carriers have penetrated into the markets of the established carriers, the criterion used to select the competitive markets for analysis must be independent of traffic share. Under a selection criterion based on market share, those markets where the penetration of a new carrier does not reach the specified level are eliminated from consideration, although the ascertainment of the existence of such pairs and of the reason for the low penetration may be of considerable value. That reason might be equipment shortage, inadequate service and sales effort, the barrier of extreme customer loyalty or unequal authorization, or some other factor or group of factors.

CHAPTER IV

Forms of Airline Competition

COMPETITION AND THE PUBLIC INTEREST

The basic commodity produced by the air transport industry is air flights between communities. This is true, whether these flights are offered by one carrier or by two or more. In this sense, the addition of a second or a third carrier to compete with an existing carrier typically adds nothing tangible that the existing carrier could not have provided alone, if he had available the necessary resources in personnel, funds, and equipment; and if he had the inclination. Therefore, the real question to be answered in evaluating the desirability of competition is whether the addition of competition in a market does in fact inspire an increase in the amount of resources applied to that market or a decrease in prices, or improvement in any of the other aspects of the product-price package available to the traveling public; and whether it does this without creating new problems which nullify the benefits.

What are the benefits which competition might be expected to provide to the traveling public? First, of course, the existence of actively competitive carriers gives the traveler a choice of firms with which to deal. This, in itself, is a desideratum. It means freedom from dependence on the ability and caprice of a monopoly carrier. It provides assurance that service or fares will not be changed irresponsibly, that personnel will behave courteously, and its very existence, by permitting the consumer to choose, contributes to the dignity and independence which we, as consumers, have come to prize.

These psychic benefits are real and important, although difficult to evaluate quantitatively. However, competition should also provide other and more tangible benefits. The existence of a competitive situation should, ideally, cause the competitors to vie with one another in seeking the patronage of the traveling public, and to do this in terms of the attractiveness of their product-price package. Competition among air carriers has been and will continue to be an important factor contributing to the public interest in air transportation as defined by the President's Air Coordinating Committee.

> The public interest requires that the benefits of air transportation in all its forms be widely available at low cost. It also requires the progressive development of new aviation services, taking maximum advantage of the technological progress of the aeronautical sciences.[1]

Of course, sometimes the various potential benefits of competition may be found to be in conflict with one another. For example, with the use of larger aircraft with higher seating capacity and higher costs per mile, carriers may find it necessary to decrease the number of flights over certain routes in order to maintain load factors. Thus, the public will be getting the benefits of technological advance in terms of speed and other aircraft characteristics, but there may be a concomitant decrease in the convenience of schedule patterns.

As noted above, the public benefits to be derived from competition depend upon the forms which competition takes, and the number of ways in which active competitive behavior may be manifested in the airline industry is very great. It may involve fare reductions, more seats, more frequent, convenient, and faster schedules, better equipment, more elaborate meals, more luxurious furnishings and decor, more charming stewardesses, ready extension of credit, increased advertising and promotional effort, more aggressive salespersons, or superior ground installations.

NON-CUSTOMER-DIRECTED COMPETITION

In addition to the familiar forms of competition listed above, whereby the carriers compete for customer patronage, the airlines also compete with one another in areas which are not immediately directed toward attracting customers. This non-customer-directed competition includes competition in efficiency, competition for equipment, and competition for routes.

Competition in efficiency. With respect to efficiency or cost reduction efforts on the part of airline managements, all airlines are, in a sense, competitive with one another, regardless of whether they serve the same routes. When two or more carriers compete over the same routes, the effect of this stimulus on costs is not clear. During the period covered by the Gill and Bates study, roughly the first decade under the Civil Aeronautics Act of 1938, according to the criteria used, Eastern Airlines was the least competitive of the major airlines,[2] yet it had the lowest costs per available seat mile.[3] It also had the highest fares,[4] presumably because of the lack of competition. Clearly there was no evidence, at least in this case, that the lack of competition deterred the management of Eastern Airlines from minimizing costs. Indeed, the effect may be in the opposite direction in that the pressure of competition may stimulate the offering of costly customer services or the purchase of newer equipment with the result that costs are raised by competition.

Competition for equipment. This consists of study and analysis of and even contribution to the creation of new aircraft designs, as well as the imaginative and aggressive ordering of new aircraft. It also encompasses the leasing of existing aircraft from various sources. As an illustration of this last form of competition, some carriers have been suspected of leasing aircraft for which their needs were not pressing, in order, among other things, to keep these aircraft from a competitor who was limited by equipment shortage and who would otherwise have leased these aircraft for use on competitive routes. A more truly "competitive" action would be hard to imagine.

Competition for routes. This is the competitive seeking for new route authorizations in proceedings before the Civil Aeronautics Board. For example, in the *Denver Service Case,* which represented the consolidation of several route applications into one proceeding, eight airlines [5] were actively competing for routes providing for east-west service over all or part of the New York, Chicago, Kansas City, Denver, Salt Lake City, San Francisco and Los Angeles route. In this, and all of the other similar large proceedings, the various parties go to great expense and effort to retain counsel, prepare exhibits, attend hearings, and argue before the Board in their attempt to secure the routes for themselves, or to preserve their exclusive rights to their monopolistic routes by arguing against the award of those routes to competitive carriers. It is common to see, in one proceeding, a particular airline extolling the benefits of competition as it seeks to enter the routes of a second carrier, while that second carrier argues equally eloquently for the maintenance of the *status quo,* and, in another proceeding, the same two airlines with their roles reversed. The following citation from a CAB decision is an interesting illustration of these two phenomena in a single proceeding.

Termination of National's Norfolk/Newport News restrictions would enable the carrier to participate in traffic between these cities and Washington and Baltimore where Capital is now the sole carrier in the market. Capital opposes elimination of these restrictions, but at the same time it seeks expanded authority to serve the New York/Philadelphia–Norfolk/Newport News markets which National now serves exclusively.[6]

CUSTOMER-DIRECTED COMPETITION

In their competitive seeking for routes, in their competition for equipment, and in other non-customer-directed areas of competition, the airlines compete vigorously, and the intensity of the struggle among the carriers rises, on occasions, to heroic proportions. This study, however, is primarily interested in customer-directed competition; that is, competition for passengers by seeking to offer them a product that is, or seems to be, a better bargain than that offered by the competing carrier or carriers. This customer-directed competition can exist only when more than one carrier is authorized to provide service over a given route, and it occurs only between such carriers.

Since air transportation is a point-to-point service, the relevant number of competitors in any intercity market is, as seen by the customers, the number of competitors actually serving that market. The number of air carriers in the entire industry is of little importance in affecting the competitive pattern in any individual market. Under current conditions, the number of truly active competitors between any two points tends to be relatively small. In most competitive markets, there are only two or three certificated competitors, and, in the extreme case, where there are ten carriers certificated (New York–Washington), not all of these are, as of this date, active competitors. Further, one may speculate that, if all restrictions to entry into this market were to be removed by the regulatory authority, the number of actual competitors might even then not be significantly changed. Clearly, any air transportation market that may be classified as "competitive" may also be described as "oligopolistic."

The many possible forms of customer-directed competition may conveniently be grouped into five classes: price, equipment, passenger service, marketing, and schedules. It must be borne in mind that these classes or forms of competition are not independent of one another, but, on the contrary, may show a high degree of interaction. For example, there are many examples of the elimination of customer services in association with price concessions. Noteworthy here is the Western Airlines experiment with the elimination of inflight meals coupled with a five percent fare decrease, and, of course, the entire coach service movement with its decrease in customer services in favor of price reductions. These modifications of the product-mix have taken place concurrently with the opposite product-mix modification represented by the "name" flights with their increase in luxury services accompanied by higher fares. In addition, there are examples of lower fares being charged in order to compensate for older equipment and higher fares or surcharges associated with new equipment. Illustrations of the latter have been noted with the introduction of most new aircraft types, particularly the jet equipment; and the former, while not so common, was seen in the case of Capital Airlines in 1948–49, when its DC–4's were competing with postwar equipment.[7]

PRICE COMPETITION

In an oligopolistic situation, particularly where the products of the various competitors are homogeneous or near homogeneous, there tends to be an emphasis on nonprice competition rather than on price competition. The reasons for this are given in Chapter III, for the general case. In the air transportation industry, where rate changes must be filed in advance with the Civil Aeronautics Board and published for all to see, each competitor knows exactly what the others are charging and what they propose to charge for their product. If competitors believe, and this is not an unreasonable expectation in the air transportation industry, that travelers will shift rapidly and in large numbers in response to a rival's price cut, then price cuts will be matched or, in vindictive situations, exceeded by the price cutter's competitors. Because of fear of such "price wars," prices tend to become and to remain homogeneous, with the price level for all competitors set by that competitor who elects to set his price lowest. This "price leadership" situation may act similarly in the case of price increases. An individual carrier fears to raise his price alone if he feels that competitors will not follow and that, therefore, traffic will shift to those competitors. On the other hand, if he has reason to suspect that the other carriers will follow his lead and raise their prices at the same time or very soon thereafter, then he can lead the price upward for all competing carriers, subject, of course, to the fact that all price changes must be approved by the Civil Aeronautics Board.

In his survey of airline managements, Paul Cherington found that they seemed to feel that price cuts are promptly matched by competitors, and that price increases will, in general, not be matched.[8] Thus, the demand curve as seen by management is one of great demand elasticity for price increases and little elasticity for price cuts. In this case of a so-called "kinked" demand curve,[9] the tendency is for management to fear to tamper with price on a unilateral basis.[10] The result of this competitive and regulatory situation is that: "Many members of the carriers' management tend to feel that price policy is something over which individual carriers have little or no control."[11]

Thus the elasticity characteristics of the demand curve of the *individual* carrier are an important factor in causing carrier managements to avoid direct price competition. The elasticity of demand for air transportation in any market; i.e., the *industry* demand curve, is also of great importance, since this determines the desirability of price cuts for all of the competitors in that market. That is, if the elasticity is sufficiently great, a price cut, even if matched by competitors, may generate enough new traffic to be a wise move.

From the point of view of the air carrier industry, the new air travel thus generated by price cuts includes all of the new air traffic whether it consisted of diversion from ground carriers, from private vehicle transportation, or whether it consisted of new trips that might otherwise not be taken. For example, in the trans-Atlantic charter service, groups or organizations (unions, social and fraternal clubs, professional societies, athletic groups, etc.) may charter a round-trip flight from a qualified carrier and travel between New York and Paris in any season for about $300 per person as against approximately $900 for the individual first-class fare, and $500 for the economy fare. A large amount of this charter traffic has been developed. This may be largely new business; i.e., traffic that would otherwise not move, and, if so, it suggests that there may also be a high price elasticity of demand for other types of service.

The airlines have not yet tried to exploit to the fullest the industry elasticity of demand. That is, the airlines have traditionally been geared to the luxury traffic market, even in the coach field. It seems obvious that air travel can be made less expensive than it is and that the airlines may be able to effect further penetration of the mass market by cutting costs and prices below their present levels. For example, costs per seat mile may be decreased further by more dense seating arrangements, no advance ticketing, and no reservations. Such an operation as this, using maximum density seating, no advance reservations, and no luxury services, might, on heavily traveled routes, if the cost savings are reflected in decreased fares, have a strong effect on traffic generation.

This kind of price competition may eventually come about. However, at present, except for a few limited efforts, the carriers seem to be more interested in service competition than in price competition. Probably some phenomenon such as the postwar "irregular" carriers or excess capacity or a new vehicle or perhaps something completely unforeseen may be necessary to provide the impetus for a new push forward on the cost and price competition front.

Rate making. Typically, in the airline industry, rates are made by applying some rate-per-mile to the all-stop mileage between two points. That is, the certificate of public convenience and necessity, which authorizes an air carrier to operate, describes the route over which the carrier operates in terms of a series of served points. For example, the route of Eastern Airlines between Miami and Boston as cited in the *New York–Florida Case,* is described in the certificate of public convenience and necessity in part as follows.

Eastern Air Lines, Inc. is hereby authorized, subject to the provisions hereinafter set forth, the provisions of Title IV of the Civil Aeronautics Act of 1938, as amended, and the orders, rules and regulations issued thereunder, to engage in air transportation with respect to persons, property and mail, as follows:

Between the terminal point Miami, Fla., the intermediate points West Palm Beach, Vero Beach, Melbourne, Orlando, St. Petersburg-Clearwater, Tampa, Ocala, Gainesville, Daytona Beach and Jacksonville, Fla., Brunswick and Savannah, Ga., Charleston, S.C., Augusta, Ga., and Columbia, S.C., and (a) beyond Columbia, S.C., the intermediate points Florence, S.C., Raleigh-Durham, N.C., Richmond, Va., Washington, D.C., Baltimore, Md., Wilmington, Del., Atlantic City, N.J., Philadelphia, Pa., Newark, N.J., New York, N.Y., New Haven, Conn., Hartford, Conn.-Springfield, Mass., Providence, R.I., and the terminal point Boston, Mass. . . .[12]

The distance between terminals may be computed as either the "non-stop" mileage or the "all-stop" mileage, the first being obvious, and the latter being the distance between the terminals given as the sum of the individual segments from point to point over all intermediate points on the route. It is this all-stop mileage which is typically used in computing the rate. However, if two or more airlines are competing for the traffic between two points, the airline that sets the lowest fare, in effect, is setting the fare for the other carriers serving the same points. If the rate-making procedure outlined above were to be used always, the route with the fewest stops would control the rate. Although usual, this is not always the case. For example, in the New York to Miami route, when National Airlines was certificated to serve this route in competition with Eastern Airlines, National adopted Eastern's fare even though National's route, on an all-stop mileage basis, was shorter than

Eastern's. The general rate-making procedure has been described by the CAB's Bureau of Air Operations as follows:

> Fares in air transportation are determined by multiplying a base rate per mile by the total mileage between the points involved. . . . Insofar as the mileage component of this equation is concerned, the bulk of air fares have been constructed using the sum of the point-to-point mileages over the carrier's certificated route, using all the intermediate points designated in its certificate. . . . This approach makes use of airport-to-airport mileage only between adjacent points on a carrier's route. This mileage is then multiplied by the base rate per mile to give the tentative fare between the two points. In similar fashion the fares between each adjacent pair of points are constructed. These fares are then added to construct the tentative fares between non-adjacent points. Thus, if the fare from A to B is $10, and the fare from B to C is $5, the tentative fare from A to C will be $15.
>
> At this point, however, other factors must be given consideration. For example, a second carrier may have a direct certificated route from A to C. Since these are adjacent points on its route, it will construct its fares from A to C in exactly the same manner as its more circuitous competitor, but because of shorter mileage, establish a fare of $14. To meet this competition, the circuitous carrier will establish $14 as the fare from A to C, notwithstanding the fact that the normal method of construction indicated a fare of $15. The carrier will then construct fares from A to points beyond C on the basis of the $14 fare from A to C.[13]

This general procedure of equalization of fares between terminals without regard for differences in the number of intermediate points has had an interesting application in the relationship between local service airlines and trunk airlines. Although it probably did not represent the original intent of the Board, there have been several instances where local lines have been in competition for terminal-to-terminal traffic with trunklines. This has been particularly the case with the newer certificates (starting in the early 1950's) which may permit the local airlines to skip stops. In certain cases, the local lines (which usually have more intermediate stops listed in their certificates) have matched the terminal-to-terminal fares of the trunklines, thus making their fares (in cents per route mile) much lower.

It will be noted that, under Section 414 of the Act, CAB approval of an agreement among the carriers frees that agreement from the operation of the federal antitrust laws. This has permitted certain agreements including the following:

In order to facilitate the equalization of competitive fares and thus prevent rate wars, airlines cooperate voluntarily through associations. As we have seen, almost all domestic fares are published by the airlines through the executive secretary of ATA's Air Traffic Conference of America as agent. A carrier desiring to initiate or to change any of its fares or other tariff provisions must furnish the agent with a statement of the new provision at least fifteen days before it is to be filed with CAB. The agent thereupon notifies the other domestic airlines, which may make appropriate changes in their fares or rules to meet the proposal on an equal, competitive basis. As a courtesy in the case of a change that may affect other airlines, an airline generally notifies the other airlines at the time it sends its statement to the agent. If the purpose of a tariff change is to meet another airline's competitive tariff provision previously sent to the agent, and the change is filed with CAB within fifteen days after the filing of the other line's tariff provision, the usual fifteen days' notice to the agent is reduced to one day's notice.[14]

The prevalence of price competition. Although the airlines have made much use of price appeal in their competition with surface carriers, traditional price competition, namely the competitive manipulation of prices for similar products in order to attract customers from competing carriers, has not been common within the certificated airline industry. On the other hand, it has not been totally absent. In the early days of lower cost "coach" or "tourist" air service in the certificated airlines industry after World War II, price competition indeed existed in those situations where one competitor was offering coach service between two points while the other competitor offered only first-class service. Outside the certificated industry, the so-called "irregular" carriers of the same period (now the "supplemental" carriers) were real price competitors. Theirs was and is traditional price competition in that they seek, by offering services at lower prices, to attract traffic away from the certificated airlines. Typically, however, within the certificated airline industry, now that coach services are offered widely, price competition is confined to the offering of special promotional fares for small areas and limited periods. These include round-trip discounts, family fares, and stop-over privileges.

The effect of competition on prices. In order to ascertain whether or not competition affects prices in the air carrier industry, one might inquire whether the rates are different for competitive and noncompetitive routes. As we have seen, there is a small effect in those cases where an air carrier has set a lower rate for a competitive segment in order to meet the rate of a competing carrier with a shorter route. Thus, at the very least, competition has affected fares to the extent that " . . . competing carriers have equalized fares between points even when economic considerations alone might have called for a higher charge by one of the carriers." [15]

In their 1949 study, Gill and Bates,[16] using data through March of 1949, concluded that, although air competition may have contributed to uniformity of rates on competitive routes, it had no appreciable effect in reducing airline fares.

With respect to the effect of competition on the price of the first-class service, a later Civil Aeronautics Board staff study has indicated that, in general, the effect of competition on air fares is discernible, but not very great. The study found, on the basis of its sample of domestic passenger fares, that, with respect to the influence of competitive factors on fares,

> 1. Except for a tendency to higher fares on the non-competitive segments of high route circuity, the Big Four carriers show little variation in fares between competitive and non-competitive segments.
>
> 2. The other trunk carriers generally reflect higher fares on non-competitive than on competitive segments.
>
> 3. Aside from non-competitive circuitous segments, the Big Four carriers' fare structure generally follows a consistent pattern, with relatively few variations for individual segments, and this same pattern also generally appears to be present on the competitive segments of the other trunklines.[17]

Thus, while there seems to be little effect on the Big Four, medium and smaller trunklines seem to elect to charge higher rates on certain of their noncompetitive segments. This reflects the fact that, barring industry-wide increases, the only way in which the carriers can increase their individual unit revenues is by rate increases on their noncompetitive routes. An interesting illustration of such a rate is the Capital Airlines fare between Cleveland and Detroit in the early 1940's. Here, because of the circuity of the rail route, the traffic could bear the higher fare, which was 8.6 cents per air mile, as against the industry average of 4.6 cents. Subsequent certification of Eastern caused the rate to be reduced.[18]

However, it is not the case that such competitive certification was the only means by which the Board could reduce this rate, since it could, at any time, have acted on the rate directly, if it had found that rate to be opposed to the public interest. The same is, of course, true for any of the individual rates of the medium and small trunklines which have caused their average rates to be somewhat higher on their noncompetitive routes as found in the study cited above. Nevertheless, the certification of a competitive airline may usually be expected to be—and was in this case—an effective means of reducing such rates. In the Cleveland–Detroit case referred to above, the traffic was so heavy that a competitive carrier would probably have been certificated regardless of the Capital rate. Of course, such high traffic is not always the case and, in fact, these higher fares tend to occur on short haul, light traffic routes, where unit costs are high.[19]

The offering of an increased proportion of coach services does, in effect, lower the price, although the service offered under the generally accepted definition of "coach service" may omit some aspects of the first class service which are important to various segments of the traveling public. Clearly, for those patrons who regard the omitted services as more important than the price differential, the coach service represents less satisfaction for the money than does the first class service. On the other hand, the popularity of the coach services indicates that, for many people, the transportation is the thing, and the features omitted from the coach service are, to them, nonessential "frills." To those people who do not mind the omission of the elaborate meals, the narrower seats, diminished leg room, and omission of certain of the first class features, the coach service is indeed a bargain relative to the first class service, and the growth of coach service has, to a considerable extent, been inspired by competition.

Competition has, in at least one case, had a perverse effect on price. This occurred in the air freight business, where the inauguration of competition actually raised the prices. Originally, air freight was carried by certificated passenger carriers, who, by carrying it at or near marginal cost, were (on a fully allocated cost basis) subsidizing the air freight business with revenues from other sources. When new all-freight carriers were certificated to compete for freight business with the established passenger carriers, they found it impossible to compete with the price, since they had no other business to absorb their overhead. The result was that the new all-freight carriers applied to the Board for a rate floor based on the costs of hauling freight in all-freight aircraft. This request was granted by the Civil Aeronautics Board thereby increasing the price of air freight and, of course, discouraging the demand for the transportation of air freight. Here, in order to create service competition between the all-freight carriers and the passenger carriers in their freight business, the Board decided to increase the price of the service. This, of course, is an unusual circumstance, and the question is really not whether competition increased the price, but rather should the air freight business be subsidized and, if so, who should provide the subsidies. In the initial period, before the certification of the all-freight carriers, the freight service was subsidized, and the subsidy was provided by the other revenues of the airlines, either from mail pay or from passenger revenues. Clearly, if, in this joint cost situation, the freight service was paying its marginal cost and making some contribution to overhead, it was good business for the passenger carriers to provide the service. However, if it did not cover its marginal costs, then this kind of subsidy; i.e., selling a product at less than its marginal cost by, in effect, overcharging for a different product in a different market, is uneconomic, in that it leads to less than optimum allocation of resources. In regulated industries such subsidy decisions should not be made by individual business managements. Rather, if it is felt by the community at large that subsidization of a particular kind of business is desirable, either for promotional purposes or on a continuing basis, then such a decision should be consciously taken by the public at large through their government, which should then provide the subsidy with funds derived from the public by a more equitable basis than that of overcharging in air passenger fares. This matter of "internal subsidy" is discussed at some length in later chapters where the question of rich routes subsidizing weak routes is raised. However, it should be noted that internal subsidy is not uncommon. It is practiced, for example, by the railroads who subsidize certain of their passenger services with revenues derived from other sources.

EQUIPMENT COMPETITION

. . . the history of equipment purchases leaves little doubt that the stimulus of competition has been in the forefront of the factors influencing airline management in its constant search for new equipment. Thus, new equipment has traditionally been placed in operation first on the most competitive segments, and the introduction of more modern aircraft by one company on such a route has been followed by a scramble on the part of competitors to introduce with the greatest possible speed comparable or more advanced types. Conversely, the introduction of new equipment has generally lagged the most in services where competition was not a prime influence. Although it is perhaps inevitable that, apart from competitive considerations, the largest carriers would have led the way in equipment advances, it is significant that these carriers operate in perhaps the most highly competitive of the major markets. It is again significant that the smaller carriers which have trailed in the acquisition of new property have promptly developed equipment programs when changes in route structures have placed them in competitive situations with carriers utilizing more modern equipment.[20]

Probably the most active and obvious form of competition among the airlines has been the striving to offer more and more attractive flight equipment. It was realized very early in the history of the industry that larger, faster, more comfortable aircraft attract more passengers in a competitive situation. Even when most airlines were using the DC-3, various airlines used different seating configurations in an attempt to better their competitive position. Indeed, the remarkable upsurge of the traffic carried by Capital Airlines in 1956 and 1957 in its competitive markets is probably due, in a large measure, to its introduction of the Vickers Viscount, the first nonpiston powered aircraft used in the domestic service in the United States. That aircraft was so successful at that time that, according to the president of Capital, a campaign of detraction had been waged against it by some of the other airlines.[21] This, too, is a form of competition!

The president of the Air Transport Association, appearing before the Celler Committee testified that, "The competitive situation in the industry as it relates to equipment is now and always has been violent, and that is one of the reasons that our fleet is the finest in the world." [22] And with respect to the jet equipment programs which were then getting under way, he noted that, "there are some carriers in vigorous competition with those who have bought the equipment that have not yet bought the equipment and they will have to get themselves in a competitive position where they can meet the competition with these new airplanes, and thus are forced to buy them." [23]

There is no question that the newer and faster airplanes have been put into service on competitive routes, and that the relative traffic balance among competing air carriers has been on many occasions observed to be shifted from one carrier to the other as newer and faster aircraft types have been put into service alternately by first one and then the other of the competing carriers. Excellent illustrations of this effect of equipment on competitors' market shares are Eastern vs. National and, later, Northeast over the New York to Miami route and the American–TWA–United competition on the transcontinental routes.

Earlier studies by Gill and Bates,[24] and Frederick [25] have also reported that competition does have a tangible and observable effect on the acquisition and use of flight equipment.

On the other hand, not all varieties of competition have had the effect of inspiring the use of the newest aircraft. For example, the competition of the irregular carriers in the early postwar years was characterized by the use, on their part, of older equipment and an appeal to the public based on price alone. This, clearly, is a pattern of competition that is quite different from that of the certificated trunkline carriers, who traditionally seek to avoid offering service with second-best equipment on competitive routes.

PASSENGER SERVICE COMPETITION

In-flight service has been a competitive factor since even before the first in-flight meal service in 1929. The competitive aspects of the many dimensions of the service, such as speed, size and comfort of the seats, seating configuration, various aspects of the meals and beverages served, soundproofing, red carpets, etc.

are well-known to anyone who flies or who takes note of the barrage of competitive advertising. These "product differentiating" factors are of varying importance to different individuals, but hardly any passengers can be said to be completely indifferent to them, with the consequence that, insofar as competition inspires the carriers to improve these aspects of their transportation service, the traveling public is benefited. If, however, these added services are offered in lieu of price decreases, the benefit to the public is not so clear, since, then, passengers are not given the choice between this and the less luxurious service at a lower price.

In addition to the in-flight service, the effects of competition may be seen in ground services, such as the speed with which reservations are made, the courtesy with which passengers are treated, the sales services, refund policies, the speed and efficiency with which baggage is handled, the "no tipping" policy, and in many other ways.

The airlines have realized that passenger services, both in the air and on the ground, are an important aspect of their product, and that, since prices, equipment, and certain other factors tend to be identical among carriers, these passenger services may well be controlling in the minds of the customers. The airlines have been outstanding in their attention to these details of customer service. It is far easier and more comfortable to buy an airline ticket than to buy a railroad ticket. Sales offices that are always pleasant and frequently luxurious may be found in several downtown locations in large cities.

Thus, competitive airlines tend to offer luxurious, but comparable, customer services. For those passengers to whom these amenities are important, this has been and continues to be a highly desirable effect of competition. On the other hand, the growth of coach service indicates that for many passengers these service features have been unnecessarily luxurious and excessively expensive, and that elimination or contraction of some of them with corresponding rate reductions is a preferable alternative.

MARKETING COMPETITION

If the existence and intensity of competition may be judged by the criterion of the amount of competitive advertising, the airlines may be characterized as highly competitive. The daily newspapers in almost any large city testify eloquently to the emphasis placed on this form of competition by the carriers. In New York, for example, at one time, one could find two advertisements, in the same newspaper, in which Capital Airlines advertised nonstop flights, New York to Chicago, "Every Hour on the Half Hour," 8:30 a.m. to 8:30 p.m., while American Airlines offered nonstops, "Every Hour on the Hour," 8:00 a.m. to 8:00 p.m. This sort of competitive advertising is commonplace in the industry. In the Celler Committee Hearings, a representative of the Air Transport Association, seeking to convince the Committee that the airline industry is indeed competitive, testified that

> . . . the certificated carriers of the United States, on another qualitative competitive level, can be found to be at least as intense, in fact more intense, than other forms of transportation.
>
> As an example, in 1954, six United States airlines, despite their reasonably comparatively meager earnings, were among the top 100 national newspaper advertisers, according to the advertising bureau of the American Newspaper Publishers Association. . . .
>
> In addition to that, on a 5-year comparison of newspaper expenditures by travel advertisers—and there you are talking of airlines, buses, railroads, steamships, and travel agents—you would find in 1954 that the certificated carriers of the United States, in terms of newspaper expenditures, spent about $13 million; $1.5 million spent by foreign carriers, $2 million by the bus operators, $5.5 million by the railroads, $2.3 million by the steamships, and less than $1 million by the travel agents. . . .
>
> . . . we find in the Washington Post of Tuesday, March 20, 6 ads by United States scheduled airlines, 1 by a foreign airline, 1 by a railroad, and 2 by buslines. . . .
>
> In the New York Times of Monday, March 19, we find 9 United States scheduled airlines ads, 1 by a United States supplemental air carrier, 5 by foreign airlines, 3 by railroads, 1 by a United States steamship company, and 1 foreign steamship line.[26]

The trunkline carriers undertake passenger marketing activities in a variety of ways other than the advertisements in newspapers and periodicals mentioned above. Advertising is also carried out on radio and television, billboards and direct mail. The distribution of schedules to potential and actual users of air transportation is another way of marketing airline service. The *Official Airline Guide,* published by American Aviation Publications, contains the schedules of all airlines and is a medium for industry and individual airline promotion as well as a valuable service to the public. The recent development of condensed schedules covering all the flights between a city pair is an outstanding example of industry marketing.

The establishment of ticket offices in midtown locations and hotels promotes airline sales both by being a visual reminder of an individual company's services and by offering a convenient location for the conduct of business. This tends to offset the relative inconvenience of out of town airports.

The reservation service of the airlines was early developed into an effective sales tool by making it quick and easy for potential passengers to make firm reservations for travel and to obtain information about an airline's service. Closely associated with the reservation service are the extensive sales staffs maintained by the airlines in major cities. The sales representatives solicit the business of organizations which have a large volume of travel. Also, they call upon travel agents in an effort to increase their share of the business that is often controlled by these organizations who, in turn, contribute to the airlines' overall marketing effort.

The use of public relations to maintain the airline's name before the public is yet another important marketing technique. The practice of some airlines of maintaining private clubs at certain terminals open only to frequent users of their service is also designed to be a sales tool.

Since, as has been noted above, the airlines do not compete in price, much of the competitive battle finds its impact in the marketing activities, and within the areas of advertising, ticket office locations, reservation service, solicitation, public relations, private clubs, etc., much ingenuity, expense, and effort are applied.

SCHEDULE COMPETITION

Schedule quality is probably the most important of the forms of competition as actively manipulated in the industry today. Also, it is rather different from the others, since schedule frequency may serve as a measure of competitive position as well as a means of affecting that position.

The several aspects of schedule quality (in addition to equipment type) which are important from a competitive viewpoint include: frequency and timing of flights, time en route, number of coach flights, number of intermediate stops, and number of available seats. These various schedule characteristics are not independent of one another. For example, the more frequent the number of flights, the more likely it is that a passenger will find one leaving or arriving at a time convenient to him. The aircraft type determines its passenger capacity and its range and, therefore, also determines whether or not it can fly a nonstop schedule. Turnaround schedules will mean more on-time departures, more seats available at all times, and usually flights at more convenient times. With newer aircraft and fewer stops, a trip is faster.

Improvements in the schedule pattern between two cities might include not only more flights, more non-stop or limited-stop flights, or more convenient hours of arrival and departure, but, perhaps less obviously, more seats might be made available between the city pair by scheduling more originating and terminating flights, or even by scheduling other flights to other cities on the route thereby freeing more seats for the city pair under consideration, although the pattern of flights between that city pair may seem unchanged.

OTHER EFFECTS OF COMPETITION

Traffic generation. One of the possible benefits of competition, and one which has figured somewhat controversially in the exhibits and testimony of various parties to Civil Aeronautics Board route cases has been the generation of new air traffic.[27] The issue was raised in 1947 in the *Detroit–Washington Service Case.*

There is testimony in the record to the effect that the injection of competition on some routes has resulted in the development of additional traffic. This would appear to have been conspicuously true of certain routes, such as the Los Angeles-San Francisco service, upon which competition was allowed since the 1940 and 1941 traffic survey dates. But the wartime boom in air traffic was at least in part responsible for the outstanding growth of traffic on such routes. Non-competitive routes, such as PCA's Route 14, have also experienced a tremendous increase in the volume of air travel since 1940 and 1941. The record is without data which would specifically assess the role competition has played as a generator of air traffic.[28]

In many route proceedings since that time, there have been exhibits submitted which were prepared on the basis of statistical inquiries into this question and which tend to suggest that competition does have some traffic generating effect. These studies have generally not been convincing. Obviously competition, as such, cannot generate traffic. Air traffic may be generated only by diverting passengers from various modes of ground transportation or by creating new travel. This may be done only by making air transportation relatively more attractive either, first, by making the product relatively more desirable or, second, by decreasing the price. Only if competition can effect these changes, can it generate new traffic. The effect of the intensive advertising, both competitive and noncompetitive, by directing the consumer's mind toward air travel, doubtless is to increase the total air travel market, and it may be included in the first category listed above; i.e., making the product more desirable.

The factors affecting traffic generation were cited in the following statement made in 1956 by Ross Rizley, then Chairman of the Civil Aeronautics Board.

> The demand for air transportation services is responsive to many factors such as the quality of service rendered—whether one-plane or one-carrier service, for example—frequency of service, type of equipment, type of service—whether first class, coach or family plan—convenience of schedules, as well as to such factors as the business and other institutional characteristics of the areas involved, general income levels and fare changes.[29]

However, any traffic generation effect of improvements in the product-price package may be expected to occur regardless of whether the improvements are stimulated by competitive factors or whether they come from a monopoly carrier. The critical question as regards competition, then, is the extent to which competition stimulates such improvements.

Tying-in of routes. One way in which the addition of competition benefits the traveling public stems from the fact that each carrier has its own distinctive route pattern. Thus, when a new competitor is added to a route to create competition over that route, the new carrier, besides providing the competition over the route in question, also usually provides new one-carrier service to those points on its old routes which previously were not certificated for such service with points on the newly competitive route. This new one-carrier and, perhaps, one-plane service does, no doubt, stimulate traffic development, because, like any new air service, it creates and develops its own market by making possible many meetings and trips that otherwise would be foregone.

CHAPTER V

Methods for Creating and Controlling Competition

THE CERTIFICATION REQUIREMENT

In the traditional economic conception of competition, high or excessive profitability in an industry attracts new firms to that industry, thereby expanding the number of competitive firms in that industry, or, more specifically, in that particular market. This, of course, cannot happen freely in the domestic scheduled air transportation industry because, under the Civil Aeronautics Act of 1938, no air carrier may engage in air transportation unless there is in force a certificate of public convenience and necessity issued by the Civil Aeronautics Board.[1]

In addition, since the traditional certificate of public convenience and necessity describes the specific route over which the carrier may operate,[2] and since it also defines the terms and restrictions under which it must operate, an existing carrier cannot, without the specific authorization of the Civil Aeronautics Board, expand its activities to encompass new routes and the offering of air transportation between additional city pairs. Thus (with the minor exception of the "supplemental" carriers) no carrier can, of its own accord, without the specific authorization of the Board, become a new competitor over any route.

ADMINISTRATIVE PROCEDURES IN ROUTE CASES

The actual administrative procedures used by the Board in formal route proceedings involve several sequential steps. After initiating actions, which might be applications of carriers or of public bodies or motion of the Board itself, or some combination of such actions, the following series of steps is usually followed, although it is possible, with the consent of the parties, to waive one or more.

1. Assigned for prehearing conference before a Board examiner: Scope of proceeding defined, issues fixed and tentative procedural dates set.
2. Public hearing before a Board examiner: Oral testimony presented, exhibits previously prepared subjected to cross-examination. Briefs to examiner filed subsequent to hearing.
3. Initial decision or recommended decision issued by examiner: Exceptions and briefs to examiner's initial or recommended decision may be filed. If no exceptions are filed, examiner's decision becomes final.
4. Oral argument before the five-man Board: If exceptions and briefs are filed, the Board hears the parties in oral argument. After argument, the case is ready for final decision by the Board.
5. Issuance of Board decision and order: Board decision made public, and copies served on parties to the proceeding. Cases involving foreign or overseas transportation require Presidential approval before issuance by the Board.[3]

The discussions and citations used and quoted frequently throughout this study are either the examiner's decision resulting from step #3 above or the actual Board decision resulting from step #5. The Board frequently attaches parts of the examiner's decision to its own decision, thereby "adopting" these statements as its own. This may vary from, in some cases, a few pages, to, in others, all or most of the examiner's decision.

ENTRY INTO THE INDUSTRY

In air transportation, there is restriction of entry on two levels. First, a new firm may not, on its own decision, enter the air transportation industry, and, second, a firm already in the industry may not freely extend its routes to points which it has previously not served. The requirement for a certificate of public convenience and necessity which specifies the cities served by the individual carrier obviously gives the Civil Aeronautics Board complete control (with the very limited exception posed by the supplemental carriers) over both of these aspects of freedom of entry.

The only economic reason for this restriction of entry both into the field of air transportation and into a particular route is to protect the existing carriers and, through them, the air transport industry from certain undesirable consequences, real or imagined, of unrestricted free entry. "Unrestricted free entry" here refers to the usual situation, typical of industries not subject to economic regulation and which, in air transportation, would mean that any firm which could comply with certain noneconomic requirements, such as those relating to safety, would be free to operate as a public carrier over any routes which it might desire to exploit.

Under the law, as cited above, entry is *controlled* rather than *closed*. The issuance of certificates of convenience and necessity to new carrier firms or to existing firms for route extensions is one of the important matters decided by the Civil Aeronautics Board in its so-called "route cases" or "route proceedings." The extent to which entry is open or closed depends upon the willingness of the Board to issue certificates, and it is not fixed by law. Rather, the law has made it a subject for the Board's discretion, and, if it so desired, the Board could create, in effect, a system of unrestricted entry by merely announcing its readiness to issue certificates of public convenience and necessity to any and all qualified applicants.

The actual policy followed by the Civil Aeronautics Board has been to permit neither the free entry of new carrier firms into the scheduled passenger air transportation industry nor unlimited competition among existing carriers in the form of free entry into any routes which they may desire to serve. The Board feels that such competitive freedom would not be in the public interest, and that, were this type of free entry into new markets to be permitted, there would be excessive duplication of air routes and a return to the chaotic conditions of 1938, conditions which led the Senate committee in charge of the bill which became the Civil Aeronautics Act to state:

> Competition among air carriers is being carried to an extreme which tends to jeopardize the financial status of the air carriers and to jeopardize and render unsafe a transportation service appropriate to the needs of commerce and required in the public interest, in the interest of the postal service and the national defense.[4]

Paragraphs (b) and (c) of Section 2 of the Act [5] instruct the Board to regulate air transportation in such manner as to "foster sound economic conditions in, such transportation . . ." and to avoid ". . . unfair or destructive competitive practices." Clearly, the Board seeks to accomplish these ends by limiting entry both into the industry and into new routes. The President's Air Coordinating Committee in discussing the general question of control of entry, agreed with this position:

> This basic obligation to maintain service can be meaningfully enforced only if entry into the business is controlled. It would be unrealistic to force a given carrier to continue serving all of its points (including the unprofitable ones) if at any time it could be subjected to competition by a new carrier entirely free to serve only profitable points. Under such circumstances carriers would naturally tend to concentrate their operations on profitable routes with a consequent decline in the quality and volume of service on more marginal routes. The broad national interest in having adequate air transport service, wherever needed, would inevitably suffer under such a situation.
>
> For the above reasons, it would be unsound to have a completely unrestricted right of entry in air transportation; it would be both unsound and inequitable to maintain a dual regulatory standard, in which some carriers are required to adhere to certificated obligations, while other carriers are free to provide competitive service without such obligations.
>
> Federal subsidy policies for the development of civil air transportation further emphasize the importance of controlling entry into the business. Only by maintaining sound economic conditions within the industry can the Government discharge its public obligation to minimize subsidy expenditures.
>
> 1. The intent of the Civil Aeronautics Act, to establish a pattern of controlled entry with regard to common air transportation, is still sound.[6]

Although the Civil Aeronautics Board has not authorized the entry of new carrier firms into the domestic certificated trunkline air transportation industry, it has, over the years, authorized all of the trunkline carriers to expand their routes by a series of carefully defined route awards, many of which, also under careful and purposeful control, permitted carriers to expand into the routes of other carriers, thus creating directly competitive authorizations over those selected routes.

The amount of growth in the trunkline systems under this policy may be seen in Table V-1, which shows the number of points served and the certificated route mileage of the trunkline carriers at the time of their original certification and on June 30, 1959.

TABLE V-1

GROWTH OF THE TRUNKLINE CARRIERS

	Points Served		*Certificated Route Mileage*	
	Original	*June 30, 1959*	*Original*	*June 30, 1959*
American Airlines	59	71	6,826	26,053
Braniff Airways	21	54	2,543	10,153
Capital Airlines	20	56	2,015	11,999
Continental Air Lines	8	37	624	7,202
Delta Air Lines	13	62	1,091	16,750
Eastern Air Lines	42	104	5,276	22,445
National Airlines	13	37	871	3,569
Northeast Airlines	16	61	648	6,611
Northwest Airlines	21	34	2,507	10,855
Trans World Airlines	27	58	5,749	21,914
United Air Lines	38	71	5,321	18,651
Western Air Lines	12	48	1,237	7,855

Source: *Annual Report of the Civil Aeronautics Board, 1959,* page 53.

THE "GRANDFATHER" CARRIERS

As has been noted, the Civil Aeronautics Act of 1938 provided that certificates of convenience and necessity were required for all commercial air carriers. The important paragraphs of the Act with respect to carrier certification are given at the end of this chapter. The paragraphs quoted are from the Federal Aviation Act of 1958, which, as noted, restated this section of the 1938 Act almost identically. The major changes in the 1958 Act are the deletion of the provisions of the 1938 Act relating to the status of the air carriers existing at the time of its passage. Parts of these are cited here.

Sec. 401. (a) No air carrier shall engage in any air transportation unless there is in force a certificate issued by the Authority [Board] authorizing such air carrier to engage in such transportation: *Provided,* That if an air carrier is engaged in such transportation on the date of the enactment of this Act, such air carrier may continue so to engage between the same terminal and intermediate points for one hundred and twenty days after said date, and thereafter until such time as the authority [Board] shall pass upon an application for a certificate for such transportation if within said one hundred and twenty days such air carrier files such application as provided herein. . . .

Existing Air Carriers

(e) (1) If any applicant who makes application for a certificate within one hundred and twenty days after the date of enactment of this Act shall show that, from May 14, 1938, until the effective date of this section, it, or its predecessor in interest, was an air carrier, continuously operating as such (except as to interruptions of service over which the applicant or its predecessor in interest had no control), the Authority [Board], upon proof of such fact only, shall, unless the service rendered by such applicant for such period was inadequate and inefficient, issue a certificate or certificates, authorizing such applicant to engage in air transportation. . . .

The routes which existed at the time of the Act—i.e., those referred to in Section 401 (e) (1), under which certificates were issued to the various carriers for routes which they had operated continuously with adequate and efficient service from May 14, 1938, to August 22, 1938—are the so-called "grandfather" routes. This previously established route system which was inherited by the Board, the so-called "grandfather system," is the basis for the domestic trunkline air transportation system of today. By the subsequent issuance of additional certificates of convenience and necessity as provided for in the Act, the Civil Aeronautics Board has expanded the routes of all of the grandfather carriers so that new service and new competitive service have been developed as the public convenience and necessity, as interpreted by the Board, required.

Thus, all of the trunklines in the domestic air transportation system today have been in the industry since before the passage of the Civil Aeronautics Act. They are all "grandfather" carriers in that some part of the route of each of these trunkline carriers, the "grandfather route" was certificated to that carrier under Paragraph (e) (1) of Section 401 of the Civil Aeronautics Act.

Since the passage of the Civil Aeronautics Act in 1938, the

number of certificated trunk airlines in the domestic service has decreased from 19 to 12 as a consequence of mergers, consolidations, and, in one case, the cessation of service by one of the grandfather carriers. Table V-2 lists the domestic "grandfather" certificated airlines.

TABLE V-2

DOMESTIC "GRANDFATHER" CERTIFICATED AIRLINES

American Airlines, Inc.
Boston-Maine Airways, Inc.
Braniff Airways, Inc.
Canadian Colonial Airways, Inc.
Chicago & Southern Air Lines, Inc.
Continental Airlines, Inc.
Delta Air Corporation
Eastern Air Lines, Inc.
Inland Airlines, Inc.
Marquette Airlines, Inc.
Mayflower
Mid-Continent Airlines, Inc.
National Airlines, Inc.
Northwest Airlines, Inc.
Pennsylvania-Central Airlines, Corp.
Transcontinental & Western Air, Inc.
United Airlines Transport Corp.
Western Air Express Corp.
Wilmington-Catalina Airline, Limited

All of the service authorized in grandfather certificates except that operated by Wilmington-Catalina,* continues in operation although there have been the following mergers or changes in corporate name:

Boston-Maine—now Northeast Airlines, Inc.
Canadian Colonial—later Colonial Airlines, Inc.,
subsequently merged with Eastern Air Lines
Chicago & Southern—merged with Delta Airlines
Delta Air Corporation—now Delta Air Lines, Inc.
Inland Airlines—merged with Western Air Lines
Marquette Airlines—certificate transferred to TWA
Mayflower—certificate transferred to Northeast
Mid-Continental—certificate transferred to Braniff
Pennsylvania-Central—now Capital Airlines, Inc.
Transcontinental & Western Air—now Trans-World Airlines
United Airlines Transport Corp.—now United Air Lines, Inc.
Western Air Express Corp.—now Western Air Lines, Inc.

* This carrier was permitted to abandon its route and its certificate was canceled on September 30, 1955. (Order No. E-9563)

Source: Answer submitted by Chairman Ross Rizley of the Civil Aeronautics Board in answer to representative Celler's letter of August 8, 1955. *Hearings before the Antitrust Subcommittee of the Committee on the Judiciary of the House of Representatives, 84th Congress, 2nd Session, Part 1, Vol. I, Airlines,* p. 492 (*Celler Committee Hearings*).

THE LIMITATION OF NEW CARRIERS

At the outset, the Board disclaimed any intention of pursuing a policy of closed entry into the industry and, in two cases in 1940, new airlines were certificated, one for international service and the other for the carriage of mail using a pick-up device for securing the mail without landing. In the *All American Case,* the Board spoke out strongly against a policy of closed entry, saying that a theory which resulted

in reserving solely for existing airlines the privilege of providing all additions to the present air-transportation system of the United States, is untenable. Our adoption of such a policy would certainly not be consistent with a sound development of air transportation, and would not be conducive to the best interests of the foreign and domestic commerce of the United States, the postal service, and the National defense.[7]

Indeed, the privilege of providing all additions to the present air transportation system of the U. S. has not been reserved solely for the existing airlines. However, such new firms as have been certificated have been certificated for local service, helicopter service, all-freight service, etc.; that is, they are authorized to perform tasks and to develop services that are different from those of the air carriers in existence in 1940 when the Board made the statement quoted above. There have been no new firms certificated to perform the functions and to enjoy the privileges of the grandfather carriers, the present "trunklines." This essentially closed entry may have been the result of a re-evaluation on the part of the Board of its policy as expressed in the *All American Case,* or it may be that the Board, in its statement in that case, did not necessarily refer to new airlines, created in the image of the existing airlines. In any event, the Board stated, in the next year, its policy with respect to new firms, and, if we define the word "particular" to refer to those circumstances surrounding the creation of helicopter service, local service airlines, and such other services as have been certificated, none of which resemble the services performed by the air carriers at the time of the following statement, this policy has not been changed.

The number of air carriers now operating appears sufficient to insure against monopoly in respect to the average new route case, and we believe that the present domestic air-transportation system can by proper supervision be integrated and expanded in a manner that will in general afford the competition necessary for the development of that system in the manner contemplated by the Act. In the absence of particular circumstances presenting an affirmative reason for a new carrier there appears to be no inherent desirability of increasing the present number of carriers merely for the purpose of numerically enlarging the industry.[8]

However, via the recent permanent certification of the local airlines, the clearly developing pattern of permitting them to skip stops, and the authorization to them of service that is competitive with trunklines, the Board seems to be creating, from the local service lines, air carriers which may be destined eventually to resemble the older trunklines. If this should happen, the Board will have increased the number of carriers in spite of the policy stated in the *Delta Case.*

In following its policy, what the Board has explicitly refused to do in its individual decisions is issue certificates creating new carriers to compete in the heavily traveled highly competitive markets for which various applicants have sought certificates. There are good reasons for this. Aside from any considerations relating to the strength or other characteristics of the applicant carriers, there are the questions of the "tying-in of routes," and the strengthening of the existing carriers as a device for balancing carrier sizes and reducing the federal subsidy.

The tying-in factor may be illustrated by consideration of one of the cases decided in 1955 by the Civil Aeronautics Board. In the *Denver Service Case,* several carriers had applied to compete with United Air Lines on the route New York–Chicago–Denver–Los Angeles, among other routes. In this case, the Board chose TWA for this route over all of the other applicant airlines, both the certificated airlines and the noncertificated. One of the reasons given by the Board for the choice of TWA was that, as a consequence of the tying-in of the new route with TWA's existing routes, new single-plane service between Denver and many other cities would become possible. On the other hand, a theretofore uncertificated carrier such as North American, an applicant in the case, could provide service only over the new route for which application had been made.

In addition to the "tying-in" factor described above, awards for new trunkline routes, both competitive and noncompetitive, have been made to existing carriers rather than to new carriers because of the general policy of extending and strengthening existing carriers. This strengthening was intended, among other things, to reduce the need for direct federal subsidy and eventually to eliminate the direct subsidy in favor of internal subsidy as the carriers achieve system-wide self-sufficiency. Under this policy, many of the grandfather carriers which were extremely small at the time of the Civil Aeronautics Act, have grown to be relatively large carriers and efficient competitors of the very largest carriers. These smaller airlines have been strengthened, they have become self-sufficient, and their growth has permitted the tying-in factor to operate to the benefit of both the new cities to which they were extended and the cities which were originally served.

Unfortunately, this policy seems to say that the "haves" shall receive more, while the "have-nots" can receive nothing. Nevertheless, with respect to the award of regular trunkline routes, this policy, judiciously pursued, seems to be in the public interest.

This failure of the Board to permit the entry of new trunkline carriers into the domestic scheduled trunkline air transportation industry has been the object of considerable attack. It has been argued that the failure of the total number of carriers to be increased indicates that there has been too little competition.[9] (On the other hand, it has been argued that, even with the restricted number of carriers in the industry, the amount of competition that has been created is excessive and that dire consequences are in store.) The question whether new interstation competition should be provided by extension of the routes of existing carriers or by the certification of new carrier firms was a matter of great interest in the decade following World War II, and it has been explored thoroughly by the Board and by various congressional committees in connection with the so-called "irregular" or "nonscheduled" carriers.

The Board's policy of increasing the amount of competition by expanding the routes of the existing carriers rather than by adding to the number of certificated carriers follows from the fact that the Board has regarded the market for air transportation as the route over which the particular transportation service is offered. For example, there are three airlines certificated to carry passengers between Denver and Chicago. The amount and intensity of competition which exists on that route is a function of this fact. If these three were the only airlines in the country, or if they were but three of a very large number of airlines operating in the country, the fact would be unchanged that there are three airlines certificated in that market. The buyer in that market is purchasing a specific service; namely, transportation between Denver and Chicago, and the only trunkline sellers in the market are the three airlines which are certificated to offer the service which he desires to purchase. If the Board feels it desirable to increase the amount of competition between Denver and Chicago, it can do this only by authorizing another carrier to serve that market. The addition of any number of other carriers to offer various other transportation services within the United States will not increase the amount of competition in the market for the transportation service between Denver and Chicago.

THE NUMBER OF CARRIERS

The competition which the Board has sought to create and which the Board has created has been limited or controlled competition in that the Board has felt that the number of carriers that should be certificated to offer service between any two points should be limited. In no case does the number of carriers exceed ten. The New York–Washington route with ten carriers certificated has more carriers than any of the other routes in the country. Even here, however, the competitive situation can be described only in terms of oligopoly. In the other routes where there are two or three or four carriers, the term oligopoly is *a fortiori* appropriate. From the economist's point of view there are just a few sellers in any of these markets, and the possibility of tacit or implied collusion, of price leadership, fear of retaliation, or of any of the other well-known phenomena which operate to decrease the intensity of competition, is present. The control of these phenomena in the absence of the possibility of increasing the number of firms to a very large number lies with the Civil Aeronautics Board.

Thus, the best in the way of competition that the Civil Aeronautics Board can create via its certification authority is an oligopolistic situation, coupled with the appropriate policing to minimize the undesirable effects of the market phenomena which are characteristic of oligopoly and which might tend to reduce the force and the public benefits of competition. This kind of policing is evident in a recent decision by the Board not to permit the carriers to meet with one another in order to discuss what were seemingly harmless matters.[10] The Board was doubtless influenced by the same thought, which, back in the year 1775, was expressed in the familiar quotation from Adam Smith that,

> People of the same trade seldom meet together, even for merriment and diversion, but the conversation ends in a conspiracy against the public, or in some contrivance to raise prices. It is impossible indeed to prevent such meetings, by any law which either could be executed, or would be consistent with liberty and justice. But though the law cannot hinder people of the same trade from sometimes assembling together, it ought to do nothing to facilitate such assemblies; much less to render them necessary.[11]

The optimum total number of air carrier firms in the domestic air transportation industry must be at least large enough to assure that there will be competition "to the extent necessary . . ." as prescribed by the Civil Aeronautics Act. On the other hand, the upper limit to the desirable or optimum number of firms in the industry is not so clearly defined. If it were required that all of the firms in the industry be self-sufficient, then the number of firms should be sufficiently small so that each firm can be profitable and have some satisfactory mix of strong and weak routes. If this has been accomplished with respect to the certificated trunkline carriers, then, by that criterion, as of the present, the number of carriers is not too large. However, if the local airlines were to be included in the requirement that airlines be self-sufficient, then, with present or foreseeable traffic levels, such self-sufficiency could be attained only by merging with the trunkline carriers, whose dense traffic routes might then provide a balance against the sparse routes presently served by the local carriers. Then, of course, the travelers on the dense routes would be in the position of subsidizing the travelers on the less dense local routes, whereas, now, these local routes are subsidized by the nation at large via direct Federal subsidy.

While such internal subsidy; i.e., subsidization of the weak routes by the strong, has undesirable theoretic economic implications with respect to the allocation of resources, it is not contrary to our national practice. As a matter of fact, this is clearly the typical practice among the trunkline carriers as well as in other utility and transportation industries. The importance of internal subsidy in the air transport industry has long been recognized and accepted. The President's Air Coordinating Committee report stated that:

> Like other forms of transportation, air transportation is characterized by a wide variation in the profitability of individual routes and stations. Some routes are capable of supporting profitable operations; other routes are marginal; and still others are inherently unprofitable. In keeping with the normal public utility concept, certificated carriers have a statutory obligation to maintain all authorized services needed by the public on both strong and weak routes. Carriers cannot abandon service without Governmental approval, and they can be compelled to expand service where needed. If carriers are to provide the full scale of service needed by the public with minimum reliance on Federal subsidy, they must be able to earn sufficient profits on strong routes to offset losses on weak routes.[12]

As indicated in Table V-2, there has been a slow but steady procession of mergers which may be expected to continue, perhaps to consolidate some of the smaller and weaker trunklines and, more probably, to consolidate local service lines with trunklines operating in the same area. However, this process should not proceed to the extent that the effectiveness of competition may be diminished. As long as the number of firms in the industry is sufficiently large to assure the effectiveness of competition in individual markets, the actual total number of firms in the industry is not a matter of great economic importance.

One other possible argument in favor of a decrease in the total number of air carriers might exist if the industry were characterized by significant economies of scale. However, the fact seems to be that, within the size range that is presently characteristic of the trunklines, and with current technology, there is evidence that there are no important economies of scale.[13]

Conversely, since competition exists on specific routes, the fact that one carrier is relatively large and another small does not necessarily affect the effectiveness of competition between the two carriers, provided the smaller of the two is financially able to provide an adequate service offering over the route in question. This is a conclusion with which the CAB agrees:

> However, it has been amply demonstrated that small carriers can compete with larger ones, and that given access to markets of adequate traffic density, sound route structure, and the exercise of sound managerial judgment, over the long run, a small carrier can obtain a fair share of the markets involved.[14]

It is indeed an enabling factor in its long-term policy of strengthening the smaller carriers by expanding their routes into new markets including those that are already served by the larger carriers.

The real problem in airline competition has to do with competition over particular routes serving particular points, and the matter of the total number of firms in the industry is not, with the limitations noted, of crucial importance. Indeed, if the traffic density mix pattern described above in the quotation from the report of the President's Air Coordinating Committee is to be followed for all airlines, there remains some question about whether or not it is feasible for a new airline to be created which would have a balanced distribution of dense and sparse routes in a well-integrated route system. If any new trunklines, as we know them today, are to be created, they will probably result from the growth of presently existing local service airlines, rather than from the certification of new firms for trunkline service over heavily traveled routes.

INTERCHANGES

On various occasions in the past, where the Board has felt that new service, either first single-plane service or competitive service should be added to a route, it has authorized *interchanges,* an interesting substitute for the certification of a new carrier. This interchange arrangement is an agreement between two or more carriers to provide service over a particular route with no change of airplane for the passengers. For example, in the *Denver Service Case,* where service between Denver and the East was at issue, one proposal which was seriously considered was equipment interchange between Continental and Capital. Continental, under the plan, was to be extended to Chicago, so that it could serve Denver–Chicago. Capital already served Chicago–New York. Under the proposed interchange arrangement, a single airplane could fiy between Denver and New York, stopping at Chicago, the "interchange point," at which point the flight changed ownership and management, all without disturbing the passengers any more than is implied by the necessity of making the intermediate stop at Chicago.

Interchange arrangements such as these have been used in both the domestic and international service for many years, and some of them have been quite successful. However, in general, they have not provided service that is as good as that of a single carrier, and, as competitors, interchanges have failed dismally in vying for business against single carriers. This results quite naturally from the fact that there is less drive on the part of carrier management to develop the market than is the case when the market is one's own, and also from the fact that the interchange flight, both in planning and operation, requires a high degree of coordination between the cooperating carriers. Manifestly such coordination is more difficult to achieve between independent business managements than within one firm.

The interchange as a *modus operandi* is becoming progressively less important. This comes both as a consequence of its inability to perform and also as a result of the development of air traffic in general. That is, the authorization of an interchange is a conservative step in that it creates the desired single-plane authorization without necessarily extending the routes of any of the carriers involved. It presumably, therefore, requires no new investment in ground facilities, limited additional sales expenses, and, in general, very little additional effort or expense on the part of the carriers. This was indeed a virtue when confidence in the future development of traffic was not high, or when there was fear of excessive traffic diversion from one of the carriers if the other were given the whole route, or, alternatively, from both of the carriers if a third carrier were given the route.

In the *Denver Service Case,* the interchange issue was given serious consideration and careful evaluation. The Examiner, in his initial report, did decide in favor of a Continental-Capital interchange to provide Denver with new services to the East. By extending Continental from Denver to Chicago, and by authorizing, at Chicago, an interchange with Capital, the Examiner hoped to create new competitive service between Denver, on the one hand, and Chicago, Detroit, Cleveland, New York, and Washington, on the other; and first single-plane service between Denver and Pittsburgh. This was possible since Chicago and all of these named cities east of Chicago were served by Capital.

The Board overruled the Examiner and authorized TWA to add Denver to its transcontinental route, thereby authorizing TWA to provide all of the services listed above, and, of course, many more:

> Although we agree with the Examiner's decision to award new regional services for Denver, we believe that the examiner did not go far enough in affording Denver a second transcontinental service . . . . we believe that the examiner was unduly concerned over the protection of the regional carriers, and underestimated the needs of Denver for competitive service to points east of Chicago.
>
> It is manifest that the proposed Capital-Continental interchange service would be inferior to a single carrier transcontinental service. This was indicated by the proposed schedules submitted by Capital and Continental which reflected a milk run type of service. And even if these schedules were altered, they would at best provide a one-stop service to New York via Chicago. While Denver showed a need for additional service to such points as Louisville, Indianapolis, Columbus and Dayton, the interchange would provide no improvement at all to these points. Furthermore, Continental would find itself faced with the problem of concentrating on its new regional services to Chicago and Los Angeles, while at the same time attempting to develop the long-haul transcontinental interchange market. There would be a serious risk that the carrier would be forced to place its primary attention on either the regional or the long-haul services, and the net result would be an impairment of the other service.
>
> As compared with single carrier, single plane service, an interchange service is more limited in its flexibility and does not as readily permit the frequent modifications in service necessary to meet the changing needs of air transportation. This arises chiefly from the fact that where

two airlines managements must agree on each schedule change, the alteration of scheduling often becomes a laborious process. We conclude that an interchange service recommended by the examiner would inhibit the experimentation necessary to produce the schedules and services which are most suited to Denver's needs.[15]

More recently, in the *Southern Transcontinental Service Case,*[16] the issues include the supplanting of the authorized interchanges by single-carrier competitive authorizations for service between southeast points and west coast points via New Orleans, Texas points, Albuquerque, Tucson, Phoenix, and Las Vegas.[17]

CREATING AND CONTROLLING COMPETITION

After the Board has decided that competition should exist between two points, the Board proceeds to certificate an additional carrier to offer competitive air service. However, this need not necessarily always produce such competitive air service. That is, although the Board can avoid competition by withholding certificates of convenience and necessity, it has not always been able to create competition by the issuance of such certificates. The certificate *permits* the offering of competitive service. It does not *create* such service. The authorized carrier must then be both willing and able to offer the appropriate number and type of flight schedules to create the kind and amount of competition which the Board had envisioned. Typically, the Board has not policed its authorizations, and the carriers as a matter of practice, have offered as much or as little service as their abilities and judgment dictated.

Examination of the record shows that there are many city pairs which were specifically and purposively authorized for competitive service by the Board, and which, after two or three years, still did not have competitive service. On the other hand, there are some city pairs for which the new carrier inaugurated service promptly and offered a considerable amount of service, but still not so much service as offered by the original carrier. The amount of service offered by the new carrier varies from segment to segment from essentially no service to a quantity of service that matches or even exceeds that offered by the original carrier.

Although the Board, under Section 404 (a) of the Civil Aeronautics Act, may enforce "adequate" service, this authority has not been exercised frequently, and, indeed, the determination of what constitutes adequate service under the Act is not a simple matter. In recent years, however, there have been some indications that this provision of the act may become more important. In the Supplemental Decision in the *New York–Florida Case,*[18] the Board mentions the possibility that an authorization might be rescinded for failure of the carrier to inaugurate service which the Board feels is necessary. More recently, in the *Toledo Adequacy of Service Investigation,* the Board took a large step in the direction of more active application of this provision. In that case, the Board said:

> This investigation was initiated by the Board, upon a joint complaint filed by the City and Chamber of Commerce of Toledo, Ohio, to determine whether Capital Airlines has failed to provide adequate service between Toledo, on the one hand, and Chicago, Cleveland, Philadelphia, and New York, on the other hand, and whether a remedial order should be issued under section 404 (a) of the Act. . . .
>
> After due notice, a public hearing was held before Examiner Paul N. Pfeiffer. Thereafter, the Examiner issued an Initial Decision in which he found that Capital had violated section 404 (a) of the Act by failing to provide any through service, either first-class or coach, in the Toledo–Chicago, Toledo–Philadelphia, and Toledo–New York markets. The Examiner decided that Capital should be ordered to provide two daily round trip coach flights in the Toledo–Chicago, Toledo–Philadelphia, and Toledo–New York markets for a period of one year. For the purpose of evaluating the operating results during this trial period, the Examiner recommended, further, that the proceeding remain open. . . .
>
> After due consideration of the entire record, we adopt as our own, except as modified herein, the findings and conclusions of the Examiner in his initial decision, which is attached hereto as an appendix. . . .
>
> We note, initially, that Capital was selected to serve Toledo in the *Detroit–Washington Case, supra,* for the purpose of providing a competitive service. . . . In selecting Capital . . . the Board clearly intended that Capital would provide a competitive spur to United. . . . The acceptance by Capital of this competitive certificate award carries with it the requirement that the carrier, *at the very least,* attempt to provide the service for which it was certificated. The record establishes that Capital has failed to provide this service with respect to Toledo. . . .
>
> It is clear from this record that Capital has not provided adequate

service in the pertinent markets, and that Capital should be ordered to comply with the provisions of Section 404 (a) of the Act. The manner in which such compliance will be ordered rests within the sound discretion of the Board. The Examiner fully and fairly explored the evidence in this case and fashioned an appropriate remedy which balances the conflicting needs of the carrier and the traveling public. Nothing presented by the parties persuades us that we should reach a different result from that prescribed in the Initial Decision. . . .

It is ordered that:

1. Commencing sixty days from the date of service of this order, and for at least one year thereafter, Capital Airlines shall provide two daily round trip through coach service flights between Toledo, on the the one hand, and Chicago, Philadelphia, and New York, on the other hand, at least one of such daily round trips in each market to be operated during daylight hours in each direction.[19]

Again, in the *Washington–Baltimore Adequacy of Service Case* the Board " . . . decided that inadequacies exist with respect to air service between Baltimore and a substantial number of cities and that these inadequacies should be remedied by Board order requiring additional air service." [20]

The development of the full implications of these seemingly far-reaching decisions lies in the future. However, in the absence of such direct action, the implementation of a decision on the part of the Board that a particular air route should become competitive or, if already competitive, should become more competitive, can be accomplished only by the appropriate Board action in issuing the service authorization, followed by the desired action on the part of the newly authorized carrier.

In general, in the past, the Board has not followed through in its procedures for creating competitive air service. It has authorized a new competitor and then assumed that the market forces would insure the creation of the competitive service that had been authorized. Clearly, this does not always happen. Indeed, until the very recent actions cited above, the only device which had been used for the purpose of policing this was the infrequently used but ever-present threat of certification of additional carriers. In the *Southwest–Northeast Case,* as cited below, and in other cases, there has been the expressed expectation that the new certifications would provide a competitive spur for improvement of services previously authorized with presumably some implication that, had the authorized services been fully exploited, the additional certifications might have been less liberally made.

Braniff's . . . notice is given of its plans to inaugurate a through service between San Antonio and New York at the start of service over its new route from Texas to the Northeast. We are confident that Braniff will provide a desirable new service for San Antonio as well as act as a competitive spur for improvement of the services of the other carriers in the markets which it serves.*

* [original note] In this connection, we note that Eastern has authority to operate nonstop service between San Antonio and the Northeast, but has not yet rendered such a service.[21]

Also, there seems to be considerable evidence that the very announcement of a new proceeding, or the holding of hearings, or some other manifestation of the imminence of a new competitive authorization can have a marked influence on the quality of the service offered by the existing carrier or carriers.

In recent months, probably under pressure of this proceeding, Eastern has provided some service improvements. . . .[22]

With respect to the new regional services we are awarding herein, we note United's exceptions to the Initial Decision which stress the improvements in United services offered since the close of the hearing. These improvements do not in our judgment obviate the need for the new services being authorized.[23]

American has introduced two new coach schedules in this market since January 1954 and offers the same one and one-half first-class trips it offered in September 1953. While these new services represent a marked improvement over the previous situation, they were not offered until long after the question of additional competitive service was posed by this proceeding.[24]

In summary, then, the Board has traditionally sought to create competition by awarding new competitive routes to the various carriers, and it has depended on the carriers to inaugurate the desired service. As a spur to stimulate the provision of this service, the Board has always held the threat of the certification of an additional carrier. The importance of this threat is seen in the alacrity with which carriers have increased their service in the wake of information about a new proceeding which might result in the certification of a new competitor. As a last resort, the Board can directly enforce standards of adequate service, and it has, in the recent past, taken such action. Although it is still too early to tell whether this new policy will be pursued vigorously, the very fact that it has happened insures that things will never be the same. The possibility of direct Board orders requiring additional service must henceforth loom large in the contemplation of all concerned.

OPERATING RESTRICTIONS

On the other hand, it is often the case that for some reason the Board wishes to limit the degree to which a new competitor can compete over a specified route. This can be controlled by the device of restrictions in the operating authority specified in the certificate of public convenience and necessity. That is, a new carrier may be required to make one or more intermediate stops between two points, thereby limiting its ability to compete with a nonstop carrier. Alternatively, a somewhat less stringent restriction might be the requirement that one of the carriers make one or more stops beyond the cities in the pair under question on all flights serving that pair of cities. There is a broad range of severity of the possible restrictions which may be and are imposed on individual carriers when the Board desires to limit the extent to which, or control the markets in which, one or more of the carriers may compete.

For example, in the *New York–Chicago Case,* Northwest's service to Chicago was restricted by the requirement that all flights serving Chicago also serve New York and further that they originate or terminate at Minneapolis or a point west thereof. The purpose of this restriction was to protect the other carriers in the market.

> Because of our imposition of a long haul restriction on Northwest's Chicago authorization we do not anticipate that Northwest will divert any serious amount of New York–Chicago traffic from existing operators, or inhibit the continued development of suitable turnaround services as contemplated by the lifting of Capital's New York–Chicago restrictions.[25]

TWA's authority with respect to Detroit and Delta's authority with respect to Dallas and the Northeast were similarly restricted for the same purpose. In the former case, the restriction was a long haul restriction, and, in the latter case, an intermediate stop was specified.

> We are requiring that TWA's flights serving Detroit must originate or terminate at Kansas City or points west, and at New York. Such a restriction will materially minimize the adverse effect on other carriers. We are satisfied that the diversionary impact of TWA's certification upon other carriers will not seriously affect the operations of those carriers.[26]
>
> The route extension granted Delta would, if not otherwise restricted, enable Delta to operate Dallas/Ft. Worth–Northeast nonstop services. In order to insure priority of opportunity for Braniff in the latter markets, we shall require Delta to stop at Atlanta on flights providing such service. The absence of nonstop rights in those markets will effectively limit Delta's competitive opportunity therein. However, the required stop will not seriously impede Delta in the provision of the new one-carrier service to the northeast sought by the Mississippi and northern Louisiana cities, and upon which Delta based a substantial part of its case for the Dallas–Northeast authority it sought.[27]

Sometimes, an additional purpose of a restriction in one market is to channel the efforts of a carrier into other markets, as in the following restrictions on United's Pittsburgh service and American's Houston service.

> However, we do not believe that it is necessary to make Denver the closest western terminal for Pittsburgh flights in order to assure that United will focus upon meeting Pittsburgh's long-haul service requirements rather than competing for its local traffic to and from Chicago and points east thereof. Our purpose can be achieved without undue burden on United, by requiring that all flights serving Pittsburgh shall originate or terminate at Omaha or a point west thereof. We shall, therefore, amend United's certificate accordingly.[28]
>
> Houston has also supported American in seeking a broader authorization of that carrier for Houston service. Our decision requires that all American flights which serve Houston shall also serve Pittsburgh. It is this restriction from which American seeks relief. American asserts that the restriction serves "no purpose whatsoever" and should be removed in order to permit American to provide Houston with additional desirable services. The purpose of the restriction is not obscure. It was designed to preserve priority for Delta in the provision of additional

competitive services in the New York–Houston and Washington–Houston markets. . . . It was also designed to insure that American would concentrate upon development of Houston–Pittsburgh traffic.[29]

The importance of such restrictions in controlling the degree to which carriers may compete is suggested in the following quotation from the opinion of Board member Josh Lee in the *Southwest–Northeast Service Case.*

Another advantage which American has over its competitors is with respect to *restrictions.* National cannot operate shuttle service between Washington and New York, but American can. Eastern has a restriction on its route from Richmond to Washington and Boston, but American is unrestricted on that route. Northwest, United, and TWA cannot operate shuttle services between Chicago and New York, but American can. United and TWA cannot operate shuttle service between Chicago and Washington or between Chicago and Detroit, but American can. United and TWA cannot operate shuttle service between Detroit and New York, but American can. Eastern and National have longhaul restrictions along the Atlantic Seaboard, but not American. In fact, of the transcontinental carriers, American alone has no longhaul restrictions in the area defined by the *New York–Chicago Case.* This gives American a strong advantage in those markets as shown by the following percentages of the traffic which each airline carried in 1953:

Between New York and Chicago:

American carried	48.2 percent
TWA carried	23.5 "
United carried	25.9 "

Between New York and Boston:

American carried	70.6 percent
Eastern carried	22.7 "
Northeast carried	5.9 "

Between New York and Detroit:

American carried	68.1 percent
Northwest carried	18.6 "
United carried	5.0 "
Capital carried	6.6 "

Between Chicago and Detroit:

American carried	65.3 percent
Capital carried	26.9 "
United carried	7.3 "

Between New York and Washington, D.C.:

American carried	68.6 percent
Eastern carried	30.6 "
National carried	0.6 "

Between Washington, D.C. and Chicago:

American carried	43.6 percent
Capital carried	32.0 "
United carried	12.0 "
TWA carried	10.4 "

Between Boston and Washington, D.C.:

American carried	74.5 percent
Eastern carried	24.9 "

These percentages show the advantage which American has over its competitors in markets where they are operating under longhaul restrictions and where American is unrestricted.[30]

Perhaps it is somewhat unwise to assign all of these observed differences to the effect of the restrictions, but there can be no doubt that the restrictions have a powerful effect on the ability of carriers to compete. For this reason, they constitute an important tool in the hands of the Board. They permit the Board to control the relative abilities of the carriers to compete over specified routes and thus add flexibility to the basic tool, the certification authority. However, the restriction device is a very difficult one to use in that the Board, by thus limiting the quality of service which the restricted carrier is authorized to offer, clearly inconveniences the traveling public. Indeed, in some cases such as the so-called "closed door" restrictions,[31] the conflicting goals of the adjustment of competitive impact and the provision of service to the public were perhaps not wisely resolved.

THE EXEMPTION AUTHORITY—THE IRREGULAR AND SUPPLEMENTAL CARRIERS

Title IV of the Civil Aeronautics Act of 1938 (restated in the Federal Aviation Act of 1958) deals with Air Carrier Economic Regulation. Its provisions include the requirement of a certificate of public convenience and necessity, the description of the terms of the certificate, the prohibition against route abandonment, labor provisions, requirements as to carriage of mail, tariff provisions, carrier's duty with respect to service rates and cost allocations, the keeping of accounts and the filing of reports, stock ownership limitations on officers and directors, consolidations, mergers, acquisition of control, pooling, etc. These are the economic rules under which the certificated carriers operate. However, Section 416 Paragraph (b) (1) provides for exemption from the provisions of Title IV under certain conditions.

(b) (1) The Board, from time to time and to the extent necessary, may (except as provided in paragraph (2) of this subsection) exempt from the requirements of this title or any provision thereof, or any rule, regulation, term, condition, or limitation prescribed thereunder, any air carrier or class of air carriers, if it finds that the enforcement of this title or such provision, or such rule, regulation, term, condition, or limitation is or would be an undue burden on such air carrier or class of air carriers by reason of the limited extent of, or unusual circumstances effecting, the operations of such air carrier or class of air carriers and is not in the public interest.

It was this provision in the Civil Aeronautics Act of 1938 which was the basis for the "irregular" or "nonscheduled" airlines industry. The growth and background of this industry was summarized by the then Chairman of the Civil Aeronautics Board, Mr. Oswald Ryan, in his statement before the Senate Select Committee on Small Business, March 31, 1953.

From its beginning in 1938, the Board recognized that there was a group of carriers which, although engaging in air transportation as common carriers and, therefore, subject to the economic regulatory provisions of the act, conducted their business in such a way that they could not comply in any substantial measure with those provisions and continue to operate. These carriers during the entire prewar period furnished a call-and-demand air service, operating generally from a fixed base, and flying where and when requested with no regard to schedule. For the most part, they operated small non-transport-type aircraft and their air transportation services were only incidental to other aviation activities in which they were engaged such as flight training, the operation of airports and the sale and service of aircraft and accessories.

While in 1938 the operations of these carriers were of limited economic significance insofar as the air transportation system of the country as a whole was concerned, their very existence indicated a need that could not be satisfied by the scheduled air carriers. It was also clear that their operations were of such a limited extent and were conducted under such unusual circumstances that compliance with the provisions of Title IV of the act would have been unduly burdensome on them. The limited nature and indefiniteness of their services as to time and place made it extremely difficult for them to sustain the burden of prosecuting an application for a certificate of public convenience and necessity, or to assume the other obligations that are imposed upon air carriers generally. It was also obvious that their operations were of a type which did not logically fit into the economic provisions of the act which were designed primarily for the regulation of the scheduled, route-type services that were, and are today, the backbone of an adequate air transportation system.

Accordingly, the Board, relying upon its authority under section 416 (b) of the act, issued in 1938 its so-called nonscheduled regulation. That regulation exempted from virtually all of the economic provisions of Title IV of the act all air carriers which did not engage in scheduled operations.

Now, what were scheduled operations? Under the regulation, an operation was deemed to be scheduled, and, therefore, not authorized under the exemption, if (1) it involved the flight of one or more airplanes from a takeoff point in one State (or Territory or possession of the United States) to a landing in another such State, Territory, or possession, or in a foreign nation, and (2) if the air carrier held out to the public by advertisement or otherwise that it would operate one or more airplanes between such points with regularity or with a reasonable degree of regularity, and (3) if the carrier permitted it to be generally understood that on such flights, and for compensation or hire, it would accept for transportation between such points such members of the public as might apply therefor, or such express or other property as the public might offer.[32]

Until the end of World War II, the operations of the nonscheduled airlines, while the subject of an investigation [33] in which the Board emphasized "the limited and sporadic nature of the services which were authorized by the non-scheduled regulation," did not constitute a serious regulatory problem.

However, after the War the nature and scope of the noncertificated airlines' operations changed radically, and the Civil Aeronautics Board did find that serious regulatory problems were created. The Board considered that many of these new carriers, a large number of which engaged solely in the carriage of passenger traffic, showed sufficient regularity of flights between fixed points that they could no longer be called "nonscheduled." Since they served primarily the heavy traffic density markets, they were able to operate on a profitable long haul, high load factor basis. The scheduled certificated carriers objected vigorously, claiming that the "nonskeds" were "skimming the cream," by taking away passengers on the profitable routes which were essential to the certificated carriers who were required to serve less dense unprofitable routes as suggested in the statement of the President's Air Coordinating Committee cited above. The Board was clearly disturbed by this situation, and, in May 1947, the Board changed the nonscheduled exemption regulation to require these carriers, now renamed "irregular air carriers," to obtain letters of registration from the Board. However,

. . . the amended regulation did not require any showing of a need for the carrier's operation or a showing of fitness and ability. The basic limitation upon frequency of operations which had been implicit in the nonscheduled regulation since 1938 was now spelled out in a more detailed and precise form.

By August 6, 1948, 147 companies had been issued letters of registration as large irregular carriers, and of those 109 were still in effect. At that time the Board provided that no further letters of registration would be issued to large irregular carriers unless an application had been filed on or before August 6, 1948. This was followed in May of 1949 by a further revision which terminated the blanket exemption of large irregular carriers but provided that any large irregular carrier which, by a specified date, filed an application for an individual exemption could continue operations under the limitations of the regulation until its application for individual exemption was disposed of. Thereafter on May 25, 1950, the Board issued its opinion in *Large Irregular Carriers, Exemption* (11 CAB 609), setting forth the policies that would guide it in disposing of the applications for individual exemptions. Without attempting a detailed review of all of the reasoning underlying these policies they can be briefly summarized.

First, the Board concluded that the applications of irregular carriers that had been conducting route services—services described by the Board as "a pattern of operations which shows a concentration of relatively frequent and regular flights between a limited number of pairs of points"—would be denied.

Secondly, the Board concluded to grant exemptions to those carriers which in the past had been furnishing truly irregular services.

Thirdly, the Board in arriving at its policies concluded that in order to insure that each such carrier will carry out and perform the type of service which it is our intention to authorize, the Board, in addition to the restrictions upon regularity which had theretofore been imposed, would permit only 3 flights in the same direction during any period of 4 successive calendar weeks between 13 named pairs of points, and only 8 flights in the same direction in such period between any other pairs of cities. The 13 pairs of cities were those between which the bulk of the operations by irregular carriers had been conducted and between which operations had been characterized by frequency and regularity.

Finally, the Board pointed out that there was a large number of irregular carriers which, although holding valid letters of registration, had not conducted in the preceding year any operations pursuant to their authority. With respect to these carriers, the Board concluded that there did not appear to be any need for their services, and that, accordingly, the applications of all nonoperators would be denied.[34]

On September 21, 1951, the Board instituted a general investigation of air services by "large irregular carriers" [35] and irregular transport carriers. The purpose of the investigation was to ascertain whether there was a public need for the services provided by the irregular carriers "in addition to and supplemental to services performed by the carriers holding certificates of public convenience and necessity."

At the time of the hearings at which Mr. Ryan presented the testimony cited here, the large irregular carrier investigation had not been completed by the Board. Since that time, it has been settled, and it will be discussed below. It is important to note however, the position which Mr. Ryan, speaking for the Board, deemed appropriate for the large irregular carriers. In response to charges made by the Committee before which he was testifying, that the Board had been hostile to the irregular carriers and that it was practicing "death by delay" and "strangulation by regulation," Mr. Ryan, speaking for the Board, replied

> We are and have been in favor of irregular air transportation and irregular air carriers. But we have felt it to be our duty under the Civil Aeronautics Act to see to it that the irregular carriers shall do the job which we authorized them to do and to supplement and not compete with the certificated air-transport structure of the Nation.[36]

Thus, although the exact status of the large irregular carriers with respect to their position in the air transport industry was not defined, it was perfectly clear that the Board did not intend that there be competition in scheduled service on an equal footing between the irregular carriers and the certificated carriers. In that connection, the Board felt it extremely important that the restriction against excessive regularity and frequency be observed. However, the so-called "3 and 8" regulation, cited above, with respect to number of round-trip flights permitted for irregular carriers, was never made effective, since its effective date was postponed each time it drew near. These postponements were made at the request of the Senate Small Business Committee, and later in response to an injunction issued by the United States District Court. The policy difference between the Senate Small Business Committee and the Civil Aeronautics Board was described by Mr. Ryan as follows:

> the Board has a responsibility of its own, given to it by Congress, which it cannot escape. The Board must consider the public interest as a whole, it must develop and promote a sound air-transportation industry, and not merely a segment of that industry. Thus, although the Board may agree that expansion of these small-business enterprises would be good for them, the question which the Board must answer is whether it would be good for the public and the entire air-transportation industry generally. While the answer may seem obvious to the irregular carriers and to a committee whose purpose is to foster and protect small business, the Board's answer must be reached in the light of the statutory standards of the Act and after affording an opportunity to other interested parties to express their views. The "large irregular carrier" investigation is the means to those ends.[37]

While it was clear that the large irregular carriers had moved far from the original function contemplated by the Board, namely, the charter and local air taxi operations, and while they had concentrated largely on the lucrative long haul high density routes, thus, to some extent, bedeviling the regulatory agency which has always sought, within limits, to maintain a balance, for any given carrier, between strong and weak markets, nevertheless the large irregular carriers had, beyond shadow of a doubt, had a considerably stimulating effect on the air transportation industry. They provided a new kind of competition, the benefits of which have been of great importance to the traveling public. They provided price competition on a grand scale—something the certificated airlines had not provided—and they stimulated the development of air coach service on the part of the certificated carriers.[38]

The competition which the large irregular carriers offered was quite different from that which existed among the certificated carriers. The certificated carriers competed with respect to luxury services, frequency and timing of schedules, and especially, in introducing new and improved flight equipment. The irregular carriers, on the other hand, generally used less advanced aircraft than the certificated airlines. Typically, they used the surplus military aircraft of the DC-3, C-46, and DC-4 types. There was some use of the truly postwar aircraft, such as the DC-6 series, but, again, this use followed that of the certificated airlines. Thus, the irregular airlines did not, by their example, provide a competitive spur to the purchase and use of newer aircraft types.

On the other hand, by concentrating on the nonluxury type of service, with higher seating density and less expensive aircraft, the irregular carriers were able to offer price competition, to assist greatly in the development of coach traffic, and, by demonstrating and exploiting the elasticity of demand for air transportation, to expand the air transportation market. There can be no question that this has been a valuable service.

The problem of the Civil Aeronautics Board, however, was to avoid any injurious effect which the irregular carriers might have on the air transportation industry as a whole. Basically, the problem was to try to find a role for the large irregular carriers so they could continue to provide the benefits which they had provided in the past without causing excessive damage to the certificated air transportation industry. The small irregular carriers, operating the originally contemplated fixed-base and charter operations, created no regulatory problems. It was the large irregular operators whose actions had raised these fundamental issues.

The President's Air Coordinating Committee, reporting to President Eisenhower, stated that the language of Section 416 of the Civil Aeronautics Act clearly did not intend that the exemption authority was to serve as the basis for large scale departures from the "controlled entry" principle. The Committee clearly preferred the certification procedure wherever it could be used. The Committee stated:

> . . . this exemption authority should not be used to authorize noncertificated operations of significant scope, particularly where such operations are competitive in nature with services authorized under regular route certificates.
>
> It is unnecessary to resort to the exemption authority merely because a given operation represents a new type of service, or one which is small or experimental. Such service can be adequately handled through the normal certification process, as evidenced by the temporary, experimental route authorizations actually granted by the Board for local service operations, all-cargo routes, a "packaged tour" operation, and helicopter services. It is significant to note, in this connection,

that many of these certificated services are much smaller in scope than are some of the operations now being conducted on a non-certificated basis under the "non-scheduled" exemption order.

The exemption authority of Section 416 of the Civil Aeronautics Act should be used only in limited and exceptional circumstances and should not be used as the basis for any significant departure from the controlled entry principle.[39]

The committee conceded that it was extremely difficult to define and enforce a meaningful standard of nonscheduled service, in view of the fact that truly irregular services are not suited to the individual passenger market because of the problem of generating plane-loads of individual passengers at points served only sporadically. The report further stated that, even though individual carriers might operate sufficiently few schedules over each route to remain truly nonscheduled, as defined, the noncertificated carriers as a whole, by rotating such operations among several routes, could provide an over-all pattern of regularity. The impact of this on the air transport system as a whole was deemed "at least as important as the question of whether the individual carriers are respectively staying within the regulatory definition of "nonscheduled." [40]

The Committee concluded that the "nonscheduled" criterion was not an appropriate basis for exempting from normal economic regulation the route-type operations of the large irregular carriers. They did not believe that further attempts to specify the limits of the nonscheduled concept could solve the basic problem. Rather, they came to the important conclusion that

The concept of non-scheduled services does not provide a meaningful basis for exempting route-type passenger services from the normal certification requirement. In the future, there should be no general use of the exemption authority as a basis for authorizing common carrier transportation to individually ticketed passengers on large transport planes.[41]

Those operations of the large irregular carriers which represent a supplementary type of service, such as bona fide charter and contract operations, should be encouraged. A new type of certificate should be developed for such operations, providing suitable flexibility in terms of areas to be served.[42]

The Large Irregular Carrier Investigation was set up to determine the future place of the large irregular (since renamed "supplemental") air carriers. Thus the purpose of the investigation was to determine the future Civil Aeronautics Board policy with respect to the supplemental air carriers and, even more basically, to ascertain whether there was a need for air transportation services which were additional to and supplemental to the services performed by the regularly certificated carriers, and which could properly be provided by supplemental carriers. These supplemental carriers, of course, felt that they had already conceived and instituted a type of air service which was "supplemental" to that of the regularly certificated carriers. Their spokesman, appearing before a Senate Committee testified:

> I should like to point out again that the independent air carriers did in fact originate the coach-type service which met both of the stated requirements of the Board. It was "additional" to the class of service supplied by the certificated lines and it was "supplemental" in that it substantially broadened the base of the air transportation industry, making it possible for the large mass of the public that could not afford to pay for luxury service to enjoy the benefits of air travel for the first time.[43]

He held that, if allowed to operate with a greater degree of scheduling freedom, the supplemental carriers could operate successfully "Without directly competing with the certificated deluxe service or even with the type of second-class service now being provided on the certificated lines. . . ." [44] However, the certificated industry argued that this service would indeed be competitive and diversionary with respect to their own first class and coach services.

Basically, the conflict between the supplemental air carriers and the certificated carriers (and the Board) was that the latter had consistently opposed "route-type" operations on the part of noncertificated carriers, while it was apparent [45] that the large airplanes could be operated economically only under reasonably regular or "route-type" operations. The other possibility, large scale charter operation, had proven too difficult to develop economically.

The Civil Aeronautics Board in its decision in the *Large Irregular Carrier Investigation* settled the controversy with respect to the place of these carriers. It recognized that they had provided ". . . useful and necessary service in meeting fluctuating demands for air transportation, specialized services, and charter operations which have not been met by the certificated air carriers . . ."; that their operations had not hurt the certificated carriers; that they were a significant part of the Nation's air transport system; and that they had rendered invaluable military service in the Berlin and Korean airlifts and in the domestic charter service. The Board concluded that its policy should ". . . be directed toward their survival and continued healthy growth, subject to the overall objectives of the Act and a proper relationship to the certificated air carrier system." [46]

Under the policy spelled out by the Board in its decision in that proceeding, these carriers were designated as "supplemental air carriers" and authorized to conduct:

> (1) unlimited charter operations on a planeload basis for the carriage of passengers and property in domestic overseas, and territorial (except intra-Alaska) operations, and of property only in international operations; (2) charter operations for the carriage of passengers in international operations on an individual exemption basis similar to that which is set forth in the *1955 Trans-atlantic Charter Policy*, E-9221, adopted May 20, 1955; and (3) individually-ticketed or individually waybilled operations by each carrier not to exceed 10 trips per month in the same direction between any single pair of points in any calendar month, except as to intra-Alaska operations and execpt as to the carriage of passengers in international operations.
>
> The authority granted under the new policy will be supplemental and additional to the services of the certificated carriers and will not be unduly competitive with the operations of the certificated carriers.

At the time of that decision, the Board had not yet heard all of the applicants, so it deferred its final decision ". . . on the nature and form of the authority to be granted to the qualified applicants and as to the identity of the carriers to receive the enlarged authority." [47] The case was continued and three years later on January 28, 1959, the Board in conformity with the recommendations of the President's Air Coordinating Committee created a new type of certificate for the qualifying carriers.[48]

These new certificates of public convenience and necessity were issued to twenty-three supplemental air carriers for domestic air service. Twelve of these certificates are effective for five years, and eleven of them for two years. They authorize unlimited domestic charter service, but they prohibit the offering of more than ten round trips per month between any domestic city pair in individually ticketed passenger and/or individually waybilled cargo service. Also prohibited were agreements with other carriers or ticket agents which might result in a joint offering that might be or seem to be the equivalent of regularly scheduled service.

The following are selected paragraphs of the Civil Aeronautics Act relating to carrier certification.

TITLE IV—AIR CARRIER ECONOMIC REGULATION

CERTIFICATE OF PUBLIC CONVENIENCE AND NECESSITY

CERTIFICATE REQUIRED

SEC. 401. (a) No air carrier shall engage in any air transportation unless there is in force a certificate issued by the Board authorizing such air carrier to engage in such transportation.

APPLICATION FOR CERTIFICATE

(b) Application for a certificate shall be made in writing to the Board and shall be so verified, shall be in such form and contain such information, and shall be accompanied by such proof of service upon such interested persons, as the Board shall by regulation require.

NOTICE OF APPLICATION

(c) Upon the filing of any such application, the Board shall give due notice thereof to the public by posting a notice of such application in the office of the secretary of the Board and to such other persons as the Board may by regulation determine. Any interested person may file with the Board a protest or memorandum of opposition to or in support of the issuance of a certificate. Such application shall be set for public hearing, and the Board shall dispose of such application as speedily as possible.

ISSUANCE OF CERTIFICATE

(d) (1) The Board shall issue a certificate authorizing the whole or any part of the transportation covered by the application, if it finds that the applicant is fit, willing, and able to perform such transportation properly, and to conform to the provisions of this Act and the rules, regulations, and requirements of the Board hereunder, and that such transportation is required by the public convenience and necessity; otherwise such application shall be denied.

(2) In the case of an application for a certificate to engage in temporary air transportation, the Board may issue a certificate authorizing the whole or any part thereof for such limited periods as may be required by the public convenience and necessity, if it finds that the applicant is fit, willing, and able properly to perform such transportation and to conform to the provisions of this Act and the rules, regulations, and requirements of the Board hereunder.

TERMS AND CONDITIONS OF CERTIFICATE

(e) Each certificate issued under this section shall specify the terminal points and intermediate points, if any, between which the air carrier is authorized to engage in air transportation and the service to be rendered; and there shall be attached to the exercise of the privileges granted by the certificate, or amendment thereto, such reasonable terms, conditions, and limitations as the public interest may require. A certificate issued under this section to engage in foreign air transportation shall, insofar as the operation is to take place without the United States, designate the terminal and intermediate points only insofar as the Board shall deem practicable, and otherwise shall designate only the general route or routes to be followed. Any air carrier holding a certificate for foreign air transportation shall be authorized to handle and transport mail of countries other than the United States. No term, condition, or limitation of a certificate shall restrict the right of an air carrier to add to or change schedules, equipment, accommodations, and facilities for performing the authorized transportation and service as the development of the business and the demands of the public shall require. No air carrier shall be deemed to have violated any term, condition, or limitation of its certificate by landing or taking off during an emergency at a point not named in its certificate or by operating in an emergency under regulations which may be prescribed by the Board, between terminal and intermediate points other than those specified in its certificate. Any air carrier may make charter trips or perform any other special service, without regard to the points named in its certificate, under regulations prescribed by the Board.

EFFECTIVE DATE AND DURATION OF CERTIFICATE

(f) Each certificate shall be effective from the date specified therein, and shall continue in effect until suspended or revoked as hereinafter provided, or until the Board shall certify that operation thereunder has ceased, or, if issued for a limited period of time under subsection (d) (2) of this section, shall continue in effect until the expiration thereof, unless, prior to the date of expiration, such certificate shall be suspended or revoked as provided herein, or the Board shall certify that operations thereunder have ceased: *Provided,* That if any service authorized by a certificate is not inaugurated within such period, not less than ninety days, after the date of the authorization as shall be fixed by the Board, or if, for a period of ninety days or such other period as may be designated by the Board any such service is not operated, the Board may by order, entered after notice and hearing, direct that such certificate shall thereupon cease to be effective to the extent of such service.

AUTHORITY TO MODIFY, SUSPEND, OR REVOKE

(g) The Board upon petition or complaint or upon its own initiative, after the notice and hearings, may alter, amend, modify, or suspend any such certificate, in whole or in part, if the public convenience and necessity so require, or may revoke any such certificate, in whole or in part, for intentional failure to comply with any provision of this title or any order, rule, or regulation issued hereunder or any term, condition, or limitation of such certificate: *Provided,* That no such certificate shall be revoked unless the holder thereof fails to comply, within a reasonable time to be fixed by the Board, with an order of the Board commanding obedience to the provision, or to the order (other than an order issued in accordance with this proviso), rule, regulation, term, condition, or limitation found by the Board to have been violated. Any interested person may file with the Board a protest or memorandum in support of or in opposition to the alteration, amendment, modification, suspension, or revocation of the certificate.

TRANSFER OF CERTIFICATE

(h) No certificate may be transferred unless such transfer is approved by the Board as being consistent with the public interest.

CERTAIN RIGHTS NOT CONFERRED BY CERTIFICATE

(i) No certificate shall confer any proprietary, property, or exclusive right in the use of any airspace, Federal airway, landing area, or air-navigation facility.

APPLICATION FOR ABANDONMENT

(j) No air carrier shall abandon any route, or part thereof, for which a certificate has been issued by the Board, unless, upon the application of such air carrier, after notice and hearing, the Board shall find such abandonment to be in the public interest. Any interested person may file with the Board a protest or memorandum of opposition to or in support of any such abandonment. The Board may, by regulations or otherwise, authorize such temporary suspension of service as may be in the public interest.

CHAPTER VI

The Policy of the Civil Aeronautics Board toward Competition

THE GROWTH OF COMPETITION

Since the passage of the Civil Aeronautics Act in 1938, the number of domestic certificated trunkline air carriers in the United States has decreased from nineteen to twelve. No new firms have entered this part of the industry, and the decrease in the number of firms has been largely the result of mergers. However, the amount of competition in the industry has increased as more and more routes have been certificated for service by more than one carrier. Indeed, in many quarters there has been fear that, since the end of 1956, the industry has become excessively competitive. It may seem at first glance that "excessive" competition is anomalous in an industry where entry of new firms and expansion of existing firms is restricted, and where the inauguration of new service is based largely on the business decisions of the private airline managements. There is typically no more competitive service than those managements create, and there is, indeed, less, in that many applications for new competitive routes are denied by the Civil Aeronautics Board. However, in Chapter VIII, where the issue of internal subsidy is discussed, it will be seen that, even under these conditions, competition may develop which may, by some criteria, be deemed to be "excessive."

The growth in the amount of domestic trunkline competition has come about as a result of the issuance of certificates of convenience and necessity extending the routes of the various airlines. These extensions were made by the Civil Aeronautics Board as a result of formal proceedings in which, typically, the airline had requested the extension in its operating authority, and in which, often, other carriers were parties to the proceeding, having themselves requested similar or related routes. Carriers are always seeking to come into one another's territory and to compete, and the Civil Aeronautics Board is always in the position of restraining the development of competition and of authorizing competitive services only over those routes where the Board decides that the public interest requires competition.

As is well known, the Civil Aeronautics Board, as well as the institution of regulatory commissions in general, has been seriously attacked [1] for this "passivity" whereby its actions are typically taken in response to applications of the carriers rather than on its own initiative as the motivating force in extending the airline system and in developing competitive service. However, it must be noted that the Board has usually had large numbers of route applications before it, and, by combining various applications into consolidated area proceedings, and by bearing in mind the implications of its decisions with respect to other proceedings being considered at the same time or projected for the near future, the Board has been able to plan its program and coordinate its decisions more than might be expected from a mere description of the formal procedures involved in individual air route proceedings.

The two great periods of growth in the amount of competition in the domestic air transportation industry are the period ending in 1947 and the period beginning with September, 1955 [2] and extending into the present. This study is concerned primarily with the later period, and, in particular, with the far reaching effects of the cases decided between September 1, 1955 and the end of 1956. These cases which changed the entire competitive picture in the industry will be examined in detail. More than five hundred city pairs received new or improved competitive authorizations in these cases, and most of the great monopolies, such as United Air Lines in Denver, American Airlines in Dallas and Fort Worth, and Trans World Airlines in Kansas City and Pittsburgh were opened to one or more competitors. The Civil Aeronautics Board wrote,

> In decisions handed down since June 30, 1955, the Board increased competition on the trunkline routes. At the time of the final decision of

the first of the trunkline-area cases, approximately 55 percent of trunkline passengers already had a choice of competitive services. On June 30, 1955, 37 of the top 50 markets and 23 of the second 50 were competitive. Logically the more extensive competition was in the more heavily traveled markets. Today only 4 of the top 50 and 12 of the second 50 remain noncompetitive, and proposals are pending for competitive service for these markets.[3]

The earlier period, that ending in 1947, was also of great importance. In addition to the increase in competitive service authorizations which resulted from the CAB decisions during the period, those decisions afforded the Board its opportunity to interpret the Civil Aeronautics Act with respect to competition, and to formulate its philosophy. It has been noted that the philosophy of the Board or, at least, certain aspects of it, may change with the membership of the Board. It also may vary in response to changes in the degree of prosperity in the industry. Nevertheless there has been considerable constancy with respect to basic philosophy. The differences that have characterized the different Board memberships have chiefly had to do more with the assessment of quantitative factors than with differences in basic policy, although in the early 1950's, the Board's attitude toward competition was sufficiently conservative to be characterized as representing a difference *in kind* rather than a difference *of degree.*

THE DEVELOPMENT OF A POLICY, 1938–1947

At the outset, the Board felt that Congress intended it "... to exercise a firm control over the expansion of air transportation routes in order to prevent the scramble for routes which might occur under a 'laissez faire' policy." [4] Thus, uneconomic duplication and wasteful competitive practices were to be avoided. Examiner Edward T. Stodola, writing in 1947, noted that, "Reference to both the language of the statute and to its legislative history compels the conclusion that the Congressional policy is one of promoting competitive service between points where the demands of traffic are great enough to support both the existing and the additional service on a sound and economical basis." [5]

He suggested that, perhaps the following statement by Senator McCarran (83 Cong. Record 6852) made in the course of Senate debate on S. 3845 expressed generally the intent of the framers of the Act on this issue:

If it could be established to the satisfaction of the Authority which is about to be set up that another line could well be operated from Chicago to Salt Lake City, although that same territory is now served by the United Air Lines, and the demand for service was so great as to support another line, then the Authority could investigate, reach a determination, establish a rule, and could say, "There is sufficient demand, there is sufficient patronage, and there is sufficient commercial life to sustain the other lines. Therefore we can grant a franchise to another line." But before that could be done, full and complete hearings would have to be had. So we are trying to set up a nonpolitical agency that will go into matters such as this one I have tried to illustrate, and if the circumstances do not justify another line, say, "No, you cannot go in; you cannot set up another line, because if you do both lines will fail; both lines will go out of business, and the public that we are looking to primarily will not be served." That is the object and purpose of this entire bill. It is not to say that any line may be "frozen" nor that any line may be perpetuated nor that any monopoly over any terrain may be established to the exclusion of the necessity which the public may present.[6]

In 1941 the Board expressed the opinion that, with respect to the development of the domestic scheduled air transportation system, the grandfather carriers themselves constituted a large enough number to provide the competition required by the Act:

The number of air carriers now operating appears sufficient to insure against monopoly in respect to the average new route case, and we believe that the present domestic air-transportation system can by proper supervision be integrated and expanded in a manner that will in general afford the competition necessary for the development of that system in the manner contemplated by the Act. In the absence of particular circumstances presenting an affirmative reason for a new carrier there appears to be no inherent desirability of increasing the present number of carriers merely for the purpose of numerically enlarging the industry.[7]

Under this doctrine, which has not changed, the Board proceeded to develop the domestic route systems and to provide such competition as, in its discretion, the public convenience and necessity required. *Public convenience and necessity,* for these purposes, was defined in 1947 by the Board as follows.

The Civil Aeronautics Act requires that before the Board may authorize air transportation it must find that such air transportation is required by the "public convenience and necessity." The principal factors which the Board is directed to consider in determining public convenience and necessity are set forth in the statement of policy incorporated in section 2 of the Act. This statement of policy makes the present and future needs of the commerce of the United States, the postal service, and the national defense the primary criteria by which we determine whether a particular proposal meets public convenience and necessity. Among other provisions of this statement of Congressional policy, is the declaration that competition must be regarded as being in the public interest to the extent to which it is necessary to assure the sound development of an air transportation system adequate to our national needs. In cases relating to the establishment of competing services the Board considers the probable effects of competition on both the existing carriers and the carrier seeking entry into new territory.[8]

In this important 1947 case, several airlines [9] were seeking authorization to serve all or part of the Detroit–Washington route, which at that time was served only by Pennsylvania-Central Airlines Corporation (now Capital Airlines). The Examiner, noting that the case raised the basic issue of the extent to which competition should be authorized, presented a careful and detailed analysis of the Board's policy toward competition as given by its opinions in earlier cases.[10]

In summary, this analysis of the Board's policy toward competition as of 1947 pointed out, first, that the Board has held that the Act does not require competition on all routes, but that the amount of competition to be prescribed lies within the Board's discretion.

We conclude that competition in air transportation is not mandatory, especially when considered in relation to any particular route or service. Clearly, Congress has left to the discretion of the Board the determination of whether or not competition in a particular area is necessary to assure the normal development of an appropriate air transportation system.[11]

Second, it was pointed out that the Board has consistently held that competition can and does produce desirable improvements in service.

The full development and technological improvement of air transportation cannot be gained by regulation alone; to achieve improvement an incentive is necessary and under the Act that incentive should flow in part from competition between air carriers.[12]

It is generally recognized that economic regulation cannot be relied upon to take the place of the stimulus which competition provides in the advancement of technique and service in air transportation. Competition invites comparison as to equipment, cost, personnel, organization, methods of operation, solicitation and handling of traffic, and the like, all of which tend to insure the development of an air transportation system as contemplated by the Act. That the domestic air transportation system of this country has reached its present position of preeminence is in large part due to the competitive spirit which has existed throughout its development. The continued maintainence of that position as well as the further development of the industry demands the encouragement of free initiative and enterprise subject only to the condition that the competitive services shall not be wasteful.[13]

Furthermore, the adequacy of the existing carrier's service does not constitute a bar to the authorization of competition, nor does the justification of competition depend upon a showing of inadequacy of service as offered by the existing carriers.

In considering the extent to which competition is necessary to assure the sound development of an air transportation system, therefore, its justification does not depend upon the inability or unwillingness of an existing carrier to render adequate service. The carrier's failure in this regard may evidence a need for competition, but its ability and willingness to furnish a sufficient volume of service does not, of itself, constitute a bar to the authorization of a competitive service. Otherwise, no competition would ever be authorized for there is no limit to the extent to which an existing carrier could expand to meet increased demand.[14]

The decision as to when competition is justified is discretionary with the Board, but the level of traffic has always been viewed by the Board as an important criterion in arriving at that decision.

The fact that Congress in this Act did not lay down any definite rule or formula for determining the measure of competition required for the fulfilment of the statutory objectives suggests the impracticability of formulating a rule of general application. While no convenient formula of general applicability may be available as a substitute for the Board's discretionary judgment it would seem to be a sound principle that, since competition in itself presents an incentive to improved service and technological development, there would be a strong, although not conclusive, presumption in favor of competition on any route which offered sufficient traffic to support competing services without unreasonable increase of total operating cost. How that competition would be provided must depend upon the facts and circumstances of each particular case.[15]

THE PRESUMPTION DOCTRINE

The above statement that, when there is sufficient traffic there is a strong, although not conclusive, presumption in favor of competition, has been referred to as the "presumption doctrine," and the relative importance of the presumption in favor of competition as against the "specific facts and circumstances" in individual cases is one of the aspects of CAB philosophy that has undergone considerable variation in the years which followed that 1943 decision. In pursuing the presumption doctrine, the Board was accused of favoring "competition for competition's sake," an expression which somehow achieved the status of a catch phrase, describing an unpopular sentiment to which one admitted at one's peril. A hearing witness favoring a competitive application might inevitably have expected to be asked in icy tones in cross-examination by opposing counsel whether he favored "competition for competition's sake," and to this a direct affirmative answer was unthinkable. The Board itself felt impelled, in the next year, to protect itself against that ubiquitous charge in a case where competitive routes were awarded to Northeast Airlines.

> . . . we have stated that where there is sufficient traffic to support competitive service there is a presumption, although not conclusive, in favor of competition. The reason that such presumption is not conclusive is because the Board considers all the circumstances surrounding each case. This declaration of policy we believe to be sound, and we are not impressed with the contention advanced in this and other cases that such a policy amounts to competition for competitions' sake.
>
> The phrase "competition for competition's sake" is meaningless, since in every case there are numerous considerations bearing on the public interest. The over-all public interest is the principle by which we measure each decision. This public interest can only be determined after the Board has considered all of the factors and circumstances surrounding the case, and in such consideration the Board does not give weight to an empty phrase, but rather to such factors as volume of potential

traffic, total operating costs, benefits to the public in the form of improved service, financial condition of the carriers, and many other factors which contribute to the constant improvement of air transportation.[16]

Continuing the trend, the presumption doctrine seems to have been abandoned or, at least, weakened soon thereafter, when the Board stated:

> The mere fact that a particular route develops a large volume of traffic does not of itself afford sufficient justification for finding that the public convenience and necessity require establishment of an additional competitive service exactly duplicating an existing operation. The public interest which must be served can only be determined after consideration of all the factors and circumstances surrounding each case.[17]
>
> While the traffic potential of the New York–Niagara Falls sector is substantial, the proposed Colonial operation would parallel that of American. The only benefits which could be anticipated from the Colonial operation would be in providing additional local service between the two cities. Parallel competition is not justified unless some substantial benefit to the public can be expected as a result of such service. The record fails to establish such public benefit in the instant case.[18]

Thus, at this point there seems to be some question about the presumption in favor of competition. The last quoted statement above seems to suggest that there must be a showing of a specific "public benefit" in order to establish the need for competition in any specific situation. Examiner Stodola noted that there did not appear any subsequent cases (as of the date of his report, March 17, 1947) in which the Board rested its award of a competitive route solely on the presumption doctrine.[19]

In the instant case, the *Detroit–Washington Service Case,* which involved competitive service on the Detroit–Washington route, Examiner Stodola assumed that "there is no longer a presumption that competition is required over a route simply because it has ample traffic flow to support competition." Nevertheless, after long analysis,[20] in which he sought to find the true direction in which the public interest lay, Examiner Stodola recommended that Northwest be authorized to serve the Detroit–Washington route in competition with PCA,[21] subject to a long-haul restriction to minimize diversion from PCA. The Board, in adopting this recommendation of the Examiner, expressed serious concern about the diversion of traffic from PCA, which, in its presentation in the proceeding, had taken the position that ". . . no case before the Civil Aeronautics Board has ever held such grave portent for it as the present proceeding . . ." [22] Nevertheless, the Board stated that such diversion was not necessarily the controlling factor.

> We have heretofore pointed out that the extent to which the proposed operations would divert traffic from the existing carriers warrants careful consideration because of the possibility that the economic stability of such carriers might be impaired, with consequent effect upon the development of a sound national air transportation system, and also because diversion from the existing facilities might reduce revenues to such an extent that the rate of mail compensation paid by the government to the present carriers might have to be increased. The effect of the proposed new service upon existing carriers, however, is not the controlling consideration where the new service offers substantial advantages to the public.
>
> That there have been large volumes of available traffic on each of the Detroit–Washington route segments is amply supported by the record. The great economic importance of Detroit, Cleveland, Pittsburgh and Washington and the close interrelation of their interests are conceded. Not only are these four cities among the country's strongest traffic generating centers, but a substantial portion of their traffic is with each other, thus making inevitable a strong local route. However, in the situation before us the carrier whose services are proposed in varying degrees to be duplicated has suffered serious financial losses over a considerable period of time; and, as previously indicated, the route over which competition is proposed has been an important source of this carrier's system revenues. Accordingly, the public advantages anticipated from the proposed new operations must be weighed against the relative detriment likely to be inflicted upon the existing carrier as well as the possible added cost to the government in the form of increased mail compensation. It is with these fundamental considerations in mind that we now turn to the proposals for new or additional service.[23]

The Board then proceeded to examine the various proposals of the several applicant carriers and to discuss the factors involved in the evaluation of the public interest. It discussed at some length the total new service available from the tying-in of the new route to the existing routes of the several applicants, and, in the case of

Northwest, noted the possibility of new service to the Pacific Northwest and to Alaska and the Orient:

While the record reveals no immediate prospects of heavy travel over Northwest's newly established route to the orient, the air transport pattern required by the Act should reflect the long-range potentialities of air service to and from that part of the world.[24]

National defense considerations are a further factor to be weighed in resolving Northwest's proposal in this proceeding. This Board must consider the requirements of national defense as one of the three primary criteria of public convenience and necessity in determining the need for new or additional air service. The Act therefore requires that careful attention be paid to the maintenance of essential services in the interest of our national security. Commercial air transportation has come to be recognized as important an auxiliary to modern military air power as the merchant marine has been to naval power. Northwest offers a short, inland air route to Alaska and also the most direct air route to Japan, Korea, China, and the Philippine Islands.[25]

. . . the important national transportation needs which would be served by the extension of Northwest from Detroit to Cleveland, Pittsburgh and Washington outweigh the possible detriment to PCA in the way of diversion of its revenue. Accordingly, we conclude that the proposed extension of route No. 3 of Northwest from Detroit to Washington via Cleveland and Pittsburgh on a restricted basis is required by the public convenience and necessity.

The present record establishes no substantial need for additional competitive local service between Detroit and Washington. The extension of Northwest will result in some competition for local traffic but the competition will be incidental to the long-haul services authorized and not the justification for the extension. Insofar as the various proposals involved herein would provide only added local competition on the various Detroit-Washington route segments they must be rejected because the adverse effect resulting from the authorization of unrestricted local service upon PCA outweighs the probable benefits such service would bring.[26]

This award to Northwest was made by a divided Board, with Vice Chairman Oswald Ryan and members Harllee Branch and Clarence M. Young concurring, but with Chairman James M. Landis and Member Josh Lee dissenting, the former because he felt that such point-to-point paralleling of the PCA route was excessively competitive and that the restriction on Northwest was inadequate to reduce this competition, since it merely stipulated that Northwest's flights east of Milwaukee must serve Washington and St. Paul, or a point west thereof.

This rather lengthy discussion of this important case is introduced here because, in it can be seen the emergence of one of the most trying problems facing the Board and students of air transportation. It may be characterized as a variation of the old hen and egg problem. That is, does the Board decide that there is a need for competition over the route and then proceed to analyze the applications of the various carriers to ascertain which carrier should be selected to provide that competitive service, or, conversely, does the Board, as this case suggests, analyze the potential public benefit of the various proposals, and, finding one which promises overwhelming benefits (national defense, carrier strengthening, etc.), create the authorization for the competitive service in order to obtain those benefits, although the competition, *per se,* may not be needed or even wanted? Or are these decisions made simultaneously as one decision so that no chronological or conceptual priority can or should be assigned?

Study of many CAB decisions indicates that although in some cases the intention of the Board and the reasoning followed by the Board are made perfectly clear in the published opinion, this is not always the case; and indeed, in many cases it is difficult to ascertain the purpose of the Board from its published decisions. This is an important obstacle to serious study and interpretation of the decisions, as for example, when an attempt is made to assess, by subsequent developments, the degree to which the Board, through its route awards, has achieved its purposes. Clearly, such evaluation is not possible if the purpose of the Board is not made clear. For this case suffice it to note that Northwest was authorized to compete over the Detroit–Washington route although it is not clear whether Northwest was selected to provide needed competition, or whether competition was authorized in order to secure the benefits of the extension of Northwest's route, or whether the decision rested in part on both of these foundations. The majority, which authorized the competition, seemed to imply the second when it said, "The present record established no substantial need for additional competitive local service between Detroit and Washington. The extension of Northwest will result in some competition for local traffic but the competition will be incidental to the long-haul services authorized and not the justification for the extension. . . ." [27] But Chairman Landis, on the other hand, dissenting and objecting that the amount of competition thereby imposed on PCA was excessive, said, "I am of the opinion that some competition should be provided Pennsylvania Central Airlines on its route 14." [28] In any event, a competitive authorization was made, and the Examiner and the Board specifically stated that their respective decisions to make such authorization did not rest on the presumption doctrine. The presumption doctrine was disowned, if not abandoned, but important new competitive authorizations were nevertheless made.

Thus, in the period from its inception through 1947 the Board increased markedly the amount of competition between the domestic trunk airlines.[29] Indeed, it was charged by many that the Civil Aeronautics Board had authorized far more competition than was economically feasible, and that this contributed significantly to the economic instability of the airline industry in the late 1940's.[30]

THE POSSIBILITY OF "EXCESSIVE" COMPETITION

The argument that the Board had authorized too much competition was based on the contention that when two carriers operate over the same route, splitting the traffic between them, each carrier is in effect serving a lower density route.

> It is clear that load factor is related to density of traffic and that higher load factors are attainable on the denser routes. Therefore, it would appear that subdividing the traffic on any given route does have the effect of lowering the load factor below what it might have been if one firm carried all the traffic.[31]

This conclusion, which assumes little or no traffic generation effect of the increased number of schedules, has led some students of air transportation to conclude that airline competition is undesirable in general.[32]

With respect to the possibility of localized excessive competition, some observers have concluded that too much competition is worse than none.

> In many long-haul markets with relatively light traffic flow, two or three-carrier competition has been created for the first time. In such markets, there is the possibility that no one of the competitors will generate

sufficient traffic to support a frequent, high quality air service. Where this happens, of course, is it not conceivable that the traveling public will be worse off with the competitive service than it was without it? [33]

Since the early days of the air transportation industry, well before the Civil Aeronautics Act, it has been generally felt by students of the industry that competition should be preserved, but that care must be taken lest competition become excessive. The Federal Aviation Commission, appointed in 1934 before the Civil Aeronautics Act, reported that:

On the other hand, too much competition can be as bad as too little. To allow half a dozen airlines to eke out a hand-to-mouth existence where there is enough traffic to support one really first-class service and one alone would be a piece of folly. To try to maintain a multiplicity of services in such a case by giving direct governmental aid to all of them would be folly thrice compounded.[34]

It has also been suggested that, although as has been pointed out above, competition has in general had the effect of stimulating the use of ever improving aircraft, excessive competition may, by jeopardizing the financial stability of the carriers, have exactly the opposite effect.

. . . it is perfectly possible for a regulatory agency such as the Board to use a short sighted policy, which will restrict the ability of the major airlines to acquire the latest possibile equipment. That can be done easily by increasing competitive forces, and it can be done in other ways.[35]

The even more extreme position that competition in any degree in the air transport industry is undesirable is not without its supporters. It has been argued that the alleged reductions in load factors caused by competition increase the cost of the provision of air service to such an extent that airline competition is unduly expensive and therefore should not be permitted and, indeed, that even the amount of competition which existed in 1953 should have been reduced.[36]

A tacit assumption in most arguments stressing the evils of competition is that higher load factors mean greater profitability and, therefore, they are to be desired. Conversely, it should be pointed out that higher load factors mean less possibility of conveniently available space for air travelers and that, beyond a certain level, higher load factors are inconsistent with adequate service. John H. Frederick [37] says that 78.8 percent is "generally regarded as being in excess of the highest load factor compatible with adequate service," and at present, in Board and industry circles, anything above 70 percent is generally regarded as incompatible with adequate service. Cost savings at the expense of quality of service may not be in the public interest.

Gill and Bates in their study [38] concluded that in general "competition has been an important force in the maintenance of a high quality, low-price airline service. . . . " However, at the same time, they noted that the type of competition which had been certificated in the postwar period (through 1949, the publication date of their study) had not in many cases contributed significantly to either improving the quality of the service or lowering its price and further that this competition had been a major reason for the failure of some carriers to become self-sufficient. Particularly, they concluded that multiple-carrier (three or more) competition was wasteful and of little if any constructive value, that it not only brought about the greatest subsidy burden on the government but afforded relatively little in improved air service to the traveler, and that "multiple-carrier competition has been the major flaw . . . in the competitive expansion of the domestic air transportation system." [39]

In spite of the dire predictions about the continuation of the requirements for government subsidy in view of the amount of authorized competition, the domestic trunkline industry in 1959 became free of subsidy.[40]

The most important problem of "excessive competition" is not whether there will be more carriers and more flights on certain of the high density routes than those routes can support. After all, the Board does not schedule the flights. It is the carriers who enter and serve the market and who add and eliminate schedules. The basic problem is the current necessity for the rich routes to subsidize the lean routes. By sharing the rich routes and decreasing their profitability to individual carriers, competition decreases the profit cushion available to these carriers who depend upon this profitability to offset their losses on the lean routes, which they also are required to serve. It is the system-wide profitability which is critical.

CONSERVATISM IN THE EARLY 1950'S

It was during and immediately following a period of recession in the airlines industry and of severe criticism of the Board for the authorization of allegedly excessive competition that the Board heard and decided the *Southern Service to the West Case,* Docket No. 1102, *et al.* on January 30, 1951. In this case the Board, in a three-to-two decision, adopted what Member Lee in his dissent termed its "anticompetitive philosophy" when it stated:

> Undoubtedly, where it appears on the record of a particular case that an air carrier is failing to attain the high standards of public service contemplated by the Civil Aeronautics Act, and where only provision for an economic competitive service would contribute effectively to the assurance of such standards, a case is made for competition. But it is not seriously contended in the present case that competition is needed for that reason. The only service shortcoming revealed by the present record is the absence of through-plane service, a defect which we here find can and should be remedied by interchange arrangements between connecting carriers.
>
> We would be less than helpful if, at this time, we did not express our considered opinion that further route expansion in our domestic trunk-line network would present problems of serious difficulty in view of the conditions which presently and during the postwar period have existed in this industry. Certainly the task of proving public convenience and necessity in satisfying the statutory requirements would place a difficult, if not insurmountable, burden upon the air carriers which would undertake to sponsor further route extensions of any substantial character.[41]

A major factor in the Board's position in this case seems to have been the then current condition of the industry. The Board said that, in deciding against new route extensions in this proceeding, they were not prejudicing possible future extensions.

A short time later in the *Reopened Southern Service to the West Case,* Docket No. 1102, *et al.,* decided December 22, 1953, the majority confirmed its stand.[42]

> It is our considered judgment, therefore, that such competition as would be offered by the interchange, including the trans-gulf route extension, would not provide "competition to the extent necessary to assure the sound development of an air transportation system adapted" to our national needs. On the contrary, approval of this interchange would signify

the adoption by the Board of a policy of competition solely for competition's sake, which policy we reject. Accordingly, we shall disapprove the agreement submitted for our consideration.

The extent to which the Board's decision in the *Southern Service to the West Case* departed from its previous policy is suggested by the following quotations from the dissent of member Josh Lee.

Had the Board followed the Examiner's recommendation or had it followed its own long established competitive policy in reaching its decision in the original *Southern Service to the West Case,* an entirely new route would have been awarded, connecting California with the Southeast and at the same time establishing a competitive service between Texas and the West Coast and also the Board would have provided additional service between Los Angeles and San Francisco as recommended by the Examiner.

But the majority did not provide competition for American's Dallas–West Coast route nor did it authorize additional service between Los Angeles and San Francisco. Had the majority stopped there and merely refused to provide such competitive service, it would have indeed represented a departure from a long line of previous decisions wherein the Board favored competition even though the traffic was substantially less than in this case. But the majority not only kept American's route free from competition, it deliberately strengthened its Dallas–West Coast route by tying on to it three separate interchanges. That decision, which is unparalled in all of the fifteen years of the Board's regulatory history, protected a monopoly route between Texas and California over which a total of approximately 400,000 passengers move annually.[43]

But now the TWA-Braniff-Eastern interchange is being disapproved on the ground that it would provide "competition for competition's sake." It should be evident that competition was the real issue in the original *Southern Service to the West Case.* As herein before pointed out that was the first of a series of decisions by a divided Board vote which changed the policy of the Board from one that was generally favorable to competition to one that opposes competition even though catch phrases rather than facts must be relied upon to try to justify its refusal.[44]

This seeming reluctance to create competitive authorizations was to be short-lived, and, despite this decision in the *Reopened Southern Service to the West Case* in December 1953 and subsequent orders in the same case decided in June and October of

1954, the Board in early 1953 had instituted three major new route proceedings intended to re-examine the need of specified major cities for competitive service. These cases, the *New York–Chicago Service Case,* the *Denver Service Case,* and the *Southwest–Northeast Service Case,* and others which followed, were destined to create large amounts of competitive service and reverse the position taken in the *Southern Service to the West Case.*

THE POLICY 1955–1956

The *New York–Chicago Case,* which was decided in September, 1955, was the first of a series of decisions by which, within less than a year and a half, the Civil Aeronautics Board under the leadership of Chairman Ross Rizley vastly increased the amount of competition among the scheduled domestic air carriers. These decisions, by expanding the route authorizations of all of the domestic trunkline carriers, created new single-plane service in many markets in which, theretofore, there had been none authorized; created competition in many routes that had been monopolistic; and created multiple-carrier competition in yet other routes which had been competitive but served by fewer carriers.

The Board, in taking these actions was following a policy of increasing competition but, at the same time, trying to serve all of the objectives which are laid down in the Act. These goals, which may often be conflicting, include: developing the air transportation industry, serving the needs of commerce, promoting the national defense, serving the needs of the postal service, fostering competition, avoiding monopoly, and minimizing subsidy payments or, in any event, maximizing the public benefit from each unit of subsidy outlay. Perhaps it is because of the multiple objectives served by the Board that the decisions are sometimes difficult to interpret and to predict and precedent is difficult to establish. Nevertheless, with respect to its policy on competition, the Board was perfectly clear. The increase in competition was the result of a conscious and expressed policy of the Board under the assumption that it is not necessary to support monopoly in order to protect existing carriers and that competition between carriers where the traffic is adequate to support the competing carriers is in the public interest. This was specifically stated by the Board:

. . . competitive air service offers greater assurance that the public will receive the quality and quantity of air service to which it is entitled.[45]

The Board's long-standing policy is to rely on competition for the vigorous development of our national air transport system with the fullest improvements in service and technological developments.[46]

We are no longer faced with the problem of heavy subsidy support for our trunkline carriers—which was a factor which necessarily inhibited the award of competitive services and, at an earlier date, made the question of diversion of particular importance. On the contrary, there has been a remarkable growth in the strength of many of our trunkline carriers, and the markets which they serve. This presents a greater opportunity than has existed heretofore for the establishment of competitive services. This does not mean, of course, that we are now free to authorize unlimited competition for an excess of competition can bring uneconomic conditions and jeopardize the development of that sound system of air transportation which is the ultimate objective of the Act. But it does mean that in sizeable markets with promising traffic potential we have greater freedom to introduce or enlarge competitive service to insure the full development of those markets without burdening the Federal Treasury.[47]

Over the years the Civil Aeronautics Board has reaffirmed its belief in the need for effective competition to assure the high quality of service which regulation alone cannot provide.[48]

In deciding the issues in these proceedings, the Board followed the policy that competition *per se* is a desideratum and the amount of traffic on the route in question is the most important consideration in evaluating the need for competition. However, it found that the problem of selecting the carrier to provide this competition was not simple. The Board's carrier selection problem will be examined in some detail in Chapter IX. Further, it became clear that the Board did not decide each case *in vacuo*. Rather, both by consolidation of applications and by coordination of the decisions in the various proceedings, the Board was in effect investigating and modifying the route structure of the entire industry, although formally accomplishing this within the framework of separate consideration of individual proceedings.

The Board had, in effect, returned to the presumption doctrine and awarded competitive authorizations where the traffic was found to be adequate. This is proclaimed by the Board in the citations which follow.

Aside from the actual volume generated in these markets the rate of growth is significant. Thus, between 1952 and 1954, the number of passengers practically doubled. The size and potential of these markets is brought into focus when it is realized that Philadelphia is the third largest city and Detroit is the fifth largest in the country. In terms of cities with which Philadelphia has exchanged the greatest number of air passengers, Philadelphia–Detroit ranks third and Philadelphia–Cleveland ninth. In this context, we are convinced that the size and potential of these markets clearly warrant competitive air service in order to insure that the traveling public will obtain the quantity and quality of service to which it is entitled.[49]

Furthermore, it is clear that the Seattle/Portland–Chicago and east market is of such size and importance as to warrant fully competitive services. During 1954, more than 122,980 passengers traveled between Seattle and Portland, on the one hand, and Chicago, New York, Detroit, Cleveland and Washington, on the other. Considering the length of the haul, and quantum of traffic, we believe that unrestricted competitive service by United and Northwest will help to insure the quantity and quality of service best suited to needs of the traveling public.[50]

Authorization of additional air service found warranted in order to provide improved service between important cities in the Southwest and Northeast areas of the United States and major cities in between where the available traffic potential is sufficient to support multiple carrier services.[51]

Traffic between Norfolk and Newport News, on the one hand, and Washington, Baltimore, Philadelphia, and New York, on the other hand, will exceed 230,000 passengers in 1956. A combined market of this size can support competitive service and is entitled to the benefits to be derived therefrom. We expect that, with the authorization of competitive service in these markets, these cities will be assured in the future of receiving a full pattern of service, including coach services, in modern equipment.[52]

This policy of authorizing competitive service on those routes which could support it was not confined to the domestic routes. The President of the United States wrote, in 1957, that: "It is this Administration's objective, wherever traffic justifies it, to provide competitive U.S. service on all international and overseas routes from all gateways." [53] However, still unanswered is the question of just how much traffic is adequate or needed to justify competitive awards. This will be discussed in Chapter VIII under the general heading, *Criteria for Competition.*

Inadvertent awards. By thus returning, in effect, to the presumption in favor of competition, the Civil Aeronautics Board, in these very important decisions rendered between September 1, 1955 and the end of 1956, increased the amount of competition in the domestic airline industry by authorizing new or improved competitive service to more than 500 pairs of cities. In these decisions, the Board, in effect, peeled the top traffic-generating noncompetitive city pairs from the top of the rankings by traffic, and authorized competitive service for them. At the same time, by virtue of these selfsame carrier route extensions, many other city pairs shared in the competitive authorizations. For example, in the *New York–Florida Case,* Docket No. 3051, TWA was authorized to offer service between Hartford-Springfield and Las Vegas, Nevada, two points which exchange very little traffic and between which neither TWA nor United, the original carrier, offered single-plane service in September, 1957. Clearly, the Board did not set out, purposely or deliberately, to create competition between these two points. It resulted from the fact that, for other purposes, Hartford-Springfield was added to TWA's route which previously contained Las Vegas.

In much the same way, many of the city pairs which received their first authorizations for single-plane service, received these authorizations as a result of route awards that were made for other reasons. In these cases, there was no clear need for the service in terms of large volumes of traffic waiting to be served, the Board did not specifically and purposively authorize the new service between those city pairs, and the carrier will probably not offer the service for some time, if at all. An illustration of this is found in the *Tucson Airport Authority Case,* Docket No. 5564, where TWA was authorized to offer single-plane service between Tucson, Arizona and many other cities on TWA's route No. 2, including, say, Reading, Pennsylvania, for which city pair, single-plane service was certainly not an issue in that case.

The Board took note of the fact that there are many implications to decisions which create even small extensions to existing large route systems when it stated:

> It is evident that the possible combinations of service that could be offered under the authority sought in a proceeding of this complexity are so myriad as to make it completely impractical for an applicant to show schedules using every conceivable routing which might be attained.[54]
>
> We cannot accept the contention that the Board, in awarding a new route, must find a need for every new service which may be offered as a result thereof. Such a contention is at war with consistent Board practice since the promulgation of the Act. In granting new routes to carriers to meet service needs demonstrated on the record in a proceeding, we have frequently described these routes to permit other new services for which a specific need was not shown in the record. In this regard, our general policy in awarding new route segments has been first to provide operating authority broad enough to permit the full development of the new services found required by the public convenience and necessity, and then to impose upon the award only such operating restrictions as may be required either as a matter of law, or by public interest considerations, including the protection of operating rights of other carriers.[55]

Because of the many possible results of these awards, some of which may not happen to have been foreseen by the Board, it is reasonable to expect that on occasion such an inadvertence may result in an award that the Board not only did not intend, but which is actually deemed to be undesirable. On such occasions the carriers who are opposed to the extension waste no time in calling this to the attention of the Board, which then may amend its decision, if that is deemed appropriate, as in the following three illustrations:

> There are three additional matters in connection with our decision on additional Detroit service that warrant comment. First, American has correctly pointed out that, in authorizing TWA to provide additional service in the Chicago–Detroit–New York market we erroneously granted to TWA the right to provide nonstop services between Detroit, on the one hand, and Phoenix and points west therefore, on the other hand. TWA's current Detroit service on segments "1" and "2" of Route No. 2 is subject to the restriction that flights serving Detroit, on

the one hand, and Los Angeles, San Francisco, Oakland or Phoenix, on the other hand, shall make an intermediate stop enroute. And TWA's application herein did not embrace modification of this restriction. Accordingly, we shall restore this restriction on service to Detroit on segments "1" and "2" to TWA's certificate. We shall also, in accordance with the limitation of this proceeding, require a stop at Chicago on all flights over TWA's new New York–Detroit–Chicago routing, which also serve points west of Chicago.[56]

The Board's second order of consolidation in the subject proceeding stated that any authorization granted Western herein would be subject to a condition against operation of "through-plane service through Denver to or from points north or east therof." However, under the restriction we placed on the award to western, the carrier would be able, for example, to provide service between Salt Lake City and the Twin Cities via Denver. We find that such service would be outside the scope of the proceeding as delineated by the consolidation order. Accordingly, Western should be additionally restricted against serving points north or east of Denver on flights serving both Salt Lake City and Denver.[57]

TWA has also called attention to the fact that in authorizing American to serve Columbus and Pittsburgh on a direct routing to New York, subject to long-haul restriction, we granted American an unrestricted Dayton–New York nonstop. Since this was an inadvertence, we shall redraft the award to American to exclude this authority which we have not found required by the public convenience and necessity.[58]

The policy. The policy which emerged during this period, and which still prevails, is one of:

(1) Certificating the maximum amount of competition consistent with the sound development of an air transportation system,
(2) Granting entry into the field in all areas which showed promise of further development of air transportation, and
(3) Using the opportunity provided by the need for more competition on the more profitable routes to provide more and better service and at the same time reducing the need for subsidy by strengthening marginal carriers. . . . [59]

Thus, the primary objective of many of the route awards was the authorization of competitive service for selected city pairs which in the judgment of the Board needed and justified competitive service. These are, typically, heavily traveled routes; and the Board indicated, as noted above, that the volume of traffic, both actual and potential, traveling between these cities was an important factor in its decisions to make the competitive awards.

In addition, the Board went further and found that in some of the very heavily traveled routes the amount of traffic was adequate to justify multiple competition; that is, competition by three or more carriers.

> In our judgment, the size and potential of the New York–Detroit market will now support three turnaround services rather than merely one heretofore operated by American. Thus, the record shows that in this area the New York–Detroit market is exceeded only by the New York–Chicago market, and yet American is the only unrestricted operator between New York and Detroit. The much smaller New York–Cleveland market has two turnaround services. Furthermore, the New York–Detroit market increased by 86 per cent from 1949 to 1954. Under such circumstances, we have no hestitation in finding that the New York–Detroit market will support two additional turnaround services.[60]

This multiple-carrier competition will be discussed in greater detail in Chapter VIII.

In effect, the mood of the Board, if not its philosophy, had made the full circle. "Competition for competition's sake" could, after these decisions, hardly have been regarded as a term of derision. Competition was no longer on trial.

CHAPTER VII

The Materials and Framework for Analysis

THE PERIOD UNDER STUDY

On June 30, 1955, 37 of the top 50 markets and 23 of the second 50 were competitive. . . . Today only 4 of the top 50 and 12 of the second 50 remain noncompetitive. . . . *Annual Report of the Civil Aeronautics Board*, 1956.

Beginning with the *New York–Chicago Case,* decided September 1, 1955, the Civil Aeronautics Board by a series of decisions awarded route extensions which broadened the route systems of all of the domestic trunkline carriers to a greater or lesser extent. Of these cases, those which were decided between September 1, 1955, and December 31, 1956, and which constitute the basis for the empirical aspects of this study, are listed in Table VII-1. The fact that the last case presented in Table VII-1 and therefore the last case analyzed in this study is the *New York–Florida Case,* the decision in which became effective December 21, 1956, should not be taken to suggest that this was the last of the important cases. On the contrary, decisions affecting competition since that time have included the *Eastern Route Consolidation Case,* and the *Service to Phoenix Case,* decided in 1957; the *St. Louis–Southeast Service Case* and the *Great Lakes–Southeast Service Case,* decided in 1958; the *Dallas to the West Service Case* and the *Chicago–Milwaukee–Twin Cities Case,* decided in 1959; and the *New York–San Francisco Nonstop Service Case,* decided in 1959 but effective in 1960. However, only those listed in Table VII-1 have been subjected to detailed analysis in this study. This is because, since the analysis includes investigation of the schedule patterns offered by the newly authorized carriers and of the resulting traffic flows under the new competition, it was necessary to consider only cases which were decided early enough for the subsequent schedule and traffic data to be satisfactorily developed under the new authorizations. Therefore, no cases later than the *New York–Florida Case* are analyzed in this study.

TABLE VII-1

CASES INVOLVING COMPETITION DECIDED BY THE CIVIL AERONAUTICS BOARD BETWEEN SEPTEMBER 1, 1955 AND DECEMBER 31, 1956

		Date	
Docket Number	*Name of Case*	*Initial Decision*	*Effective*
986, *et al.*	New York–Chicago Service Case	9/1/55	10/31/55
1789, *et al.*	Reopened Milwaukee–Chicago–New York Restriction Case	9/1/55	10/31/55
2190	United Restriction Case, Supplemental Opinion	9/1/55	10/31/55
7253	Louisville–New York Nonstop Investigation	9/1/55	10/31/55
6503 *et al.*	Southwest Airways Renewal Case	9/27/55	11/26/55
986, *et al.*	New York–Chicago Case—Supplemental Opinion and Order on Deferred Applications *	11/14/55	12/30/55
1841, *et al.*	Denver Service Case	11/14/55	12/30/55
2355, *et al.*	Southwest–Northeast Service Case	11/21/55	1/20/56
5564	Tucson Airport Authority Application	7/27/56	9/25/56
4294	Northwest Airlines, Pittsburgh–Cleveland and Detroit Restriction Case	8/21/56	10/20/56
986, *et al.*	New York–Chicago Service Case—(Deferred Portion of Eastern's Application)	8/21/56	10/20/56
8134, 8139, 8175	Eastern Airlines, Inc., Huntsville–Madison County Airport Authority and Southern Airways, Inc.	8/28/56	8/28/56
5701, *et al.*	Florida–Texas Service Case	9/24/56	12/31/56
3051, *et al.*	New York–Florida Case	9/28/56	12/21/56

* This deferred portion of the *New York–Chicago Case,* Docket No. 986, is designated *1986* in the appendices.

THE STATISTICAL FRAMEWORK

City pairs. The route awards made in the decisions listed in Table VII–1 are analyzed in this study in terms of the *city pairs* affected by these awards. There are three compelling reasons for analyzing the data in terms of city pairs. First, data are available for both traffic and schedules in these terms. Second, the data are more amenable to certain kinds of statistical investigation and analysis when expressed in terms of city pairs than in any other form. Third, regardless of the intent of the Board with respect to considerations such as the total route configurations of various carriers or of service between groups of cities or geographical areas, the eventual impact of all service authorizations and of the resulting flight schedules operated by the carriers is the offering of air transportation between city pairs. Similarly, the transportation services available to the traveling public exist only in terms of city pairs. A traveler wishing to purchase transportation between Philadelphia and Cincinnati or between Tampa and Boston is concerned with the service available between those specific city pairs, and the total service between Ohio and the East or between Florida cities and New England cities is of little consequence to him. Therefore, although, in the deliberations of the Board and in the operations of the carriers, there may be many considerations over and above that of the requirements for service between the city pair, it is, in a real sense, the city pair which defines the unit of transportation that is offered, that is sold, and that is consumed.

Single-plane service authorization. In order to study the implications of these decisions with respect to the specific city pairs for which new service was authorized, it was necessary to adopt a standard definition of what constitutes "service authorization" for single-plane service between two cities. In this study, a pair of cities is considered to have "authorized single-plane service" if:

1. a carrier is authorized to offer single-plane service between the two points with circuity of not more than 15% with respect to the most direct alternative authorized routing, be it single-plane or connecting, or
2. when there is no alternative routing, a carrier is authorized to offer *any* single-plane service, provided that the circuity is less than 100 percent with respect to the nonstop distance.

It should be noted that "single-plane service" as here used refers always to single-plane single-carrier service. None of the authorizations in the cases considered here involved interchange service.

Since some of these city pairs received such single-plane service authorizations in more than one case, the sum of the city pairs

TABLE VII-2

CITY PAIRS RECEIVING NEW OR IMPROVED COMPETITIVE SINGLE-PLANE SERVICE AUTHORIZATIONS IN MORE THAN ONE OF THE PROCEEDINGS

City Names	*Docket Numbers*		
Akron–Pittsburgh	986	986 *	
Atlanta–Philadelphia	986	2355	
Baltimore–New York	2355	3051	
Baltimore–Philadelphia	2355	3051	
Baltimore–Richmond	2355	3051	
Baltimore–Washington	2355	3051	
Birmingham–Philadelphia	986	2355	
Boston–Houston	2355	3051	
Boston–Pittsburgh	2355	3051	
Chattanooga–Philadelphia	986	2355	
Cleveland–Pittsburgh	986	986 *	4294
Denver–New York	1841	2355	
Denver–Washington	1841	2355	
Detroit–Pittsburgh	986	986 *	4294
Hartford–Louisville	7253	3051	
Hartford–San Francisco	1841	3051	
Houston–New Orleans	2355	5701	
Houston–Providence	2355	3051	
Houston–Savannah	2355	5701	
Huntsville–New York	7253	2355	
Huntsville–Philadelphia	2355	8134	
Knoxville–Philadelphia	986	2355	
Los Angeles–Pittsburgh	986 *	2355	
Memphis–Philadelphia	986	2355	
Nashville–New York	7253	2355	
New Orleans–Philadelphia	986	2355	
New York–Newport News	2355	3051	
New York–Norfolk	2355	3051	
New York–Philadelphia	986	2355	3051
New York–Pittsburgh	986	986 *	2355
New York–Richmond	2355	3051	
New York–Washington	2355	3051	
New York–Wheeling	2355	3051	
Newport News–Philadelphia	2355	3051	
Norfolk–Philadelphia	2355	3051	
Philadelphia–Pittsburgh	986 *	2355	
Philadelphia–Richmond	2355	3051	
Philadelphia–Washington	2355	3051	
Philadelphia–Wheeling	986	2355	3051
Pittsburgh–San Francisco	986 *	2355	

* Deferred portion. See Table VII-3, note ‡.
Source: Appendix One.

affected by the decisions in all of the listed cases exceeds the number of unduplicated city pairs. For example, in a deferred portion of Docket No. 986, *et al.*, United Air Lines was authorized to operate single-plane service between Pittsburgh and Los Angeles in competition with TWA. Later, in Docket No. 2355, *et al.*, American Airlines was also authorized to provide service between these points. Thus, the "geographical city pair," Pittsburgh–Los Angeles,

TABLE VII-3

NUMBER OF CITY PAIRS RECEIVING NEW OR IMPROVED COMPETITIVE SINGLE-PLANE AUTHORIZATIONS IN EACH OF THE PROCEEDINGS

		Number of City Pairs		
Docket Number	*Name of Case*	*First Competition* *	*Additional Competition* †	*Total*
986, *et al.*	New York–Chicago Service Case	22	13	35
986 ‡ *et al.*	New York–Chicago Case—Supplemental Opinion and Order on Deferred Applications	13	6	19
1841, *et al.*	Denver Service Case	38	12	50
1789, *et al.*	Reopened Milwaukee–Chicago–New York Restriction Case		1	1
2190	United Restriction Case		18	18
2355, *et al.*	Southwest–Northeast Service Case	138	81	219
3051, *et al.*	New York–Florida Case	77	82	159
4294	Northwest Airlines, Pittsburgh–Cleveland and Detroit Restriction Case		2	2
5564	Tucson Airport Authority Application	22	1	23
5701, *et al.*	Florida–Texas Service Case	6	2	8
6503, *et al.*	Southwest Airways Renewal Case	5		5
7253	Louisville–New York Nonstop Investigation		12	12
8134, *et al.*	Eastern Airlines, Inc., Huntsville–Madison County Airport Authority and Southern Airways, Inc.	7	1	8
Total		328	231	559

* These city pairs had no more than one airline authorized to offer single-plane service before September 1, 1955.

† This list includes not only those awards resulting in multiple-carrier (three or more carriers) competition but also those which represented improved authorization to one or more of the carriers where competitive awards existed before September 1, 1955.

‡ In the Appendices, *1986* is used to represent the deferred portion of Docket No. 986, the *New York–Chicago Case.* The decision in this deferred portion was issued November 14, 1955 contemporaneously with the decision in the *Denver Service Case.*

appears in two cases as receiving new or improved competitive authorizations and thereby is represented by two "docket-city-pairs" (i.e., "LAX PIT 986" and "LAX PIT 2355") for the purpose of authorization analyses. New or improved single-plane service authorizations for approximately 1,550 docket-city-pairs, involving 1,500 geographical city pairs, result from the decisions in the cases listed in Table VII-1.

Of the 1,500 geographical city pairs involved in these decisions, 514 received competitive authorizations; i.e., were authorized single-plane service by two or more carriers as of December 31, 1956. Actually thirty-five of these appeared in two of these cases, and five of them appeared in three of the cases with the result that, when summed over the various cases, there were 559 docket-city-pairs authorized competitive service in these cases. The forty city pairs which received new or improved competitive single-plane service authorizations in more than one of the proceedings are listed in Table VII-2 which also shows the docket numbers of the Cases involved. The 559 docket-city-pairs are shown in Appendix One, which also shows certain details of the authorizations and the carriers involved.

Among the 514 geographical city pairs receiving new or improved competitive single-plane service authorizations were some receiving their first competitive authorizations, some their second, some their third, and, in the extreme, New York–Washington, its ninth (ten trunk and local service airlines certificated). The number of airlines involved in each city pair may be seen in Appendix One. Actually, 328 of the 559 docket-city-pairs represented first competitive service authorizations. These, naturally, since they are the *first* competitive authorizations, are unduplicated and represent also 328 different geographical city pairs. Table VII-3 shows the number of first competitive and additional or improved competitive authorizations resulting from each of the decisions.

Among those city pairs which received their first competitive authorizations as a result of these cases were many heavily traveled pairs such as: Buffalo–New York, Dallas–New York, Denver–Los Angeles, Houston–New York, Detroit–Philadelphia, Kansas City–New York, Norfolk–Washington, and Boston–Miami.

SUPPLEMENTS TO THE CITY PAIR FRAMEWORK

Although the decisions may be analyzed in terms of the city pairs affected by the decisions, and although the Board in its statements of purpose and intent as printed in the opinions has often thought and acted in terms of the city pairs involved and in terms of the effects which it desired for those city pairs, it would be wrong to conclude that the Board thought only or even always primarily in terms of *city pairs* in arriving at its decisions. At least four other criteria have been cited in the Board's opinions.

Geographical areas. One of these bases for judgment has been the geographical area in which was located one or more of the cities involved. For example, service was found needed to or from "the Southwest," "New England points," or "Florida cities."

Service for a city. The second criterion was the characteristics of the individual city involved without any specific pairing considerations. This basis was used by the Board in at least one case as a factor in formulating its decision to create competitive authorizations. The general concept of competitive air service for a city is based on reasoning that a particular city, because of its geographical, economic, and demographic characteristics, should have competitive air service with many points and thus not be dependent upon only one major carrier. Here the Board deems it unnecessary to find that there are specific cities, groups of cities, or areas, with which competitive service is required, and, therefore, the expressed purpose of the award is not to create competition with named points, but rather to create general transcontinental competition for that city's traffic. Thus the traffic with specifically named points is not the important determinant of need, but rather the total traffic or traffic potential of the city with *all* other points is cited as the controlling criterion. This central concept is illustrated in the *Tucson Airport Authority Case,* in which the Board stated:

> Thus, the number of passengers boarded by American at . . . [Tucson] . . . rose from 46,255 in 1951 to approximately 79,000 for the year 1955. In terms of percentage growth, the 1955 passengers boarded by American exceeded the 1954 experience by 30 percent.

An indication of Tucson's importance as an air traffic center is the fact that only 42 cities developed more revenue passenger miles during the latest survey period (March 1955). And, it is noteworthy that during the same survey period, Tucson produced more revenue passenger miles than did both Tulsa and Oklahoma City, both of which were recently given a second transcontinental service. The evidence leaves no doubt that Tucson has developed into a city of such size and importance in terms of air traffic potential as to justify service by a second transcontinental trunkline carrier.

The importance of air transportation to Tucson is underscored by the city's high degree of isolation. With the exception of Phoenix, the distances between Tucson and other major cities is considerable, and there are mountain barriers separating Tucson from every major city except Phoenix. The record shows that Tucson is highly dependent upon good air transportation to sustain its economy, particularly with respect to its tourist business.[1]

Carrier route configurations. Third, the Board, in attempting to satisfy all of the goals which it seeks to optimize, thinks also in terms of carriers and in terms of those carriers' route configurations. In this connection, one of the primary objectives of the Board in these decisions has been the strengthening of the smaller carriers. Chairman Rizley, in a letter to Representative Celler, which has already been cited, referred to the policies followed by the Board of:

(1) Certificating the maximum amount of competition consistent with the sound development of an air transportation system,
(2) Granting entry into the field in all areas which showed promise of further development of air transportation, and
(3) Using the opportunity provided by the need for more competition on the more profitable routes to provide more and better service and at the same time reducing the need for subsidy by strengthening marginal carriers.[2]

However, it has not always been clear whether the Board's primary objective in granting competitive route extensions was: (1) the creation of competition, with the policy of strengthening the weaker carriers given expression in the choice of carrier to provide that competition, or whether (2) the primary objective was the strengthening of the weaker carriers. It seems difficult to ascertain, in some of the decisions, which of these two motives was the more important. In any event, the decisions did have the effect of expanding and, hopefully, strengthening the weaker carriers. In the words of the Celler Committee,

> the smaller trunklines were permitted to participate in lucrative routes and traffic centers where they previously had been excluded. The Board's action to strengthen the smaller domestic trunklines and to increase the amount of competition among the trunklines was long overdue.[3]

Regional route configurations. Fourth, the Board considers the *entire route structure of the region* under consideration or, in some cases, of the entire country. It has been noted above that the Board does not treat each case in isolation and that the decision in any case may be expected to be related to some extent to the developments and the thinking of the Board in other cases that are being considered at the same time or are in prospect. For example, there is evidence that, in some ways, the Board considered the important 1955–56 cases as something akin to a single consolidated proceeding. Indication of such unofficial—and of course highly desirable—coordination of proceedings is seen in the following quotations.

> This case is the third in a series of major area route cases in which the Board is reappraising important portions of the national air route structure.[4]
>
> Contemporaneously herewith, in the *Denver Service Case* we are authorizing TWA to serve Denver. Consequently, Denver–Pittsburgh service by both United and TWA will be authorized.[5]
>
> The benefits to the traveling public of a competitive service outweigh the diversion of revenue which Capital will suffer. With the recent extensions of Capital's system, the importance of these markets to Capital has diminished greatly. The loss of revenue which Capital will sustain can be absorbed by the carrier without difficulty.[6]
>
> Capital's request for extension to Dallas/Fort Worth and Houston, Texas denied, in view of Braniff's and Delta's greater need for route strengthening, and the fact that Capital will have to devote a major portion of its resources and efforts to the development of the new markets in the New York–Chicago area which we recently authorized it to serve.[7]

Here, again, in the last quotation, is evidence of the Board's policy of strengthening the weaker carriers by route extensions in order to achieve a better competitive balance among the carriers. In Chapter IX, which deals with the problem of selection of the carrier to provide needed new services, this criterion is discussed as a factor in carrier selection.

THE INTENT OF THE BOARD AND ITS IMPORTANCE

It has been noted that the Board, in its decisions during the period under study, made route authorizations or route changes resulting in new or improved competitive single-plane service authorizations to 514 unduplicated city pairs. Actually, there were 559 "docket-city-pairs," as defined above. It has also been noted in Chapter VI that when a route change is made for the purpose of improving the service authorization over a particular route, there may be and usually are some other city pairs whose service authorizations are affected by the change. The decisions under consideration here created 559 new or improved competitive service authorizations, but, by no stretch of the imagination or of the facts, could it be said that it was the purpose of the Board to effect all of the 559 changes. Clearly, some of these were brought about because it was the purpose of the Board to do so, but on the other hand, many city pairs received authorizations for new or improved competitive single-plane service as a consequence of route changes made for other reasons. This has always been recognized by the industry and by the Board. In some cases, the Board has thus inadvertently created authorizations which it preferred not to let stand, and it has later made the appropriate changes to the certificates involved. The general policy of the Board in this matter is stated in the *Denver Service Case,* where, after the decision, United objected that Western, under its new authority to serve Reno–San Francisco, could also offer service between Reno and points north and south of San Francisco on Western's previous routes. United claimed that the issue in the case was, for Reno "additional east-west service," and that the record showed no need for such north-south service. The Board replied that:

> Western's authority to provide service via San Francisco between Los Angeles and Reno, for example, will flow from its pre-existing authority to operate between Los Angeles and San Francisco, and the new San Francisco–Reno authority which we found required by the public

convenience and necessity. As we have previously pointed out herein, similar additional service authorization, flowing from the addition of new route segments to existing route systems, frequently result from Board decisions in route proceedings. Our general policy in awarding new route segments has been first to provide operating authority broad enough to permit the full development of the new services found required by the public convenience and necessity, and then to impose upon the award only such operating restrictions as may be required as a matter of law or by the public interest. United has not demonstrated where we are required either as a matter of law or for sound policy reasons to so restrict our award to Western of a San Francisco/Oakland–Reno service as to prevent the carrier from providing additional service on this segment to points on Western's present route north or south of the Bay Area.[8]

It is important for the purposes of this study to differentiate between those city pairs which received their authorizations because the Board intended to award them and those which received their authorizations as a result of route changes made for other purposes. There are two main reasons for this. First, it permits study of the *criteria* used by the Board in arriving at its decisions, and second, it makes it possible to judge whether the *effect* of each decision is as the Board intended it to be.

The criteria for decision. The Board, in making the awards to the various city pairs, clearly used some criteria for deciding which city pairs needed and justified competitive service, and which did not. The traffic levels prevailing at the time of the awards were an important, if not the most important, basis for judgments about the advisability of making competitive route authorizations.

Over the years the Board has reaffirmed its belief in the need for competition to assure the high quality of service which regulation alone cannot provide. The Board has also repeatedly asserted its belief in the benefits of competition, particularly in markets where no competition exists, requiring only that there be a showing of sufficient traffic to support competitive service and that the record establish public benefits to be derived from additional operations.[9]

Clearly, all 559 docket-city-pairs did not have levels of traffic sufficient to cause the Board to conclude that the public convenience and necessity required new or improved competition. Some did and some did not, but nevertheless, all 559 received the service improvements. The only clue to permit separation of these lies in the intent of the Board as expressed in the published opinions. The level of traffic which characterized those city pairs for which the Board purposively created new or improved competitive authorizations must necessarily have been an important factor in the Board's decision process. It would, on the other hand, be unfair to the Board to suggest that the traffic levels of those other, the unintended, city pairs constituted, in the eyes of the Board, a criterion for decision.

The effect of the decisions. The Board is committed by the Act of 1938 and by its statements of intention to the use of competition as an adjunct to and a substitute for direct regulatory action. With the exception of the recent departures represented by the *Toledo Case* discussed above, the Board does not compel competitive service—it merely authorizes it. The effectiveness of the Board's actions in this effort may be measured by the extent to which the Board's authorizations have produced the desired changes in the service offered to the public. For this purpose, those authorizations which were intended to produce new service must be identified, since it is only on those routes that service changes (or lack of service changes) are relevant.

INTENT AND THE PUBLISHED OPINIONS

While the *intent* of the Board is often expressed clearly in the published opinions, this is, unfortunately, not always the case. There are many reasons for this, an important one of which is probably the fact that the opinions are not written by the Board members themselves, but by an "Opinion Writing Division" on the Board staff. This group, which is a branch of the General Counsel's office, consists of about seven or eight people who upon instructions from the Board (given in the conference at which the decision is made), prepare the Board's decisions. This practice of delegating the writing of opinions, not uncommon among administrative agencies, has long been recognized as a source of weakness in both the conclusions and the written opinions. James M. Landis pointed out long ago that the delegation of opinion writing means

> . . . that the laborious process of articulation is not indulged in by the individual who has the responsibility of judgment. Any judge can testify to the experience of working on opinions that won't write with the

result that his conclusions are changed because of his inability to state to his satisfaction the reasons on which they depend. Delegation of opinion writing has the danger of forcing a cavalier treatment of a record in order to support a conclusion reached only upon a superficial examination of that record. General impressions rather than that tightness that derives from the articulation of reasons may thus govern the trend of administrative adjudication.[10]

Former CAB Member Louis J. Hector took a very strong position on this matter in his memorandum to President Eisenhower, dated September 10, 1959. In this memorandum, which was submitted soon after his resignation from the Board, Mr. Hector said in part:

One of the most important reasons for the failure of the agencies to enunciate principles is the fact that commissioners in most cases do not personally give the reasons for their votes and hence have no need to think in general policy terms. As explained below, in the CAB and other regulatory agencies, the members of the agency merely vote on the outcome of a case and the opinion justifying the outcome is written by a professional staff. Members of these opinion writing staffs explain that they consciously avoid statements of general principle as much as possible in the opinions they write, because they must be able to write an opinion justifying an opposite conclusion the next day, and hence must not be hampered by prior statements of general principles.[11]

There have been times when the Board made decisions in executive session and then told the opinion-writers what answer the opinion should come out with. Major decisions of the Board have been made in that way. More often, the opinion-writers sit with the Board when a case is discussed. There can be no real claim, however, that the Board tells the opinion-writers in detail what to put in the opinion. . . . Nor can it be claimed that the opinions prepared by the staff are mere drafts and that the Board carefully reviews, edits, modifies, and rewrites the opinion. . . . If the opinions of the Board express what actually goes on in the minds of the deciding members, this is coincidental or the result of the intuition that a good staff can develop over the years.[12]

In a 1959 report, the Committee on Interstate and Foreign Commerce of the United States House of Representatives,[13] after long hearings, recommended legislation to end this practice.

The subcommittee has been impressed with the need for change in the practices followed by some commissions of letting the commission staff rather than individual commissioners assume responsibility for the preparation of commission decisions and opinions. It is the view of the subcommittee that inconsistencies in commission decisions over the years are traceable to a considerable extent to the failure of following the practice of having the commission, or the majority of the commission, designate individual commissioners to assume responsibility for the preparation of the decisions or opinions of the commission, or the majority of the commission. It is the view of the subcommittee that this practice, which is traditional with the courts and which has been followed by some commissions, should be adopted by all commissions. It is the hope of the subcommittee that this change will produce a sense of personal responsibility of individual commissioners for the decisions and opinions of the commission and will avoid the practice of having commission staffs assume the burden of reconciling inconsistent decisions reached by the commissions.[14]

The recommendation of the subcommittee was that:

Each commission should be *directed by law* that the commission, or the majority of the commission, as the case may be, designate a commissioner to prepare or have prepared under his personal direction the opinion or decision of the commission, or of the majority of the commission, in any case submitted to the commission for decision, and that the commissioner thus designated shall sign his name to the opinion or decision. . . .[15]

While there is thus, under the present system, the possibility of considerable looseness in the relationship between the true reasons for a Board decision and the reasons as given in the published opinions, it does not necessarily follow that such looseness is inevitably present. The Civil Aeronautics Board current practice involves the circulation of the draft opinions to the Board members before release. The Board members then request such changes as they desire, and their final approval before release is indicated by their signatures.

Although there is the possibility that in at least some cases the reasons and reasoning given in the published decisions may not adequately or even accurately represent the true thought processes and purposes of the Board members, nevertheless for the present, with respect to the decisions of the Civil Aeronautics Board, the published decisions as written by the Opinion Writing Division are the only source of information about the reasoning followed by the Board in reaching its decisions. It is these opinions which have been used in this study for ascertaining the intent of the Board as discussed below at some length. Although these opinions have not been written by the Board members, they have been read and approved by the Board members and adopted and published as their own decisions, and the responsibility for their contents must rest solely with the Board.

The classification of the intent of the Board has been, for each of the city pairs discussed, determined by intensive study of the published opinions. Since the statements in the opinions are not always clear, nor always amenable to this kind of rigorous analysis, it is possible that different students might arrive at somewhat different interpretations of the precise intent of the Board in some of the cases. The classification given below is the result of the reconciliation of the interpretations derived from independent reading and study of the opinions by three persons—the author and two associates. It was found that adequate description of the various degrees and kinds of intent of the Board required as a minimum seven categories of "intent" as described below.

THE CLASSIFICATION OF INTENT

All of the city pairs which were authorized for new or improved competitive single-plane air service in any one of these 1955–56 decisions were classified according to how the Board, as indicated by its statements in the published opinion, intended to treat that particular city pair. Actually, the opinion writers, by judicious selection of words, are able to suggest an infinite number of gradations of intensity of intent to create the new authorizations. However, for the purposes of this study, the various city pairs affected by the decisions were classified into seven categories, coded as follows:

1. *Purposive-specific.* Those city pairs for which the Board created competitive authorizations because it was the stated purpose of the Board to do so. The following quotation is such a Board statement in connection with the Dallas–New York and Dallas–Washington city pairs. "The predominant purpose of this new route is to provide a new service competitive with American between Dallas and Ft. Worth, on the one hand, and New York and Washington, on the other hand." [16]

2. *Purposive-group (or area)*. Those city pairs which received authorizations because of the Board's stated purpose to create competitive authorizations between a named city and a group of cities or between two groups of cities, but where the actual *city pair* is not specified. "Authorization of additional air service found warranted in order to provide improved service between important cities in the Northeast and in Florida where the available traffic potential is sufficient to support multiple carrier services." [17]

3. *Noted-specific*. Those city pairs which were given competitive authorization in the decision and which were specifically noted by the Board in its opinion as receiving such competition, although the Board did not indicate that the route modifications that resulted in this competition were made in order to create competition between these city pairs. "It is highly significant that the first one-plane competitive service proposed by TWA relates to four of Tucson's five leading passenger markets, namely, Los Angeles, Chicago, New York and San Francisco. First competitive service will also be available to a number of other cities . . . Albany, Baltimore, Boston, Cincinnati, Columbus, Dayton, Detroit, Indianapolis, Louisville, Philadelphia, Phoenix, St. Louis, Scranton and Washington." [18]

4. *Noted-group*. These city pairs correspond to those classified under code "3" above except that, instead of individual cities or city pairs being named, the Board statement is in terms of groups of cities or of areas. "Delta will also be able to provide Charlotte and Birmingham with needed new services to the southwest and northeast." [19]

5. *Corrective-specific*. Those city pairs which received competitive awards because the Board felt that there should be single-plane service between those specific city pairs, and the existing certificated carrier was not offering such services. "In addition, TWA proposes to operate through plane services between the Oklahoma cities and points in the Ohio Valley including Detroit and Cleveland, a service which American is authorized to render but has failed to provide." [20]

6. *Corrective-group*. These city pairs correspond to those classified under code "5" above with the exception that the Board

spoke in terms of groups of cities or areas instead of in terms of specific city pairs.

> The Examiner found correctly that Hartford should be added to route No. 2 as requested, in order that it be enabled to receive needed through service to the important Ohio Valley cities served by TWA. Both American and United assail the decision on the ground that American can now, as a result of our award in the *Southwest–Northeast Case, supra,* meet all the needs of the important Ohio Valley cities for Hartford/Springfield service. However, the Official Traffic Guide for September 1956, more than six months after our decision in the *Southwest–Northeast Case, supra,* does not show any direct through plane service by American between Hartford/Springfield and any of the Ohio Valley points. It is clear, therefore, that American's interest or ability with respect to the desired service is minimal and constitutes no bar to the granting of TWA's application.[21]

7. *Mentioned.* Those city pairs which received competitive authorization in the decision, and which, although mentioned in the decision as receiving new or improved authorizations, were not referred to as receiving *competitive* authorizations. These are city pairs such that the Board made no mention of competition or of the existence of a competitive carrier. Thus, with respect to *competition,* they were not "noted." The statement: "route modifications consist principally of an extension of route No. 51 north of Washington to New York/Newark via Baltimore and Philadelphia. . . ." [22] qualifies all pairs of these named cities for code "7," since they are specifically mentioned, but there is no mention of competition or competitive carriers for them here or elsewhere in the decision.

The remaining category, code "0," contains all city pairs of which there was no mention, either in terms of the specific city pair or of areas or groups of cities, which could be construed as referring to the city pair in question. Whether the Board was concerned about or even aware of these implications of the decisions cannot be ascertained from study of the opinions.

An important difference between code "1" and "2," and "3" and "4," is that decisions made which fall into the latter categories were made for the purpose of carrier or route strengthening, or some other reason such as in the Tucson Case, rather than to create competition. The fact that they resulted in competitive authorizations was noted as an incidental benefit, although it was not the purpose of the action.

THE ROUTE AWARDS

Of the 559 route "awards" or "docket-city-pairs," roughly half were mentioned in the decisions; that is, 253 of the 559, or 45 percent, were coded "0" as seen in Table VII-4. For the first competitive city pairs, this figure was 54 percent, while only 33 percent

TABLE VII-4

DOCKET CITY PAIRS CLASSIFIED BY INTENT OF THE BOARD

	Intent Classification								
	1	*2*	*3*	*4*	*5*	*6*	*7*	*0*	*Total*
First Competition	39	49	40	2	4	12	6	176	328
Increased Competition	70	46	29	2	0	2	5	77	231
Total	109	95	69	4	4	14	11	253	559

of the multiple competitive awards were not mentioned. Thus, of those competitive awards that were made in this period, the Board was more likely to have taken some note of them when it authorized multiple competition than when it authorized first competition for the city pair. This may be due to a greater concern of the Board in the multiple competition cases and a greater chariness about creating multiple competition where it might not be justified than about creating first competition. It also may be due to characteristics of the national route pattern which make it more likely that a given route extension will create more unintended cases of first competitive awards than of multiple competitive awards. The observed difference is probably due in part to both causes.

The twelve cases decided during the period of this study were, of course, not all equally productive of competitive awards as seen in Table VII–3. The four great cases, the *New York–Chicago Case* (Docket No. 986), the *Denver Service Case* (Docket No. 1841), the *Southwest–Northeast Case* (Docket No. 2355), and the *New York–Florida Case* (Docket No. 3051), accounted for 482, or 86 percent, of the 559 docket-city-pairs. The information of Table VII-4, giving the intent classifications, is analyzed by docket numbers in Table VII-5. Here, the importance of each of the cases is seen both in terms of its effect on the total number of competitive pairs and in terms of the Board's intent to create competition.

In later chapters, many of these will be analyzed with respect to the amount of the traffic both before and after the decisions, the identities and nature of the newly authorized and previously authorized carriers, and the quality of the service schedules as offered before the awards by the original carrier or carriers and, after the awards, by both the original and the newly authorized carriers.

TABLE VII-5

AWARDS CLASSIFIED BY DOCKET AND INTENT OF THE BOARD

Docket	*Code for Intent of the Board*								
Number	*1*	*2*	*3*	*4*	*5*	*6*	*7*	*0*	*Total*
				PART A: ALL AWARDS					
986	6		8				4	17	35
986 *	5		3					11	19
1789			1						1
1841	19		6					25	50
2190	10							8	18
2355	37	52	18	4	4	8	7	89	219
3051	29	43	9			5		73	159
4294	2								2
5564			19					4	23
5701								8	8
6503			5						5
7253	1					1		10	12
8134								8	8
Total	109	95	69	4	4	14	11	253	559
				PART B: FIRST COMPETITION					
986	4		4				1	13	22
986 *	5							8	13
1789									0
1841	13		4					21	38
2190									0
2355	11	18	9	2	4	8	5	81	138
3051	6	31				4		36	77
4294									0
5564			18					4	22
5701								6	6
6503			5						5
7253									0
8134								7	7
Total	39	49	40	2	4	12	6	176	328

PART C: INCREASED COMPETITION

Docket Number	*Code for Intent of the Board* 1	*2*	*3*	*4*	*5*	*6*	*7*	*0*	*Total*
986	2		4				3	4	13
986 *			3					3	6
1789			1						1
1841	6		2					4	12
2190	10							8	18
2355	26	34	9	2			2	8	81
3051	23	12	9			1		37	82
4294	2								2
5564			1						1
5701								2	2
6503									0
7253	1					1		10	12
8134								1	1
Total	70	46	29	2	—	2	5	77	231

* Deferred portion.
Source: Appendix One.

CHAPTER VIII

The Bases for Decision—Criteria for Competition

THE ROLE OF CRITERIA

The Civil Aeronautics Board has, throughout its history, been faced with two decisions in all cases involving new competition; first, the determination of whether public convenience and necessity require a competitive award and, second, the selection of the carrier to receive the competitive award. It is the first question which is the subject of major interest in this chapter. The second question; the selection of the carrier, is the subject of the next chapter.

In the view of the Board, direct competition exists or is created between two points when more than one carrier is authorized to serve these points with essentially similar authority. Therefore, the mandate of Section 2 of the Civil Aeronautics Act with respect to fostering "competition to the extent necessary . . ." has been and is executed through the medium of route awards.

Thus, by the mechanism of route awards, the Board has sought to create competition, and it has selected among the potential competitors according to various criteria for judging the public need and convenience. As might well be expected, these criteria have not been immutable and consistently applied over the two decades of the history of the Act. However, this does not constitute an indictment of the Board. The relative importance of consistency *per se* in successive decisions as against a willingness to modify a previous position to take account of technical and quantitative change, and to profit from past experience is questionable. It is the serving of the goals of the Act rather than the use of the various economic and legal criteria for route awards and choice of carrier that should be characterized by consistency.

This leads to a knotty problem, however, since the establishment and consistent use of criteria for decision is certainly desirable on the part of any judicial or semi-judicial body. One of the functions of any official body with judicial powers is the setting of precedents. Unless judicial and administrative power is to be capriciously wielded, interested parties must be able to determine, from the past, the probable bases of future decisions. Certainty is, of course, impossible, but a reasonable expectation about a future decision should be ascertainable from examination of precedents.

The Board's problem in the application of its criteria is complicated by the fact that air transportation is a rapidly growing industry in which all of the important factors such as equipment characteristics, traffic levels, and service standards are constantly changing. Indeed, the criteria themselves must be ever re-examined in the light of current developments.

Actually, the task of the Board has been to decide *when* rather than *whether,* since, as the industry has developed, competition has naturally become more and more general. Many markets, which some years ago were not deemed ready for competition, are now competitive, and similarly many of those which are now noncompetitive, will eventually become competitive.

Since the passage of the Act, one of the tasks of those affected by Civil Aeronautics Board decisions has been the search for understanding of the criteria used by the Board. The various parties to the CAB proceedings, especially those who are seeking competition, be they the carriers who are seeking new certifications, or municipalities seeking new competitive services, must, in the preparation of their cases, address themselves to those criteria which they believe are used and useful to the Board. This must, of course, be done in very specific terms. The Board has often, in general terms, listed the criteria which it uses in making these decisions about new competition. In the following quotation, the Board lists the general criteria but states clearly that a high degree of precision has not been attempted. The criteria are:

(1) Whether the new service will serve a useful public purpose, responsive to a public need;
(2) Whether this purpose can and will be served as well by existing lines or carriers;
(3) Whether it can be served by the applicant without impairing the operations of existing carriers contrary to the public interest; and
(4) Whether the cost of the proposed service to the government will be outweighed by the benefit which will accrue to the public from the new service.

Although the Board has consistently recognized the congressional policy contained in the act favoring sound and healthy competition, it has also recognized that in determining whether new services will bring about such sound competition the weight to be given the various factors that must necessarily be taken into consideration will vary depending on the facts of each particular case. It has therefore not attempted to spell out any rule that can be applied to every case with mathematical precision.[1]

Although the Board has " . . . not attempted to spell out a rule that can be applied to every case with mathematical precision," the more closely such a state is approached the easier and more economical becomes the task of all parties concerned in CAB route cases. This chapter will explore the recent Board decisions in order to ascertain what the Board's criteria actually have been, and how consistently the Board has applied them. Both the statements of the Board as given in the published opinions and the actual consequences of the decisions will be examined.

The four bases for decision which are listed above must, for analytical purposes, be transformed into criteria which are subject to more nearly objective evaluation or measurement. Four criteria which seem thus operationally feasible are:

1. Quality of service by the currently certificated carrier(s)
2. Level of traffic
3. Size, strength, and profitability of the existing carrier(s)
4. Size, strength, and profitability of applicant carrier(s).

In addition it will be noted that the route configurations of the carriers involved constitute an important complicating factor. The fourth of these criteria will be discussed in the next chapter, which deals with the selection of the new carrier, since it is used in making that part of the decision. The first three; those which constitute the criteria for deciding whether competitive authorizations should be added to a given route, will be examined in detail here, with reference primarily to the actions and statements of the Board in the period under study; i.e., September 1, 1955 to December 31, 1956. This period, characterized by the decisions listed in Table VII-1, represents the most recent stage of Civil Aeronautics Board policy—a policy, which, as of this writing, is essentially unchanged.

QUALITY OF SERVICE BY THE PRESENTLY CERTIFICATED CARRIER

The Civil Aeronautics Act provides, in Section 404, that:

> (a) It shall be the duty of every air carrier to provide and furnish interstate and overseas air transportation as authorized by its certificate, upon reasonable request therefor and to provide reasonable through service in such air transportation in connection with other carriers; to provide safe and adequate service, equipment, and facilities in connection with such transportation. . . .

Later, in Section 1002, the Act states:

> (a) Any person may file with the Authority [Board] a complaint in writing with respect to anything done or omitted to be done by any person in contravention of any provision of this Act, or of any requirement established pursuant thereto. If the person complained against shall not satisfy the complaint and there shall appear to be any reasonable ground for investigating the complaint, it shall be the duty of the Authority [Board] to investigate the matters complained of. Whenever the Authority [Board] is of the opinion that any complaint does not state facts which warrant an investigation or action on its part, it may dismiss such complaint without hearing.

Under these provisions of the Act, a municipality, a firm, or an individual may file a complaint with the Board if it feels that the airline which is certificated to offer a particular service has not been providing service that is "adequate." Presumably, then, the Board would take action to enforce certain standards of adequacy. In spite of this provision, and perhaps as a most eloquent testimony to the relative ineffectiveness of such a purely regulatory or administrative device as compared with competition in assuring adequacy of service, it has become common for municipalities (and even applicant airlines) to bring before the Board a showing of alleged inadequacy of service by the currently certificated carrier as a demonstration that a competitive certification was required rather than as the basis for a complaint proceeding to secure better service from the presently certificated carrier. This clearly implies, on their part, a judgment that competition is a more effective route to improved service than is the complaint proceeding or the threat of a complaint proceeding. The following statement in an Examiner's initial decision which was subsequently adopted by the Board summarizes this process as it developed in one of the most important of the route cases:

> . . . there has also been set forth in the earlier part of this decision in varying degrees of detail the facts which have been advanced by the cities and applicants in support of additional services, much of this data being related to the justification of competition. This type of material dominated the presentations of most of the cities and is typified by the witnesses appearing for Dallas and Atlanta. On behalf of the cities in general it has been clearly established that services of the single carrier fail to satisfy a great many representative users of air transportation. While most of these witnesses used the word inadequate in describing the existing services the various situations described fall short of establishing conditions of inadequacy in the technical sense of the word as it is used in section 404 of the Civil Aeronautics Act. On the other hand they have established some situations where the standard of service on the one-carrier segments is below that available on competitive segments out of the same city. Illustrations are Atlanta and Dallas where competitive services to Chicago can be compared with non-competitive services to the Northeast. And quite appropriate is the point made by Houston that Eastern proposes more service at Dallas, as a competitor of American, than it has been giving at Houston where it has no competition.
>
> While the cities may have fallen short of establishing inadequacy in the technical sense, they have established in general a situation where mature services under present day standards do not exist. . . . Eastern, according to American, has failed to provide Houston a present day standard of air service to the Northeast; the entry of American is necessary to assure this standard; but American does not contend that the traffic volume between Houston and the Northeast is sufficient for two carriers.[2]

The Board, in the same case, added:

> . . . Houston points out, as detailed in the Initial Decision (p. 80), that Eastern in support of its application to serve Dallas, where it would compete with American, proposed more service in the Dallas–New York market than it was providing for Houston–New York, where it is the sole carrier. And Delta points to a comparison of the Atlanta–New York market, which Eastern monopolizes, and the Atlanta–Chicago market, which has effective competition, to show the difference in service provided monopoly and competitive markets. For example, the Atlanta–Chicago market, which in the September 1954 survey period had only 1,758 passengers, received 12 nonstop schedules daily in both directions from Delta and Eastern, whereas in the Atlanta–New York market which had 3,742 passengers, Eastern provided only 8 nonstop schedules.[3]

This policy on the part of municipalities of seeking competitive authorizations as a means of correcting alleged service inadequacies has struck a responsive note with the Board, and it has been fruitful. For example, in improving Eastern's authorization at Tampa, the Board commented that:

> Our decision should provide the competitive spur leading to needed improvements in Tampa service, such as nonstop service to New York, improvements which National, the only unrestricted carrier in the market, has been loath to provide. In addition, Eastern will be able to offer desirable new one-carrier and through plane services between Tampa and other points on route No. 6 south of Washington.[4]

The effectiveness of this policy may be seen in many cases where the very announcement of a proceeding which could result in new competitive authorizations seems to have had the effect of causing the existing carriers to improve their service. In authorizing new competition in the New Orleans-Northeast markets, the Board noted that:

> The complaints of the City of New Orleans with respect to the relative inconvenience of its service to the Northeast are detailed in the Initial Decision and need not be here repeated.* The need for effective competitive services between New Orleans and the Northeast, and the ability of this market to support multiple services is clearly evident.
>
> * [original note] Initial Decision, pp. 83–84. We note, however, that the recent Official Airline Guides indicate that in recent months, probably under pressure of this proceeding, Eastern has provided some serv-

ice improvements. However, the October Traffic Guide indicates that New Orleans still has no nonstop service northbound, and only one such service southbound, and only one daily coach service in each direction which provides a multi-stop service.[5]

This approach; namely, the reliance on competition where feasible rather than enforcement of service standards as the device for securing the desired quality of service, has been traditional with the Board. Whether the new adequacy of service enforcement approach taken in the *Toledo Case* will become generally used remains to be seen. It will be recalled that, in that case, Allegheny Airlines petitioned the Board, seeking to replace Capital between Toledo, on the one hand, and Cleveland, Philadelphia, and New York, on the other, in the event that the Board found Capital's service between these points to be inadequate. The Board denied Allegheny's petition, declaring that, if it should find Capital's service inadequate in these markets, its action would be to order Capital to take prompt remedial action.[6] This is, of course, exactly what happened.

Before that case, the Board had not, to a significant extent, used its powers directly to enforce a desired level of quality or "adequacy" of service. On the other hand, it has, and still does, consider deficiency of service as evidence that competitive service is needed, and it has stated on many occasions that such shortcomings have been factors in its decisions to create competitive authorizations.

The record shows that space difficulties have occurred at Tucson despite the 14 daily arrivals and departures of American, and that, even in an off peak period, American flights in and out of that city have often operated at load factors in excess of 70 percent. Moreover, there are certain deficiencies in the timing of Tucson's present services. American's two morning westbound flights miss northbound connections out of Los Angeles to many California and Pacific Northwest points. Eastbound, American's schedules during the morning do not make important gateway connections possible via El Paso, Ft. Worth–Dallas, or Oklahoma City. Between noon and midnight there is only one schedule available to reach Tucson from Pheonix, thus neutralizing service from Phoenix as a connecting point to reach Tucson. It may be that the number of connections and layovers could be reduced by adjusting or increasing American's transcontinental schedules. It appears, however, that the needed schedule frequency can best be assured by the services of an additional carrier serving many points in common with American.[7]

Moreover, Eastern has continued to provide first class service in the New York–Houston market in aircraft with high seating density long after it had introduced equipment with a more standard configuration in competitive markets. In addition, it is to be noted that the coach service which Eastern has provided in this market has been of a multi-stop nature and at relatively inconvenient hours. It is evident from the foregoing that, with the spur of competitive service, Houston should receive a greater volume of better quality first class service and more convenient coach service.[8]

While Capital's service between these points cannot be considered legally inadequate, the record is convincing that Capital has not fully exploited the potential, and that the growth of these markets has lagged behind that of comparable route segments where services of several unrestricted carriers are available. In addition, the extremely high load factors enjoyed by Capital in this area reflect the inability of passengers to secure space during peak periods. Clearly, the size and importance of these markets and the current service deficiencies warrant the authorization of a second unrestricted service, as proposed by Northwest. And we fully agree with the Examiner that the public benefits flowing from this authorization outweigh the diversionary effect it will have upon Capital.[9]

It is further apparent that, while not inadequate within the meaning of Section 404 of the Act, the service provided by the existing carriers has not fully met the needs of the traveling public. The Initial Decision adequately summarizes the evidence of record which discloses that, during the prime winter season when travel to Florida is at its high point, it is necessary to obtain New York–Miami reservations as much as three or four weeks in advance of a planned departure in order to obtain the traveller's choice of service and departure time, that extended wait lists are not uncommon, and that the carriers' efforts to meet space demands by too tight scheduling of aircraft has resulted in an impairment of on-time reliability with a consequent inconveniencing of the traveling public. In addition, there is no doubt that Eastern and National have concentrated heavily on the New York–Miami market, and have not provided comparable quality or quantity of service to many other markets here involved. These factors of passenger inconvenience are at least comparable to those found in recent cases to warrant additional air service.

> We recognize that the New York–Miami market in particular has been aggressively developed, and has already received many benefits from the vigorous competition between Eastern and National, such as a large volume of coach service and the early introduction into service of the most modern available equipment. Moreover, the extensive re-equipment programs of the two carriers promise to provide similar benefits in the future and possibly some alleviation of space shortages. However, in our judgment the needs of the traveling public for service between the Northeast and Florida cities are not now being fully met by Eastern and National, and in these circumstances it would not be consistent with our statutory obligations under the Act and the course of our decisions thereunder, to merely maintain the status quo, and rely upon the carriers assurances as to their willingness and ability to remedy the situation. The present shortcomings in service have been shown to exist over a substantial period of time, and the existing carriers have not demonstrated their ability to overcome them. Moreover, as we have on a number of occasions pointed out, the Congress in adopting the Civil Aeronautics Act, clearly considered competition to hold the greatest prospect for vigorous development of our national air route system "with the fullest improvements in service and technological developments." The extent of competition warranted in given markets necessarily turns upon the facts and circumstances peculiar to those markets. In the present case, we are convinced that a third carrier is required.[10]

Thus, clearly, the Civil Aeronautics Board has considered the quality of service offered by the presently certificated carrier as an important factor in its decisions to award competitive routings. This has become so well accepted as a criterion that the Board has, on occasion, felt it desirable to state, in denying a request for an additional service authorization, that the service has not been found inadequate. This is not because adequacy of service is a bar to such an award. Indeed, we shall see presently that it is not. Rather, it is because, had inadequacy been shown, that would constitute prima facie evidence of need for a competitive authorization.

> Request of Eastern Air Lines for authority to provide a second trans-Gulf service in addition to National Airlines between Houston, Texas/New Orleans, Louisiana, and Tampa/Miami, Florida, denied; trans-Gulf route does not have the traffic potential to support two through services; National's trans-Gulf service has not been shown to be unsatisfactory.[11]

Adequacy not a bar. While a finding of inadequacy does influence the Board and help move it toward a decision favoring a new carrier, such a finding of inadequacy is not essential.

We have made it clear on several recent occasions that the benefits of competitive air service will not be withheld from the traveling public merely because the existing carrier may be rendering sufficient service to satisfy the legal "adequacy" test. Of course, the markets in question must be of sufficient size and importance to warrant the new service; and the new service must be shown to be economically feasible and consistent with the overall development of a sound system of air transportation. But subject to qualifications of this character, the establishment of competitive air service is an important statutory objective. . . .[12]

The Board has not let adequacy of service on the part of the existing carrier (or carriers) stand in the way of its authorization of additional competitive carriers. It has often been argued by existing carriers that, regardless of the fact of high traffic levels, there is no need for competitive authorizations where their own present service offerings are adequate. The Board has disagreed with this argument and has restated this position many times in answering such attempts by existing carriers to forestall competitive awards by showing that their currently offered services were adequate.

American does not contend, nor could it properly do so, that a market of this size cannot support competitive air services. American asserts, however, that its services for these markets are not inadequate, and that in the absence of a finding of inadequacy we may not authorize a competitive air service.

Such an argument completely misconceives the nature of our responsibilities under the Civil Aeronautics Act and the Board's long standing policy for discharging these responsibilities. Fundamental to the Act is the provision that the Board shall regard as in the public interest "Competition to the extent necessary to assure the sound development of an air transportation system properly adapted to . . ." our national needs. In the application of this provision, along with the other relevant factors bearing upon the public convenience and necessity, the Board has, over a period of years, authorized the expansion of our air transportation system in such a manner as to bring more and more competitive service to more and more communities. In taking these actions, the Board has not been guided by the negative concept of determining first whether the existing services met minimum standards of legal adequacy. Rather the Board has been influenced, in accordance with its statutory mandate, by the concept that competitive service holds the greatest prospect for vigorous development of our national air transport system with the fullest improvements in service and technological developments. Our recent decisions in the *New York-Chicago Case* and in the *Denver Service Case* fully reflect this policy.[13]

This statement has been cited in at least two subsequent decisions [14] and, in both, the general position has been summarized in the following words:

Where the markets are of sufficient size and importance to warrant a new service, and such service is shown to be economically feasible and consistent with the overall development of a sound air transportation system, the benefits of a competitive service by TWA will not be withheld from the traveling public merely because the existing carrier may be rendering adequate service within the legal minimum specified by Section 404(a) of the Act.[15]

THE LEVEL OF TRAFFIC

As is amply indicated in the published opinions, the most important single criterion in judging the need for competitive authorizations is the level of traffic. There is good reason for this. The basic reason for restriction of entry in the first place was to avoid excessive competition and to protect the certificated carriers and thereby the Federal subsidy. The Civil Aeronautics Board policy has been to increase competition as markets have grown thereby seeking to gain the best of both worlds; the safety and continuity of restricted and protected public utilities; and the benefits of the world of competition.

As markets become large enough, the Board creates competitive authorizations.

. . . we are convinced that the size and potential of these markets clearly warrant competitive air service in order to insure that the traveling public will obtain the quantity and quality of service to which it is entitled.[16]

We shall also authorize American to provide service to Columbus on a routing through Pittsburgh to New York. The Columbus–New York market was 69th among the first 100 pairs of points, ranked by passengers, and is one of the top markets in which there is now no competitive service available.[17]

In the international sphere, the same policy with respect to the importance of traffic levels has been followed.[18] The President of the United States, with reviewing authority of all CAB certifications in overseas and foreign air transport,[19] has said:

> It is this Administration's objective, wherever traffic justifies it, to provide competitive U.S. service on all international and overseas routes from all gateways.
>
> I request the Board to review periodically U.S.–Tokyo traffic with a view to achieving this objective on that segment of our international air routes as soon as possible, and to report to me at least once a year on the results of such reviews.[20]

Despite the obvious importance of traffic levels in formulating decisions in route cases, the Board has never felt able to say just how large the volume of traffic should be, in the general case, to indicate the need for a competitive authorization. On the contrary, the Board has stated that it believes that there is no single figure that is generally applicable.

> The question remains, of course, as to just how large a market need be before it will support competition or additional competition. No ready formula is available for this purpose; the decision must turn upon all the surrounding facts and circumstances. This has been true in the past and must continue to be true under our statute. But with the establishment of the larger domestic trunkline carriers on a firm subsidy-free footing, and the great growth and potential in existing markets, we feel warranted in enlarging competitive service in the manner authorized in this proceeding.[21]

Surely, if it had been possible for the Board to state that competition is required when the origin and destination traffic between a pair of cities exceeds, say 15,000 passengers per year, or 30,000, or some other figure, the task of the Board and of the parties to the various route proceedings would have been vastly simplified. However, although the Board has clearly felt that there is no firm figure which is applicable to a wide variety of geographical, economic and demographic situations, and although it has felt constrained to consider each case as a new situation, there is certainly some relationship among city pairs in this respect. Indeed, there has been implied acceptance of the fact that there is some relationship from one situation to another in the Board's frequent statement, as above, in the Columbus–New York citation, that the instant city pair is the "most traveled," or "one of the most traveled," of the remaining noncompetitive city pairs. This, of course, implies that the traffic level which was adequate to call forth competition in one case is adequate (or, at least not irrelevant) for the same conclusion in another.

This importance of the level of traffic has evoked bitter criticism on the part of airline managements who had worked hard to develop markets which, because of their success, became so heavily traveled that, as a result, competitive carriers were authorized. The charge that competition has been, in effect, the punishment of successful operators may not be without some element of truth, but this characteristic of CAB regulation is not unfamiliar elsewhere. Indeed, the promptness with which competition follows the successful operator is doubtless far swifter in the unregulated sectors of our economy. Thus, rather than punishing success with competition, regulation has, by its very slowness and deliberateness, protected profitable markets more and longer than might have been the case without regulation. In addition, the fact that the Board does not create competitive service but merely competitive authorizations, assures that the actual inauguration of competitive service and its timing and amount are business decisions made by airline management and based largely on the usual criteria of the business world. In this sense, the inauguration of competition can seldom, if ever, be faster nor the amount greater under regulation than without it. Indeed, the reverse is by far the more usual.

The Board's policy is that it is not consistent with the philosophy of the Act or the spirit of our economic system for a single carrier to enjoy the exclusive monopoly right to serve a particular market when the traffic level is sufficient to permit the profitable operation of more than one carrier over the route; that, unlike the electric or gas utilities, or the telephone service, the air transportation industry is not a "natural" monopoly; that competition is feasible, economical, and desirable; and that, in the absence of compelling reasons to the contrary, competition should be authorized where the traffic is sufficient. The aggressive carrier who develops a new market and who thereafter finds himself in competition with a newly authorized carrier in the same market, must depend upon his continued aggressiveness, reputation, and established historical participation in the market to avoid excessive traffic diversion to the new carrier.

INTERNAL SUBSIDY

Thus, as traffic levels have increased in particular markets, competitive carriers have been certificated to serve them. The anguish on the part of the original carriers with which these awards have been greeted is not without an important economic basis. That is, the carriers, because of their obligation to serve sparse routes as well as rich ones, must rely on the rich routes to provide excess income to compensate for the lower income or even losses incurred on the weak routes. If competition on the rich routes drives the income to the carriers on those routes down to the theoretic traditional marginal level, then the losses on the weak routes will cause the carriers to show overall losses. The absence of unhindered exit from these weak routes implies the existence of and the insistence on internal subsidy, and, indeed, this has been the policy of both the regulatory agency and the carriers in the air transport industry. This state of affairs, whereby some of the customers of a business firm pay more than their share of the firm's costs of doing business in order that the firm may serve other customers at rates that do not fully cover the costs of serving them, is widely accepted today, especially in various areas of government enterprise and in certain of the regulated industries.

For example, the post office charges a uniform rate for the domestic delivery of a letter regardless of whether the sender and addressee are in the same city or a continent apart. Surely the costs per letter are quite different in the case of a letter from a rural village in Florida to a farm in central Oregon as against a letter from one firm to another in downtown Boston. If the price charged for all letters is such as to cover the total costs of the letter mail service, then, clearly, the more costly service is being subsidized by the less costly.

Similarly the question of internal subsidy is of extreme importance in the regulated industries. This is a natural consequence of the fact that industries such as the local gas and electric utility industries, the telephone industry, and the transportation industries, have a mandate to serve all customers on an equal basis, coupled with a traditional drive on the part of these industries to expand their service wherever feasible and to serve more and more customers. Almost invariably, this has been accomplished via the use, usually consciously, of internal subsidy. Typically, the newer customers are outlying high cost customers, and they are served at rates that often do not adequately take the cost differentials into account. The telephone industry has actually charged higher rates for the local service in the large cities than in the smaller towns, with the differentials based on a concept of "value of the service" under which the relative costs of serving the different classes of customers are not considered important. Often this and similar use of internal subsidy is the only way in which the new customers can be added, since rates that cover their service costs would be intolerably high for the potential new customers.

Although internal subsidy may also be observed in private unregulated businesses, especially in the area of absorption of freight costs, delivery costs, equipment service costs, etc., the relative unimportance of this consideration is evident from the fact that, in private business, there is seldom a conscious attempt to serve customers who cannot be served profitably.

In the airline industry, which, as clearly stated in the Civil Aeronautics Act, serves as a medium of national defense and commercial development, the drive for expansion of service stems from factors other than the potential profitability of new services. Service to unprofitable routes or points may not be discontinued without the authorization of the regulatory body, and this authority may not be easily obtained. In the absence of government subsidy, whenever an airline provides a service that is unprofitable, those passengers who use that service are being subsidized by the passengers who use the profitable services and who are paying more than the costs of serving them.

Of course, it is not feasible to differentiate among all conceivable services and set rates that are related to their costs, because the factors affecting the costs of the various services are many and complex; i.e., individual passengers differ in their demands and therefore in their costs, and, even on the same flight, the costs per mile of the short haul passenger are quite different from those of the long haul passenger, who, to compound the burden, is obliged to pay the costs of the intermediate stops which he personally finds undesirable. Even here, however, the point must be made that, possibly, if the intermediate stops were not made and the short haul passengers not carried, the through flight might not be profitable. Indeed, it may often be the case that, in their early stages many services are unprofitable, and that the promotional effect of offering these services at an unprofitable price helps to develop them into profitable services, to strengthen the entire system and to benefit all of the customers. Also, it may be the case that, although they may not cover fully allocated total costs, the less profitable services do contribute something to overhead, thus benefiting all of the customers of the firm.

Clearly, the implications of the fact of different costs for different customers and the resulting internal subsidies are very complex. In any event, whenever an unprofitable service is offered, the customers of that service are subsidized. This is an internal subsidy if the costs are made up by the other customers of the same firm, or it may be a direct governmental subsidy if the government makes up the deficit from the general treasury.

The most important application of the principle of internal subsidy in the airline industry is in the serving, by the trunk carriers, of unprofitable routes. The accepted condition here is that the profitable routes shall make up the deficit.

If such internal subsidization causes the rates over the rich routes to be higher than would otherwise be the case, then potential customers on the rich routes are faced with two alternatives, both of which are undesirable to them and which cause uneconomic allocation of their resources. That is, they must use the service and pay rates which are unduly in excess of the costs of providing the service, or they must forego air trips which they would willingly have made at the lower rate. In the latter case, the airline's resources are also uneconomically allocated since they are not providing and selling the service to potential customers who would be willing to pay the normal costs (including profit) of the service. It has often been argued that direct governmental subsidization, by avoiding this kind of economic dislocation, is a more equitable technique for making service available to customers who cannot be served profitably but who, according to some national interest criterion, should nevertheless be served. The funds for the subsidization then come from the general treasury, and are therefore presumed to be more equitably derived for the subsidization purpose than is the case when the source of the funds is the excess air transportation payments resulting from the higher rates charged the customers on the profitable routes.

The difference between the two kinds of subsidy; i.e., internal vs. direct, and an illustration of a disagreement among the Board members on this very subject is seen in the dissent of CAB Member Denny in the *New York–Florida Case*.

The case of Northeast is built from beginning to end upon its need for subsidy. However, in my opinion, the fact that Northeast requires subsidy for its present local service operations in New England is *no* proper basis for extending its system over 1,200 miles to Florida. I am convinced that there are other avenues for improving Northeast's position in the industry without granting such an illogical and unsound extension. The logical solution would be to reclassify Northeast as a local service carrier, recognizing that it is in fact a Local Service Carrier and like other such carriers will require subsidization until their load factors increase, their routes are strengthened in their local areas and until a more efficient short-haul aircraft is developed. Another sound approach would be that Northeast merge or consolidate with another strong regional or local service carrier which would assure the elimination of subsidy. In my judgment, either of the above alternative solutions would solve Northeast's problem in a much more effective manner than would the proposed extension.[22]

Member Denny's first alternative involved direct subsidy of the weak routes by the government, and his second alternative, the merger, involved internal subsidy for the merged system, with the patrons of the rich routes of the other merging carrier providing the source of the subsidy funds. The Board, as is well known, did extend Northeast Airlines to Florida in this proceeding thereby seeking to strengthen that carrier and to exploit the possibility of internal subsidy by giving it access to the rich east coast route.

In any event, the principle of internal subsidy is well established in the airline industry. It was the defense of this principle which constituted the most telling charge against the large irregular carriers of the postwar period. They were charged with "skimming the cream" by flying the most heavily traveled routes and thereby diverting passengers from the certificated airlines who needed these rich markets to make up their losses elsewhere. Thus, in Board decisions about whether the irregular carriers could fly over particular routes, even though they were the richest routes in the country, the level of traffic (or, more particularly, the fact of low load factors) over the *other* routes of the certificated carriers was a crucial factor.

Similarly, in certificating a competitive certificated carrier over a particular route, the Board considers the number of passengers available to the various carrier parties over all of their routes as well as the level of traffic over the route in question.

DIFFICULTIES IN THE INTERPRETATION AND USE OF TRAFFIC DATA

In the following sections, we shall examine what the Board has said about traffic levels and then we shall study the traffic levels of the city pairs for which competitive authorizations were made. However, before examining the actual traffic levels, there are certain limitations in the traffic data and in their application which must be considered. In using the traffic level as a criterion in assessing the need for competitive services over a route, the amount of traffic over the route whether measured by the number of passengers, passenger-miles, or some other factor, must be considered in the light of current technology. As the technology of the industry —particularly the characteristics of the flight equipment—changes, so the standard may change. The standard for the DC-3 may be quite different from that for the DC-8 or even the F-27. If changing technology acts to decrease the traffic level which is the standard for competition, then today's correct decisions will always be correct, and even today's premature competitive authorizations will eventually be vindicated. On the other hand, if technology acts to raise that standard (and this may well be the effect, at least temporarily, of the large jet aircraft) then even correct decisions made in the light of today's technology may be regretted tomorrow.

Another factor to be considered in assessing the traffic level is the position of the city pair on the carriers' routes with respect to other traffic-generating cities. That is, if all of the traffic flying on the segment between the two cities under consideration is traffic that originates or terminates at those two cities, then a much higher level of such "origin and destination" traffic over that segment is required than would be the case if this segment also carried considerable traffic to and from points beyond one or both of the two cities in question. For example, the number of nonstop flights between New York and Chicago is larger than would be the case if all of the nonstop flights or, *a fortiori,* all of the passengers, originated or terminated at Chicago. Actually, many of these flights go on to the West, and much of the New York–Chicago traffic originates or terminates beyond Chicago, but this enables the carriers to offer frequent service between New York and Chicago. This through traffic, for the most part, is not recorded in the origin and destination traffic data, and, for that reason, the number of flights offered may seem excessive when related to those reported data. As a matter of fact, it is quite generally the case that the origin and destination traffic between two points does not support the frequency of flights that is offered. The importance of this may be illustrated by a simple computation. If "minimum" service between two points may be defined (as it often is) as four trips per day, one in each direction early in the day and one in each direction late in the day, thereby permitting a daily round trip in each direction, and if we assume a 44-passenger airplane, then the number of seats available between the two points in both directions per day is 176 seats. Multiplying this by 365, the product is approximately 65,000 available seats per year for passengers between the two cities. For a 60 percent load factor, 39,000 annual origin and destination passengers must travel between the two cities. This is a sizable traffic! For example, roughly 40,000 passengers traveled in 1955 between Cincinnati and Cleveland, between Dallas and Oklahoma City, between Atlanta and Birmingham, and between Cleveland and Washington. For a 25-seat DC-3, the last figure would be 22,000 passengers, which would correspond to the 1955 traffic between Atlanta and New Orleans or between Memphis and New York. Clearly, if single-plane "minimum" service of one round trip in each direction were restricted to pairs of large cities such as these, we should have a vastly less developed national air transportation system than we have today. In the other cases, it is the traffic on the route beyond and between the two cities which helps to fill the airplanes on the route segment between the two cities in question and therefore makes the service to the city pair economical.

Thus, the origin and destination traffic between two points constitutes only part of the information necessary for a determination of whether or not there is adequate traffic over the segment to support competition. The use of a fixed number of origin and destination passengers as a measure of the traffic justification for competitive service and as a standard of comparison from one city pair to another implies the tacit assumption of a constant relationship between the origin and destination traffic between two points and the amount of other traffic also passing between the two points, but originating or terminating at points beyond or between the cities in question. This is not a correct assumption, and its inapplicability constitutes a limitation on such use of the origin and destination data as a measure of the total number of persons traveling between two points.

On the other hand, these data from the *Airline Traffic Survey* do give, as measured by ticket purchases, the number of passengers who originate at one of the points and terminate at the other, and therefore, they do, subject to these limitations, measure the expressed demand for flights that serve both points. Therefore, the use of the origin and destination data in connection with the evaluation of the service needs of the city pair is not without considerable justification. Indeed, there is no other single available passenger measure which can approach it in usefulness.

Certain serious limitations in the published origin and destination traffic data stem from the methods by which the data were obtained. The ticket sales of all of the airlines for the periods March 1–14 and September 17–30 of each year were reported to the Civil Aeronautics Board and subsequently published. For the estimation of annual totals, these two two-week periods, one in the spring and one in the fall, were combined, and the sum multiplied by 13 to yield a 52-week estimate for the year. This procedure has at least three inherent sources of error. First, the data themselves are in error to the extent that ticket sales in the period do not represent trips made during the period, or even trips made at all, in view of the possibility of ticket returns. Second, through passengers may not buy through tickets, but rather may purchase separate tickets for the individual portions of trips involving connections. Third, these two two-week periods may not adequately represent annual traffic patterns. This is especially disquieting for many of the city pairs which have wide seasonal traffic variations. However, for the period under study, there are no better data available, and, indeed, it should not be inferred from the above that these data are not extremely useful. In spite of the fact that much should be and is being done to improve the traffic data in the future,[23] the origin and destination traffic data reported to the CAB for the years covered by this study and presented here are a highly illuminating and useful tool for analysis. It is those data which are used extensively throughout this study.

TRAFFIC AND THE DECISIONS

In some of the cases in which the Civil Aeronautics Board awarded new route authorizations, it cited the traffic volumes between the city pairs in question and noted that these were clear indications of the need for the new authorizations. These statements will be examined below in order to ascertain the level of traffic which the Board thought merited this kind of specific identification. Then the actual awards will be examined in their entirety in order to ascertain what the traffic levels were for all of the city pairs which received new competitive awards in the decisions.

First competition. In authorizing first competition over routes that, at the time of the decision, were served by only one carrier, (in a few cases where two new carriers were authorized at the same time, competition was created between city pairs which were, at the time of the award, not authorized for any single-plane service) the Board indicated that certain traffic levels were such as to require and justify competitive service. For example, the Board referred to Buffalo's ". . . dominant need for a competitive service, namely to points such as New York and Detroit . . ." [24] when the estimated 1954 origin and destination traffic between Buffalo and these two points was 170,000 and 31,600 passengers respectively.[25] Also, with 51,500 annual passengers in 1954 between Kansas City and New York, the Board said: "The Kansas City Market fully justifies the establishment of a vigorous competitive trunkline service to the major markets in the east, particularly New York." [26] More specific traffic citations by the Board include:

We agree with the City of Philadelphia that the importance of the communities involved and the volume of traffic already developed indicates the need for a second carrier in this market. The record shows that in 1954 (based upon March and September 1954 surveys) Philadelphia–Detroit generated 60,000 local passengers and Philadelphia–Cleveland developed 44,000 local passengers.[27]

. . . we estimate an annual market of over 75,000 passengers between Houston and New York, and over 102,000 passengers annually between Houston, on the one hand, and New York, Philadelphia, Baltimore and Washington, on the other hand. Many smaller markets than this are supporting multiple services to New York, and in our judgment, Houston needs and can support competitive service to the northeast.[28]

As previously indicated, we agree with the Examiner's conclusion that a competitive air service should be established between Dallas/Ft. Worth and the Northeast and that Memphis and Nashville should be served as intermediate points on this route. The predominant purpose of this new route is to provide a new service competitive with American between Dallas and Ft. Worth, on the one hand, and New York and Washington, on the other hand. In 1954, there were over 86,000 passengers exchanged between these cities; the New York–Dallas/Ft. Worth segment alone was, in terms of revenue passenger miles, the largest noncompetitive market in the country.[29]

Traffic between Norfolk/Newport News–Hampton–Warwick, Va., and Washington, D. C., Baltimore, Md., Philadelphia, Pa., and New York, N.Y.–Newark, N.J., can support competitive service and is entitled to the benefits to be derived therefrom; to provide such competition National is relieved from restrictions prohibiting service between Norfolk/Newport News–Hampton–Warwick and Baltimore and Washington where Capital is now the sole carrier, and Capital is authorized to provide nonstop turn-around service between New York and Philadelphia and Norfolk/Newport News–Hampton–Warwick; National's temporary authority to serve Newport News–Hampton–Warwick, Va., is made permanent.[30]

This last quotation, upon analysis, involves the following:

City Pairs	*1954 Passengers*
Baltimore–Newport News	1,270
Baltimore–Norfolk	6,640
Newport News–Washington	14,500
Norfolk–Washington	51,500
New York–Newport News	6,000
New York–Norfolk	70,800
Newport News–Philadelphia	1,120
Norfolk–Philadelphia	21,300

Of these, the first four were in this decision given their first competitive authorization (National), and the latter four were given improved competitive authorizations in that restrictions on Capital's authority were removed. Capital had been added to these four city pairs in the *Southwest-Northeast Service Case* a year earlier. Capital had enjoyed unrestricted authority in the first four and National in the second four before that decision. Clearly, it was the intention of the Board to create competitive authorizations for all eight city pairs. However, it does not necessarily follow that the traffic level for each and every one is sufficient such that, were it geographically alone, the Board would still seek to add competition in that market. Rather, because of the unique spatial configuration of airports and population, the Board created the authority described in the quotation given above. Thus, the Board, *with full intent* created a competitive authorization for Baltimore–Newport News, but by no stretch of the imagination could it be maintained that the level of traffic between these two points was the controlling factor in the decision. It is situations such as this which confound precise analysis of the traffic levels at which competitive authorizations were made for all city pairs.

The situation described above was one in which the traffic level was the major criterion used to determine the need for the new service. The relationship between the traffic level and the decision is less close when there are other important criteria used in the decision as in the Memphis and Nashville award (below), and the relationship may be completely absent for city pairs which received their awards without the specific intent of the Board as noted in the Board's answer to Eastern's proposals in the *Texas–Florida Case* also cited below. The traffic between any of the city pairs cited is to be found in Appendix Two.

In the Memphis and Nashville situation, the Board had decided that the size of the market between Dallas/Fort Worth and the East Coast warranted the addition of Braniff to compete with American. The Board included Memphis and Nashville on the route, stating:

> There can be no doubt that competition for American between Dallas/Ft. Worth and the East Coast is fully warranted by the size and scope of this market and its ultimate potential. The potential for the

East Coast service is substantially greater than for the Dallas/Ft. Worth–West Coast service where American's monopoly route was recently subjected to an alternate service.

Braniff's new route to the Northeast will gain strength from the naming of Memphis and Nashville as intermediate points. Both these communities are now reliant pricipally upon American's services to the Northeast as well as the Southwest, and are of sufficient size and traffic potential to warrant an additional service as part of a new competitive routing between Dallas/Fort Worth and the Northeast. Memphis and Nashville in 1954 generated over 79,000 passengers to and from New York and Washington, and Dallas and Ft. Worth. The great bulk of this traffic is carried by American; only in the Memphis–New York and Nashville–New York/Washington markets does any other carrier obtain as much as 5 percent of the traffic.

Both Memphis and Nashville seek the addition of competitive services. Nashville in particular, as detailed in the Initial Decision, points to the fact that the volume of service which it has received in recent years has lagged behind that furnished comparable cities which have received effective competitive services, and that as a consequence it has not reflected the same rate of increase in use of air transportation experienced by the other cities. Moreover, the quality of Nashville's air service to the Northeast has not kept pace with that provided at other cities both in terms of first class four engine service and coach service. The provision of additional service to the Southwest and Northeast should lead to substantial service improvement for Nashville, as well as for Memphis.[31]

Here the other factors in the decision such as strengthening the carrier's new route and adequacy of service were of comparable or greater importance than the level of traffic. Again, competitive authorizations were created with full intent, but the traffic levels between the city pairs involved may not necessarily be taken to be the traffic levels at which the Board felt that competition was required and justified.

This very award was discussed a year later in the opinion in the *Florida–Texas Service Case*. Then Eastern sought authorization to offer competitive service on the Houston–New Orleans–Tampa–Miami route. The Board said:

Eastern asserts that in 1957, there will be 52,868 on-line passengers between New Orleans and Houston, on the one hand, and Tampa and Miami, on the other hand,* and that this is considerably more traffic than generated by many other cities for which we have authorized multiple carrier competitive services in recent cases. In support of this contention, Eastern refers to several city pairs on routes where we have recently added competitive services which generate less traffic than that here involved. However, in each instance the comparative pair referred to by Eastern for which competitive service has recently been authorized, is but one of several on the route involved and in no instance does the referenced pair constitute the major economic justification for the new route. For example, Eastern refers to the authorization of competitive service between Nashville and the Northeast—where there is alledgedly less traffic than over the trans-Gulf route—ignoring the fact that Nashville contributes only a small part of the traffic supporting American's and Braniff's service between Texas and the Northeast. As National has forcefully pointed out, comparisons are only valid when placed in their proper context. In each instance cited, Eastern has torn the facts from their context.

* [original note] Eastern's traffic forecast is set forth below:

Between: New Orleans	and	Tampa	10,622
		Miami	28,279
Houston	and	Tampa	4,152
		Miami	9,815
			52,868 [32]

The Board thus made it clear that when routes are extended, in order to improve service to certain city pairs, other city pairs may enjoy similarly improved service authorizations for reasons other than their own traffic levels and that it is not reasonable to point to the traffic levels under which awards were made and to interpret these levels as always representing, in the Board's judgment, the major economic justification for the award.

In any event, it is clear that the traffic levels which prevailed on that route were not adequate to convince the Board that competition was needed.

Finally, in the *Southwest–Northeast Case,* the Board noted that

The community of interest between New Orleans and the Northeast is a strong one, New York being its largest air travel market, both in terms of number of passengers and in revenue passenger miles. In 1954, there were over 145 passengers daily in this market. In 1956, we estimate that this market, with the addition of effective competitive services, should exceed 65,800 passengers annually, and that New Orleans will exchange over 97,000 passengers with the four Northeast points.[33]

Here the Board in addition to pointing to the 65,000 passengers expected between New Orleans and New York cited the 97,000 passengers between New Orleans and the four Northeast points, including New York. This suggests that the Board meant to imply that the traffic to the other three points was a useful contribution, although they alone or any one of them alone would not necessarily have been able to show a need for a competitive service to New Orleans.

Thus, although certainly more crucial than quality of service, traffic levels are similarly interpreted by the Board in that high traffic inspires new awards, but failure to meet any particular standard does not constitute a bar to a competitive award.

Similarly, when traffic levels are even higher, the Board admits two, three, and even more competitive carriers.

Multiple-carrier competition. The level of traffic has also been used as the criterion for determination of the need for multiple competitive services. The practice of the Board has been based on the concept that there is some level of traffic at which competitive service is needed, or justified, or both, and that there is another, higher level at which multiple competitive services are indicated. This reasoning is seen clearly in the following quotations:

> As to Northwest's New York–Detroit service, we find that removal of that carrier's long haul restriction is required by the public convenience and necessity. In our judgment, the size and potential of the New York–Detroit market will now support three turnaround services rather than merely one heretofore operated by American. Thus, the record shows that in this area the New York–Detroit market is exceeded only by the New York–Chicago market, and yet American is the only unrestricted operator between New York and Detroit. The much smaller New York–Cleveland market has two turnaround services. Furthermore, the New York–Detroit market increased by 86 percent from 1949 to 1954. Under such circumstances, we have no hesitation in finding that the New York–Detroit market will support two additional turnaround services.[34]
>
> Authorization of additional air service found warranted in order to provide improved service between important cities in the Northeast and in Florida where the available traffic potential is sufficient to support multiple carrier services.[35]

The record shows that the major long-haul markets here involved have had outstanding traffic growth in recent years. Between 1948 and 1954 the volume of passenger travel between the principal Florida and northeast cities has increased more than threefold. And there is no indication that this growth has reached a plateau. Not only have the applicants forecast substantial traffic increases in future years, but the evidence of the civic intervenors indicating a continuing high level of economic activity and future industrial, commercial and recreational expansion requires the conclusion that traffic growth will continue at a high rate. In short, there can be little question that the markets here involved are in material aspects more than comparable to those for which in recent cases we have authorized service by more than two carriers.[36]

The Bay area points out that in terms of air traffic, Chicago ranks second in its leading traffic segments, and that this market is of sufficient size and importance to justify an effective service by a third transcontinental carrier. We believe that the record fully supports this conclusion, and we will therefore authorize American to operate directly between Chicago and San Francisco/Oakland. This will be done by adding a new segment on Routes Nos. 7 and 25, extending between the terminal point Chicago and the coterminal points San Francisco/Oakland. As a result of this action, San Francisco, as in the case of Los Angeles, will have three effective services by transcontinental carriers, to and from Chicago. We are cognizant that this action will give American entry into a highly lucrative market, and that this carrier's vigorous participation will result in substantial diversion from United and TWA. Nevertheless, we find that the public need for this additional competitive service, and the benefits that will flow therefrom, outweigh the factor of diversion from other carriers.[37]

What we have already pointed out about Houston and New Orleans is equally true of Atlanta. It too is a strong, rapidly growing hub in an important area having substantial commercial ties with the Northeast. Atlanta is the sixth largest air traffic generating city without effective competitive air service to and from New York, and Atlanta–New York is the largest market, in terms of number of passengers, without such service. As a matter of fact, air traffic at Atlanta has just about doubled since the Board first found competitive air service warranted in this market. In 1954, there were more than 265 passengers daily between Atlanta and New York. In 1956, we estimate that this market with the addition of effective competitive services, will grow to over 110,000 passengers annually, and that there will be over 159,000 passengers annually between Atlanta, on the one hand, and New York, Philadelphia,

Baltimore and Washington, on the other hand. . . . We think it equally patent that markets of the size heretofore indicated can well support multi-carrier services.[38]

This last was a split decision, with two members feeling that there was adequate traffic to justify two-carrier competition, but not three-carrier competition. The dissenting Board members wrote that:

With respect to Capital's proposed air service via Route No. 51 between Atlanta, Birmingham, Mobile and New Orleans, on the one hand, and Washington and Baltimore, on the other, both Capital and Delta seek authority to provide competitive services in this market. At the present time, Eastern operates between all of these points and carries the bulk of the traffic. The record clearly indicates that the above markets are without an effective competitive service. Accordingly, we concur with the majority in authorizing a competitive service, but *disagree* with the majority that these markets are large enough to support two additional competitive services at this time. We cannot find on the record, as the majority have found, that the public convenience and necessity require the authorization of both Delta and Capital in addition to Eastern to provide service between these points.

Even a cursory examination of the facts reveals that no need has been shown for a third carrier in these markets and the record does not provide any economic justification for two additional carriers. For example, the record shows that in 1954 (based upon March and September 1954 survey) Atlanta–Washington generated 2,156 local passengers or approximately 39 passengers daily in each direction, New Orleans–Washington generated 1,363 local passengers or approximately 24 passengers daily in each direction, and Mobile–Washington developed 308 local passengers or approximately 5 passengers daily in each direction. Available traffic between the other pairs of cities is of similar proportions. It is self-evident that the quantity and character of the air traffic involved herein requires the services of only one additional carrier. In our opinion, the majority action in granting the applications of both Delta and Capital will make available services in these markets out of all proportion to the traffic potential and cannot be economically justified.

The majority action in triplicating the service over these route segments will result in affecting both the operations of Delta and Capital contrary to the public interest. Such an excess of competition will stretch the available traffic so thin that both carriers' financial and competitive position in this area will be substantially weakened rather than strengthened. As a consequence, the public will be denied the benefits flowing from a vigorous and effective competitor to Eastern in these markets. With these considerations in mind, it is our conviction that only one additional competitive service is warranted. In our judgment, Delta should be selected over Capital to provide the new service. The Board would thus be substantially strengthening Delta and at the same time assuring the most effective improved service to the public.[39]

On the other hand, there have been many cases in which the Board denied applications for multiple-carrier competitive authorizations saying that the traffic was adequate for the present number of competitive carriers, but not for more.

We cannot find on this record that the Cleveland–New York nonstop market is large enough to support an additional service by American. Accordingly, we will deny American's application for additional New York–Cleveland nonstop service. We also agree with the Examiner that the public convenience and necessity do not require the authorization of additional Cleveland–Chicago service. As the Examiner points out, it is more than likely that TWA would divert more than the estimated 15 percent of the Chicago–Cleveland market. American's application would give only a slight amount of new first one-carrier service while providing a competitive service which would divert traffic from Capital and United. We agree with the Examiner that the price of any benefits which TWA and American could supply to Cleveland–Chicago traffic would be the diversion of substantial volumes of traffic now hauled by the existing carriers. We also find that this market is not large enough to support any additional competitive services at this time.[40]

We do not believe that the Detroit–New York market will adequately support the additional service which United would be enabled to provide, and that, in addition, the probable impact on Northwest's services of the additional proposed service would adversely affect the competitive balance between these carriers essential to the development of a sound national air route system.[41]

Thus it may be concluded that when the traffic reaches some level —albeit loosely defined and quite variable from situation to situation—then the Board authorizes competition. Further, when it reaches some higher level, then multiple carrier competition is deemed appropriate. However, this relationship between traffic level and number of carriers does not persist at higher traffic levels, but seems to change in that, above some levels, the Board seems to lose interest in the problem of diversion and it feels free to authorize new carriers to such an extent that restriction of entry has all but disappeared.

This may be seen in the East Coast cities, New York, Baltimore, Philadelphia, Washington where new carriers were added as parts of awards made largely for other purposes until there were, in January 1957, ten airlines authorized to serve New York–Washington. Nine of these were trunklines authorized to offer nonstop service, and four were completely unrestricted and thus authorized to offer turnaround service. Although this was viewed with some apprehension by at least two of the Board members:

> It should also be pointed out that as a result of the decision herein, *four* additional carriers have been authorized to operate between Washington and New York, making a total of *seven*. Even though several of these services have been established on a restricted basis, the resulting incidental operations bid fair to saturate this market, and to present major problems of air traffic control. While we do not consider this factor to be controlling, it seems to us to be still another weakening element to be taken into account in assessing the soundness of the awards to Braniff and Capital.[42]

Nevertheless, these additions, and the subsequent additions in the *New York–Florida Case,* seem to have been made by the majority without great concern about diversion.

THE LIFE CYCLES OF CITY PAIRS

The many city pairs which entered into the decisions considered in this study differ widely in their traffic levels and in the kinds of response which they evoked from the Civil Aeronautics Board in connection with its consideration of their needs for additional air service. Also, the characteristics of the various city pairs have progressively changed over their history as city pairs between which air service is certificated and offered. They seem to progress through successive stages of development with their stage at any point in time a function of their traffic level (but not *only* of the traffic level). Although the various city pairs move through the successive stages at different rates of speed, and although many, if not most, of the city pairs never experience all of the stages, their sequence being truncated at either or both ends of the scale, nevertheless, there is a discernible common sequence, which may be regarded as the life cycle of the city pairs. The stage of the cycle in which a given city pair finds itself at any time is a function primarily of the level of traffic, and it is characterized by the attitude of the regulatory agency and the carriers with respect to restriction of entry and desirability of entry.

Although the stages may be more finely divided and defined, there are essentially six, the first two and the last one of which differ from the other three, in that for them, both the regulatory agency and the carriers find questions of freedom of entry of minor importance. The importance of these considerations in the intermediate stages is well known.

Stage I—no service. In this stage there is very little traffic between the city pairs. There may or may not be single-plane service authorized, and there may even be competitive service authorized as is the case in many of the 514 city pairs for which competitive service was authorized in the period under study. However, the Civil Aeronautics Board was not concerned about the authorizations to these city pairs because of the low traffic or traffic potential between the cities of the pair. Also, the carrier or carriers which may be certificated to offer single-plane service between the pair do not offer such service for the same reason. No carrier is interested in serving the market, and no carrier has an interest in protecting the market for itself. There just is not enough traffic.

Stage II—unwilling or unprofitable service. Service may be offered between the city pair because of the carrier's public spirit, hope for development, or because it cannot obtain CAB permission to discontinue this service. Then the carrier is subsidizing the service between that pair of cities with revenues obtained from the government as direct subsidy or from the other passengers via the medium of internal subsidy. In the trunkline industry, the latter, internal subsidy, is the general situation, while direct subsidy applies in the case of the local airlines. In the case of the trunklines, the existing carrier would often like to discontinue, and he would have no objection to the certification of a second, usually local service, carrier. In fact, that eventuality may be welcomed as a possible avenue to permission to discontinue service.

Stage III—exclusive authorization and service. One carrier is authorized to serve the city pair, but both the carrier and the Board do not wish a second carrier to be authorized to serve the pair; the carrier because the market is worth serving, and worth protecting, and the Board because there is not enough traffic to require and justify competition according to its standards.

Stage IV—two-carrier competition. The traffic levels here are such as to induce the Board to certificate a second carrier to compete with the original carrier, although, of course, the carrier objects strenuously to this addition of a competitive carrier. Conversely, the carrier which is newly certificated or seeking certification in this market is interested in serving the market, argues eloquently for the benefits of competition in the market, and, once authorized, serves the market.

Stage V—multiple-carrier competition. Traffic levels here are adequate to induce the Board to accede to the applications of one or more new carriers for authorization to enter these markets which are already competitive.

Stage VI—quasi-free entry. These city pairs are so situated and so heavily traveled that they constitute valuable terminals for routes which serve them and thence branch out in various directions. Also, the two cities may be expected to be relatively close to one another. The traffic levels are sufficiently high for the Board to be comparatively unconcerned about the diversionary effect of the addition of competitive carriers. Also, the newly certificated carriers do not necessarily attempt to compete actively with the earlier established carriers for the local traffic over these routes, although they may have comparable authorizations. Of course, it may be that, in time, they will attempt to compete over these routes, but there is at present no indication that this development is imminent.

At present, there are but few of the city pairs which have arrived at this final stage of competitive development. It may be expected that, as traffic continues to develop, the ranks of these city pairs will be augmented, and that the characteristics of route structure which have been described in the last paragraph will be found to be unnecessarily limiting; that is, perhaps pairs such as New York–Chicago, Chicago–Washington, or Los Angeles–San

Francisco will move into this group to join New York–Washington, New York–Philadelphia, and the others. Also, perhaps, the closer the cities are to one another, the lower is the traffic level which is necessary to qualify the city pair for entry into this group, since, after all, it is passenger-miles shared, which is the most important measure of potential lost revenue and profitability, and the generator of active protest by existing carriers.

The level of traffic historically associated with the attainment of each of these stages has varied widely as a consequence, to a considerable extent, of the fact that the level of traffic was not the only element, or even the only important one. The other two important factors are the characteristics of the carriers involved and the route configurations of the carriers on whose routes the various city pairs lie.

ANALYSIS OF THE TRAFFIC LEVELS

The basic data for the following analyses are presented in Appendix Two, which shows the identification data and traffic data for all of the 559 city pairs which, in the cases decided in the period under study, received new or improved competitive authorizations. That is, the number of airlines authorized to serve these city pairs was increased, or, alternatively the airlines authorized to serve the city pairs had some or all of their operating restrictions removed or lessened so that they were thereby authorized to offer better competitive service than they could before the decisions.

The only city pairs involved were those which, because of their location or routes, could emerge with new or improved authorizations from the cases which the Board considered in the period studied. The sampling process, if it may be dignified by that term, is the sampling of the mental processes and standards of the Civil Aeronautics Board with the hope that the decisions reflect what the Board would have done in comparable cases, if they had been presented. There is good reason to believe—and subsequent decisions confirm—that there is such continuity in the decisions of the Board.

In any event, these are the decisions made by the Board in this period. The Board considered those cases before it, and made the many important competitive awards analyzed here. The primary purpose of the analysis is to find the criteria and standards which the Board used in its decisions to increase the amount of authorized competition. Clearly, the important criterion was usually the level of traffic. What were the traffic levels under which the various awards were made?

In making the 559 route awards, the Civil Aeronautics Board created route changes which varied from the mere lessening of certain operating restrictions to the certification of as many as three or four new competitive carriers to serve a given city pair. The city pairs in turn emerged from the decisions with two to ten carriers authorized to serve them. Table VIII-1 shows the 559 docket-city-pairs classified according to the number of authorized carriers before and after the decisions.

The 559 city pairs represent 514 geographical city pairs, of which 35 appear twice and 5 appear three times. Thus there are 40 city pairs which received awards in more than one of the cases. These are listed in Table VII-2, which shows the cases in which each appears. If all of the cases decided in this period are treated as one grand case, New York–Washington as the extreme example, moved from 4 to 10 carriers. The detailed information about this and the other duplicated city pairs may be found in Appendices One and Two.

Table VIII-1 indicates that as the number of carriers becomes high the Board seems less inclined to omit reference to the route changes in the published opinion, even though the award may not have been "purposively" made. The "non-O" intent designation, it will be recalled, merely means that the Board opinion refers, however briefly, either to the city pair in question or to a group of city pairs which includes that pair.

In Table VIII-1 those city pairs which were affected only by the lessening or removal of restrictions are identified as those with the same number of carriers before and after the decision. Of the 559 docket-city-pairs ("awards"), 109 were of this type. In these awards, although the number of carriers was not increased, the lessening of restrictions did increase the amount of competition and, in some cases, the impact was essentially equivalent to that of the addition of a new carrier. Again, in the individual awards, these restrictions might have been lessened because the Board

TABLE VIII-1

THE DOCKET CITY PAIRS CLASSIFIED BY NUMBER OF CARRIERS AND INTENT

Number of Carriers			*Number of City Pairs*		
			Intent Code		
Before the Decision	*After the Decision*		*Purposive, Noted, or Mentioned ("non-0")*	*Not Mentioned ("0")*	*Total*
0	2		3	3	6
1	2		123	172	295
2	2		48	38	86
1	3		25	1	26
2	3		54	21	75
3	3		9	5	14
1	4		1		1
3	4		10	6	16
4	4		6	3	9
2	5		3	3	6
3	5		1	1	2
4	5		5		5
2	6		3		3
3	6		3		3
4	6		1		1
5	6		1		1
4	7		1		1
6	7		1		1
4	8		1		1
6	8		2		2
7	9		2		2
8	9		2		2
8	10		1		1
		Total	306	253	559

Source: Appendix One.

desired to do this in order to create improved competitive service as in the *United Restriction Case,* where the Board removed United's intermediate stop restriction on service between Seattle/Portland and points east of Denver:

Furthermore, it is clear that the Seattle/Portland–Chicago and east market is of such size and importance as to warrant fully competitive services. During 1954, more than 122,980 passengers traveled between Seattle and Portland, on the one hand, and Chicago, New York, Detroit, Cleveland and Washington, on the other. Considering the length of the haul, and quantum of traffic, we believe that unrestricted competitive service by United and Northwest will help to insure the quantity and quality of service best suited to needs of the traveling public. Furthermore, the lifting of United's restriction together with our action on Northwest's applications in the *New York–Chicago Service Case* should result in a better balance in competition between . . . Seattle/Portland and Chicago–east.[43]

However, in others of these awards, the Board lifted the operating restrictions between a city pair for reasons completely unrelated to the traffic levels. For example, in the *United Restriction Case* noted above, the same action made possible nonstop service between Seattle and other cities such as Milwaukee, which, with only some 700 annual passengers in 1954, could hardly be said to merit additional or improved competitive service, with Northwest already authorized for unrestricted service. As noted before, the Board could not possibly create the new awards which it desired without either creating others at the same time or, alternatively, loading the certificates with burdensome and voluminous restrictions. The Board has chosen the former course, conceding that many awards that are neither sought nor especially desired do occur, but reserving the use of preventive restrictions for those cases where a resulting award is felt to be clearly contrary to the public interest. Of the 109 city pairs receiving improved competitive service authorizations as a consequence of the lifting of restrictions, 46 were not mentioned or referred to in the opinion, and the remaining 63 represented various degrees of intent or interest on the part of the Board. The distribution of these city pairs according to the number of carriers, the intent of the Board, and the level of traffic is shown in Table VIII-2. The 1954 traffic figures used here are the most recent annual data available to the Board at the time it made its decisions.

The remaining 450 city pairs, all of which received one or more new competitive carriers, are summarized in Tables VIII-3 and VIII-4, which summarize the awards in terms of passengers and passenger-miles. Many of these city pairs are, of course, characterized by lessened restrictions for the original carriers as well as new route extensions for the new competitors.

Although it is abundantly clear from these tables that the level of traffic is an important factor in the Board's decision to create

TABLE VIII-2

PASSENGER LEVELS FOR AWARDS CONSISTING ONLY OF LESSENED RESTRICTIONS

		Number of City Pairs Classified by Passengers, 1954									
Number of Carriers	*Intent Code*	*Under 1,000*	*1,000 but under 5,000*	*5,000 but under 10,000*	*10,000 but under 15,000*	*15,000 but under 25,000*	*25,000 but under 50,000*	*50,000 but under 100,000*	*100,000 and Over*	*Total*	*Median Number of Passengers*
TWO	1		5	3	3	1	2	1		15	8,000
	3					1	1			2	32,000
	2	15	12	2	1					30	1,000
	6		1							1	2,000
	0	21	15	1		1				38	700
	Non-0	15	18	5	4	2	3	1	0	48	2,000
THREE	1					2	2	1	1	6	44,000
	3								1	1	196,000
	2		2							2	2,000
	0	2	1	1				1		5	3,000
	Non-0	0	2	0	0	2	2	1	2	9	44,000
FOUR	1		1		1		3			5	38,000
	2		1							1	4,000
	0		1	1		1				3	10,000
	Non-0	0	2	0	1	0	3	0	0	6	24,000
Total 0		23	17	3		2		1		46	1,000
Total non-0		15	22	5	5	4	8	2	2	63	3,000
Total specific *		0	6	3	4	4	8	2	2	29	20,000

Intent code: 1: specific purposive; 2: group purposive; 3: specific noted; 4: group noted; 5: specific corrective; 6: group corrective; 7: mentioned; 0: no reference.

* Codes 1 and 3.

Source: Appendix Two.

TABLE VIII-3

PASSENGER LEVELS FOR AWARDS CONSISTING OF NEW ROUTE EXTENSIONS

Number of Carriers after the Decision	Intent Code	Number of City Pairs Classified by Passengers, 1954: Under 1,000	1,000 but under 5,000	5,000 but under 10,000	10,000 but under 15,000	15,000 but under 25,000	25,000 but under 50,000	50,000 but under 100,000	100,000 and Over	Total	Median Number of Passengers
TWO	1	2	4	5	4	3	3	4	1	26	14,000
	3	13	12	7	3	2	1	2		40	3,000
	2	17	14	4	1	1				37	1,000
	4	1	1							2	3,000
	5		4							4	2,000
	6	5	6							11	1,000
	7	2	4							6	3,000
	0	90	61	15	3	4	1	1		175	1,000
	Non-0	40	45	16	8	6	4	6	1	126	3,000
THREE	1	1	10	9	5	5	8	7	1	46	13,000
	3		1	1	1	1	1	2		7	19,000
	2	6	6	4		3				19	4,000
	4				1	1				2	18,000
	6		2							2	3,000
	7					1	2			3	38,000
	0	7	8	1	2		3	1		22	3,000
	Non-0	7	19	14	7	11	11	9	1	79	10,000
FOUR OT MORE	1		1		1	1	1	4	3	11	61,000
	3	2	1	2			7	1	6	19	42,000
	2		2	1	1			2		6	11,000
	7						1		1	2	111,000
	0		1	2		2	4	1		10	27,000
	Non-0	2	4	3	2	1	9	7	10	38	44,000
Total 0		97	70	18	5	6	8	3		207	1,000
Total non-0		49	68	33	17	18	24	22	12	243	6,000
Total specific *		18	29	24	14	12	21	20	11	149	12,000

Intent code: 1: specific purposive; 2: group purposive; 3: specific noted; 4: group noted; 5: specific corrective; 6: group corrective; 7: mentioned; 0: no reference.

* Codes 1 and 3.

Source: Appendix Two.

TABLE VIII-4

PASSENGER-MILES FOR AWARDS CONSISTING OF NEW ROUTE EXTENSIONS

Number of Carriers after the Decision	Intent Code	Number of City Pairs Classified by Millions of Passenger-Miles, 1954									Median Number of Passenger-Miles (millions)
		Under 1 Million	1 but under 5	5 but under 10	10 but under 15	15 but under 25	25 but under 50	50 but under 100	100 Million and Over	Total	
TWO	1	2	6	7	1	5	3	2		26	8
	3	15	17	2	1	5				40	2
	2	21	8	6	1	1				37	1
	4	1	1							2	2
	5		4							4	2
	6	7	4							11	1
	7	2	3	1						6	1
	0	98	58	16	2	1				175	1
	Non-0	48	43	16	3	11	3	2	0	126	2
THREE	1	2	10	11	3	7	5	7	1	46	10
	3	2	1	2		1	1			7	6
	2	6	6	3	1	2	1			19	2
	4		1			1				2	13
	6		2							2	2
	7		2	1						3	4
	0	8	5	2	1	5		1		22	2
	Non-0	10	22	17	4	11	7	7	1	79	6
FOUR OR MORE	1		1	2		2	1	2	3	11	27
	3	5	4	2	1		1	3	3	19	8
	2	2	1	1	2					6	4
	7		1					1		2	32
	0	1	6	1	1			1		10	4
	Non-0	7	7	5	3	2	2	6	6	38	10
Total 0		107	69	19	4	6		2		207	1
Total non-0		65	72	38	10	24	12	15	7	243	4
Total specific *		26	39	26	6	20	11	14	7	149	7

Intent code: 1: specific purposive; 2: group purposive; 3: specific noted; 4: group noted; 5: specific corrective; 6: group corrective; 7: mentioned; 0: no reference.

* Codes 1 and 3.

Source: Appendix Three.

additional competition, there is great variance in the levels at which the various kinds of awards were made. This is, of course, a necessary consequence of the chain of events that led to the singling out of these 559 city pairs for consideration here. The city pairs which received these route awards were not selected by a sampling process, random or otherwise, from some larger universe of city pairs, nor were they individually selected for consideration by the Civil Aeronautics Board. On the contrary, the Board decided those cases which came before it in this period by combining them into this series of proceedings which, in effect, constituted a re-examination of the airline route structures covering a large part of the United States. In making its decisions, the Board made route awards which increased the amount of authorized competition for some city pairs while it refused to do the same for many other city pairs.

The city pairs which were eligible for such new services as a consequence of decisions which might be made in these cases constitute the set of city pairs from which the Board selected the subset of city pairs which did receive these awards, and, as noted before, this selection procedure did not involve the conscious selection of these 559 city pairs, but was rather a consequence of the nature of the applications before the Board and of the existing route configurations of the carriers involved. There are many city pairs which the Board had no specific desire to select, but whose awards the Board found tolerable since they followed as consequences of route changes that were desirable for other reasons, and, on the other hand, there are many city pairs which the Board might long before have certificated for competitive service, if the same Board, with the same criteria for decision, had had earlier occasion to consider them for such increases in competitive route authorizations.

Thus, the 559 city pairs include many city pairs whose traffic levels are well below any reasonable criteria for the route changes which they received, and, conversely, there are many whose traffic levels are well above any minimum levels which might be appropriate. Also, there is no reason to suspect that the number of city pairs in each of these two extreme groups is equivalent, so that averages are of doubtful utility. For that reason, the complete distributions are shown on the tables. The medians are given to the nearest thousand passengers and the nearest million passenger-miles, respectively. However, they are of only minor descriptive importance.

The tables describe the Board's actions in terms of traffic levels, but their analytical usefulness is limited. Unfortunately, the facts of reality are too complex to permit the drawing of sweeping conclusions about the Board's traffic standards. That is, the authorization procedure must not be regarded as one in which: (1) the Board has a list of all of the city pairs in the United States, arrayed in descending order of origin and destination traffic, (2) origin and destination passengers are the only passengers traveling between two cities, (3) the Board, as a more or less continuous process improves the service authorizations for the top city pairs on the list, as the traffic levels become high enough, and finally, (4) the route awards affect no city pairs other than those singled out for these improvements. On the contrary, none of these conditions are in fact met.

In addition to the many departures from this ideal state which have already been discussed, there are two other sets of factors which contribute to the variance of traffic levels among those city pairs receiving seemingly equal treatment in terms of the number of certificated carriers. These are the matters which the Board considered in addition to the traffic level, and which caused the Board to modify its traffic criteria for specific city pairs. They are, first, the size and strength of the existing carriers and their consequent ability to withstand additional competition, and, second, the existing carrier route configurations and the positions of the various cities and city pairs on the existing and contemplated routes of the various carriers. These two important factors will each be considered in turn.

SIZE, STRENGTH, AND PROFITABILITY OF THE EXISTING CARRIERS

In addition to the traffic level, the Board has always paid considerable attention to the condition of financial strength or weakness of the presently certificated carrier as part of its decision about the authorization of competitive carriers. Here, of course, the Board's object is to avoid unduly burdensome traffic diversion. For example, in the *Denver Service Case,* the Board refused to certificate a competitive carrier for certain routes although traffic levels, *per se,* were adequate because of the effect that it might have on the existing weak carriers.

In accordance with our practice in other areas, we will qualify TWA's authority to serve Denver in such a way as to minimize the diversionary effect upon regional carriers without serious interference with improvements in service to the public. Thus, we will prevent TWA from serving Denver with Kansas City or St. Louis on the same flight, and we will subject TWA's service between Denver and Los Angeles or San Francisco to a long-haul restriction. The latter restriction will in effect permit TWA to haul overflow traffic between Denver and the West Coast, after the regional carriers have provided the services specifically designed to meet the regional needs of Denver.[44]

As in the case of TWA's certification at Denver, we will qualify United's authorization at Kansas City to the extent necessary to protect the regional carriers, without undue interference with needed improvements in service to the public. Thus, we will prohibit United from serving Kansas City on flights serving Denver or Chicago. This will afford Continental ample protection between Denver and Kansas City, and protection for both Braniff and Continental between Kansas City and Chicago. With such restrictions, we believe that the regional carriers and the trunkline will be suitably confined to their primary spheres, and the public will be able to enjoy the benefits of their combined services.[45]

Here, the Board took pains to avoid certification of TWA to serve Denver–Kansas City and to avoid certification of United to serve either Denver–Kansas City or Chicago–Kansas City. Since, before this decision, TWA served Kansas City and United served both Denver and Chicago, the extension of TWA to Denver and of United to Kansas City would have made these services possible, if the Board had not imposed the restrictions cited above. For these two city pairs, the existing carriers, the carriers added in this case, and the 1954 annual origin and destination passenger traffic levels (these were the most recent annual traffic figures available to the Board at the time it made its decision) were:

	Carriers		
	Existing	*Added*	*1954 Traffic*
Denver–Kansas City	Continental	None	15,400
Chicago–Kansas City	Braniff, TWA Ozark	Continental	79,200

Source: Appendices One and Two.

For the city pair, Chicago–Kansas City, Continental was added in this decision with the restriction that it serve this city pair only on flights that serve Los Angeles. Ozark, the local carrier, was not a true competitor in that it was required to make two intermediate stops. Thus, with respect to trunklines, the Board saw three trunklines, two of them "small" or "regional" trunklines, authorized, when it spoke as cited above.

For the city pair, Denver–Kansas City, no competition was awarded although 15,400 passengers exceeded that of many city pairs involving one or the other of these same two cities for which competitive authorizations were awarded. These city pairs are listed in Table VIII-5. It is noteworthy that, in the case of Denver–Pittsburgh, United and TWA were both newly authorized at the same time, and the particularly low traffic is the result of the absence of any single-carrier service in 1954. In this case, the two trunklines could be authorized at the same time without great

TABLE VIII-5

CITY PAIRS INVOLVING EITHER DENVER OR KANSAS CITY WHICH RECEIVED COMPETITIVE ROUTE AWARDS IN THE DENVER SERVICE CASE WITH LESS THAN DENVER–KANSAS CITY TRAFFIC *

City Pairs	*Existing Carrier*	*New Carrier*	*1954 Passengers*
Denver–Washington	United	TWA	13,800
Denver–Detroit	United	TWA	6,100
Denver–Cleveland	United	TWA	4,500
Denver–Philadelphia	United	TWA	4,000
Denver–Boston	United	TWA	3,700
Denver–Reno	United	Western	1,400
Denver–Pittsburgh	—	United †-TWA	1,300
Kansas City–San Francisco	TWA	United	13,800
Kansas City–Detroit	TWA	United ‡	11,800
Kansas City–Cleveland	TWA	United	7,700
Kansas City–Pittsburgh	TWA	United **	6,100
Kansas City–Boston	TWA	United	4,500
Kansas City–Moline	Braniff	United	2,000
Kansas City–Toledo	TWA	United	1,700
Kansas City–Baltimore	TWA	United	1,600
Kansas City–Las Vegas	TWA	United	1,000

* This list includes only those city pairs with 1,000 or more 1954 passengers. Eleven others may be found in Appendix Table 2, but these are not important for the purpose of this table.

† United required intermediate stop at Chicago.

‡ United subject to long-haul restriction.

** United required intermediate stop at Chicago and also required to serve Omaha or a point west thereof.

concern about diversion since neither carrier had an important source of income to protect, as did Continental in Denver–Kansas City.

This suggests that the important criterion here is not only the strength of the existing carrier, but also the importance of the particular market to that carrier's profitability and its ability to survive and continue to provide its services, despite such traffic diversion as might result. The Denver–Kansas City route was, from this standpoint, of great importance to Continental.

In the Chicago–Kansas City award discussed above and in the Denver–Los Angeles and Denver–San Francisco awards in the same case, once the Board had decided to certificate Continental in the first and second and Western in the third, it, in its consideration of the further addition of other carriers, weighed the necessity of protecting these so-called "regional" carriers on these routes. For this reason the Board made service by other carriers impossible in the Chicago–Kansas City award and, in the other two, imposed a long-haul restriction on TWA. Thus, the Board in its authorization of a route to more than one carrier considers, and rightly so, the effect of the additional new competitors on each other as well as on the original carrier or carriers. That is, given a traffic situation in which the Board might add two carriers to a route, the Board might decide to add both carriers, if they were both strong carriers. But, if of the two logical candidates for the route extension one were strong and one were weak, the Board might add only the weaker in order both to maximize the strengthening of the weaker carrier and to protect it from the competition on the new route of the additional strong carrier. Thus, the Board considers in such multiple-carrier cases the size, strength, profitability, and susceptibility to traffic diversion of newly added carriers as well as of the original carriers.

The Board has ever been mindful of the possibility that excessive competition might affect the economic stability of the carriers involved. In the period under consideration, the large trunklines, so-called the "Big Four", (American, Eastern, TWA, and United) were considered to be economically healthy and therefore able to withstand reasonable increases in competition.

Diversion. We recognize that our decision herein will result in more competition than recommended in the Initial Decision and that the diversionary effect on Eastern will be substantially greater. However, as we have previously pointed out in the *New York-Chicago Case, supra,* the diversion resulting from the newly authorized services will be, at least in part, offset by normal traffic growth in the markets involved. In any case, considering the size and economic strength of Eastern, we find that the diversion resulting from our decision will not have a serious adverse effect on its financial strength or ability to provide certificated services.[46]

. . . the impact on Eastern and American of the additional competition should be cushioned by the growth of traffic in the markets. In any case, we do not believe that the certificated services or economic soundness of any of the air carriers herein will be impaired by traffic diversion occasioned by our decision.[47]

In the cases decided in this period most of the trunklines became subject to, or "burdened" by, the addition of new competition on their routes, and the amount of new competition to which each carrier became subject varied from carrier to carrier with the larger carriers being affected in this way by a greater absolute burden than the smaller carriers. There are three reasons for this. First, the big carriers with the larger, richer, and more mature routes were more likely to have profitable monopoly routes for which the certification of competition might be found desirable. Second, the Board followed a conscious policy of strengthening the smaller carriers and thereby moving toward a balance among carrier sizes. Finally, and of primary importance here, the Board was more concerned about diversion of traffic from smaller carriers. This, of course, means that the Board looked at the size and strength of the existing carrier and applied different standards and arrived at different decisions according to these characteristics of the existing carrier and the importance of the particular route segment to its economic health.

Tables VIII-6 and VIII-7 show the extent to which the formerly monopolistic routes of the various carriers became subject to competition. That is, of the 559 awards, 322 were the award of the authority to offer competitive single-plane service on routes previously served by only one carrier. These "existing" car-

TABLE VIII-6

DISTRIBUTION OF THE BURDEN OF THE NEW FIRST COMPETITION, PASSENGERS

Existing Carrier	*City Pairs Classified by Origin and Destination Passengers, 1954*									*Traffic (thousands of passengers)*			
	Under 1,000	*1,000 but under 5,000*	*5,000 but under 10,000*	*10,000 but under 15,000*	*15,000 but under 25,000*	*25,000 but under 50,000*	*50,000 but under 100,000*	*100,000 and Over*	*Total*	*1954*	*1955*	*1956*	*1957*
American	36	34	12	5	4	2	2	1	96	699	812	998	1,095
Eastern	57	33	11	1	2	1	3		108	431	582	710	812
TWA	6	10	5	3	5	1	1		31	294	339	410	449
United	12	10	3	1	1	5	2		34	420	502	571	634
Braniff		3							3	9	11	11	13
Capital	6	9	3	1			1		20	114	138	165	173
Continental	1	1							2	2	2	3	4
Delta	2	1							3	5	6	8	8
National	8	4	1		2		1		16	129	141	170	165
Northwest	2	1							3	5	6	7	7
Allegheny	1								1	1	1	1	1
Pacific	1	1	2	1					5	35	40	61	88
Total													
Big Four									269	1,844	2,235	2,689	2,990
Other Trunklines									47	264	304	364	370
Local Lines									6	36	41	62	89
Total									322	2,144	2,579	3,115	3,449

Source: Appendices One and Two.

TABLE VIII-7

DISTRIBUTION OF THE BURDEN OF THE NEW FIRST COMPETITION, PASSENGER-MILES

Existing Carrier	City Pairs Classified by Millions of Passenger-Miles, 1954: Under 1 Million	1 but under 5	5 but under 10	10 but under 15	15 but under 25	25 but under 50	50 but under 100	100 Million and Over	Total	Traffic (millions of passenger-miles): 1954	1955	1956	1957
American	36	37	11	4	6	1	1		96	467	542	669	724
Eastern	59	31	13	1	2		2		108	376	503	637	726
TWA	8	10	5	2	3	2	1		31	274	313	386	423
United	11	10	5		3	4	1		34	298	369	428	484
Braniff	2	1							3	2	3	3	4
Capital	11	8	1						20	30	38	44	48
Continental	2								2	1	1	2	2
Delta	3								3	1	1	2	2
National	12	3			1				16	33	35	43	41
Northwest		2	1						3	10	13	15	16
Allegheny	1								1				
Pacific	3	2							5	7	8	12	19
Total													
Big Four									269	1,415	1,727	2,120	2,357
Other Trunklines									47	77	91	109	113
Local Lines									6	7	8	12	19
Total									322	1,499	1,826	2,241	2,489

Source: Appendices One and Three.

riers generally carried the bulk of the traffic before the new awards in that, any competing service necessarily involved, at best, two-plane connections. Table VIII-6 shows the number of city pairs and their traffic distributions for those 322 city pairs. The annual traffic figures for 1954, 1955, 1956, and 1957 serve to indicate the extent of the burden imposed on each of these existing carriers. The 1954 traffic is the amount of business which, as the Board viewed it at the time of the decision, the existing carrier had exclusive certification to serve on a single-plane basis, and which, at some time before the end of 1956, it was forced to share with one or more new carriers. Of course, the extent of the actual sharing depended upon the amount and efficiency of the competitive service offered by the new carrier. This, the extent to which the Board's decisions actually produced new and improved services for the traveling public will be discussed in Chapter X. Table VIII-7 corresponds to Table VIII-6, but it is based on passenger-miles.

Clearly, the Big Four trunklines bore the bulk of the burden of the new competitive route certifications. Of the routes and traffic thus shared, 83 percent of the city pairs, 86 percent of the 1954 passengers, and 94 percent of the 1954 passenger-miles was accounted for by these four carriers. Of the 34 city pairs with more than 15,000 1954 passengers, 30 were originally exclusive to one of the Big Four, and the other four were distributed among only two of the other carriers; Capital and National, accounting for 1 and 3, respectively. Two of the trunklines, Northeast and Western, do not appear in this list; but two of the local lines, Allegheny and Pacific (formerly Southwest), do appear.

ROUTE CONFIGURATIONS

Many of the route decisions and resulting changes in authorizations between city pairs are the direct consequences of the particular route configurations with which the various carriers came into the case. For example, it is clear that almost any extension made to the route of an air carrier affects the amount and quality of service which the carrier is authorized to offer to other cities previously on that carrier's routes. It is because of the many possible unintended and even slightly unwanted consequences of almost any route change that the intent of the Board has been used in this study. Only in this way could the Board's traffic level criteria be examined. That is, the traffic level for a pair is most meaningful as an indication of the Board's criterion, if the Board took action intentionally on the basis of that traffic level.

Similarly, a route extension to a particular terminal might include the naming of intermediate points which, on the basis of their traffic alone, would not merit being added to the route, but which, as intermediates, may make useful contributions to the new route. The service authorization between various city pairs involving these may thus become better than might otherwise be the case.

One other consequence of the nature of the existing route configurations looms important in the Board's decisions about competition between city pairs. For example, many route extensions might not be feasible at all, if there were only one city in the region to which the extension is being considered. That is, there are many cases in which there is no city in the region whose traffic, *per se,* justifies the route extension into the region, but where there is a group of two or more cities whose combined traffic does make the extension desirable. It is also important in cases where one large city, such as New York in the following example, which does have a traffic level high enough to merit the extension, has neighboring cities which individually could not justify the extension, but which, when added to the traffic level of the large city, may make a useful incremental contribution.

> Similar considerations warrant the authorization of competitive services in the New Orleans–Northeast markets. New Orleans population exceeds 760,000 and the usual economic indices give abundant evidence of a healthy and expanding economy. The community of interest between New Orleans and the Northeast is a strong one, New York being its largest air travel market, both in terms of number of passengers and in revenue passenger miles. In 1954, there were over 145 passengers daily in this market. In 1956, we estimate that this market, with the addition of effective competitive services, should exceed 65,800 passengers annually, and that New Orleans will exchange over 97,000 passengers with the four Northeast points.[48]

The area grouping of cities has made the relationship between the propensity to authorize service between a specific city pair and the traffic between that pair less precise than would be the case if each city pair had to stand on its own.

Finally, the route configurations of the applicant carriers are of great importance in the selection of the carrier to provide the new services. Here, the size of that carrier's routes, their configuration, and the characteristics of the cities served play important parts. This will be discussed at length in Chapter IX.

CHAPTER IX

The Bases for Decision—Selection of the New Carrier

THE PROBLEM OF CHOICE OF CARRIER

Any decision by the Civil Aeronautics Board that results in additions to the route systems of the certificated carriers is necessarily composed of two basic parts. First, there is the decision about the route. Should it be given new or additional service authorizations? The various criteria involved in this decision have been discussed in the previous chapter.

The second part of a route authorization decision is the selection of the carrier to receive the route extension. The importance of this aspect of the decision as a separate problem varies from case to case. In some proceedings, the decision to add a carrier is made, and then the Board must address itself to the problem of selection of the carrier; but, in other cases, the selection of the carrier may not pose a separate problem at all, since sometimes the carrier to be authorized and the route under consideration are so bound together that the Board decision is a compound one. Such for example is the decision to create new service authorizations for specified city pairs by the removal of a restriction on a carrier that already serves all of the cities involved.

In most of the large trunkline cases, however, the Board has been faced with the problem of selection of carrier as a more or less distinct problem.

> On the record made in this case, we are convinced that Denver's long-haul needs are of such a character, size, and importance as to justify service by a second transcontinental carrier. . . . We believe that

a second transcontinental carrier at Denver would insure better development of the coach potential to and from that point, particularly to New York and Washington. We have chosen TWA to supply competitive trunkline service for Denver.[1]

We have already noted that these markets are of sufficient size and importance to warrant competitive service, and that Capital should be selected to provide it rather than Eastern, in part because Capital is already an established carrier in Norfolk, and can meet Norfolk's need for competitive service to the Northeast without undue exposure to diversion of revenue from National's services between Norfolk and the south.[2]

We therefore conclude that notwithstanding the probable benefits that the introduction of competition would bring to the local New Orleans–Tampa market, the interests of the Gulf area and the nationwide air transportation system would be better served by National's extension to Houston and endangered by the alternative, Eastern's extension across the Gulf.[3]

In the selection of the carrier, just as in the decision about whether or not a route should be served, the Board must somehow reconcile its many objectives as stipulated in and suggested by the Act. A technical approach to rational decision making, which prescribes the optimization of some objective function presupposes the creation and construction of such a function combining the objectives of the decision making body. In the case of the Civil Aeronautics Board route decisions, the function to be optimized is some measure of public interest, and the ingredients of the function are specified in the Act. However, the relative importance of the various factors is not only difficult to determine, but it changes from one period to another, and certain of the goals are in conflict with one another to the extent that a decision to optimize on some specific desideratum often runs counter to the best interests of another. The historical intractability of the concept of public interest and the changing ingredients of this concept in a dynamic world have given rise to inconsistencies in specific airline route decisions.

An excellent and provocative study by Howard C. Westwood, published in 1948, analyzing the reasons given by the Board for its selection of particular carriers in the cases decided by the Board from its inception until the time of the study,[4] concluded that the Board has not been consistent in its decisions with respect to criteria for the selection of new carriers. In deciding against the award of new trunkline authorizations to nontrunkline applicants, the Board in its reasoning was found to look with disfavor on new companies, on surface carriers desiring to enter the air transportation industry, on carriers engaged in other non-air business, and on carriers engaged in different types of air transportation that might result in conflicting interests if they were granted the new routes. Westwood also found that priority of application was not controlling where two carriers had applied at different times for the same route, and that the carriers' economy or efficiency records were also not controlling. However, he found that the Board generally gave favorable consideration to locational factors for the purpose of developing strong regional carriers, and to a record of pioneering, optimism, and initiative. Other factors which Westwood found to be important, and which are still of extreme importance today, are those having to do with the effectiveness of competition and the general quality of the nation's air route pattern. Specifically, the Board has tried to avoid making one carrier too powerful, thereby impairing the ability of other carriers to compete. In the same spirit, the Board has granted route extensions to weak carriers for the purpose of strengthening those carriers in order, first, to assist them in becoming self-sustaining and, second, to permit them to compete effectively on new and existing routes. With respect to the emerging route pattern, the Board has given considerable importance, in the selection of carriers for new routes, to the ability of the various carriers to integrate the new route into their existing routes, to operate economically, and to tie in with the existing routes thereby creating many more needed new services.

The policy and history of the Board decisions with respect to choice of carrier have been described more recently by Civil Aeronautics Board Hearing Examiner Edward T. Stodola. In discussing this question in connection with his own recommended decision in a situation involving selection of a carrier to serve a route, he said:

> Beyond the requirements of legal fitness or qualification, which, except in unusual circumstances, are not subject to comparative measurement, the choice of carrier in this instance is wholly a matter of some preference—though not necessarily in each instance substantial pre-

ference—in terms of the principal aims and objectives of the Civil Aeronautics Act. This question of preference is mainly an economic one. There is obviously no single established criterion governing the matter of preference. While the Board has in past proceedings sought to establish general principles governing a choice of carrier, its criteria for that choice have often changed under the varying facts and circumstances of case-to-case adjudication. Among the readily familiar standards employed by the Board in the past, have been the need for revamping a particular carrier's route pattern to insure its greater economic strength; the requisite integration of a proposed route to the rest of a carrier's system; the recognition of pioneering and developmental activities; the comparative operating costs (i.e., relative efficiency) of competing applicants; the promise of effective competition; and the fear of monopoly or competitive dominance. Except for such general principles and their function in Broad decisions regarding the choice of carrier, the only certainty in Board policy with respect to the choice of carrier law is that there are no immutable criteria for such choice and certainly no readily available formula to support a final determination under a particular set of facts and circumstances.

The nature of comparative determinations, of course, makes a specific formula virtually impossible. A choice between competing proposals usually rests upon the significant differences in the proposals based upon the facts of record adduced with respect to each. In other words, the selection of carrier for the services needed to be operated is primarily a process of choice made in terms of the relative advantages of each proposal under consideration. The Board's several criteria of choice for selection between competing proposals are the guideposts to ascertaining the applicant whose proposal gives promise of best serving the public interest.[5]

THE APPLICANT CARRIERS

The domestic airlines of the United States may be divided into three groups: the Big Four trunklines, the other trunklines, and the local service lines. Only the first two groups, the trunklines, are of interest here. The local lines, for reasons which will be discussed presently are not now, except in very rare instances, serious competitors of the trunklines. The relative sizes of the carriers in these three groups are found in Table IX-1, which shows the revenue passenger-mile range for the members of these groups in 1954, before the decisions considered in this study, and in 1957, after the decisions.

TABLE IX-1

PASSENGER-MILE RANGE FOR INDIVIDUAL CARRIERS
BY CARRIER GROUPS, 1954 AND 1957
(*thousands of revenue passenger-miles*)

	1954	*1957*
Big Four Trunklines	2,611 to 3,372	3,662 to 5,042
Other Trunklines	98 to 787	246 to 1,513
Local Lines	8 to 62	24 to 107

Source: 1954—*Materials Relative to Competition, op. cit.*, p. 18. 1957—*American Aviation,* April 21, 1958, pp. 40, 79.

Local airlines. Although this study is concerned primarily with the domestic trunklines, there are a few city pairs in which one of the competing carriers is a local line. In the early days of the local airlines, there was no intention of fostering or even of permitting competition between local airlines or between local and trunk lines. However this policy seems to have been weakened, if not reversed, in recent years.

The local airlines were certificated after World War II in what was essentially an experiment to determine the need for and the response to local airline services on short-haul routes, primarily between regional centers and small cities and towns, but also, between these small urban points. The experiment was controlled by the fact that the early local airline certificates were all temporary certificates, which, unless renewed, expired after a period of, usually, three years. These carriers were not expected to be self-sufficient, but, rather, their subsidy requirements were and are generally regarded as appropriate Federal expenditures under the promotional mandates of the Civil Aeronautics Act of 1938. Of the 23 local airlines which have been certificated by the CAB, 13 are still in operation, and they now enjoy permanent route certification.

At the inception, it was anticipated that the local airlines would not find a large ready market for several reasons.[6] First, they would be serving communities which were far smaller than the average of those already served by the certificated carriers. Second, they would be competing with a highly developed rail and highway transportation system. And third, since the distances over which they were going to operate were relatively short, the importance of the speed advantage of the airplane would be minimized. Thus, the Board sought to avoid the award of competitive routes to local carriers, and in order to insure the local nature of their operations, the local lines were required, in general, to stop at all points on their routes. Their role was clearly to supplement the trunklines by feeding passengers into their routes, rather than to compete with these larger carriers, or with each other. The Board was, in 1949, quite clear on the subject of competition.

From the information now before the Board we are of the general opinion that feeder service should seldom if ever be competitive. The traffic potential is so limited in most feeder territory that duplicate operations by two or more carriers can seldom if ever be economical. We have reached the conclusion that in general where a feeder carrier's route is duplicated by a trunk-line carrier and such route is not necessary to the trunk-line carrier's operation, then such route should be served by the feeder carrier alone. Conversely, where a route is a necessary and integral part of a trunk-line carrier's system and essential to its economical operation, then such route should not be served by a feeder carrier. Where two feeder carriers substantially duplicate service between certain communities, then the feeder routes should be adjusted to avoid such duplication. Of course, these general objectives cannot be achieved immediately in many cases and may not be possible to fulfill in particular situations, but they represent salutary principles which are of importance in working out the appropriate relationship between our feeder carriers and the other certificated carriers (*Southwest Airways Co., Pioneer Airlines, Inc., and Trans-Texas Airways Show Cause Order* [*Order Serial No. E-2680, dated April 4, 1949*]).[7]

Over the years, the Board has granted and extended skip-stop permission in many cases, and in many certificates has changed the requirement to read that the carrier must stop at some minimum number of points, which the carrier can select from all of the points on the segment. However, this was done for cost reduction and traffic generation purposes. The Board, in 1952, was careful to point out that such competition as resulted from this was ". . . an unavoidable byproduct of the basic objective." [8] The Board felt that the competition which existed between the local airlines and the surface carriers would provide any necessary competitive spur, and that, at that early stage of development, there was no economic justification for competition between local airlines.

However, in more recent years nonstop and nonstop competitive routes have been given to local carriers. For example, in the

Syracuse–New York City Case, the Board gave Mohawk Airlines nonstop authorization over the 195–mile segment between Syracuse and New York City in competition with American Airlines. Here the Board insisted that it was not breaking with its precedent:

In reaching a decision in this case we fail to find any need for labeling the Syracuse–New York route as reserved exclusively for either a local service or trunkline carrier. Nor do we believe our decision herein should be viewed as a landmark case which reverses, modifies or changes the essential characteristics of the local service concept heretofore developed by the Board.[9]

More recently, the Board authorized three local service carriers to operate relatively longer haul services than were typical of their route systems. North Central was authorized to serve Duluth–Chicago (414 miles) nonstop, Frontier received nonstop authority for Denver–Grand Junction (200 miles), and Bonanza was awarded nonstop authority between Phoenix and Salt Lake City (500 miles).[10] These distances should be compared with 74 miles, 95 miles, and 112 miles, which were the average distances on these three local carriers respectively.

Thus have the sizes and the authorizations of the local airlines grown and evolved in the first fifteen years of their history. There is reason to believe that they will continue to grow and that, perhaps, eventually, some of them will not differ from the trunklines in many important respects.

The following question and answer by Representative Celler and CAB Chairman Rizley respectively suggest the above-mentioned weakening of the Board's anticompetitive position with respect to the local airlines.

Question. Does Board policy contemplate that local service carriers be competitive with trunkline carriers?

Answer. The principal characteristic of local air services is the provision of relatively short-haul transportation. There are many short-haul routes in the neighborhood of large metropolitan cities where the traffic may increasingly require more convenient and frequent service than now available. The public interest in many instances can better be served by flights local in character even though there may be competition with trunkline carriers between certain pairs of cities. Therefore, upon completion in the near future of the local service permanent certification proceedings, implementing the recently enacted section 401

(e) (3) of the Civil Aeronautics Act, the Board expects to conduct area proceedings involving review of the local service carrier route patterns throughout the country, with the objective of authorizing desirable and needed modifications of local service routes. The further objective will be to strengthen the economic position of the carriers so that the subsidy now provided by the Government may be reduced through the progress of the carriers toward self-sufficiency.[11]

The domestic trunklines. The twelve trunkline carriers are those carriers whose permanent operating rights were granted to them or to predecessor companies under the "grandfather" provisions of the Civil Aeronautics Act of 1938. The Big Four: American, Eastern, TWA, and United, constituted in 1955 a group, the members of which were far larger than the other carriers. The quantitative difference between these four and the other trunklines was large enough to constitute a real difference in kind. The other eight domestic trunkline carriers were not only smaller than the Big Four, but they were relatively more variable in size, as is indicated by the range as given in Table IX-1. Indeed, some observers have treated these carriers as two groups; i.e., "small" and "medium-sized," but this seems no longer desirable. Table IX-1 clearly indicates that there has been a lessening of the relative size spread between the Big Four carriers and the other trunklines. This has been the result of a conscious policy of the Civil Aeronautics Board. That policy has been one of seeking a more balanced pattern of carrier sizes, and it has been implemented by the selection of the smaller carriers to provide new services. Thus, although all of the carriers have grown, the smaller carriers have grown relatively more than the Big Four, with the result that the gap has been somewhat closed. Although the objective of strengthening the smaller carriers has been a dominant factor in the Board's decisions with respect to carrier selection for route awards, there have been many other factors involved in those decisions. The three most important factors are carrier strength, carrier policies, and route configurations.

CARRIER STRENGTH AS A SELECTION CRITERION

The size, strength and economic well-being of the applicant carriers has entered into the decisions of the Board in several ways. In some cases, it has been argued that the Board should decide against a particular applicant carrier on the ground that it was too small or too weak to offer the kind of competition which was found to be desirable. On the other hand, the Board has been implored to deny the applications of some carriers on the ground that they were already too large or too strong, and that others of the applicant carriers were more in need of strengthening by the award of the route extensions. The Board has considered both of these positions and has clearly rejected the first and vigorously espoused the second.

THE ARGUMENT FOR STRONG CARRIERS AS VIGOROUS COMPETITORS

The large carriers in seeking route extensions have argued their own causes by contending that if it is competition which the Board wants, the Board should award the new routes to them, the strong applicants, rather than to the smaller and weaker carriers who would presumably be unable to compete effectively, especially if the existing carrier or carriers on the route are large. The Board has conceded, at least on some occasions, that the smaller carriers, if given the routes, might not be able to offer equivalent strong competition quite so soon as the large carriers, but has insisted that in the long run there is no reason why the smaller carriers cannot compete effectively with the large ones. Also, it must be noted that the very award of such route extensions to the smaller carriers mitigates their smallness and thereby, if that argument is at all valid, increases their ability to compete. Thus, the Board has in the period under study repeatedly rejected and reaffirmed its rejection of this argument.

However, the Board opinions which rejected this argument have frequently been divided opinions in which, although the majority decided in favor of the weaker carriers, the dissenting member or members of the Board argued for the stronger carriers on the ground that the weaker carriers could not do the job properly. This position is forcefully presented in the following citations from the dissenting opinions in cases in which the majority of the Board did give the new routes to the smaller carrier.

In the *Southwest–Northeast Case,* CAB Members Gurney and Denny wrote, in a separate opinion, that:

Our basic difficulty with the Braniff authorization is that it represents an illogical extension of the carrier's system into highly competitive markets in such a manner that it will weaken, rather than strengthen, Braniff's overall economic position.[12]

The majority of the Board held, however, that:

It has been suggested that the smaller trunks are not able to compete effectively with Eastern and American in these monopoly markets, and that the end result of any action authorizing them to do so would weaken rather than strengthen them. Were we to accept this point of view it would spell stagnation for the smaller trunklines. Our recent actions in other areas underscore the Board's program for strengthening smaller carriers, and doing so in part by certificating them to serve rich markets already served by one or more of the Big Four. For example, we recently awarded Capital a substantial route extension from Detroit to New York, via Buffalo and Rochester, where American was the sole trunkline carrier. And even more recently, Western and Continental were granted substantial new segments in markets served exclusively by United.[13]

Later, in the *New York–Florida Case,* where the lucrative east-coast route was at stake, Members Denny and Gurney, in separate dissents, wrote respectively:

There is no question that the East Coast–Florida route is an extremely competitive market. It is crystal clear that in order for Northeast to effectively compete in the market it would require the constant and complete attention on the part of management. However, it is equally clear that such attention would diminish the effectiveness of management in administering their local service routes in New England. In view of such conflicts of interest, the conclusion is inescapable that a diffusion of management energy would take place with the inevitable result that the quality of both of Northeast's operations would be adversely affected. In my opinion, I do not believe that Northeast's management can afford the diffusion of energy which would result if the carrier makes a serious attempt to exploit the East Coast–Florida route to attain an effective competitive status.[14]

Northeast has neither the aircraft nor the know-how to operate the route competitively and effectively. I note that only three of Northeast's ten DC-6B aircraft on order are scheduled for firm delivery during the first three months of 1957. Because of this late delivery, Northeast is in no position to commence service in time for the peak traffic period this winter. The Board's decision, therefore, does nothing to relieve the immediate need for improved service to the public. Furthermore, the DC-6B aircraft on order will not be an effective competitive force against the DC-7's presently operated by Eastern and National. In addition the jet aircraft soon to be placed on the route by Eastern and National relegates Northeast to a third rate competitor from the standpoint of improved service to the public.[15]

But the majority held:

As we have heretofore pointed out, in connection with the authorization of Northeast over the New York–Florida route, even though it may not be able to meet as quickly as other applicants the need for additional service, our basic statutory responsibility is to develop a sound national air route structure and we cannot let short term objectives hamstring our long range objectives in this regard.[16]

The following additional citations from the majority opinions in others of the cases show the determination with which the Board held to its position of rejection of this argument, and the last of these citations, again from the *Southwest–Northeast Case,* effectively summarizes the Board's position.

It has been contended that the award of the requested routes to Capital "will stretch it so thin" that it will be unable to compete with the existing operations of the transcontinental carriers. Thus, on the one hand, the objectors to the selection of Capital contend that Capital will not develop sufficient traffic participation to justify the award. On the other hand, they argue that Capital's participation will result in so much diversion from them as to warrant denial of Capital's application . . . . We are unable to accept the contentions that Capital will inflict destructive diversion upon the existing carriers and we are satisfied that Capital will be able to compete successfully with the existing operators.[17]

Eastern has pointed to its equipment purchase program which, it says, exceeds that of any other carrier in magnitude and argues that it will be able to provide greater quantity and quality of service than Northwest. If this were the test in selection of carriers, we would always be forced to choose the strongest and richest carrier. The Board has therefore refused to follow such a course. The record shows that Northwest is fully capable of inaugurating the necessary competitive service at this time. Northwest contemplates providing three turnaround round trips per day between Pittsburgh and Detroit, using DC–6B equipment. And we are confident that Northwest will obtain such newer types of aircraft as may be necessary to maintain the competitive spur in these markets in the future.[18]

We recognize, as the Examiner points out, that in this case, breaking into the markets where American and Eastern now provide monopoly service will not be an easy task. However, we do not believe that the task can only be successfully undertaken by a Big Four carrier. Thus, Delta, for example, is without doubt an effective competitor with Eastern for Chicago–Atlanta and Chicago–Miami traffic. National competes on practically equal terms with Eastern for New York–Florida traffic, and Braniff competes successfully with American for traffic between Chicago and Dallas/Ft. Worth. Although the greater resources of the larger carriers may enable them to attain effective competitive status in a new market at an earlier date than the smaller trunks, we have little doubt that in the long run a smaller trunk can, provided it operates over a sound route system, attain a fair share of the markets here in question and provide the competitive spur essential to development of a full pattern of air service to the communities they are authorized to serve.[19]

THE ARGUMENTS FOR WEAK CARRIERS

The Civil Aeronautics Board has, on balance, preferentially awarded new routes to the smaller and weaker carriers rather than to the Big Four. The reasons for this are not hard to find, and indeed, they have been emphasized often in the published opinions. The stated purposes are: (1) the minimization of the need for direct Federal subsidy, (2) the strengthening of the weaker carriers in order to make them more effective competitors for the large carriers, and (3) the improvement of the "balance of carrier sizes." In some cases the Board's opinion has emphasized one of these three considerations, and in other cases, two or even all three. An attempt will be made to examine them separately, but the nature of the opinions as vehicles for justifying as well as explaining the decisions motivates the Board and its staff to include all arguments that might be applicable in any case, thus minimizing their separate use. Also, of course, in many cases, more than one of these purposes may well have combined additively in the Board's consideration so that it was their total effect which swayed the Board's decision.

Subsidy minimization. In the *New York–Florida Case,* the selection of Northeast Airlines to serve the rich east coast route in competition with Eastern and National was inspired, in large measure, by the desire to strengthen Northeast, and hopefully, to eliminate the need for subsidy.

The development of a sound national air route structure requires that in selecting the carrier or carriers to provide needed new and additional air service, consideration be given to the applicants' relative route strength and to their need for subsidy assistance for present and future operations over their current routes.[20]

We have selected Northeast as the third carrier. Northeast is the only domestic trunk system which today requires subsidy. Extension of Northeast to Florida will, in our judgment, eliminate the carrier's current subsidy need of more than $1.5 million annually and at the same time enhance the carrier's ability to provide needed short-haul services within the New England regional area which it now serves. Northeast is the smallest of the trunklines and has received less in the way of strengthening route awards than any of the original "grandfather" carriers. All of the other regional air transportation systems have achieved self-sufficiency largely as a result of the Board's policy of authorizing these carriers to expand their services into the long-haul high density markets. Bureau Counsel, the applicant, and the New England civic intervenors call attention to the fact that this case provides the last opportunity to accord similar treatment for Northeast.[21]

Strengthening of the weak carriers in this way is a device which serves not only to remove the need for subsidy, but also, when a weak carrier is already self-sustaining, to assure that the carrier will remain free from subsidy, even in the event of general business decline.

We recognize that most of the smaller trunks are now operating on a service rate basis and are competing effectively in many markets with the larger carriers. However, in many instances, the margin between a commercially self-sufficient operation and one that would require subsidy assistance is a close one. Our objective is to so strengthen the smaller trunks as to insure that they will in the future be able to continue operations without subsidy even during periods of economic adversity. Thus, in the *New York–Chicago Case, supra,* we so enlarged Capital Airlines operating authority, and improved Northwest's route structure as to provide greater strength for these carriers. And in the recent *Denver Service Case,* similar considerations influenced us in granting additional operating authority to Western and Continental. . . .

The problems faced by the smaller trunks in their efforts to maintain operations on a service rate basis, and to compete effectively with the Big Four will tend to be accentuated in the immediate future as the carriers embark upon re-equipment programs involving turbo-prop and jet aircraft requiring substantially greater capital investment than ever before, and also involving in all probability the new and costly operational problems that have heretofore been associated with the transition into newer categories of equipment. Unless the relative economic opportunity—and basically this means route systems—of the smaller carriers approaches more closely that of the Big Four, their competitive position and ability to weather economic adversity are bound to suffer.[22]

As a matter of fact, Braniff alone among the small trunk applicants herein has had a deteriorating industry position. Its portion of the total domestic traffic in the year ended December 31, 1954, was only 3.24 per cent, whereas in 1940 it was 4.04 per cent. Only Western, among the nonsubsidized trunks, has a smaller share of the total domestic market, and we have recently taken steps to strengthen Western in the *Denver Service Case, supra.* In fact, in each of the previously mentioned indices of economic strength (total revenue passenger miles flown, average length of passenger haul, density of passenger traffic per route mile, etc.), Braniff in the first six months of 1955 ranked either lowest or next to lowest among the nonsubsidized trunks.[23]

Increasing competitive effectiveness. In addition, looking toward greater effectiveness of competition among the various air carriers, the Board indicated that one of the benefits of extension of the weaker carriers was that the resulting general strengthening would enable them to compete more effectively over the routes which they were already authorized to serve. This factor should not be taken to indicate that the Board feels that carriers of different sizes cannot eventually compete effectively over individual routes.[24]

We cannot ignore the fact that substantial route awards to the larger carriers would tend to create a greater unbalance in carrier size, and thereby adversely affect the ability of the smaller trunks to compete effectively in markets which they jointly serve with the larger carriers. We believe that the benefits to be derived from effective competition will be spread to a greater number of cities if the size disparity between the smaller and larger carriers is reduced. In many markets which are jointly served today by a small trunk and a Big Four carrier there is no effective competitive service because the smaller carriers' resources and route systems inhibit them from challenging their larger competitors. To the extent that we choose a small trunk instead of a Big Four carrier to provide a needed new service in high density markets, we enlarge the small carrier's opportunity to render effective competitive service in other markets which they are already authorized to serve.

It is also likely that as the smaller carriers' route systems are strengthened they will be in a better position to experiment with the provision of low cost transportation in markets which are currently served only with first class service. As we pointed out, in the *General Passenger Fare Investigation Case,* there is a greater risk in developing coach over the shorter and medium haul segments, which form the bulk of the services performed by the small trunks, than on the high density long haul segments. However, we believe that there is a profitable future for coach services in these markets, and are hopeful that with the strengthening of the smaller trunk's route systems there will be created the economic climate which will lead the carriers to expand coach services in shorter haul markets.[25]

Also, the granting of the new Denver–San Francisco segment to Western is of importance in further strengthening that carrier as a regional operator. The strengthening of such carriers is of substantial importance in our ultimate goal of preventing undue imbalance in the size of carriers that are expected to compete with each other.[26]

Delta is the only one of the ten trunkline air carriers operating an appreciable measure of its services east of the Mississippi River which does not have access to important Northeast markets. We have already pointed out the enormous significance of access to the Northeast, and it need not be here repeated. It is clear that, if Delta were denied such access Delta would remain in an inferior position to its principal competitors. Extension of Delta to the Northeast will, in our judgment, substantially strengthen the carrier and thereby contribute to a more balanced, and therefore more effective competition among air carriers.[27]

The goal of improved competitive balance among carrier sizes is not a new one. Indeed, it has been advocated since the early days of the industry by bodies of Congress as well as by the Civil Aeronautics Board, and it has been applied in international as well as domestic routes.

Obviously, an extension of Pan American to the Northeast would give that carrier the undoubted competitive advantage flowing from single-plane, single-carrier service and would further handicap Braniff, despite its interchange with Eastern, in its efforts to obtain effective competitive status with Pan American in South America. It is, therefore, clear that granting Pan American's application would serve to frustrate the Board's and the President's efforts to obtain competitive balance between our carriers in South America.[28]

The Antitrust Subcommittee of the Committee on the Judiciary of the House of Representatives in its 1957 report following its investigations of the Airlines commended the Civil Aeronautics Board for its record in developing competition among the carriers and decreasing the dominance of the Big Four between 1938 and 1956. However, the Committee concluded that:

It must be recognized, however, that among the certificated carriers there is much yet to be done by the Board to bring about the more balanced route structures and the greater participation by the small carriers in major traffic markets that is needed for effective competition. A greater equalization of the disparities in strength that now characterize the certificated industry would permit competitive forces to work more effectively and result in benefits both to the industry and to the public. To this end new and additional competition on the Big Four's routes and segments of their routes should continue to be a major objective of the Board in the immediate future. Now that air transportation has progressed to an established industry status, where domestic certificated carriers for the most part no longer need subsidy support, and where continued growth of the industry is predicted on all sides, it is encumbent upon the Board to take the steps necessary to assure that all elements of the certificated industry are placed in a position to offer viable competition to their rivals.[29]

Finally, the balancing of carrier sizes has been given expression not only in the selection of the carrier to receive new route awards, but also in the refusal of the Board to authorize competition that might injure one of the weaker carriers. This was seen in the *Denver Service Case,* where Continental's monopoly was protected between Kansas City and Denver, and it is seen in the following quotation from the decision in the *Southwest–Northeast Case,* in which the Board defends its protection of Delta's monopoly in the Dallas–Atlanta market.

In reaching this conclusion, we recognize that Delta will retain an exclusive right to serve important markets, such as the Dallas/Fort Worth–Atlanta market, for which Eastern's proposal would offer a first competitive service. However desirable competition in these markets may be, the price for such competition as is embodied in the Eastern proposals is in our judgment unwarranted, if we are to achieve the more balanced competition among carriers which we believe is required to obtain a sound national air route system.[30]

Thus, the Board in its eagerness to extend the smaller carriers has used two seemingly inconsistent arguments. That is, it has awarded competitive routes to the smaller carriers, asserting that they can compete effectively despite their smallness, while on the other hand, it has argued for extending their routes on the basis that such strengthening will make them better able to compete with the larger carriers. Perhaps this seeming inconsistency may be resolved by noting that failure to have reasonable confidence in the first argument, *ex ante,* makes it impossible ever to extend the smaller carriers, and that *ex post,* the extensions will so have strengthened the carrier in question that the need for reliance on the first argument is reduced. In summary the argument would be that although some small carrier may seem too small to be extended into a particular route where it would be expected to compete with a Big Four carrier, once it is so extended it will be less small. Therefore, it will be a stronger competitor on all of its routes although its size increase *per se* is probably not essential to insure its ability to offer adequate competition over any particular route.

Improving the "balance" of carrier sizes. In addition to its stated objectives of minimizing subsidy requirements and of making the smaller carriers more effective competitors, the Civil Aeronautics Board has also preferentially extended the smaller carriers as a means of achieving a "balance" of carrier sizes.

The need of a carrier for additional strength is a significant factor in selection of carrier where the strengthening is not required for the advantage of the individual carrier as such but for the sound development of the national system of which it is a part.[31]

The development of a sound air route structure for the nation requires in the selection of a carrier, a consideration, among other things, of the applicants' comparative positions and their relative needs for strengthening.[32]

While United could provide public benefits to much of the same traffic as Capital, it is not in a position to provide those advantages which Capital can toward the promotion of a better balanced air transport system.[33]

Whether this means that the Board will continue to add to the weaker carriers until all carriers are approximately equal with respect to some measure of size or strength cannot be foreseen at this time, but it is clear that the size variation which existed before 1955 was considered to be too great, that the Board has striven to reduce this variation by extending the smaller carriers into the rich routes, and that the size variation which remained at the end of 1956 was still considered to be too great, so that this "balancing" process may be expected to continue well beyond the period of the cases considered here. Thus, the Board in examining the size and strength of the smaller carriers as possible recipients of route extensions looks not only at their own absolute strength, but looks also, and perhaps with even greater weight, at their size and strength relative to that of the largest carriers. Then the Board acts on the basis that smallness and weakness relative to the larger carriers is at least as strong an argument for extending the smaller carriers as is absolute weakness as measured by some profitability potential criterion.

The goal of balance of carrier sizes was the subject of considerable disagreement among Board members in certain of these cases, including the *New York–Florida Case* in which Northeast was authorized to compete with Eastern and National, and the *Southwest–Northeast Case* in which Braniff was authorized to compete with American in the Dallas/Ft. Worth–Northeast market. Both of these are cases in which the Board extended the weak carrier in order to strengthen it and thereby guard against possible financial problems. In each of these cases minority opinions expressed the fear that the newly authorized weak carriers would not be able to offer effective competition to the larger carriers who were already established in these markets.

In the *New York–Florida Case,* Board Members Gurney and Denny, who objected to the authorization of Northeast Airlines, did not argue for a Big Four carrier. Rather they contended that Delta was the best choice because of its superior equipment and because it was already serving most of the points involved, although on different routes. However, the majority felt that the benefits to be derived from strengthening Northeast were controlling, not only because of the financial need for strengthening, but also because of the general objective of balancing carrier sizes.

The *Southwest–Northeast Case* is discussed in great detail below, because in it is found the Board's most careful and eloquent defense of the principle of balance, both for increasing competitive effectiveness and for improving the national air route structure. The need for this articulation of its motivations seems to have stemmed from the disagreements among the Board members which resulted in the rendering of separate opinions involving this problem by three of the five members.

That proceeding, which involved applications for additional service between designated major cities in the southwest, northeast, and midway areas, raised the issue of new competitive service over Eastern Air Lines' route between Houston and the Northeast and over American Airlines' route between Dallas/Ft. Worth and the Northeast. The majority opinion of the Board stated:

> Adoption of the Initial Decision's position selecting American to provide first competitive service in the rich Houston–New York market and Eastern to compete with American in the equally important Ft. Worth/Dallas–Northeast market would tend to solidify the economic superiority of the Big Four over the smaller carriers. We think it clear that we should not reach this result unless satisfactory alternate solutions are not available.[34]
>
> As we pointed out in the *New York–Chicago Case* the statutory objective of a sound national air route structure requires, in the selection of a carrier to provide needed new services, consideration of the applicants' competitive positions and their relative need for strengthening. It is vital, in our opinion, to so develop the national air route structure as to tend to decrease rather than increase the gap between the relative size of the Big Four carriers and the smaller trunks.[35]
>
> *Braniff*. We have selected Braniff for the service between Ft. Worth/ Dallas and the Northeast. This route extension will meet Braniff's urgent need for access to long-haul, high density markets comparable to those served by its competitors. Based upon past experience, Braniff is the most marginal of the unsubsidized trunkline carriers. It is the last of those to have achieved self-sufficiency. Braniff participates in fewer of the total top 100 city pairs than any of the other nonsubsidized trunklines, and the three major markets which it serves are less productive of passenger miles than those enjoyed by the others. . . . As previously noted, the

Dallas/Ft. Worth–Northeast route is the strongest in this proceeding which will logically integrate into Braniff's route system. . . .[36]

This grant to Braniff was attacked in a separate opinion rendered by Members Gurney and Denny, who wrote:

We are cognizant of Braniff's position as a marginal carrier and the desirability of strengthening its route structure. However, we cannot conclude either that Braniff could operate the route granted herein profitably or that Braniff could provide effective competition in the Southwest–Northeast markets. In our judgment, to grant the route herein to Braniff is inconsistent with our responsibility under the Act to foster sound economic conditions in air transportation.[37]

The Majority went on to award the Houston route to Delta, saying:

Extension of Delta to the Northeast will, in our judgment, substantially strengthen the carrier and thereby contribute to a more balanced, and therefore more effective competition among air carriers. . . . With these considerations in mind, we find that the public convenience and necessity require extension of route No. 24 [Delta] north of Atlanta, as requested by Delta, and west of New Orleans to Houston. The route so authorized will enable Delta to provide the first single-carrier competitive service in the Houston–Northeast markets, as well as needed additional competition in the important New Orleans–Northeast and Atlanta–Northeast markets.[38]

In thus extending Delta, the majority had rejected American's application; but, nevertheless, they did award to American route extensions to Houston and Pittsburgh, as indicated below:

American. American sought three principal route extensions in this proceeding: (1) extension . . . to Houston and New Orleans; (2) addition . . . of Pittsburgh; (3) inclusion of San Antonio. . . . Except for New Orleans' Service, the Initial Decision indicated approval of American's proposal. For reasons heretofore stated we reject the principal basis for the Examiner's conclusion with respect to the authorization of American to provide the primary competition with Eastern in the important Northeast–Houston market. . . . There remained a need for (a) first single carrier service between Pittsburgh and important points in the Southwest, such as Dallas/Ft. Worth and Houston . . . (b) more direct service to Memphis and Nashville, and (c) a third service to California. . . . This could be provided by placing Pittsburgh on [American's] route No. 4 which we decided to do. . . . We shall also add Houston to route No. 4 in order to provide a usable one carrier service between Houston and Pittsburgh. . . . We think that American will be able to provide Houston with satisfactory service to Pittsburgh, without an undue impact on the Houston–New York market, if Houston is placed on route No. 4 subject to a restriction requiring all flights serving Houston to also serve Pittsburgh.[39]

This award to American was the subject of attack in a dissenting opinion of Board Member Lee, who agreed strongly with the majority in its desire for size balance among carriers, but felt that the Board had violated that policy by its award to American.

I concur with the majority decision on most of the issues in this case, but I cannot agree to grant American a new route from Houston to the Northeast by way of Pittsburgh because such an award will increase the already unhealthy dominance of that carrier and worsen the competitive unbalance which now exists in the airline industry. While it is true that the majority is making very substantial extensions and improvements to the route systems of Baniff, Capital, and Delta, yet the majority is also adding size and strength to American in this case which should go to Braniff and Capital as follows: I would select Braniff instead of American to serve Pittsburgh, and Capital instead of American to serve Houston.[40]

THE BALANCING OF GAINS AND BURDENS WITHIN THE SAME OR JUXTAPOSED CASES

On rare occasions, the Board has explained its selection of a new carrier on the basis that the new carrier is moving into the route of another carrier which in the same or another proceeding was given or is being given extensions to its authorizations. Alternatively, when two carriers seek additions in two cases, the Board might be inclined to select one of the carriers in each of the cases.

. . . selection of Northwest over United will help to offset the impact of our contemporaneous action favoring United in the *United Restriction Case*.[41]

Northeast will initially divert less traffic from National and Eastern than any of the other passenger trunkline applicants, which is a factor in selecting Northeast; normal traffic growth, exploitation of long-haul markets other than New York–Miami, and route improvements granted National and Eastern herein, *infra,* should go far to offset traffic lost to Northeast.[42]

The possibility of complementary exchange is illustrated in the Examiner's report in the *Southwest–Northeast Case:*

The Examiner, as previously indicated, chose Eastern and American to provide service over two of the most important routes in the proceeding. Eastern was selected for the Ft. Worth/Dallas–Northeast service, where American now has a lucrative monopoly route, and American was selected for the equally rich Houston–Northeast route, where Eastern provides the sole single carrier service. The Examiner reasoned that effective competition in these monopoly markets could thereby be provided and that this "complementary exchange" between American and Eastern would reduce to a minimum any concern about diversion.[43]

It will be recalled that the Board reversed this decision, preferring to award the route extensions to smaller carriers (Braniff and Delta) in order to improve the balance of carrier sizes. However, a complementary exchange such as that suggested by examiner William J. Madden, can minimize concern about diversion.

CARRIER POLICIES AS SELECTION CRITERIA

Of minor importance, but worthy of passing note, is the effect that carrier policies might have on the propensity of the Civil Aeronautics Board to award particular routes. In the *New York–Chicago Case* the Board cited Capital's demonstrated interest in promoting coach service as a factor in its decision to extend Capital's routes, "We also take note of Capital's interest in promoting coach service and its effectiveness as a competitive spur in markets of this size." [44] and, in the same case, Northwest's interest in the market was cited as a factor in the selection of that carrier.

We have already selected Capital as the logical regional operator to perform one of these additional turnaround services. We now find that Northwest should be selected to provide the second additional service. It is true that United also seeks turnaround authority between New York and Detroit, but we believe that Northwest has a superior claim to this market over United. Whereas United has made only meager use of its existing nonstop authority between Detroit and New York, Northwest has done so and has carried over 3½ times the passengers carried by United, (based on September 1953 and March 1954 survey figures). Thus, Northwest is a much more substantial participant in the market than United. Furthermore, Northwest was the earlier participant in the market.[45]

In the *Denver Service Case,* the selection of TWA to provide transcontinental service to Denver in competition with United was based on both of these policies; i.e., interest in coach service and interest in the market, as well as the particular route configuration of that carrier.

We have chosen TWA to supply competitive trunkline service for Denver. Our selection of TWA over American is motivated by several factors. TWA has had a sales office in Denver for the past nine years, and in 1953 alone sold ¾ million dollars worth of business. TWA is already a substantial participant in Denver traffic to the cities to which it proposes new one-carrier service, and in terms of passenger miles it has participated in Denver traffic to an extent double that of American. Furthermore, TWA has been more aggressive than American in promoting coach service, and would offer greater assurance of improved tourist service for Denver. Based upon 1954 survey figures, American would be in a position to offer new one carrier service to a slightly greater volume of traffic moving to points east of Chicago than could TWA. However, TWA's proposed schedules would offer first single plane service to more than three times as many passengers moving to points east of Chicago than the schedules proposed by American.[46]

ROUTE CONFIGURATION AS A SELECTION CRITERION

Whenever the routes of an air carrier are extended to a new point, new single-carrier and single-plane service become possible between that new point and many if not all of the points already served by that carrier. This is of great importance, particularly to the citizens and businesses located in the cities which are to receive the new authorizations. For example, before the *Denver Service Case,* the transcontinental service, and indeed most of the east-west service through Denver was exclusively offered by United Air Lines. Thus, there was no single-carrier service between Denver and cities not served by United or other carriers serving Denver. The expressed desires of the City of Denver in that proceeding were summarized by Examiner Ferdinand D. Moran as follows:

The city believes that its air travel market is strongly oriented toward transcontinental routings requiring (a) competitive service to Chicago, Kansas City, Los Angeles, New York, Salt Lake City and San Francisco; (b) noncompetitive, nonstop service to Pittsburgh and St. Louis;

and (c) single-carrier, noncompetitive, multi-stop service to Buffalo, Cincinnati, Columbus (Ohio), Dayton, Indianapolis, Louisville, and Peoria.[47]

By the single action of authorizing TWA to serve Denver, the Board satisfied all of these requirements except those involving Salt Lake City, St. Louis, and Buffalo. It will be recalled that, although Denver–Kansas City service by TWA would have been possible under the award, this was specifically prohibited by the Board in order to protect Continental. The Board rejected the Examiner's proposed Capital–Continental interchange, and instead, awarded the transcontinental route through Denver to TWA, stating: "While Denver showed a need for additional service to such points as Louisville, Indianapolis, Columbus and Dayton, the interchange would provide no improvement at all to these points."[48] In the same case, it will be recalled, United was authorized to serve Kansas City. Again, the tying of the new route into United's existing routes was cited as an important factor.

The Kansas City market fully justifies the establishment of a vigorous competitive trunkline service to the major markets in the east, particularly New York, and United is well qualified to meet this need. Furthermore, the certification of United will provide two important services to the west not available under the examiner's proposed pattern, namely, competitive single plane service to San Francisco, and first single plane service to the Pacific Northwest. Kansas City stressed the importance of these services, and has persuaded us that they should be authorized. The addition of Kansas City to United's system will permit new one carrier service to numerous points on United's present system. As to points east of Chicago, United can offer improved nonstop service to four major Kansas City markets now served by TWA, namely, Detroit, Cleveland, Washington and New York.[49]

The other extreme; i.e., that of no tying-in benefits would have resulted if, in that case, the Board had certificated applicant carrier North American Airlines, which as a noncertificated carrier applying for the transcontinental route through Denver had no routes to tie in with the new route. Then the pattern of services to the cities involved would be improved only to the extent of the newly created routes.

This tying-in factor was cited by the Board as one of the

reasons for rejecting the application of other noncertificated airline applicants for the east coast route in the *New York–Florida Case:* "Applications of Riddle Airlines, Resort Airlines and Trans American Airlines denied because they (a) do not offer any new one-carrier service benefits. . . ." [50] On the other hand, a factor of at least some importance was that only by extending Northeast could the Board create the possibility of single-plane service to Florida and other southern points for the New England cities served by Northeast. The Board said:

Northeast is also to be preferred over the other applicants because it alone among them can provide needed new one-carrier services for the New England cities to and from points south of New York. It is a fact that there are only seven points in the six New England states which have any through trunkline service whatsoever to any point beyond New York City. The entire state of Maine, and New Hampshire, and all but two cities in Vermont and Massachusetts must use two-carrier connecting air service, not merely to travel to Washington, but to any point south of New York. Three of the four state capitals in the United States which do not have one-carrier air service to the nation's capital are located in New England. No other comparable area in this country is similarly situated with respect to air travel.[51]

Similarly, in adding TWA to Tucson, the Board noted that:

Authorization of a second transcontinental carrier at Tucson is warranted by that city's isolation, its rate of growth and rapidly increasing use of air transportation, and by the new and additional services which will result from the entry of TWA.

TWA's authorization will make first one carrier service available to 17 cities or over 12,000 annual passengers, and produce substantial time, mileage and fare savings. The development of low fare air transportation will also be stimulated by the availability of TWA's first tourist service to San Francisco and the cities to which TWA will bring new one plane service, as well as competitive tourist service to New York, Chicago, Phoenix and Los Angeles.[52]

It seems evident that the most important factor in the selection of the carrier to receive new route authorizations has been the policy of the Board of strengthening the smaller carriers and of thereby moving toward a "balance" of carrier sizes. This factor has dominated other considerations, including that which seems to rank second; namely, the route configurations of the applicant carriers. When there is a conflict between these two factors it may be expected usually to be resolved in favor of the weaker carrier. The thought expressed in the following statement may be expected to continue to be important: "As we have frequently observed, if single carrier service were the criterion for selection of carrier, new routes would inevitably go to the largest carrier applying." [53] This position was illustrated unequivocally in the *New York–Chicago Case,* where the benefits of route tie-in advantages of larger carriers were foregone in order to strengthen the regional carrier, although some of the foregone service was deemed desirable.

The objection has been raised that the selection of Capital fails to provide Buffalo with a competitive service to points west of Chicago, such as would be provided by United. We have taken cognizance of this fact, but we find that the selection of Capital meets the dominant need for a competitive service, namely to points such as New York and Detroit, and that the choice of a regional carrier such as Capital holds promise for the most effective competition in these regional markets. We do not find at this time a sufficient need for competitive service to the west to override the benefits of selecting a regional carrier for the route here involved.[54]

THE SELECTED CARRIERS—1955–56

In the cases decided in the 1955–56 period covered by the statistical compilations of this study, the Civil Aeronautics Board awarded new or improved competitive service to 514 different city pairs. There were actually 559 "docket-city-pairs" in that some of the 514 city pairs received awards in more than one case. Also, because some of the city pairs received new or improved competitive awards involving more than one carrier in some of the cases, there were actually 700 new or improved awards to carriers. These different definitions may be clarified by the following illustrations. The city pair, Cleveland–Pittsburgh, appears in three cases, as may be seen in Appendix One. In the *New York–Chicago Case,* (Docket No. 986 *et al.*) Eastern was authorized to serve that city pair. Later, in the deferred portion of that same case, which was considered and decided separately, United was authorized to serve that pair and, still later, in the *Northwest Airlines, Pittsburgh, Cleveland and Detroit Restriction Case* (Docket No. 4294), Northwest's long haul restrictions were removed. Thus, this single geographical city pair represents three docket-city-pairs, and it represents three carrier awards, two of which are for new carriers and one for an improvement. On the other hand, the city pair, Detroit–New York, appears in only one case and therefore is only one docket-city-pair. However, it also represents three carrier awards since, in the *New York–Chicago Case,* TWA was newly authorized to serve Detroit–New York; and both Capital and Northwest were relieved of certain operating restrictions. Thus, here one of the awards was for a new carrier and two for improvements. For all of the cases considered in the statistical compilations of this study, the number of carrier awards is shown in Table IX-2.

Table IX-2 may be read as follows. There were 108 docket-city-pairs which were characterized by the improvement of one carrier and the addition of no new carriers. There were 360 which were characterized by only the addition of one new carrier. There were five docket-city-pairs which were characterized by the addi-

TABLE IX-2

CARRIER AWARDS INVOLVED IN THE 559 DOCKET CITY PAIRS

Number of Carriers Receiving Awards in the Case			*Number of Carrier Awards*		
New Carriers (*N*)	*Improved Carriers* (*I*)	*Number of Docket City Pairs* (*D*)	*To New Carriers* ($N \times D$)	*Improved Carriers* ($I \times D$)	*Total* ($ND + ID$)
0	1	108	0	108	108
0	3	1	0	3	3
1	0	360	360	0	360
1	1	34	34	34	68
1	2	1	1	2	3
2	0	30	60	0	60
2	1	5	10	5	15
2	2	1	2	2	4
2	3	4	8	12	20
3	0	4	12	0	12
3	1	7	21	7	28
4	0	1	4	0	4
4	1	3	12	3	15
Total		559	524	176	700

Source: Appendix One.

tion of two new carriers and the improvement of one. These resulted in fifteen carrier awards, ten new carrier authorizations and five improvements to previously authorized restricted carriers. Over all, there were 700 carrier awards, 176 of which were improvements to existing carriers, and 524 of which were awards to carriers not previously authorized to serve the city pair in question.

In the following discussion, we shall be concerned primarily with the 524 new carrier awards. In each of these instances a new carrier was authorized by the Civil Aeronautics Board to provide service between some city pair. We shall investigate the identity and characteristics of these carriers.

As has been emphasized in earlier chapters, not all of these 524 new awards represented plums, eagerly sought by the carriers. Indeed, some of them are quite unimportant and will doubtless not be served by the new carrier in the near future, if ever. On the other hand, some of the choicest city pairs in the country are involved, and, in those instances, the new carrier labored long and hard to obtain the award and, immediately upon certification, hastened to compete in the market. The importance of the various awards of new routes granted to the individual carriers may be ascertained from the number of passengers and the number of passenger-miles represented by each of the city pairs. The Civil Aeronautics Board has in its published opinions strongly defended the position that the smaller carriers should be strengthened by the award of new routes. There are two basic reasons for this. The first is to strengthen them financially so that they would remain self-sufficient and therefore free of need for federal support, and the second is to improve the balance of carrier sizes in order to make competition more effective. The extent to which the Board has put into practice the doctrine which it has espoused may now be ascertained from the actual distribution of the new route awards among the various carriers.

The 524 awards of city pairs to carriers in the period under consideration represented, in 1954, 13.2 million origin and destination passengers and 6.2 billion passenger-miles. By 1957, this traffic had grown to 19.5 million passengers and 9.6 billion passenger-miles. These 524 awards and their traffic figures do not represent unduplicated city pairs, but, indeed must necessarily include double counting of those city pairs which were awarded to more than one carrier during the period. This double counting is essential for the following discussion which considers the distribution of these awards (and their traffic) among carriers. The amount of double counting is seen in Appendix Three and Table IX-2. The unduplicated figures are: 424 different geographical city pairs, 7.3 million passengers, and 4.3 billion passenger-miles in 1954, and 10.9 million passengers and 6.7 billion passenger-miles in 1957.

Table IX-3 shows the distribution of the 524 awards among the twelve trunkline carriers. The city pairs are grouped according to their 1954 traffic, so that the reader may evaluate the total number of city pairs as given in the "Total" Column. Thus the importance of the awards to each of the carriers may be judged by consideration of the number of city pairs, the number of important city pairs, and the amount of traffic involved in all of the awards to that carrier. Table IX-4 shows the same data organized in terms of passenger-miles instead of passengers. The 1954 traffic figures are used throughout, because these were the latest data available to the Civil Aeronautics Board at the time of these decisions.

The variation among carriers in the importance of their awards is great, and it is clearly due to many factors. One of which, the conscious Civil Aeronautics Board selection of carriers, is of primary interest here. However, there were other factors, the most important of which was the nature and geographical configurations of the matters involved in the cases decided during this period. Clearly, the Board could not reasonably have granted the Boston–Miami route to Western, the Buffalo–New York route to Continental, nor could it have added Tucson to Northeast's route and achieved its purposes. Also, adding a new city to a large route creates new authorizations for service to more city pairs than would the addition of the same city to a smaller route. For example, the addition of Tucson to TWA's route No. 2 created new authorizations for competitive service between Tucson and 23 TWA cities, ranging from Los Angeles which exchanged 42 thousand passengers with Tucson in 1957 to Scranton with only 100 passengers to and from Tucson. Large differences in the size of the awards to the various carriers are, therefore, naturally to be

TABLE IX-3

NEW AIR ROUTE AWARDS TO TRUNKLINE CARRIERS, 1955–56
PASSENGER ANALYSIS, ALL AWARDS

	Number of City Pairs Classified by Passengers, 1954									*Origin and Destination Passengers (thousands)*			
Airline	*Under 1,000*	*1,000 but under 5,000*	*5,000 but under 10,000*	*10,000 but under 15,000*	*15,000 but under 25,000*	*25,000 but under 50,000*	*50,000 but under 100,000*	*100,000 and Over*	*Total*	*1954*	*1955*	*1956*	*1957*
Big Four													
American	3	9	3		4	1	1	1	22	430	528	627	670
Eastern	14	7	2		1	2			26	140	150	162	177
TWA	47	39	14	6	4	9	2	5	126	2,484	2,892	3,348	3,604
United	15	21	7	5	5	5	6	3	67	2,107	2,420	2,810	3,129
Other Trunklines													
Braniff	10	13	7	5	5	2	2	1	45	936	1,107	1,258	1,323
Capital	4	10	10	3	3	9	5	2	46	1,569	1,804	2,097	2,332
Continental					1	2	1	1	5	323	375	437	469
Delta	25	19	8	2	4	6	5	1	70	1,242	1,468	1,697	1,837
National	23	16	3	2		1	6	1	52	1,033	1,212	1,433	1,618
Northeast	15	15	7	3	2	5	7	2	56	1,937	2,399	2,817	3,060
Northwest								2	2	770	904	1,013	983
Western	1	2			1	2	1		7	187	208	241	252
Big Four, total									241	5,161			7,580
percent									46	39			39
Others, total									283	7,997			11,873
percent									54	61			61
All Carriers, total									524	13,158			19,453

Source: Appendices One and Two.

TABLE IX-4

NEW AIR ROUTE AWARDS TO TRUNKLINE CARRIERS, 1955–56
PASSENGER-MILE ANALYSIS, ALL AWARDS

Airline	*Number of City Pairs Classified by Millions of Passenger-Miles, 1954* Under 1 Million	1 but under 5	5 but under 10	10 but under 15	15 but under 25	25 but under 50	50 but under 100	100 Million and Over	Total	*Origin and Destination Passenger-Miles (millions)* 1954	1955	1956	1957
Big Four													
American	2	13	2		2	1	2		22	277	343	420	453
Eastern	18	7	1						26	34	40	44	50
TWA	49	42	13	5	7	4	3	3	126	1,011	1,206	1,423	1,538
United	25	19	8	4	3	4	2	2	67	669	773	923	1,022
Other Trunklines													
Braniff	14	8	10	1	7		4	1	45	619	735	864	913
Capital	7	19	9	3	4	2	1	1	46	467	541	631	705
Continental						4		1	5	384	440	518	552
Delta	26	20	11	1	7		4	1	70	667	791	931	1,013
National	25	15	6	2	1	1	1	1	52	316	408	507	573
Northeast	22	14	8	4		2	4	2	56	1,279	1,631	1,952	2,099
Northwest							1	1	2	445	521	592	576
Western	1	2	1		2	1			7	79	89	104	110
Big Four, total									241	1,991			3,063
percent									46	32			32
Others, total									283	4,256			6,541
percent									54	68			68
All Carriers, total									524	6,247			9,604

Source: Appendices One and Three.

expected. It is the general level of awards to the smaller carriers that is of interest and, of course, the differences between the awards to the Big Four carriers on the one hand, and the smaller carriers on the other.

It is clear from Tables IX-3 and IX-4 that all of the awards did not go to the smaller carriers. Indeed, the awards to TWA and United exceed the awards to any of the smaller carriers in terms of passengers, and are second only to Northeast, in terms of passenger-miles. However, the Big Four group as a whole received less favorable treatment because of the paucity of the awards to American and, particularly, to Eastern. The percentage figures at the bottom of the tables may be interpreted in the light of the fact that, for the year ended September 30, 1955, the Big Four carriers accounted for 44 percent of the route miles operated by the domestic trunkline industry, for 68 percent of its passengers and 75 percent of its revenue passenger-miles.[55]

The data given in Tables IX-3 and IX-4 are, in an important sense, gross data which require some modification in order to show the true value of the awards to the various carriers. That is, in some of the awards, the authorization of the new carrier is restricted so that it cannot compete on equal terms with the existing carrier or carriers. For example, in the awards to Delta, there is included the city pair, Dallas–New York. As a result of the *Southwest–Northeast Case,* Delta is authorized to serve that market in addition to American and Braniff. However, American and Braniff are unrestricted, while Delta must serve this city pair via the intermediate point Atlanta. This severely handicaps Delta in this market and limits its ability to compete effectively. The data of Tables IX-3 and IX-4 may be made more illuminating by taking such restrictions into account.

Second, the value of a route to a carrier depends on the number of competitors. That is, in the airlines industry, with its completely controlled entry (except for supplemental and charter carriers), the number of carriers in any route is fixed until changed by Civil Aeronautics Board action, and, all other things being equal, the fewer the number of competitors, the happier those competitors are, and presumably, the more profitable. Thus, the value of a new route to a carrier depends among other things on the amount of traffic, the degree of freedom from restrictions in the certificate, and the number of other carriers with whom the market must be shared. These two additional factors have been taken into account in Tables IX-5 to IX-14.

Tables IX-5, IX-6, and IX-7 and their passenger-mile counterparts, Tables IX-8, IX-9, and IX-10, take into account the number of other carriers with whom the newly certificated carrier must share the market. That is, these six tables contain the data from Tables IX-3 and IX-4 distributed according to whether the market must be shared with one, two, or three or more other carriers.

Table IX-11 and its passenger-mile counterpart, Table IX-12, take the restrictions into account. They show the data for all of the awards of Tables IX-3 and IX-4 for which the new carrier was unrestricted, or, if restricted, was subject to restrictions which were not more limiting than those of the least restricted of the competing carriers. Thus, these tables are labeled "New Service Authorizations Equivalent to or Better than that of the Least Restricted Other Carrier." Finally, Table IX-13 and its passenger-mile counterpart, Table IX-14, show the choicest awards from the point of view of both restrictions and number of competitors; that is, those where the service authorization is optimal with respect to restrictions and where the market is shared with only one other carrier.

Tables IX-3 and IX-4 indicate that, in terms of total size of markets to which new access was gained, Big Four carriers received 39 percent of the gains in terms of passengers and 32 percent in terms of passenger-miles, with TWA and United accounting for about nine-tenths of the passengers and 84 percent of the passenger-miles. The other two Big Four carriers did not fare nearly so well. Eastern gained least of all carriers, and American gained less than any of the others with the exception of Western and, in terms of passengers, Continental.

When restrictions and number of carriers are taken into account as in Tables IX-5 to IX-14, the picture is changed considerably. In terms of unrestricted or, at least, equivalent competitive opportunity, the Big Four group's share fell from 39 percent and 32 percent to 12 percent and 17 percent respectively (Tables IX-11, 12), indicating that the restrictions fell heaviest

TABLE IX-5

NEW AIR ROUTE AWARDS TO TRUNKLINE CARRIERS, 1955–56
PASSENGER ANALYSIS, ONE OTHER AUTHORIZED COMPETITOR

	Number of City Pairs Classified by Passengers, 1954									*Origin and Destination Passengers (thousands)*			
Airline	*Under 1,000*	*1,000 but under 5,000*	*5,000 but under 10,000*	*10,000 but under 15,000*	*15,000 but under 25,000*	*25,000 but under 50,000*	*50,000 but under 100,000*	*100,000 and Over*	*Total*	*1954*	*1955*	*1956*	*1957*
Big Four													
American	3	9	2		2	1			17	124	154	183	203
Eastern	13	7	2						22	39	51	59	64
TWA	45	33	8	3	1	1			91	252	307	366	408
United	14	16	5	4	2		1		42	226	250	334	373
Other Trunklines													
Braniff	8	12	2		1				23	73	95	97	106
Capital	3	7	8	3	2	2	3	1	29	600	701	833	936
Continental													
Delta	21	13	2		1		1		38	138	179	207	227
National	17	8	1	1			1		28	97	121	139	160
Northeast	8	2	1						11	13	15	27	44
Northwest													
Western	1	2			1	1	1		6	156	170	197	205
Big Four, total									172	641			1,048
percent									56	37			38
Others, total									135	1,077			1,678
percent									44	63			62
All Carriers, total									307	1,718			2,726

Source: Appendices One and Two.

TABLE IX-6

NEW AIR ROUTE AWARDS TO TRUNKLINE CARRIERS, 1955–56
PASSENGER ANALYSIS, TWO OTHER AUTHORIZED COMPETITORS

Airline	*Number of City Pairs Classified by Passengers, 1954*									*Origin and Destination Passengers (thousands)*			
	Under 1,000	*1,000 but under 5,000*	*5,000 but under 10,000*	*10,000 but under 15,000*	*15,000 but under 25,000*	*25,000 but under 50,000*	*50,000 but under 100,000*	*100,000 and Over*	*Total*	*1954*	*1955*	*1956*	*1957*
Big Four													
American			1		2				3	48	57	71	80
Eastern	1				1	2			4	100	99	103	113
TWA	1	5	5	2	1	5			19	254	311	369	394
United		2			2		2		6	185	235	271	324
Other Trunklines													
Braniff	2	1	5	4	3	2	1		18	277	332	398	423
Capital		3	1		1	3			8	149	151	190	213
Continental					1	2			3	98	121	145	165
Delta	3	5	5	2	3	2	2		22	333	388	465	506
National	6	5	1				2		14	138	201	254	277
Northeast	6	10	3	2	1	1	5	1	29	1,086	1,398	1,669	1,787
Northwest													
Western						1			1	31	38	45	47
Big Four, total									32	587			911
percent									25	22			21
Others, total									95	2,112			3,418
percent									75	78			79
All Carriers, total									127	2,699			4,329

Source: Appendices One and Two.

TABLE IX-7

NEW AIR ROUTE AWARDS TO TRUNKLINE CARRIERS, 1955–56
PASSENGER ANALYSIS, THREE OR MORE OTHER AUTHORIZED COMPETITORS

	Number of City Pairs Classified by Passengers, 1954									*Origin and Destination Passengers (thousands)*			
Airline	*Under 1,000*	*1,000 but under 5,000*	*5,000 but under 10,000*	*10,000 but under 15,000*	*15,000 but under 25,000*	*25,000 but under 50,000*	*50,000 but under 100,000*	*100,000 and Over*	*Total*	*1954*	*1955*	*1956*	*1957*
Big Four													
American							1	1	2	258	317	372	387
Eastern													
TWA	1	1	1	1	2	3	2	5	16	1,978	2,274	2,612	2,803
United	1	3	2	1	1	5	3	3	19	1,697	1,934	2,205	2,434
Other Trunklines													
Braniff				1	1		1	1	4	587	679	763	793
Capital	1		1			4	2	1	9	821	953	1,073	1,183
Continental							1	1	2	225	254	292	304
Delta	1	1	1			4	2	1	10	771	901	1,026	1,104
National		3	1	1		1	3	1	10	798	891	1,039	1,181
Northeast	1	3	3	1	1	4	2	1	16	838	985	1,122	1,228
Northwest								2	2	770	904	1,013	983
Western													
Big Four, total									37	3,933			5,624
percent									41	45			45
Others, total									53	4,810			6,776
percent									59	55			55
All Carriers, total									90	8,743			12,400

Source: Appendices One and Two.

TABLE IX-8

NEW AIR ROUTE AWARDS TO TRUNKLINE CARRIERS, 1955–56
PASSENGER-MILE ANALYSIS, ONE OTHER AUTHORIZED COMPETITOR

	Number of City Pairs Classified by Millions of Passenger-Miles, 1954									*Origin and Destination Passenger-Miles (millions)*			
Airline	*Under 1 Million*	*1 but under 5*	*5 but under 10*	*10 but under 15*	*15 but under 25*	*25 but under 50*	*50 but under 100*	*100 Million and Over*	*Total*	*1954*	*1955*	*1956*	*1957*
Big Four													
American	2	12	2		1				17	69	86	106	117
Eastern	17	5							22	18	23	27	30
TWA	45	32	8	2	3		1		91	280	343	413	461
United	20	12	4	2	2	1	1		42	218	242	313	345
Other Trunklines													
Braniff	12	7	4						23	45	58	61	69
Capital	5	13	6	1	2	2			29	205	244	286	328
Continental													
Delta	21	10	5		2				38	97	124	145	163
National	17	9	2						28	35	48	57	68
Northeast	9	1	1						11	14	16	30	50
Northwest													
Western	1	2	1		2				6	50	53	62	66
Big Four, total									172	585			953
percent									56	57			56
Others, total									135	446			744
percent									44	43			44
All Carriers, total									307	1,031			1,697

Source: Appendices One and Three.

TABLE IX-9

NEW AIR ROUTE AWARDS TO TRUNKLINE CARRIERS, 1955–56
PASSENGER-MILE ANALYSIS, TWO OTHER AUTHORIZED COMPETITORS

	Number of City Pairs Classified by Millions of Passenger-Miles, 1954									*Origin and Destination Passenger-Miles (millions)*			
Airline	*Under 1 Million*	*1 but under 5*	*5 but under 10*	*10 but under 15*	*15 but under 25*	*25 but under 50*	*50 but under 100*	*100 Million and Over*	*Total*	*1954*	*1955*	*1956*	*1957*
Big Four													
American		1			1	1			3	59	74	98	112
Eastern	1	2	1						4	17	17	17	20
TWA	2	5	3	2	4	3			19	218	270	320	343
United	1	1	1		1	2			6	86	109	128	147
Other Trunklines													
Braniff	2	1	5	1	6		3		18	357	423	507	542
Capital	1	3	2	1	1				8	52	55	71	80
Continental						3			3	96	118	141	160
Delta	3	7	4	1	5		2		22	291	336	405	438
National	5	4	3		1		1		14	115	172	230	254
Northeast	8	8	5	2		1	4	1	29	1,076	1,391	1,667	1,769
Northwest													
Western						1			1	29	36	42	44
Big Four, total									32	380			622
percent									25	16			16
Others, total									95	2,016			3,287
percent									75	84			84
All Carriers, total									127	2,396			3,909

Source: Appendices One and Three.

TABLE IX-10

NEW AIR ROUTE AWARDS TO TRUNKLINE CARRIERS, 1955–56
PASSENGER-MILE ANALYSIS, THREE OR MORE OTHER AUTHORIZED COMPETITORS

	Number of City Pairs Classified by Millions of Passenger-Miles, 1954									*Origin and Destination Passenger-Miles (millions)*			
Airline	*Under 1 Million*	*1 but under 5*	*5 but under 10*	*10 but under 15*	*15 but under 25*	*25 but under 50*	*50 but under 100*	*100 Million and Over*	*Total*	*1954*	*1955*	*1956*	*1957*
Big Four													
American							2		2	149	183	217	223
Eastern													
TWA	2	5	2	1		1	2	3	16	514	593	690	733
United	4	6	3	2		1	1	2	19	365	421	482	530
Other Trunklines													
Braniff			1		1		1	1	4	217	255	295	302
Capital	1	3	1	1	1		1	1	9	209	242	273	297
Continental						1		1	2	288	323	377	392
Delta	2	3	2				2	1	10	279	332	381	413
National	3	2	1	2		1		1	10	167	189	220	251
Northeast	5	5	2	2		1		1	16	189	224	255	280
Northwest							1	1	2	445	521	592	576
Western													
Big Four, total									37	1,028			1,486
percent									41	36			37
Others, total									53	1,794			2,511
percent									59	64			63
All Carriers, total									90	2,822			3,997

Source: Appendices One and Three.

TABLE IX-11

NEW AIR ROUTE AWARDS TO TRUNKLINE CARRIERS, 1955–56
PASSENGER ANALYSIS, NEW SERVICE AUTHORIZATION EQUIVALENT TO OR BETTER THAN THAT OF THE LEAST RESTRICTED OTHER CARRIERS

Airline	Number of City Pairs Classified by Passengers, 1954									Origin and Destination Passengers (thousands)			
	Under 1,000	*1,000 but under 5,000*	*5,000 but under 10,000*	*10,000 but under 15,000*	*15,000 but under 25,000*	*25,000 but under 50,000*	*50,000 but under 100,000*	*100,000 and Over*	*Total*	*1954*	*1955*	*1956*	*1957*
Big Four													
American	1	5							6	12	14	23	26
Eastern	8	3			1				12	30	36	40	43
TWA	40	36	12	4	3	3			98	389	477	562	608
United	5	6	3	3	2		1		20	172	184	237	277
Other Trunklines													
Braniff	9	4	5	3	4		1		26	218	263	320	333
Capital	1	4	2	2	1	4	4	1	19	681	780	931	1,078
Continental					1	2		1	4	244	284	338	365
Delta	10	7	4		3	1	3		28	343	405	475	519
National	18	13	3	2		1	6	1	44	1,020	1,196	1,413	1,595
Northeast	15	15	7	3	2	5	7	2	56	1,937	2,399	2,817	3,060
Northwest													
Western	1	2			1	2	1		7	187	208	241	251
Big Four, total									136	603			954
percent									42	12			12
Others, total									184	4,630			7,201
percent									58	88			88
All Carriers, total									320	5,233			8,155

Source: Appendices One and Two.

TABLE IX-12

NEW AIR ROUTE AWARDS TO TRUNKLINE CARRIERS, 1955–56
PASSENGER-MILE ANALYSIS, NEW SERVICE AUTHORIZATION EQUIVALENT TO OR BETTER THAN THAT OF THE LEAST RESTRICTED OTHER CARRIERS

	Number of City Pairs Classified by Millions of Passenger-Miles, 1954									*Origin and Destination Passenger-Miles (millions)*			
Airline	*Under 1 Million*	*1 but under 5*	*5 but under 10*	*10 but under 15*	*15 but under 25*	*25 but under 50*	*50 but under 100*	*100 Million and Over*	*Total*	*1954*	*1955*	*1956*	*1957*
Big Four													
American	1	5							6	13	15	24	28
Eastern	11	1							12	5	6	6	7
TWA	40	36	10	4	6	1	1		98	404	497	591	648
United	8	5	2	2	1	1	1		20	158	167	208	228
Other Trunklines													
Braniff	10	3	6	1	5		1		26	236	280	344	358
Capital	2	7	3	1	3	2	1		19	244	279	330	375
Continental						3		1	4	351	403	477	509
Delta	11	5	5		4		3		28	333	396	464	505
National	22	12	4	2	1	1	1	1	44	298	385	479	541
Northeast	22	14	8	4		2	4	2	56	1,279	1,631	1,952	2,099
Northwest													
Western	1	2	1		2	1			7	79	89	104	110
Big Four, total									136	580			911
percent									42	17			17
Others, total									184	2,820			4,497
percent									58	83			83
All Carriers, total									320	3,400			5,408

Source: Appendices One and Three.

TABLE IX-13

NEW AIR ROUTE AWARDS TO TRUNKLINE CARRIERS, 1955–56
PASSENGER ANALYSIS, NEW SERVICE AUTHORIZATION EQUIVALENT TO OR BETTER THAN THAT OF THE OTHER CARRIER, ONE OTHER AUTHORIZED COMPETITOR

	Number of City Pairs Classified by Passengers, 1954									*Origin and Destination Passengers (thousands)*			
Airline	*Under 1,000*	*1,000 but under 5,000*	*5,000 but under 10,000*	*10,000 but under 15,000*	*15,000 but under 25,000*	*25,000 but under 50,000*	*50,000 but under 100,000*	*100,000 and Over*	*Total*	*1954*	*1955*	*1956*	*1957*
Big Four													
American	1	5							6	12	14	23	26
Eastern	7	3							10	12	17	19	19
TWA	40	32	7	3	1	1			84	239	288	345	384
United	5	6	3	3	1		1		19	149	157	207	241
Other Trunklines													
Braniff	7	3							10	9	11	13	14
Capital	1	2	2	2		2	2	1	12	420	494	586	665
Continental													
Delta	8	4	1		1				14	38	46	54	57
National	13	6	1	1			1		22	89	110	127	145
Northeast	8	2	1						11	13	15	27	44
Northwest													
Western	1	2			1	1	1		6	156	170	197	205
Big Four, total									119	412			670
percent									61	36			37
Others, total									75	725			1,130
percent									39	64			63
All Carriers, total									194	1,137			1,800

Source: Appendices One and Two.

TABLE IX-14

NEW AIR ROUTE AWARDS TO TRUNKLINE CARRIERS, 1955–56
PASSENGER-MILE ANALYSIS, NEW SERVICE AUTHORIZATION EQUIVALENT TO OR BETTER THAN THAT OF THE OTHER CARRIER, ONE OTHER AUTHORIZED COMPETITOR

	Number of City Pairs Classified by Millions of Passenger-Miles, 1954									*Origin and Destination Passenger-Miles (millions)*			
Airline	*Under 1 Million*	*1 but under 5*	*5 but under 10*	*10 but under 15*	*15 but under 25*	*25 but under 50*	*50 but under 100*	*100 Million and Over*	*Total*	*1954*	*1955*	*1956*	*1957*
Big Four													
American	1	5							6	13	15	24	28
Eastern	10								10	2	2	3	3
TWA	39	31	8	2	3		1		84	296	365	437	521
United	8	5	2	2	1		1		19	128	132	167	180
Other Trunklines													
Braniff	8	2							10	5	7	8	9
Capital	1	5	2	1	1	2			12	137	162	189	216
Continental													
Delta	9	2	2		1				14	39	47	55	58
National	14	7	1						22	25	34	41	49
Northeast	9	1	1						11	14	16	30	50
Northwest													
Western	1	2	1		2				6	50	53	62	66
Big Four, total									119	439			732
percent									61	62			62
Others, total									75	270			448
percent									39	38			38
All Carriers, total									194	709			1,180

Source: Appendices One and Three.

on the large carriers. For example, of the over 2 million passengers in 1954 to whom United gained access, less than 200,000, or 8 percent, were in the markets to which United had equivalent access. For TWA this figure was 16 percent. On the other hand, the figure for Northeast was 100 percent, National—99 percent, Capital—43 percent, Delta—27 percent, and Braniff—23 percent. Similarly, in terms of individual city pairs, Big Four carriers moved into 9 city pairs with over 100,000 annual passengers and 9 more with between 50,000 and 100,000 annual passengers. In only one of the latter 9 and none of the first 9 was the access granted on an equivalent basis. On the other hand, other trunklines gained access to 10 pairs with over 100,000 passengers and 27 pairs with between 50,000 and 100,000 passengers. Of these, 5 of the first group (50 percent) and 21 of the second (78 percent) were entered on an equivalent basis. As evidence of the Board's sincerity in its avowed objective of approaching competitive balance, Tables IX-11 and IX-12 argue more convincingly than do Tables IX-3 and IX-4.

Tables IX-13 and IX-14 show that only 194, or 37 percent of the 524 awards represented equivalent entry into markets with but one other competitor. These accounted for only 9 percent of the passengers and 11 percent of the passenger-miles of all of the 524 awards. As seen in Table IX-15, a larger part of the decline from 100 percent to 9 percent in passengers takes place between Tables IX-3 and IX-5 than between IX-3 and IX-11, suggesting the growing scarcity of high density monopolistic markets. More and more, the competitive authorizations of the Civil Aeronautics Board will consist of entry as one of several competitors and less as first competitor.

TABLE IX-15

RELATIVE IMPORTANCE OF NUMBER OF CARRIERS AND RESTRICTIONS

Table Number	*Award Characteristics*	*Passengers*	
		Thousands	*Percent*
IX-3	All awards	13,158	100
IX-5	Shared with one other carrier	1,718	13
IX-11	Equivalent (or better) competition	5,233	40
IX-13	Equivalent (or better) competition and shared with one other carrier	1,137	9

In any event, the data shown indicate quite clearly that the Civil Aeronautics Board by its route awards has moved toward a balance in carrier sizes. The steps in that direction have not been enormous, but the smaller carriers as a group have grown relative to the Big Four, and some of the smaller trunklines, particularly Northeast, National, and Capital, have gained access to important markets on favorable terms. All of the trunk carriers have gained to some extent in terms of authorizations.

SUMMARY

The Civil Aeronautics Board has by its route certification policies pursued its mandate to foster competition in the air transport industry. It has extended the routes of the various carriers for the clear purpose of creating competitive services between the points involved, and equally important, it has in the selection of the carrier to provide this competition favored the weaker and smaller carriers in order, chiefly, to strengthen them so that they might, first, become economically strong and permanently free of any need for federal subsidy, and second, so that they might become strong enough to compete on equal terms with the largest of the carriers so that ultimately the domestic trunkline industry may consist of air carriers whose size and strength range will not be too large to preclude effective competition between any two of them. This objective of what the Civil Aeronautics Board has called a "balanced" system is solely an expression of the policy of creating and fostering competition.

Clearly, then, the Board has awarded route extensions to selected carriers in a manner calculated to increase competition. We have examined the extent to which, and the manner in which, the Civil Aeronautics Board has within the limitations of its powers acted to create the conditions for competition. Now, there remains an additional important question or series of questions. That is, to what extent have these new authorizations resulted in new service? Did the new carriers try to compete? Have they been able to compete effectively? Has the Civil Aeronautics Board created the competition it sought?

Within the realm of route awards, the competition which has been sought by the Board has been largely service and schedule competition. This suggests that success in the creation of competition exists when a new carrier is added who offers flight schedules and services of an amount and quality such that, first, the total service pattern offered over the route in question is expanded and improved, and, second, the air traveler has some degree of choice in his selection of the carrier to receive his patronage.

CHAPTER X

The Resulting Competition

The Civil Aeronautics Board has by selective use of its certification power sought to bring about a controlled increase in the amount of competition in the domestic trunk airline industry. It has attempted to find and identify those air travel markets in which the traffic or traffic potential was sufficient in its opinion to justify or require new or additional competitive air service. Having made the decision that there should be such increased service in specific markets, the Board then faced the problem of selecting the carrier to be authorized to provide this additional service.

In general, the Board has favored the medium and smaller airlines as part of a policy of decreasing the relative size range of the carriers. The policy of fostering and protecting the smaller carriers is evident not only in the selection of the carriers to receive the new authorizations, but also in the Board's seeking to avoid imposing what it considers to be unduly burdensome competition on routes initially served by the smaller carriers. This last objective has been implemented by selective avoidance of competitive authorizations for such markets or, when this is not feasible, by the imposition of operating restrictions on the newly authorized competitive carriers.

When the Civil Aeronautics Board seeks to create additional competition over a particular route, it does this by authorizing a new carrier to offer such service. With the exceptions of the recent *Toledo Case* and the even more recent *Washington–Baltimore Adequacy of Service Case,* the Board has not gone beyond the act of authorization. In these two cases, the Board found that service inadequacies existed and that the inadequacies should be remedied by Board order requiring additional service. While these pioneering cases are of extreme interest, there are as yet only fragmentary indications that the Board will develop this concept to the extent of making broad changes in its long-established policy of relying on competition rather than such direct regulatory action as the primary tool for assuring a desirable quality of air service. Under the traditional policy, which was dominant until the *Toledo Case* decision on November 10, 1959, and which, in all probability, will continue to be of great importance, the Board does not go beyond the authorization of the desired new service.

This decision on the part of the Board to authorize new or additional competitive service is merely the enabling action which makes it possible for the selected carrier in its turn to make a decision to offer competitive service. This carrier, then, also determines the amount and kind of service to be offered. Under this policy, the effectiveness of the Civil Aeronautics Board in creating competition can be judged only in terms of the operating decisions of the various carriers, a matter over which the Board has exercised essentially no control.

A basic difficulty in evaluating the extent to which the Board has achieved its objectives in creating competition arises in the accurate identification of those routes, or city pairs, for which the Board sought additional competition.[1] That is, when the Board sought to authorize new service between two points, it did this by extending the route of some carrier, thereby usually making it possible for that carrier to offer new service between that city pair. However, this route extension frequently made it possible for the carrier to offer, in addition, new service between one or more other city pairs. When these additional city pairs were such that the Board clearly wished to prevent the new service, this could be and was often accomplished by the imposition of appropriate operating restrictions. However, the Board has wished to be sparing in its use of these restrictions and has, therefore, used them only when it felt that the need was compelling. The result is that, for most of the route extensions granted by the Board, there were new service authorizations for city pairs for which the Board sought the new service, other city pairs for which the Board thought that the resulting new authorizations were a desirable, though not essential, by-product, and yet other city pairs for which the Board considered the new service a useless or perhaps even slightly undesirable resultant, but not sufficiently harmful to merit the imposition of restrictions. Also, there were many city pairs receiving authorizations, but for which the traffic and traffic potential were so low that the new authorizations were of no concern to the Board or to any of the carriers involved.

Unfortunately, it is not always possible to discover the true intent of the Board with respect to each of the various city pairs. Yet, the extent to which the Board has accomplished its ends in terms of quanta of service can be assessed for each air traffic market only when these ends are defined. It is apparent that the presence of service between a city pair where competitive service has been newly authorized may represent either success for the Board's aims, or it may represent failure, depending upon the intention of the Board with respect to that specific city pair. The same is true with respect to the absence of such service. Therefore, all of the city pairs which received competitive authorizations in the cases covered in this study have been classified according to the intent of the Board as interpreted from the statements in the published opinions.

The Board, in deciding whether to make competitive awards, seems to have made its decisions on the basis of the following criteria. It has decided to authorize new or additional competitive carriers between a city pair upon a finding of one of these four conditions.

1. There is a need for competition to improve the service or to assure optimum service for the traveling public. There is adequate traffic, and the existing carrier will not be unduly damaged by the competition. Adequacy of service by the existing carrier is not a bar to a competitive authorization.
2. Competition is permissible because there is so much traffic that additional carriers can also survive, and there is no need to limit the number of carriers to the present number. Here, adequacy of service is irrelevant. (In this and the previous case, the Board is afforded an opportunity in the selection of the competitive new carrier to serve the additional goal of strengthening selected weaker carriers.)

3. Competitive authorizations can do no harm because there is so little traffic that no existing carrier can be hurt by being forced to share the market, and probably neither the original carrier nor the new carrier will be interested in exploiting the market.
4. A competitive carrier should be authorized because, although there may not be sufficient traffic to justify two active competing carriers, the presently authorized carrier is not offering adequate service.

However, competitive awards may be denied because

1. The market is extremely important to the existing carrier, and although that particular market may be large enough to be profitable to both the existing carrier and the new carrier, the authorization of a new competitor might damage the existing carrier, taken as a whole, sufficiently to endanger its financial stability and, therefore, its ability to perform in all of the markets it serves, and it might have undesirable consequences such as the creation of a need for additional Federal subsidies. It must be remembered that the rich high density routes provide the carriers with a profit cushion which makes service to the leaner routes possible with the maintenance of carrier solvency, so that the profitability criterion for these routes must involve something more than the minimal satisfactory rate of return for the carrier as a whole. Here the Board is acting to protect the source of internal subsidy.
2. The traffic level is not adequate to require competition. Here the Board is, in effect, saying that there is no need for additional competitive service and that the existing carrier's service is adequate to serve the public's convenience and necessity. Looking beyond this statement, the Board is taking the position that the traffic level is not adequate for that route to be sufficiently profitable for all, with additional service by a new carrier. (In a sense, this seems to be the least defensible position in favor of restriction of entry, since the decision to enter the market, once certificated, is presumably made by rational airline management which would not extend into an unprofitable market. This is especially true if there is any loyalty of the market to the established carrier.)

The city pairs which received competitive authorizations because of their fulfillment of the first condition listed above constitute the most important group for analysis to ascertain the extent to which the purposes of the Board were achieved by the awards. These are the city pairs for which the Board sought competition, and from these we can find whether the Board was able to implement its desire for competitive service. Did the existing carrier improve its service in order to meet the competition? Or did it reduce its service offering? Did the new carriers offer comparable service patterns? Were the new carriers able to penetrate the established markets of the existing carriers? Did the total service offering improve? Did the traveling public gain?

The most readily understandable city pairs in this group are those which had but one carrier before the decision to create competitive authorizations and two carriers after the decision. For these, we find that, as measured by the characteristics of the schedule pattern, the public seems to have gained.

There were 328 city pairs which received new first competitive authorizations in the proceedings covered by this study. These are distributed by number of carriers and by intent of the Board as shown in Table X-1. Of these, there were 295 city pairs (lines 2

TABLE X-1

CITY PAIRS WHICH RECEIVED NEW FIRST COMPETITION DISTRIBUTION BY NUMBER OF CARRIERS AND INTENT OF THE BOARD

Number of Carriers			*Intent of the Board*								
New	*Improved*	*Original*	*1 Specific Purposive*	*2 Group Purposive*	*3 Specific Noted*	*4 Group Noted*	*5 Specific Corrective*	*6 Group Corrective*	*7 Mentioned*	*0 No Reference*	*Total*
2	0	0		2	1					3	6
1	0	1	25	33	39	2	4	11	6	170	290
1	1	1	1	2						2	5
2	0	1	11	9				1		1	22
2	1	1	1	3							4
3	0	1	1								1
Total			39	49	40	2	4	12	6	176	328

Source: Appendix One.

and 3) which had one carrier authorized before the decision and two after the decision. In five of these cases, in addition, the original carrier had its authorization improved by the removal of restrictions. Of these 295, there were 26 specifically and purposively made competitive by the Board, and 35 were members of some group of city pairs which were, as a group, purposively made competitive by the Board.

In the case of the 26 specific purposive city pairs, the new carrier was, by September 1957, offering service in 21 of the pairs. The 5 seemingly neglected city pairs included Fort Worth–Nashville, which could receive some service via Dallas (Dallas–Nashville was one of the 21 which were served by the new carrier, in this case, Braniff). Baltimore–Houston, another of the 5, was served by neither the original carrier, Eastern, nor the new carrier, Delta. (However, both carriers served Houston–Washington.) The other 3 (Baltimore–Newport News, Cleveland–Kansas City, and Denver–Washington) continued, as of September, 1957, to be served exclusively by the original carrier. However, in one (Pittsburgh–Portland, Ore.) of the 21, the original carrier discontinued service with the result that, in September, 1957, that city pair was being offered single-plane service by only the new carrier. Thus, the Board's

TABLE X-2

ANNUAL PASSENGERS AND AMOUNT OF SERVICE FOR THE THIRTEEN SPECIFIC PURPOSIVE CITY PAIRS WHICH WERE CERTIFICATED TO AND SERVED BY ONE CARRIER BEFORE THE DECISION AND BY TWO UNRECTRICTED CARRIERS AFTER THE DECISION

		Seats Flown per Week			
		Original Carrier		*New Carrier*	*Both Carriers*
City Pair	*Annual Passengers 1955*	*Sept., 1955*	*Sept., 1957*	*Sept., 1957*	*Sept., 1957*
(*1*)	(*2*)	(*3*)	(*4*)	(*5*)	(*6*)
Baltimore–Norfolk	9,425	480	770	528	1,298
Buffalo–Detroit	36,868	5,892	5,372	2,184	7,556
Buffalo–New York	190,177	13,094	12,206	4,824	17,030
Dallas–Nashville	4,160	2,828	3,200	1,344	4,544
Denver–New York	44,616	10,860	9,470	2,674	12,144
Denver–Salt Lake City	26,741	5,976	5,152	1,848	7,000
Detroit–Philadelphia	73,229	3,654	5,008	2,288	7,296
Kansas City–New York	51,948	15,660	11,991	1,862	13,853
Kansas City–San Francisco	14,768	5,271	4,718	732	5,450
Kansas City–Washington	16,783	4,746	5,942	854	6,796
Newport News–Washington	15,145	2,261	3,102	528	3,630
Norfolk–Washington	61,399	7,588	6,881	1,056	7,937
Reno–San Francisco	102,401	4,840	4,532	1,848	6,380
Total		83,150	78,344	22,570	100,914

Sources: Appendix Two, and *Official Airline Guide.*

TABLE X-3

TRAFFIC PENETRATION OF THE NEW CARRIER FOR THE THIRTEEN SPECIFIC PURPOSIVE CITY PAIRS WHICH WERE CERTIFICATED TO AND SERVED BY ONE CARRIER BEFORE THE DECISION AND TWO UNRESTRICTED CARRIERS AFTER THE DECISION

	Carrier		*New Carrier's Percentage of Both Carriers, Sept., 1957*		
City Pair (*1*)	*Existing* (*2*)	*New* (*3*)	*Seats Flown* (*4*)	*Origin and Destination Traffic Carried* (*5*)	*Months Since Decision Effective* (*6*)
Baltimore–Norfolk	Capital	National	40.7	8.5	8
Buffalo–Detroit	American	Capital	28.9	20.9	22
Buffalo–New York	American	Capital	28.3	28.7	22
Dallas–Nashville	American	Braniff	29.6	32.5	19
Denver–New York	United	TWA	22.0	15.3	20
Denver–Salt Lake City	United	Western	26.4	32.3	20
Detroit–Philadelphia	United	Capital	31.4	46.2	22
Kansas City–New York	TWA	United	13.4	8.3	20
Kansas City–San Francisco	TWA	United	13.4	16.7	20
Kansas City–Washington	TWA	United	12.6	22.4	20
Newport News–Washington	Capital	National	14.5	4.1	8
Norfolk–Washington	Capital	National	13.3	1.7	8
Reno–San Francisco	United	Western	29.0	18.7	20
			22.4	23.0	

Source: Columns (2), (3), and (6), Appendix One; Column (4), Table X-2, columns (5) and (6); Column (5), *Airline Traffic Survey*.

purposive action resulted in the provision of competitive single-plane service in 20 of these 26 markets, in September, 1957.

In 10 of these 20 markets, the original carrier offered fewer seats in September, 1957 than in September, 1955, but the new carrier, although offering fewer seats than the original carrier in 18 of the 20 markets, more than made up the original carrier's decline in all but 2 with the result that for 18 of the markets there was competitive service, and the total number of seats offered by both carriers was greater in September, 1957 than the original carrier had offered 2 years earlier.

In 7 of the 20 city pairs the new carrier was restricted; i.e., was required to stop between or operate beyond the city pair. Tables X-2 and X-3 refer to the remaining 13, where both carriers were unrestricted. Table X-3 shows that in September, 1957 for these 13 city pairs the new carrier offered between 13 and 41 percent of the seats and carried between 2 and 46 percent of the origin and destination passengers.

As might be expected, the variation in the degree of market penetration is much greater than the variation in the percentage of seats flown by the new carrier. There are many reasons for this. Some of these have to do with the nature of the customer relationships enjoyed by the original carrier. That is, for some markets there may be a high degree of loyalty to the original carrier while, for others, the arrival of a new competitor may have been joyfully greeted as a welcome relief. In addition, the comparative marketing effort of the new carrier as well as the length of time since it entered the market helps determine its market share. Also, there are the many factors in addition to number of seats flown which affect the relative quality and attractiveness of the schedule offerings. These include, among other things, aircraft type, time of flights, number of intermediate stops, number of coach flights (and seats), and number of originating and terminating flights (and seats). For example, in September, 1957, (as seen in Table X-3 in the Kansas City–New York market) United, as the new carrier competing with TWA, offered 13.4 percent of the seats but carried only 8.3 percent of the traffic, while in the Kansas City–Washington market, with the same carriers, United, as the new carrier, offered 12.6 percent of the seats but carried 22.4 percent of the passengers. Examination of the schedules discloses what may be important factors in this big difference. The two daily flights (one in each direction) which United offered on the New York–Washington–Kansas City route were nonstop between Washington and Kansas City. These flights also stopped at New York, making them one-stop flights for Kansas City–New York passengers. The other two United flights between New York and Kansas City were four-stop (Chicago, Detroit, Pittsburgh, Philadelphia) coach flights which could not be expected to compete for the terminal-to-terminal traffic against TWA's daily express service which included two nonstop, originating and terminating flights, as well as 13 one-stop and 1 two-stop flights. Thus, in the Kansas City–Washington market, United offered 12.6 percent of the seats, but these were all nonstops and constituted 38.7 percent of the nonstop seats. In the Kansas City–New York market, United's service offering had no nonstops and was far less competitive. This, no doubt, accounts for a large measure of the difference in the carriers' relative market shares as seen in Table X-3. Similar analyses could be applied to help account for much of the other variation in market penetration as noted in Table X-3. In any event, the new carriers did move into these markets in varying degrees, and they captured market shares which were clearly related to the amount of their service and the time elapsed since the decision. Table X-3 gives no indication that the large carriers were the more efficient competitors. Indeed, the highest values for percentage of seats flown and for percentage of traffic carried were scored by smaller carriers. TWA and United, the only two Big Four carriers represented on the Tables as new carriers, did not move into these new markets with the speed of these smaller carriers. Statistical generalization from this small group to other city pairs is not warranted. There are no other city pairs with the characteristics of these thirteen. They are not a representative sample of some large groups of city pairs. However, their experience may provide useful insights into carrier attitudes and behavior.

It is clear that the Board's desire for competitive service was essentially realized in this group of city pairs. Of the twenty-six city pairs, where one new carrier was added to one original carrier, with the expressed intent of the Board to create competition, the new carrier offered service, in September 1957, in all but five. Of the twenty-one in which the new carrier offered service, that carrier was restricted [2] in eight. Of the remaining thirteen, only one experienced a decrease in the number of seats available to the traveling public as seen in Columns (3) and (6) of Table X-2. For the other twelve city pairs, the number of seats available increased, and Table X-3 shows the participation of the new carrier in both the service and the traffic.

For 185 of the 295 city pairs which had one carrier before the decision and in which one carrier was added, the new carrier's authority was unrestricted or, if restricted, was not more restricted than that of the original carrier. That is, the new carrier's authority was "equivalent or better." For these decisions, regardless of the intent of the Board, the decision of the carrier to inaugurate service or not to inaugurate service provides an illuminating and use-

TABLE X-4

1957 SERVICE BY THE NEW CARRIER AS RELATED TO 1955 TRAFFIC LEVEL AND INTENT OF THE BOARD FOR THE 185 CITY PAIRS WITH ONE CARRIER BEFORE THE DECISION AND WITH A NEW SECOND CARRIER HAVING EQUIVALENT OR BETTER AUTHORIZATION AFTER THE DECISION

	Number of City Pairs			*Number of City Pairs Served and Not Served as Related to 1955 Traffic Level (Annual Passengers)*									
				Under 2,500		*2,500 but Less than 5,000*		*5,000 but Less than 7,500*		*7,500 but Less than 10,000*		*10,000 and Over*	
Intent of the Board	*Total*	*Served*	*Not Served*	*Served*	*Not Served*	*Served*	*Not Served*	*Served*	*Not Served*	*Served*	*Not Served*	*Served*	*Not Served*
1	18	13	5	0	3	1	0	0	1	1	0	11	1
2	33	12	21	6	16	0	4	3	0	2	1	1	0
3	31	17	14	5	13	1	0	2	1	1	0	8	0
4	0	0	0										
5	4	0	4	0	3	0	1						
6	11	5	6	1	6	4	0						
7	1	1	0			1	0						
0	87	16	71	7	61	1	7	3	2	2	1	3	0
Total	185	64	121	19	102	8	12	8	4	6	2	23	1

Source: Appendices One, Two, and *Official Airline Guide.*

ful insight into the effect of the size of the market in the collective judgments of airline managements. As we have seen before, especially in Chapter VIII, the Civil Aeronautics Board, as well as the spokesmen for carriers, municipalities, and other parties to route proceedings, has not been able, definitely and firmly, to identify that traffic level for which competitive single-plane service should be considered to be needed and justified. Rather this point has, in CAB hearings, traditionally been the subject of *ad hoc* arguments involving conflicting traffic standards. These 185 city pairs provide at least a partial answer to this question, since, in these cases, the carriers had the authority to enter the market on an equivalent basis, and, presumably, made their decision on some rational basis, in which the traffic level would seem to have to play an important role.

The 185 city pairs, as distributed with respect to Board intent, 1955 traffic, and 1957 service by the new carrier, are shown in Table X-4. Although 16 percent of the city pairs in the lowest traffic level group and 40 percent of the city pairs with traffic between 2,500 and 5,000 annual origin and destination passengers were served by the new carrier, this must not be interpreted to mean that the carrier action was necessarily determined by the traffic level for that city pair. Rather, it is clear that these low-traffic city pairs were, for the most part, served because they fell conveniently on routes which were served for other reasons. For example, Houston–Pensacola with only 1,027 1955 passengers was served on the flight between Jacksonville and Houston which stopped at several relatively low traffic points between Jacksonville and New Orleans. Surely origin and destination traffic between Houston and Pensacola was not controlling in National's decision to extend this flight from New Orleans to Houston, when it received the New Orleans–Houston extension.

At the other end of the Table, where traffic was high, service was inaugurated. For the last group, with pairs ranging from 11,000 to 200,000 passengers, all but one (Denver–Washington, with 17,000) were served by the new carrier in September 1957. Of course, O and D traffic is not the sole factor in the carriers' decisions to serve. Cities which develop over 10,000 passengers with each other may be expected to develop sizeable traffic with other points.

TABLE X-5

1957 SERVICE BY THE NEW CARRIER AS RELATED TO 1955 TRAFFIC LEVEL AND INTENT OF THE BOARD FOR THE 50 CITY PAIRS WITH TWO CARRIERS BEFORE THE DECISION AND WITH A NEW THIRD CARRIER HAVING EQUIVALENT OR BETTER AUTHORIZATION AFTER THE DECISION

	Number of City Pairs			*Number of City Pairs Served and Not Served as Related to 1955 Traffic Level (Annual Passengers)*									
				Under 2,500		*2,500 but Less than 5,000*		*5,000 but Less than 7,500*		*7,500 but Less than 10,000*		*10,000 and Over*	
Intent of the Board	*Total*	*Served*	*Not Served*	*Served*	*Not Served*	*Served*	*Not Served*	*Served*	*Not Served*	*Served*	*Not Served*	*Served*	*Not Served*
1	32	19	13	1	4	2	0	2	2	1	3	13	4
2	4	0	4	0	3	0	1						
3	2	2	0					1	0			1	0
4	1	1	0									1	0
5	0	0	0										
6	1	0	1	0	1								
7	0	0	0										
0	10	3	7	1	3	0	2	0	1	0	1	2	0
Total	50	25	25	2	11	2	3	3	3	1	4	17	4

Source: Appendices One, Two, and *Official Airline Guide.*

Table X-4 suggests that city pairs with more than 10,000 annual origin and destination passengers and authorized to only one carrier have, by the criterion of carrier decision, been considered large enough to receive competition. Smaller traffic generators may well be able to support competition because of their location, with respect to other points on the carriers' routes, but somewhere in the vicinity of 10,000 passengers, the second carrier generally finds it advisable to try to compete in the market.

A somewhat similar approach may be used to examine the traffic level at which three-carrier competitive service is inaugurated. There were fifty city pairs which had two carriers before the decision and to which a third carrier was added with authority to offer service equivalent to the best authorized for the original carriers. Again, as seen in Table X-5, when the 1955 traffic level exceeded 10,000 origin and destination passengers, the new carrier tended to offer service. The four city pairs which, as indicated in Table X-5 were not served by the new carrier although their traffic exceeded 10,000 passengers, involved Northeast's new authorizations to Florida cities. These city pairs showed 1955 traffic levels of 13,000 for Jacksonville–Washington, 16,000 for Tampa–Washington, 52,000 for Jacksonville–New York and 79,000 for Miami–Tampa. These city pairs have since been served by Northeast, and that carrier's slowness in inaugurating service was doubtless due to both the highly seasonal nature of the traffic in those markets and the equipment and personnel problems which faced that carrier as it grew cataclysmically from an operation which was, in the words of the Board, comparable in many respects to that of the larger local service carriers.

Clearly, for those city pairs which received new or improved competitive awards, regardless of the intent of the Board, the new carrier tended to inaugurate the service on those city pairs which had over 10,000 annual origin and destination passengers in 1955, at approximately the time of the decision. Naturally there are many pairs with less origin and destination traffic which, for other reasons, did receive the new service. However, above 10,000 passengers, the inauguration of the service seems to occur with a high degree of dependability.

This means that the Civil Aeronautics Board can effectively

increase the number of active competitors as well as the number of authorized competitors on the relatively heavily traveled routes. These high density routes are sufficiently attractive to the carriers so that, when authorized, they do expand into these routes, even though there may be one or more carriers already offering full complements of service.

Possibly this means also that, when the Board wishes to obtain improved service for a smaller market it may find it more expedient and effective to resort to an adequacy of service investigation rather than to authorize competitive service which may or may not be implemented.

THE SUBSIDY DILEMMA

Clearly, the long-haul high density routes are profitable and the high density points are desirable additions to the carriers' exist-

TABLE X-6

COMPARISON OF ORIGIN AND DESTINATION PASSENGER LOAD FACTORS OF THE ORIGINAL CARRIER, SEPTEMBER, 1955 *vs.* SEPTEMBER, 1957 FOR THE THIRTEEN CITY PAIRS OF TABLES X-2 AND X-3

(*All data refer to the original carrier only.*)

	Sept., 1955			*Sept., 1957*		
	Average Weekly		*O and D Passenger Load Factor (in percent)*	*Average Weekly*		*O and D Passenger Load Factor (in percent)*
City Pair (*1*)	*Seats* (*2*)	*Passengers* (*3*)	(*4*)	*Seats* (*5*)	*Passengers* (*6*)	(*7*)
Baltimore–Norfolk	480	180	37.5	770	81	10.5
Buffalo–Detroit	5,892	799	13.6	5,372	702	13.1
Buffalo–New York	13,094	4,324	33.0	12,206	4,144	34.0
Dallas–Nashville	2,828	86	3.0	3,200	72	2.3
Denver–New York	10,860	938	8.6	9,470	996	10.5
Denver–Salt Lake City	5,976	506	8.5	5,152	490	9.5
Detroit–Philadelphia	3,654	1,790	49.0	5,008	846	16.9
Kansas City–New York	15,660	1,010	6.5	11,991	1,088	9.1
Kansas City–San Francisco	5,271	283	5.4	4,718	282	6.0
Kansas City–Washington	4,746	316	6.7	5,942	312	5.3
Newport News–Washington	2,261	304	13.4	3,102	320	10.3
Norfolk–Washington	7,588	1,166	15.4	6,881	1,332	19.4
Reno–San Francisco	4,840	2,144	44.3	4,532	2,048	45.2
	83,150	13,846	16.7	78,344	12,713	16.2

Sources: Columns (2) and (5), *Official Airline Guide;* Columns (3) and (6), *Airline Traffic Survey;* Column (4) is column (3) divided by column (2); Column (7) is column (6) divided by column (5).

TABLE X-7

COMPARISON OF ORIGIN AND DESTINATION PASSENGER LOAD FACTORS: SEPTEMBER, 1955 FOR THE ORIGINAL CARRIER AND SEPTEMBER, 1957 FOR THE ORIGINAL AND NEWLY ADDED CARRIERS FOR THE THIRTEEN CITY PAIRS OF TABLE X-6

City Pair	Original Carrier Sept., 1955 O and D Passenger Load Factor (in percent)	Both Carriers Sept., 1957 Average Weekly		Both Carriers Sept., 1957 O and D Passenger Load Factor (in percent)
		Seats	Passengers	
(1)	(2)	(3)	(4)	(5)
Baltimore–Norfolk	37.5	1,298	88	6.8
Buffalo–Detroit	13.6	7,556	886	11.7
Buffalo–New York	33.0	17,030	5,815	34.1
Dallas–Nashville	3.0	4,544	106	2.3
Denver–New York	8.6	12,144	1,176	9.7
Denver–Salt Lake City	8.5	7,000	724	10.3
Detroit–Philadelphia	49.0	7,296	1,573	21.6
Kansas City–New York	6.5	13,853	1,186	8.6
Kansas City–San Francisco	5.4	5,450	339	6.2
Kansas City–Washington	6.7	6,796	403	5.9
Newport News–Washington	13.4	3,630	333	9.2
Norfolk–Washington	15.4	7,937	1,356	17.1
Reno–San Francisco	44.3	6,380	2,520	39.5
	16.7	100,914	16,505	16.4

Sources: Column (2) is column (4) of Table X-6; Column (3), *Official Airline Guide;* Column (4), *Airline Traffic Survey;* Column (5) is column (4) divided by column (3).

ing routes in that they strengthen the carriers' whole route patterns. However, as new carriers move into the high density routes as competitors, they may tend to drive down the profitability of these markets and make it more difficult for the original carriers to earn relatively high profits on these routes. Under the present system of regulation which requires that the carriers serve less dense, unprofitable markets, such relatively high profits from the rich routes are essential to maintain carrier solvency. Table X-6 indicates that the origin and destination passenger load factors for the original carriers serving the 13 city pairs of Tables X-2 and X-3 have moved in both directions. In 7 of the 13 city pairs, this measure of capacity utilization has increased for the original carrier in the face of new competition. However, in all of these cases of increased origin and destination passenger load factor for the original carrier, the original carrier reduced its service offering over the period, and, in one of the city pairs, Kansas City–New York, the new carrier did not make up for the decrease in the original carrier's offering, with the result that, for that city pair, although the new carrier did inaugurate service, the service available to the public actually decreased, as seen in Table X-2.

Comparison of column (3) of Table X-6 with column (4) of Table X-7 shows that the number of origin and destination passengers was higher in September 1957 than in September 1955 for all but Baltimore–Norfolk and Detroit–Philadelphia. For the thirteen city pairs, the total weekly traffic increased from 13,846 passengers for the original carrier in September 1955 to 16,505 passengers for both carriers in September 1957. Also, the new carrier, which offered 22.4 percent of the total seats in September 1957, carried 23.0 percent of these passengers.

The "origin and destination (O and D) passenger load factor" for a carrier may be defined as the number of origin and destination passengers carried between two points expressed as a percentage of the seats flown between those two points. This, although similar to the more general definition of "load factor" is not so precise a measure of aircraft capacity utilization, but it can be computed from published data, and it does relate specifically to a unique city pair. Although, as a measure of capacity ulitization, it suffers from severe limitations arising from the variability in the number of passengers to and from points located between and beyond the cities in question, it nevertheless provides useful insights into the competitive history of the various carriers.

The sums over the thirteen pairs, as given in the totals in Tables X-6 and X-7 represent the traffic and schedule data for hypothetical composite "original" and "combined" carriers respectively. These sums show that the actual O and D passenger load factor of the composite "combined" carrier (original plus new—treated as a unit) over all thirteen city pairs in 1957 was 16.4 percent, as compared to the 16.7 percent enjoyed by the composite original carrier in September 1955. The composite original carrier's comparable load factor figure in 1957 had decreased to 16.2 percent. Behind this load factor comparison is the change in the amount of service offered. The composite original carrier reduced its offering from 83,150 weekly seats in September 1955 to 78,344 seats in September 1957, while the new carrier more than made up the slack by offering 22,570 seats for a total of 100,914. Therefore, in sum, the result was that the number of seats offered increased slightly more than did the number of passengers, yielding a lower O and D load factor and perhaps, therefore, better space availability for the public.

The mixed nature of the shifts among the thirteen city pairs in most of the quantities referred to above suggest that generalizations from totals may be of limited usefulness. However, within this limitation, the totals suggest that when a new competitor was added to a monopolistic route in stage four of its life cycle (enough passengers to make the original carrier eager to protect the market, and at the same time, to cause other carriers to seek to enter the market), the new carrier entered the market usually within a year, and often sooner. The new carrier offered a lesser amount of service than did the original carrier, and although the original carrier cut its service by a significant amount, the total service was nevertheless greater than before. The new carrier seemed able to capture a share of the market that was roughly related to its share of the total number of seats offered and to the time elapsed since the new authorization became effective. The original carrier decreased his service offering, but his traffic loss was relatively greater with the result that his O and D load factor declined from 16.7 percent to 16.2 percent. The new carrier's O and D load factor was 16.8 percent.

The Civil Aeronautics Board must, as it has already recognized (e.g., the Denver–Kansas City route in the *Denver Service Case,* where Continental's monopoly was maintained), view the problem of determination of the optimum amount of competition on a route as a function of the importance of that route's excess profitability to the overall profitability of the existing carrier or carriers on that route. The question of carrier self-sufficiency cannot be ignored in the dispensing of new competitive route awards as long as the low traffic routes are required to be served and, thus, internally subsidized by the individual carriers. While it is true that there has been an increasing tendency for some of the trunklines to seek to suspend service to certain small cities, this will, in all probability not be carried far enough to eliminate internal subsidy.

One consequence of this conclusion is that the rich routes

served exclusively by the smaller carriers will necessarily tend to receive competitive authorizations fewer and later than would be the case if they were served by larger carriers.[3] This handicap to the cities and travelers on these routes could not have been avoided in the past or even in the present, but, for the future, their outlook is brightened by the expansion of the smaller carriers into more of the rich markets thereby decreasing their dependence on the relatively few rich markets to which they had previously been limited. The continuance of this selective carrier growth, described in Chapter IX, coupled with the general growth of air traffic, promises eventually to equalize the treatment of the various cities and routes with respect to their service by competitive carriers.

The dilemma with respect to the desirability of competition on the rich routes may be summed up as follows. The rich routes can support competition. New carriers are eager to be certificated to serve them, and, once certificated, they expand their operations and offer the service. This competition is highly desirable for the public and, as in any other industry, vigorous competition, legally and ethically pursued, may be expected to redound to the benefit of the customers in those markets. The dilemma arises from the fact that the carriers also serve less profitable routes and, indeed, are legally required to serve these poorer markets even though these markets may not be able to be served on a break-even basis. This creates a need for offsetting profits from the relatively richer routes. However, new competition on these rich routes may reduce their profitability and tend to shrink these offsetting profits.

Now, with this increase in competitive awards on the more heavily traveled routes, the certificated carriers are, in effect, doing to one another exactly what they so bitterly objected to in the case of the irregular carriers of the first postwar decade. That is, they are skimming each other's cream, and the carriers originally serving the routes fear that their ability successfully to effectuate this internal subsidization may be threatened.

It is difficult at this time to ascertain whether this process has progressed in such a way that it has seriously weakened any of the carriers in this respect. Of course, the extent to which it has affected the individual carriers has varied widely among carriers with respect to both the burdens and the gains, as has been described in detail in Chapters VIII and IX. However, for the industry as a whole, present indications are that the Civil Aeronautics Board has not been unduly liberal in the issuance of competitive certificates of convenience and necessity. The data presented in Tables X-6 and X-7 suggest that, for these markets, the original carriers have not suffered substantially. Perhaps, whatever profit deterioration they may have suffered, in the markets which they served originally, has been more or less compensated by their gains in the markets to which they were given access. Indeed, the data available for this study suggest that the Board's rate of issuance of competitive awards may have kept pace with traffic growth so that it could allow the public to share in the benefits derived from the general growth in air traffic by having more and more competition made available, while, at the same time, this traffic growth made it possible for the carriers to accept this new competition while continuing to operate as private enterprises, free of subsidy.

It is to be hoped, of course, that traffic will grow and technology improve to the extent that more and more of the thinner routes become profitable. Perhaps this will occur when the development of new equipment, such as VTOL (vertical takeoff and landing) or, at least, STOL (short takeoff and landing) aircraft on a truly economic basis ushers in another great revolution in air travel. Then the progressive decrease in the profit cushion will be offset by a decreasing need for subsidization, either internal or governmental.

If this does not happen, or if it does not happen fast enough, the whole question of service to the smaller traffic points must be examined. One solution is to permit the trunklines to suspend service at more and more of these points and to certificate them to the Federally subsidized local service carriers. This solution, which has been tried in many recent cases, results in decreasing the amount of single-carrier (and possible single-plane) service available to the traveling public. While the concept of a feeder line system, feeding passengers into the trunkline points, may have some merit, there is no indication that it is in the public interest to raise the minimum standards for the size and traffic potential of the points in the trunkline system. With connecting service, the passengers to and from these smaller points would at best be deprived of much of the time savings which the higher and higher aircraft speeds are providing to air passengers in general.

On the other hand, the desirability of keeping these smaller points on the trunkline routes must not be permitted to prevent the certification of competition on the richer routes. The solution may well be in the direct subsidization of these individual low traffic points by the government, either Federal or state. As noted in Chapter VIII, the subsidization of such service by the government may be far more equitable in terms of sources of funds than the involuntary internal subsidization by the customers on the richer routes.

One solution which has been put forward and which may see some development in the near future is the decrease in competition on the rich routes as a result of merger. The argument for this solution is that the new jet aircraft, with their huge passenger-mile generation capacity, make competition, especially multi-carrier competition, less economically feasible and less important to the public than heretofore. This merger solution would seem to make internal subsidy more palatable and more manageable for the surviving carriers, but one of the current merger proposals, as of early 1961, nevertheless stipulates the dropping of a sizeable number of small points from the routes of the weaker carrier. The dropping of the points is far preferable to the merger. They can easily be put back at some later date when conditions permit, but mergers tend to be irreversible. The merger solution, though perhaps predestined in some degree, is a perilous one. It would be far preferable for weak points or routes to revert to direct subsidy, if the only alternative is to be the preservation of internal subsidy at the cost of mergers significantly reducing the amount of competition available on those air routes which can readily support competitive carriers. One of the consequences of such a decrease in competition would, of course, be a requirement for more direct regulatory policing by the Board.

CONCLUSION

It is clear that both competition and direct regulation can, in the appropriate circumstances, be substituted one for the other, as mechanisms for seeking to serve the public good in the economic phases of the air transportation industry. The difficult problem, and that which is yet unresolved, is the determination of the optimum blend of these two mechanisms. Whether the current blend is viable is not yet clear. There are those who argue for modification in both directions. What is clear is that some blend is superior to the exclusive use of one or the other mechanism; i.e., a single monopoly carrier for the nation, or alternatively, unrestricted competition. Indeed, the industry and its customers and the nation are fortunate that competition in air transport is feasible and that, therefore, it is not necessary for the industry to be guided by the ill-defined and generally unsatisfactory criteria which assume so much importance in the regulation of the noncompetitive public utility industries. That is, because of the existence of competition and of competitive yardsticks, the industry has been—and can continue to be—less dependent upon arbitrary standards as, among others, some rate-of-return standard applied to some concept of value of assets all computed on the basis of what may be capricious and irrational cost allocations. Recent CAB concern about rate-of-return may presage a shift of the balance toward less competition and more regulation. In any event, the existence of competition can and does give the industry a far more desirable structure of prices, costs, and profits as well as more objective standards for judging efficiencies, service standards, and management performance. For this among other reasons, competition should be preserved and strengthened, and any steps which may tend to decrease the amount or effectiveness of competition should be avoided if at all possible.

The optimum blend of competition and regulation is a dynamic quantity. Its movement through the transition from reciprocating engine to jet to supersonic equipment as well as to short and vertical takeoff equipment with its repercussions on alternative modes of surface travel cannot be predicted. However it is to be hoped that the Civil Aeronautics Board, in making its decisions about competition and the many related economic and financial problems, will as a general policy and whenever feasible, act to preserve and strengthen rather than weaken competition in the air transportation industry.

Notes

I: INTRODUCTION AND EARLY HISTORY

1. *The Civil Aeronautics Act of 1938,* Title I, Section 2. *Aeronautical Statutes and Related Material,* Revised June 1, 1954, Civil Aeronautics Board, Washington, D.C., pp. 10–11. *The Federal Aviation Act of 1958,* Public Law 85-726, August 23, 1958, in Title II, continued the Civil Aeronautics Board and its economic regulatory functions by restating the appropriate sections of the 1938 Act. The quotation given above appears in Section 102 of the 1958 Act.

2. Excluding Slick Airways and AAXICO Airlines which, while authorized, are not now operating scheduled cargo service.

3. *Report of the Antitrust Subcommittee (Subcommittee No. 5) of the Committee on the Judiciary, House of Representatives, Eighty-fifth Congress, first session, Pursuant to H. Res. 107 . . . on Airlines, Washington 1957* (hereafter referred to as the *Celler Committee Report*), p. 8 ff.

4. For a comprehensive history of this early period, see Gilbert Goodman, *Government Policy Toward Commercial Aviation,* New York, King's Crown Press, 1934.

5. *Annual Report of the Civil Aeronautics Board,* 1959.

6. Aaron J. Gellman, "The Regulation of Competition in United States Domestic Air Transportation: A Judicial Survey and Analysis," *Journal of Air Law and Commerce,* Vol. 24, No. 4 (Autumn, 1957), p. 412.

7. Col. Edgar S. Garrell, President, Air Transport Association, *Hearings on H.R. 5234, Seventy-fourth Congress, first session* (1937), p. 66, cited in *Celler Committee Report,* p. 14.

8. Stanley Gewirtz, Executive Assistant to the President, Air Transport Association, *Hearings Before the Antitrust Subcommittee (Subcommittee No. 5) of the Committee on the Judiciary, House of Representatives, Eighty-fourth Congress, second session, 1956* (hereafter referred to as the *Celler Committee Hearings*), III, 1539.

9. *Hearings before a Subcommittee of the Select Committee on Small Business, United States Senate, Eighty-third Congress, first session (1953) on Future of Irregular Airlines in United States Air Transportation Industry* (hereafter referred to as *Thye Committee Irregular Airlines Hearings*), Testimony of Mr. Ryan, p. 14.

10. *Celler Committee Hearings,* I, 418, Letter from Mr. Rizley to Congressman Celler dated November 8, 1955.

11. "Memorandum Submitted by Senator Joseph C. O'Mahoney with Respect to the Right of Entry in Air Transportation Under the Civil Aeronautics Act," *Celler Committee Hearings,* II, 923–41.

12. *Ibid.,* p. 926.
13. *Ibid.,* p. 925 ff.
14. *Thye Committee Irregular Airlines Hearings,* p. 186.
15. *Celler Committee Report,* p. 14.

II: REGULATION OF THE DOMESTIC AIRLINES

1. Irston R. Barnes, *The Economics of Public Utility Regulation,* New York, Crofts, 1942, p. 173.

2. *Ibid.,* p. 151.

3. *Report of the Antitrust Subcommittee (Subcommittee No. 5) of the Committee on the Judiciary, House of Representatives, Eighty-fifth Congress, first session, Pursuant to H. Res. 107 . . . on Airlines, Washington 1957* (hereafter referred to as the *Celler Committee Report*), pp. 2–7. *Hearings Before the Antitrust Subcommittee (Subcommittee No. 5) of the Committee on the Judiciary, House of Representatives, Eighty-fourth Congress, second session, 1956* (hereafter referred to as the *Celler Committee Hearings*), Testimony of Professor Marver H. Bernstein, pp. 59–76. Testimony of Professor Louis B. Schwartz, pp. 89–107. *Civil Air Policy,* The President's Air Coordinating Committee, Government Printing Office, Washington, D.C., May, 1954, p. 8.

4. *Celler Committee Report,* p. 2.

5. *Hearings before a Subcommittee of the Select Committee on Small Business, United States Senate, Eighty-third Congress, first session (1953) on Future of Irregular Airlines in United States Air Transportation Industry* (hereafter referred to as *Thye Committee Irregular Airlines Hearings*), Testimony of Warren Lee Pierson, Chairman of the Board of TWA, p. 77.

6. *Ibid.,* Testimony of George E. Hatch, Western Regional Sales Manager of Northwest Airlines, Inc., p. 87.

7. *Ibid.,* Testimony of Joseph H. Fitzgerald, Director of the Alaska Office of the CAB, p. 27.

8. *Celler Committee Report,* pp. 70–71.

9. *Civil Aeronautics Act of 1938,* Titles V and VI, *Aeronautical Statutes and Related Material,* Revised June 1, 1954, Civil Aeronautics Board, Washington, D.C., pp. 44–53.

10. *Annual Report of the Civil Aeronautics Board,* 1959, p. 1.

11. Aaron J. Gellman, "The Regulation of Competition in United States Domestic Air Transportation: A Judicial Survey and Analysis," *Journal of Air Law and Commerce,* Vol. 24, No. 4 (Autumn, 1957), p. 414.

12. 2 CAB 447, 480 (1941).

13. *Celler Committee Hearings,* I, 153.

14. *Aeronautical Statutes and Related Materials,* Revised June, 1954, Civil Aeronautics Board, Washington, D.C., pp. 10–11, restated with minor changes in *Federal Aviation Act of 1958,* Section 102.

15. The section number is the same in both the 1938 and 1958 Acts.

III: THE CONCEPT OF COMPETITION

1. Corwin D. Edwards, *Maintaining Competition,* New York, McGraw-Hill, 1949, pp. 1–2.

2. *Ibid.,* p. 6.

3. *Ibid.,* pp. 8–9.

4. *Report of the Antitrust Subcommittee (Subcommittee No. 5) of the Committee on the Judiciary, House of Representatives, Eighty-fifth Congress, first session, Pursuant to H. Res. 107 . . . on Airlines, Washington 1957* (hereafter referred to as the *Celler Committee Report*), p. 2.

5. Section 2.

6. *Transcontinental and Western Air, Inc., et al.—Additional North–South California Services,* 4 CAB 373, 374 (1943).

7. *Materials Relative to Competition in the Regulated Civil Aviation Industry,* transmitted by the Civil Aeronautics Board to the Select Committee on Small Business, United States Senate, April 18, 1956, Government Printing Office, Washington, D.C., 1956. Letter from Mr. Rizley to Senator Sparkman transmitting replies of the CAB to the Committee's questions, December 14, 1955, p. 9.

8. F. W. Gill and G. L. Bates, *Airline Competition,* Graduate School of Business Administration, Harvard University, Boston, 1949. Also *Competition Among Domestic Air Carriers,* Civil Aeronautics Board, Washington, D.C., now issued by Air Transport Association, Washington, D.C.

9. *Competition Among Domestic Trunk Air Carriers,* Civil Aeronautics Board, Office of Carrier Accounts and Statistics, Washington, D.C., September 1954, Foreword.

10. Gill and Bates, *Airline Competition,* p. 23.

11. *Ibid.,* p. 23 n.

12. *Ibid.,* p. 23.

IV: FORMS OF AIRLINE COMPETITION

1. *Civil Air Policy,* The President's Air Coordinating Committee, Government Printing Office, Washington, D.C., May, 1954, p. 1.

2. F. W. Gill and G. L. Bates, *Airline Competition,* Graduate School of Business Administration, Harvard University, Boston, 1949, p. 41.

3. *Ibid.,* p. 518.

4. *Ibid.,* p. 446.

5. TWA, American, Continental, North American (later Trans American), United, and Western were original applicants. Capital and Braniff became parties by direction of the Board. In the *Dallas to the West Case,* Docket No. 7596 *et al.,* there were nine original applicants: American, Braniff, California Eastern, Continental, Delta, Eastern, National, Trans American, and Western, and in later stages of the case, Bonanza, Pacific, Trans-Texas, and Slick participated.

6. Civil Aeronautics Board Order No. E-10645, *The New York–Florida Case,* Docket No. 3051, *et al.,* dated September 28, 1956, page 31 (mimeographed decision).

7. Paul W. Cherington, *Airline Price Policy,* Graduate School of Business Administration, Harvard University, Boston, 1958, pp. 189, 340.

8. *Ibid.,* pp. 300, 437, 439.

9. Paul M. Sweezy, "Demand Under Conditions of Oligopoly," *Journal of Political Economy,* XLVII (1939), pp. 568–73.

10. Cherington, *Airline Price Policy,* pp. 453, 455.

11. *Ibid.,* p. 453.

12. Certificate of Public Convenience and Necessity, Eastern Air Lines, Inc., Route No. 6, as given in *The New York–Florida Case.*

13. *Preliminary Report on the Domestic Passenger Fare Structure Based on a Sampling of Individual Fares,* Prepared by the Commercial Rates Section, Rates Division, Bureau of Air Operations, Civil Aeronautics Board, June 7, 1954, p. A-1.

14. Air Traffic Conference of America, *Trade Practice Manual,* p. 92, as quoted in William L. Grossman, *Air Passenger Traffic,* Brooklyn, New York, Remsen Press Division, Chemical Publishing Co., Inc., 1947. This fifteen day advance notice is voluntary. The Board, in the *Air Freight Tariff Agreement Case,* Docket No. 2719, Decided August 23, 1951, refused to permit it to be compulsory.

15. *The Role of Competition in Commercial Air Transportation,* Report of the Civil Aeronautics Board submitted to the Subcommittee on Monopoly of the

Select Committee on Small Business, United States Senate, November 24, 1952, Government Printing Office, Washington, D.C., 1952, p. 15.

16. Gill and Bates, *Airline Competition,* pp. 448–49, Appendix D.

17. *Preliminary Report on the Domestic Passenger Fare Structure,* CAB staff study, June 7, 1954, p. 15.

18. This case is discussed in great detail in Cherington, *Airline Price Policy,* pp. 157–58, 176–79.

19. *Ibid.,* pp. 415–16.

20. *The Role of Competition in Commercial Air Transportation,* pp. 12–13.

21. New York *Times,* April 5, 1957.

22. *Hearings Before the Antitrust Subcommittee (Subcommittee No. 5) of the Committee on the Judiciary, House of Representatives, Eighty-fourth Congress, second session, 1956* (hereafter referred to as the *Celler Committee Hearings*), III, 1516.

23. *Ibid.,* p. 1515.

24. Gill and Bates, *Airline Competition,* Chapter 2.

25. John H. Frederick, *Commercial Air Transportation,* Homewood, Illinois, Richard D. Irwin, Inc., 1955, 4th Edition, p. 14.

26. *Celler Committee Hearings,* Testimony of Stanley Gewirtz, III, 1998–1999.

27. See Gill and Bates, *Airline Competition,* pp. 30–35. They conclude that the introduction of competition does not demonstrably develop traffic.

28. *Detroit–Washington Service Case,* Docket No. 679, *et al.,* Report of Examiner Edward T. Stodola, p. 78 n.

29. *Materials Relative to Competition in the Civil Aviation Industry,* transmitted by the Civil Aeronautics Board to the Select Committee on Small Business, United States Senate, April 18, 1956, Government Printing Office, Washington, D.C., 1956, p. 68.

V: METHODS FOR CREATING AND CONTROLLING COMPETITION

1. It will be recalled that this Act was in large part restated in the Federal Aviation Act of 1958. Unless otherwise noted in this text, the statements referred to are essentially identical in both Acts.

2. This was uniformly true until the decision in the *Large Irregular Carrier Investigation,* Docket No. 5132, decided January 28, 1959.

3. *Annual Report of the Civil Aeronautics Board,* 1956, p. 42.

4. *Hearings before a Subcommittee of the Select Committee on Small Business, United States Senate, Eighty-third Congress, first session (1953) on Future of Irregular Airlines in United States Air Transportation Industry* (hereafter referred to as *Thye Committee Irregular Airlines Hearings*), Testimony of Mr. Ryan, p. 14.

5. Section 102 of the Federal Aviation Act of 1958.

6. *Civil Air Policy,* The President's Air Coordinating Committee, Government Printing Office, Washington, D.C., May, 1954, p. 19.

7. *American Export Airlines, Certificate of Public Convenience and Necessity,* 2 CAB 16 (1940) and *All American Aviation, Certificate of Public Convenience and Necessity,* 2 CAB 133 (1940).

8. *Delta Air Corporation et al.,* 2 CAB 447, 480 (1941).

9. *Report of the Antitrust Subcommittee (Subcommittee No. 5) of the Committee on the Judiciary, House of Representatives, Eighty-fifth Congress, first session, Pursuant to H. Res. 107 . . . on Airlines, Washington 1957* (hereafter referred to as the *Celler Committee Report*), Statement of Robert R. Nathan, p. 5.

10. New York *Times,* July 17, 1958.

11. Adam Smith, *The Wealth of Nations,* New York, Random House, 1937, p. 128.

12. *Civil Air Policy,* p. 18.

13. *Materials Relative to Competition in the Regulated Civil Aviation Industry,* transmitted by the Civil Aeronautics Board to the Select Committee on Small Business, United States Senate, April 18, 1956, Government Printing Office, Washington, D.C., 1956. Letter from Mr. Rizley to Senator Sparkman transmitting replies of the CAB to the Committee's questions, December 14, 1955, p. 9. Also Harold D. Koontz, "Domestic Airlines Self-Sufficiency: A Problem of Route Structure," *American Economic Review,* March 1952, pp. 103–14.

14. Civil Aeronautics Board Order No. E-10645, *New York–Florida Case,* Docket No. 3051, *et al.,* dated September 28, 1956, p. 9 (mimeographed decision).

15. Civil Aeronautics Board Order No. E-9735, *Denver Service Case,* Docket No. 1841, *et al.,* dated November 14, 1955, pp. 3–5 (mimeographed decision).

16. Docket No. 7984, *et al.*

17. Civil Aeronautics Board Order No. E-13132, dated November 4, 1958. defines the scope of the case.

18. Civil Aeronautics Board Order No. E-10884, *New York–Florida Case,* Docket No. 3051, *et al.,* Supplemental Opinion and Order on Reconsideration, dated December 21, 1956, p. 12 (mimeographed decision).

19. Civil Aeronautics Board Order No. E-14629, *Toledo Adequacy of Service Investigation,* Docket No. 8851, dated November 10, 1959, pp. 1–7 (mimeographed decision) and Order, p. 1.

20. Civil Aeronautics Board Press release of January 26, 1960.

21. Civil Aeronautics Board Order No. E-9915, *Southwest–Northeast Service Case,* Docket No. 2355, *et al.,* Supplemental Opinion and Order on Reconsideration, dated January 16, 1956, p. 7 (mimeographed decision).

22. Civil Aeronautics Board Order No. E-9758, *Southwest–Northeast Service Case,* Docket No. 2355, *et al.,* dated November 21, 1955, p. 19 (mimeographed decision).

23. *Denver Service Case,* Order no. E-9735, p. 3 n.

24. Civil Aeronautics Board Order No. E-9537, *New York–Chicago Service Case,* Docket No. 986, *et al.,* dated September 1, 1955, p. 12 (mimeographed decision).

25. *Ibid.,* p. 7.

26. *Ibid.,* p. 15.

27. *Southwest–Northeast Case,* Order No. E-9758, p. 21.

28. Civil Aeronautics Board Order No. E-9886, *New York–Chicago Service Case,* Docket No. 986, *et al.,* Opinion and Order on Reconsideration of Supplemental Opinion, dated December 30, 1955, p. 2 (mimeographed decision).

29. *Southwest–Northeast Case,* Order No. E-9915, pp. 8–9.

30. *Southwest–Northeast Case,* Order No. E-9758, Opinion of Member Lee, concurring and dissenting, Docket No. 2355, *et al.,* dated November 21, 1955, p. 14. Member Lee erred with respect to TWA and United between Chicago and New York. They, too, were unrestricted.

31. This restriction prohibited an airline from carrying originating and terminating passengers between two cities, although its flights might serve both cities.

32. *Thye Committee Irregular Airlines Hearings,* pp. 419–20.

33. *Investigation of Non-scheduled Air Services,* 6 CAB 1049.

34. *Thye Committee Irregular Airlines Hearings,* Statement of Mr. Ryan continued.

35. Large Irregular Carriers were defined as those using aircraft with a maximum certificated take-off weight in excess of 12,500 lbs., while those using smaller aircraft were termed "small irregular carriers" and later, "air taxi operators."

36. *Ibid.,* p. 8.

37. *Ibid.,* pp. 424–25.

38. *Future of Irregular Airlines,* Report of the Select Committee on Small

Business, United States Senate, Report No. 822, Eighty-third Congress, first session, Washington, D.C., 1953.

39. *Civil Air Policy,* pp. 19–20.

40. *Ibid.,* p. 20.

41. *Ibid.*

42. *Ibid.,* p. 22.

43. *Thye Committee Irregular Airlines Hearings,* Statement of Hamlin B. Johnston, General Manager, Air Coach Transport Association, p. 127.

44. *Ibid.*

45. *Ibid.,* Memorandum of Louis W. Goodkind, p. 129.

46. Civil Aeronautics Board Order No. E-9744, *Large Irregular Carrier Investigation,* Docket No. 5132, *et al.,* decided November 15, 1955. reprinted in *Celler Committee Hearings,* I, 542.

47. *Ibid.*

48. Civil Aeronautics Board Order No. E-13436, *Large Irregular Carrier Investigation,* Docket No. 5132, *et al.,* dated January 28, 1959.

VI: THE POLICY OF THE CIVIL AERONAUTICS BOARD TOWARD COMPETITION

1. For example, see *Hearings Before the Antitrust Subcommittee* (Subcommittee No. 5) *of the Committee on the Judiciary, House of Representatives, Eighty-fourth Congress, second session, 1956* (hereafter referred to as the *Celler Committee Hearings*), I, 62–64, testimony of Professor Marver H. Bernstein.

2. Gilbert L. Bates, "Current Changes in Trunkline Competition," *Journal of Air Law and Commerce,* Vol. 22, No. 4 (Autumn, 1955), pp. 379–405.

3. *Annual Report of the Civil Aeronautics Board,* 1956, p. 2.

4. *Northwest Airlines, Duluth–Twin Cities Operations,* 1 CAA 573 (1940).

5. *Northwest Airlines Inc. et al., Detroit–Washington Service Case,* CAB Docket No. 679, *et al.,* Report of Edward T. Stodola, Examiner, March 17, 1947 (mimeographed), p. 70.

6. *Ibid.,* p. 70 n.

7. *Delta Air Corporation et al.,* 2 CAB 447, 480 (1941).

8. Civil Aeronautics Board Order No. E-861, *Northwest Airlines Inc., et al., Detroit–Washington Service,* Docket No. 679, *et al.,* dated September 30, 1947, p. 50 (mimeographed decision).

9. Northwest, United, TWA, Eastern, National, and Colonial.

10. *Northwest Airlines Inc., et al., Detroit–Washington Service Case,* CAB Docket No. 679, *et al.,* report of Edward T. Stodola, Examiner, pp. 69–78. (My indebtedness to this report is obvious.)

11. *American Export Air., Transatlantic Service,* 2 CAB 16, 31 (1940).

12. *Transcontinental and Western Air Inc. et al., Additional North–South California Services,* 4 CAB 373, 375 (1943).

13. *Colonial Air. et al., Atlantic Seaboard Op.,* 4 CAB 552, 555 (1944).

14. *Transcontinental and Western Air Inc. et al., Additional North–South California Services,* 4 CAB 373, 375 (1943).

15. *Ibid.*

16. *Northeast Air. et al., Boston Service,* 4 CAB 686, 690 (1944).

17. *Northwest Air. et al., Chicago–Milwaukee–New York Service,* 6 CAB 217, 228 (1944).

18. *Ibid.,* p. 232.

19. *Northwest Airlines Inc., et al., Detroit–Washington Service Case,* Examiner Stodola's report, p. 75.

20. *Ibid.,* pp. 78–89.

21. Now Capital Airlines.

22. *Northwest Airlines Inc., et al., Detroit–Washington Service,* Order No. E-861, p. 40.

23. *Ibid.,* pp. 51–52.

24. *Ibid.,* p. 56.

25. *Ibid.,* p. 57.

26. *Ibid.,* p. 58.

27. *Ibid.*

28. *Ibid.,* Dissent In Part of Chairman Landis, p. 1.

29. F. W. Gill and G. L. Bates, *Airline Competition,* Graduate School of Business Administration, Harvard University, Boston, 1949. G. L. Bates, "Current Changes in Trunkline Competition," *Journal of Air Law and Commerce,* Vol. 22, No. 4 (Autumn, 1955). The criterion used in these works for the determination of the existence of competition is the above-cited "ten percent rule" with respect to the amount of traffic carried. However, the results are of course related to the nature of the new authorizations.

30. John H. Frederick, *Commercial Air Transportation,* Homewood, Illinois, Richard D. Irwin, Inc., 1955, 4th Edition, p. 180 n. 15; David W. Bluestone, "The Problem of Competition Among Domestic Trunk Airlines," *Journal of Air Law and Commerce,* Vol. 20, No. 4 (Autumn, 1953), also Part II, Vol. 21, No. 1 (Winter, 1954).

31. *Materials Relative to Competition in the Regulated Civil Aviation Industry,* transmitted by the Civil Aeronautics Board to the Select Committee on Small Business, United States Senate, April 18, 1956, Government Printing Office, Washington, 1956. Letter from Mr. Ross Rizley, Chairman, Civil Aeronautics Board, to Senator Sparkman transmitting replies of the CAB to the Committee's questions, December 14, 1955, p. 68.

32. David W. Bluestone, "The Problem of Competition Among Domestic Trunk Airlines—Parts I and II."

33. G. L. Bates, "Current Changes in Trunkline Competition," p. 393.

34. *Report of the Federal Aviation Commission,* Senate Document No. 15, Seventy-fourth Congress, first session, p. 61.

35. *Hearings Before a Subcommittee of the Select Committee on Small Business, United States Senate, Eighty-third Congress, first session (1953) on Future of Irregular Airlines in United States Air Transportation Industry* (hereafter referred to as *Thye Committee Irregular Airlines Hearings*), testimony of Gordon M. Bain, Director, Bureau of Air Operations, CAB.

36. David W. Bluestone, "The Problem of Competition Among Domestic Trunk Airlines—Parts I and II."

37. John H. Frederick, *Commercial Air Transportation,* p. 96.

38. Gill and Bates, *Airline Competition,* p. 628.

39. *Ibid.,* pp. 506, 630, 631.

40. *Annual Report of the Civil Aeronautics Board,* 1959, pp. 18–19.

41. 12 CAB 518, 533–34.

42. Civil Aeronautics Board Order No. E-7988, *Reopened Southern Service to the West Case,* Docket No. 1102, *et al.,* decided December 22, 1953 (mimeographed decision), p. 12.

43. *Ibid.,* pp. 45–46. Dissent of Member Lee.

44. *Ibid.,* p. 49.

45. Civil Aeronautics Board Order No. E-9735, *Denver Service Case,* Docket No. 1841, *et al.,* dated November 14, 1955, p. 7 (mimeographed decision).

46. Civil Aeronautics Board Order No. E-9758, *Southwest–Northeast Service Case,* Docket No. 2355, *et al.,* dated November 21, 1955, p. ii (mimeographed decision).

47. *Ibid.,* pp. 35–36.

48. *Annual Report of the Civil Aeronautics Board,* 1956, p. 1.

49. Civil Aeronautics Board Order No. E-9537, *New York–Chicago Service*

Case, Docket No. 986, *et al.,* dated September 1, 1955, p. 16 (mimeographed decision).

50. Civil Aeronautics Board Order No. E-9539, *United Restriction Case,* Docket No. 2190, *et al.,* dated September 1, 1955, p. 6 (mimeographed decision).

51. *Southwest–Northeast Service Case,* p. i.

52. Civil Aeronautics Board Order No. E-10645, *New York–Florida Case,* Docket No. 3051, *et al.,* dated September 21, 1956, p. 31 (mimeographed decision).

53. Letter from President Eisenhower to CAB Chairman Durfee, August 2, 1957, cited in *American Aviation,* August 12, 1957, p. 87.

54. Civil Aeronautics Board Order No. E–9692, *New York–Chicago case.* Docket No. 986, *et al.,* Supplemental Decision, dated October 27, 1955, p. 7 (mimeographed decision).

55. Civil Aeronautics Board Order No. E–9887, *Denver Service Case,* Docket No. 1841, *et al.,* Supplemental Decision, dated December 30, 1955, p. 3 (mimeographed decision).

56. *New York–Chicago Case,* Order No. E–9692, p. 5.

57. *Denver Service Case,* Order No. E–9887, p. 5.

58. Civil Aeronautics Board Order No. E–9915, *Southwest–Northeast Ser*vice Case, Docket No. 2355, *et al.,* Supplement Opinion and Order on Reconsideration, dated January 16, 1956, p. 7 (mimeographed decision).

59. *Hearings Before the Antitrust Subcommittee (Subcommittee No. 5) of the Committee on the Judiciary, House of Representatives, Eighty-fourth Congress, second session, 1956* (hereafter referred to as the *Celler Committee Hearings*), I, 418. Letter from Chairman Rizley to Representative Celler dated November 8, 1955.

60. *New York–Chicago Case,* Order No. E–9537, pp. 7–8.

VII: THE MATERIALS AND FRAMEWORK FOR ANALYSIS

1. Civil Aeronautics Board Order No. E–10487, *Tucson Airport Authority Application,* Docket No. 5564, dated July 27, 1956. pp. 1–2 (mimeographed decision).

2. *Hearings Before the Antitrust Subcommittee (Subcommittee No. 5) of the Committee on the Judiciary, House of Representatives, Eighty-fourth Conggress, second session, 1956* (hereafter referred to as the *Celler Committee Hearings*), I, 418.

3. *Report of the Antitrust Subcommittee* (Subcommittee No. 5) *of the Committee on the Judiciary, House of Representatives, Eighty-fifth Congress, first session, Pursuant to H. Res. 107 . . . on Airlines, Washington 1957* (hereafter referred to as the *Celler Committee Report*), p. 21.

4. Civil Aeronautics Board Order No. E–9758, *Southwest–Northeast Service Case,* Docket No. 2355, *et al.,* dated November 21, 1955, p. 1 (mimeographed decision).

5. Civil Aeronautics Board Order No. E–9737, *New York–Chicago Case,* Docket No. 986, *et al.,* Supplemental Opinion and Order on Deferred Applications, dated November 14, 1955, p. 3 n (mimeographed decision).

6. Civil Aeronautics Board Order No. E–10550, *Northwest Airlines, Pittsburgh–Cleveland and Detroit Restriction Case,* Docket No. 4294, *et al.,* dated August 21, 1956, p. i (mimeographed decision).

7. *Southwest–Northeast Service Case,* Order No. E–9758, p. iii.

8. Civil Aeronautics Board Order No. E–9887, *Denver Service Case,* Docket No. 1841, *et al.,* Supplemental Order and Opinion on Reconsideration, dated December 30, 1955, p. 7 (mimeographed decision). It might be noted that the city pairs to which United objected were not considered, in this study, as competitive authorizations since they failed to meet the circuity test.

9. *Dallas to the West Service Case,* Docket No. 7596, *et al.,* Initial Decision of Examiner Thomas L. Wrenn, dated March 10, 1958, p. 139 (mimeographed decision).

10. James M. Landis, *The Administrative Process,* Yale University Press, New Haven, 1938, p. 106.

11. P. 26.

12. Pp. 36–38.

13. *Independent Regulatory Commissions,* Report of the Special Subcommittee on Legislative Oversight, House Report No. 2711, Union Calendar No. 1411, Government Printing Office, Washington, D.C., 1959.

14. *Ibid.,* p. 41.

15. *Ibid.,* p. 11, emphasis supplied.

16. *Southwest–Northeast Service Case,* Order No. E–9758, p. 9.

17. Civil Aeronautics Board Order No. E–10645, *New York–Florida Case,* Docket No. 3051, *et al.,* dated September 28, 1956, p. i (mimeographed decision).

18. *Tucson Airport Authority Application,* Order No. E–10487, pp. 3–4.

19. *Southwest–Northeast Service Case,* Order No. E–9758 p. 21.

20. *Ibid.,* p. 25. The expression "Oklahoma Cities," as is clear from the context, refers to Tulsa and Oklahoma City.

21. *New York–Florida Case,* Order No. E–10645, p. 39.

22. *Southwest–Northeast Service Case,* Order No. E–9758, p. iii.

VIII: THE BASES FOR DECISION—CRITERIA FOR COMPETITION

1. *The Role of Competition in Commercial Air Transportation,* Report of the Civil Aeronautics Board Submitted to the Subcommittee on Monopoly of the Select Committee on Small Business, United States Senate, November 24, 1952, Government Printing Office, Washington, D.C., 1952, pp. 6–7.

2. *Southwest–Northeast Service Case,* Docket No. 2355, *et al.,* Initial decision of Examiner William J. Madden, p. 236 (mimeographed).

3. Civil Aeronautics Board Order No. E-9758, *Southwest–Northeast Service Case,* Docket No. 2355, *et al.,* dated November 21, 1955, p. 18 (mimeographed decision).

4. Civil Aeronautics Board Order No. E–10645, *New York–Florida Service Case,* Docket No. 3051, *et al.,* dated September 28, 1956, p. 28 (mimeographed decision).

5. *Southwest–Northeast Service Case,* Order No. E-9758, p. 19.

6. Civil Aeronautics Board Order No. E-13119, *The City of Toledo, Ohio and The Toledo Chamber of Commerce vs. Capital Airlines, Inc.,* Docket No. 8851, dated October 31, 1958 (mimeographed decision).

7. Civil Aeronautics Board Order No. E-10487, *Tucson Airport Authority Application,* Docket No. 5564, dated July 27, 1956, p. 4 (mimeographed decision).

8. *Southwest–Northeast Service Case,* Order No. E-9758, p. 19.

9. Civil Aeronautics Board Order No. E-10550, *Northwest Airlines, Pittsburgh–Cleveland and Detroit Restriction Case,* Docket No. 4294, *et al.,* dated August 21, 1956, p. 3 (mimeographed decision).

10. *New York–Florida Service Case,* pp. 3–5.

11. Civil Aeronautics Board Order No. E-10902, *Florida–Texas Service Case,* Docket No. 5701, *et al.,* Supplemental Opinion and Order, dated December 31, 1956, p. i (mimeographed decision).

12. *Tucson Airport Authority Application,* p. 6.

13. *Southwest–Northeast Service Case,* Order No. E-9758, p. 10.

14. *Tucson Airport Authority Application,* p. 6; also *Northwest Airlines, Pittsburgh–Cleveland and Detroit Restriction Case,* p. 3 n.

15. *Ibid.,* pp. ii and i respectively.

16. Civil Aeronautics Board Order No. E-9537, *New York–Chicago Service Case,* Docket No. 986, *et al.,* dated September 1, 1955, p. 16 (mimeographed decision). Also see preceding quotation from the *Tucson Case.*

17. *Southwest–Northeast Service Case,* Order No. E-9758, p. 31.

18. See *The Role of Competition in Commercial Air Transportation,* pp. 38–45, esp. p. 41.

19. Section 801, Civil Aeronautics Act.

20. Letter from President Eisenhower to CAB Chairman Durfee, August 2, 1957, cited in *American Aviation,* August 12, 1957, p. 87.

21. *Southwest–Northeast Service Case,* Order No. E-9758, p. 36.

22. *New York–Florida Service Case,* Dissent of Member Denny, p. 16.

23. Effective January 1, 1959, a new continuous sample method was inaugurated. This was the first basic revision in the twenty-year history of the origin–destination *Airline Traffic Survey.*

24. *New York–Chicago Service Case,* p. 22.

25. The annual estimates of origin and destination passengers are computed here, and throughout this book, by adding the figures reported in the *Airline Traffic Survey* for the two two-week periods, March 1–14 and September 17–30, and multiplying the total by 13.

26. Civil Aeronautics Board Order No. E-9735, *Denver Service Case,* Docket No. 1841, *et al.,* dated November 14, 1955, p. 7 (mimeographed decision).

27. *New York–Chicago Service Case,* p. 16.

28. *Southwest–Northeast Service Case,* Order No. E-9758, p. 18.

29. *Ibid.,* p. 9.

30. *New York–Florida Service Case,* p. iv.

31. *Southwest–Northeast Service Case,* Order No. E-9758, pp. 11–12.

32. *Florida–Texas Service Case,* p. 3.

33. *Southwest–Northeast Service Case,* Order No. E-9758, p. 19.

34. *New York–Chicago Service Case,* p. 7.

35. *New York–Florida Service Case,* p. i.

36. *Ibid.,* p. 2.

37. *Denver Service Case,* p. 10.

38. *Southwest–Northeast Service Case,* Order No. E-9758, p. 20.

39. *Ibid.,* Separate Opinion of Members Gurney and Denny, p. 6.

40. *New York–Chicago Service Case,* p. 19.

41. Civil Aeronautics Board Order No. E-9692, *New York–Chicago Service Case,* Docket No. 986, *et al.,* Supplemental Opinion and Order on Reconsideration, dated October 27, 1955, p. 5 (mimeographed decision).

42. *Southwest–Northeast Service Case,* Order No. E-9758, Separate Opinion of Members Gurney and Denny, p. 7 n.

43. Civil Aeronautics Board Order No. E-9539, *United Restriction Case,* Docket No. 2190, *et al.,* Supplemental Opinion, dated September 1, 1955, p. 6 (mimeographed decision).

44. *Denver Service Case,* p. 6.

45. *Ibid.,* p. 8.

46. *Southwest–Northeast Service Case,* Order No. E-9758, p. 35.

47. *New York–Florida Case,* p. 41.

48. *Southwest–Northeast Service Case,* Order No. E-9758, p. 19.

IX: THE BASES FOR DECISION—SELECTION OF THE NEW CARRIER

1. Civil Aeronautics Board Order No. E-9735, *Denver Service Case,* Docket No. 1841, *et al.,* dated November 14, 1955, p. 5 (mimeographed decision).

2. Civil Aeronautics Board Order No. E-10645, *New York–Florida Service*

Case, Docket No. 3051, *et al.,* dated September 28, 1956, p. 34 (mimeographed decision).

3. Civil Aeronautics Board Order No. E-10635, *Florida–Texas Service Case,* Docket No. 5701, *et al.,* dated September 24, 1956, p. 13 (mimeographed decision).

4. Howard C. Westwood, "Choice of the Air Carrier for New Air Transport Routes," Parts I and II, *George Washington Law Review,* Vol. 16, Nos. 1 and 2, December, 1947 and February, 1948.

5. *New York–Mexico City Nonstop Service Case,* Docket No. 2909, *et al.,* Recommended Decision of Edward T. Stodola, Examiner, dated April 25, 1957, pp. 31–32 (mimeographed decision).

6. *The Role of Competition in Commercial Air Transportation,* Report of the Civil Aeronautics Board Submitted to the Subcommittee on Monopoly of the Select Committee on Small Business, United States Senate, November 24, 1952, Government Printing Office, Washington, D.C., 1952, p. 18.

7. *Ibid.,* p. 19.

8. *Ibid.,* p. 20.

9. Civil Aeronautics Board Order No. E-11173, *Syracuse–New York City Case,* Docket No. 6179, *et al.,* dated March 27, 1957, pp. 3–4 (mimeographed decision).

10. *Annual Report of the Civil Aeronautics Board, 1958,* pp. 13–14.

11. *Hearings Before the Antitrust Subcommittee (Subcommittee No. 5) of the Committee on the Judiciary, House of Representatives, Eight-fourth Congress, second session, 1956* (hereafter referred to as the *Celler Committee Hearings*), I, 494.

12. Civil Aeronautics Board Order No. E-9758, *Southwest–Northeast Service Case,* Docket No. 2355, *et al.,* dated November 21, 1956, Separate Opinion of Members Gurney and Denny, p. 1 (mimeographed decision).

13. *Ibid.,* Majority opinion, p. 6.

14. *New York–Florida Service Case,* Separate Opinion of Member Denny, p. 5.

15. *Ibid.,* Separate Opinion of Member Gurney, p. 1.

16. Civil Aeronautics Board Order No. E-10884, *New York–Florida Case,* Docket No. 3051 *et al.,* Supplemental Opinion and Order on Reconsideration, dated December 21, 1956, p. 15.

17. Civil Aeronautics Board Order No. E-9537, *New York–Chicago Service Case,* Docket No. 986, *et al.,* dated September 1, 1955. p. 5 (mimeographed decision).

18. Civil Aeronautics Board Order No. E-10550, *Northwest Airlines, Inc., Pittsburgh–Cleveland and Detroit Restriction Case,* Docket No. 4294, *et al.,* dated August 21, 1956, p. 6 (mimeographed decision).

19. *Southwest–Northeast Service Case,* p. 7.

20. *New York–Florida Service Case,* Order No. E-10645, p. i.

21. *Ibid.,* p. 5.

22. *Southwest–Northeast Service Case,* pp. 3–5.

23. *Ibid.,* p. 9.

24. See page 202 for the Board's position on this question.

25. *Southwest–Northeast Service Case,* p. 4.

26. *Denver Service Case,* p. 18.

27. *Southwest–Northeast Service Case,* p. 16.

28. *New York–Florida Service Case,* Order No. E-10645, p. 18.

29. *Report of the Antitrust Subcommittee (Subcommittee No. 5) of the Committee on the Judiciary, House of Representatives, Eighty-fifth Congress, first session, Pursuant to H. Res. 107 . . . on Airlines, Washington 1957* (hereafter referred to as the *Celler Committee Report*), p. 113.

30. Civil Aeronautics Board Order No. E-9915, *Southwest–Northeast Service Case,* Docket No. 2355, *et al.,* Supplemental Opinion and Order on Reconsideration, dated January 16, 1956, p. 4 (mimeographed decision).

31. *New York–Chicago Service Case,* Order No. E-9537, p. i.

32. *Northwest Airlines, Inc., Pittsburgh–Cleveland and Detroit Restriction Case,* p. i.

33. *New York–Chicago Service Case,* Order No. E-9537, p. 23.

34. *Southwest–Northeast Service Case,* p. 6.

35. *Ibid.,* p. 2A.

36. *Ibid.,* pp. 8, 9, 13.

37. *Ibid.,* Separate Opinion of Members Gurney and Denny, p. 6.

38. *Ibid.,* Majority opinion, pp. 16, 20, 21.

39. *Ibid.,* pp. 28, 30, 31.

40. *Ibid.,* Concurring and Dissenting Opinion of Member Lee, p. 1.

41. *New York–Chicago Service Case,* Order No. E-9537, p. 8.

42. *New York–Florida Service Case,* p. ii.

43. *Southwest–Northeast Service Case,* p. 2A.

44. *New York–Chicago Service Case,* Order No. E-9537, p. 17.

45. *Ibid.,* p. 8.

46. *Denver Service Case,* p. 5.

47. *Ibid.,* Appendix A, p. 6.

48. *Ibid.,* Opinion, p. 4.

49. *Ibid.,* pp. 7–8.

50. *New York–Florida Service Case,* p. ii.

51. *Ibid.,* p. 6.

52. Civil Aeronautics Board Order No. E-10487, *Tucson Airport Authority Application,* Docket No. 5564, *et al.,* dated July 27, 1956, p. i (mimeographed decision).

53. *Florida–Texas Service Case,* p. 7.

54. *New York–Chicago Service Case,* Order No. E-9537, p. 22.

55. *Monthly Report of Air Carrier Traffic Statistics,* September, 1956, Civil Aeronautics Board, Office of Carier Accounts and Statistics, Washington, D.C., pp. 50, 66.

X: THE RESULTING COMPETITION

1. This matter is discussed at length in Chapter VII.

2. These, as may be studied in detail in Appendix One, are:

	Serial Number	*New Carrier*
Atlanta–Philadelphia	0083, 0084	Capital, Delta
Columbus, Ohio–New York	0526	American
Detroit–Kansas City	0604	United
Kansas City–Pittsburgh	0935	United
Los Angeles–Pittsburgh	1010, 1011	United, American
Pittsburgh–Portland, Ore.	1357	United
Pittsburgh–San Francisco	1367, 1368	United, American
Pittsburgh–Seattle	1371	United

In three of these city pairs as indicated, a later decision added a third carrier, but, in only the first, Atlanta–Philadelphia, was the expressed intent of the Civil Aeronautics Board "specific purposive" with respect to the third carrier. In that case, Delta, the new carrier, did offer service in 1957.

3. See Table VIII-6, p. 186.

APPENDICES

Key for Decoding City Names

ABE	Allentown-Bethlehem-Easton, Pa.
ABQ	Albuquerque, N.M.
ALB	Albany-Schenectady, N.Y.
AMA	Amarillo, Texas
ATL	Atlanta, Ga.
AVP	Wilkes Barre-Scranton, Pa.
BAL	Baltimore, Md.
BHM	Birmingham, Ala.
BNA	Nashville, Tenn.
BDL	Hartford, Conn.–Springfield, Mass.
BOS	Boston, Mass.
BRO	Brownsville, Texas
BTR	Baton Rouge, La.
BTV	Burlington, Vt.
BUF	Buffalo, N.Y.
CAE	Columbia, S.C.
CAK	Akron-Canton, Ohio
CHA	Chattanooga, Tenn.
CHI	Chicago, Ill.
CHS	Charleston, S.C.
CHW	Charleston, W. Va.
CLE	Cleveland, Ohio
CLT	Charlotte, N.C.
CMH	Columbus, Ohio
CRP	Corpus Christi, Texas
CSG	Columbus, Ga.
CVG	Cincinnati, Ohio
DAB	Daytona Beach, Fla.
DAL	Dallas, Texas
DAY	Dayton, Ohio
DCA	Washington, D.C.
DEN	Denver, Colo.
FAT	Fresno, Calif.
FTW	Ft. Worth, Texas
FWA	Fort Wayne, Ind.
GEG	Spokane, Wash.
GSO	Greensboro-High Point, N.C.
HAR	Harrisburg, Pa.
HLG	Wheeling, W. Va.
HOU	Houston, Texas
HSV	Huntsville, Ala.
ILG	Wilmington, Del.
IND	Indianapolis, Ind.
INT	Winston-Salem, N.C.
JAX	Jacksonville, Fla.
LAS	Las Vegas, Nev.
LAX	Los Angeles, Calif.
LEX	Lexington-Frankfort, Ky.
LGB	Long Beach, Calif.
LIT	Little Rock, Ark.
MCN	Macon, Ga.
MEM	Memphis, Tenn.
MGM	Montgomery, Ala.
MIA	Miami, Fla.
MKC	Kansas City, Mo.
MKE	Milwaukee, Wis.
MLI	Moline, Ill.
MOB	Mobile, Ala.
MRY	Monterey-Del Monte, Calif.
MSY	New Orleans, La.
NHV	New Haven, Conn.
NYC	New York City, N.Y.–Newark, N.J.
OKC	Oklahoma City, Okla.
ORF	Norfolk, Va.
ORL	Orlando, Fla.
PBI	West Palm Beach, Fla.
PDX	Portland, Oregon
PHF	Newport News, Va.
PHL	Philadelphia, Pa.
PHX	Phoenix, Ariz.
PIA	Peoria, Ill.
PIE	St. Petersburg-Clearwater, Fla.
PIT	Pittsburgh, Pa.
PNS	Pensacola, Fla.
PVD	Providence, R.I.
RDG	Reading, Pa.
RDU	Raleigh-Durham, N.C.
RIC	Richmond, Va.
RNO	Reno, Nev.
ROC	Rochester, N.Y.
SAN	San Diego, Calif.
SAT	San Antonio, Texas
SAV	Savannah, Ga.
SBA	Santa Barbara, Calif.
SBN	South Bend, Ind.
SDF	Louisville, Ky.
SEA	Seattle-Tacoma, Wash.
SFO	San Francisco-Oakland, Calif.
SHV	Shreveport, La.
SLC	Salt Lake City, Utah
SSI	Brnnswick, Ga.
STL	St. Louis, Mo.
TLH	Tallahassee, Fla.
TOL	Toledo, Ohio
TPA	Tampa, Fla.
TUL	Tulsa, Okla.
TUO	Tucson, Ariz.
TYS	Knoxville, Tenn.
YIP	Detroit-Ypsilanti-Ann Arbor, Mich.
YNG	Youngstown-Warren, Ohio–Sharon, Pa.

APPENDIX ONE: *559 Competitive Docket City Pairs*

Civil Aeronautics Board Authorizations, Carrier Identities, and Restrictions for All New, Improved, and Original Authorizations

SOURCES AND CODES

Column

(1) City pairs are numbered serially in alphabetical order. Numbers are not consecutive because these are the *competitive* pairs.

(2) Standard three-letter codes for airline stations.

(3) Docket number for the decision affecting competition. The deferred portion of Docket 986 is shown as 1986.

(4) Number of carriers

First digit: number of *new* carriers authorized in the instant decision.

Second digit: number of carriers with authorizations *improved* in the instant decision.

Third digit: number of carriers authorized before the instant decision (the *original* carriers).

(5), (6), (7) Each carrier is represented by a four-digit code. First two digits: *Airline Code*

Code	*Airline*	*Code*	*Airline*	*Code*	*Airline*	*Code*	*Airline*
	Trunkline		Trunkline		Local Service		Local Service
11	American Airlines	18	Northeast Airlines	31	Allegheny Airlines	38	Ozark Air Lines
12	Braniff Int'l. Airways	19	Northwest Orient Airlines	32	Bonanza Airlines	39	Piedmont Airlines
13	Capital Airlines	20	Trans World Airlines	33	Central Airlines	40	Southern Airways
14	Continental Air Lines	21	United Air Lines	34	Frontier Airlines	41	Southwest Airways **
15	Delta Air Lines	22	Western Air Lines	35	Lake Central Airlines	42	Trans-Texas Airways
16	Eastern Air Lines	26	Colonial Airlines *	36	Mohawk Airlines	43	West Coast Airlines
17	National Airlines			37	North Central Airlines	50	Mackey Airlines †

* Merged with Eastern Air Lines, 1956.

** Now Pacific Airlines.

† Operates local domestic segment between Tampa/St. Petersburg, on the one hand, and West Palm Beach and Ft. Lauderdale, on the other hand, in addition to its international segments.

(5), (6), (7) Last two digits: *Restriction Code*

First digit

1	I	Intermediate stops are the only restriction.
2	L	Long haul restriction. Carrier must stop at some point beyond one city of the pair, but carrier has some choice of points.
3	R	Required stop beyond one city of the pair. Carrier must stop at a point specified in the certificate.
4	LL	L on both sides (2 + 2 = 4).
6	RR	R " " " (3 + 3 = 6).
7	R-2	Two required stops beyond one city of the pair.

Second digit (When first digit is 1–7): number of required intermediate stops.

Special codes:

00	Unrestricted.
85	L beyond either of the cities of the pair (carrier's choice); less restrictive than L.
88	R beyond either of the cities of the pair (carrier's choice); less restrictive than R.
99	For improved authorization only. Same restrictions as before but changed routing results in less circuity.

Serial (1)	City Names (2)		Docket (3)	Number of Carriers (4)		New Carriers (5)			Improved Carriers (6)			Original Carriers (7)
0003	CAK	BOS	3051	101	2121					1111		
0004	CAK	BDL	3051	101	2121					1111		
0008	CAK	PHL	0986	101	1300					2100		
0009	CAK	PIT	0986	101	1620					1300		
0010	CAK	PIT	1986	102	2150					1300	1620	
0012	CAK	PVD	3051	101	2122					1112		
0021	ALB	OKC	2355	101	2000					1111		
0023	ALB	SFO	1841	012					1111	1112	2000	
0025	ALB	TUO	5564	101	2000					1111		
0026	ALB	TUL	2355	101	2000					1111		
0028	ABQ	OKC	2355	101	2000					1400		
0029	ABQ	TUL	2355	101	2000					1400		
0037	ABE	BOS	3051	200	2000	2121						
0038	ABE	DEN	1841	101	2000					2100		
0039	ABE	BDL	3051	200	2000	2121						
0041	ABE	MKC	1841	101	2100					2000		
0045	ABE	PIT	1986	101	2150					2000		
0060	AMA	NYC	2355	101	1211					2000		
0061	AMA	OKC	2355	101	2000					1200		
0063	AMA	TUL	2355	101	2000					1200		
0064	AMA	DCA	2355	101	1211					2000		
0072	ATL	BAL	2355	112	1500				1300	1311	1600	
0073	ATL	BHM	2355	102	1320					1500	1620	
0074	ATL	CLT	2355	113	1520				1320	1311	1600	4013
0076	ATL	GSO	2355	012					1320	1311	1600	
0077	ATL	HOU	2355	101	1500					1600		
0079	ATL	MOB	2355	101	1320					1600		
0080	ATL	MSY	2355	102	1300					1500	1600	
0081	ATL	NYC	2355	102	1500					1300	1600	
0083	ATL	PHL	0986	101	1311					1600		
0084	ATL	PHL	2355	112	1500				1300	1311	1600	
0085	ATL	PIT	2355	101	1611					1300		
0086	ATL	RDU	2355	012					1320	1311	1600	
0087	ATL	RIC	2355	012					1320	1311	1600	
0089	ATL	DCA	2355	112	1500				1300	1311	1600	
0090	ATL	INT	2355	012					1320	1311	1600	
0118	BAL	BTR	2355	101	1511					1600		
0120	BAL	BHM	2355	112	1500				1300	1311	1600	
0122	BAL	BOS	3051	412	1700	1800	2020	2120	1600	1100	1620	
0123	BAL	BTV	3051	101	1800					1611		
0124	BAL	CLT	2355	112	1530				1330	1311	1600	
0125	BAL	CHA	2355	012					1300	1311	1600	
0126	BAL	CSG	2355	101	1530					1600		
0128	BAL	DAL	2355	101	1511					1100		
0129	BAL	DEN	1841	101	2000					2100		
0132	BAL	FTW	2355	101	1511					1100		
0133	BAL	GSO	2355	012					1330	1311	1600	

Serial (1)	City Names (2)		Docket (3)	Number of Carriers (4)	Carriers' Identifications and Restrictions	New Carriers (5)	Improved Carriers (6)	Original Carriers (7)
0135	BAL	BDL	3051	312	1800	2020 2120	1600	1100 1650
0138	BAL	HOU	2355	101	1500			1600
0140	BAL	HSV	8134	101	1611			1330
0143	BAL	JAX	3051	102	1800			1600 1700
0144	BAL	MKC	1841	101	2100			2000
0146	BAL	TYS	2355	012			1300	1100 1311
0150	BAL	MCN	2355	101	1511			1611
0153	BAL	MEM	2355	013			1300	1100 1311 1611
0155	BAL	MIA	3051	102	1800			1600 1700
0156	BAL	MOB	2355	012			1330	1311 1600
0159	BAL	MGM	2355	101	1530			1600
0164	BAL	NHV	3051	012			1600	1100 1650
0166	BAL	MSY	2355	112	1500		1300	1311 1600
0167	BAL	NYC	2355	304	1330	1530 2030		1100 1600 1720 3113
0168	BAL	NYC	3051	237	1800	2120	1398 1700 2020	1100 1330 1530 1600 1720 2030 3113
0169	BAL	PHF	3051	101	1700			1300
0170	BAL	ORF	3051	101	1700			1300
0171	BAL	OKC	2355	101	2000			1100
0175	BAL	PHL	2355	303	1330	1530 2030		1100 1600 1720
0176	BAL	PHL	3051	236	1800	2120	1398 1700 2020	1100 1330 1530 1600 1720 2030
0181	BAL	PVD	3051	312	1700	1800 2121	1600	1100 1650
0182	BAL	RDU	2355	012			1330	1311 1600
0183	BAL	RIC	2355	014			1330	1100 1311 1600 1720
0184	BAL	RIC	3051	014			1700	1100 1330 1600 1720
0187	BAL	PIE	3051	112	1800		1600	1611 1700
0193	BAL	TPA	3051	112	1800		1600	1611 1700
0194	BAL	TUO	5564	101	2000			1100
0195	BAL	TUL	2355	101	2000			1100
0199	BAL	DCA	2355	108	1530			1100 1300 1600 1730 2000 2100 2600 3100
0200	BAL	DCA	3051	118	1800		1700	1100 1300 1530 1600 1730 2000 2100 3100
0203	BAL	INT	2355	012			1330	1311 1600
0211	BTR	CLT	2355	101	1550			1600
0212	BTR	NYC	2355	101	1511			1600
0213	BTR	PHL	2355	101	1511			1600
0214	BTR	DCA	2355	101	1511			1600
0253	BHM	CLT	2355	113	1520		1320	1311 1600 4015
0255	BHM	GSO	2355	012			1320	1311 1600
0256	BHM	HOU	2355	101	1530			1600
0257	BHM	NYC	2355	102	1500			1300 1600
0260	BHM	PHL	0986	101	1311			1600
0261	BHM	PHL	2355	112	1500		1300	1311 1600
0262	BHM	PIT	2355	101	1611			1300
0263	BHM	RDU	2355	012			1320	1311 1600
0264	BHM	RIC	2355	012			1320	1311 1600

Serial (1)	City Names (2)	Docket (3)	Number of Carriers (4)		New Carriers (5)	Improved Carriers (6)	Original Carriers (7)
				Carriers' Identifications and Restrictions			
0266	BHM DCA	2355	112	1500		1300	1311 1600
0267	BHM INT	2355	012			1320	1311 1600
0296	BOS CHS	3051	101	1700			1600
0297	BOS CHW	3051	012			1611	1111 1621
0298	BOS CLE	3051	102	2021			1100 2100
0299	BOS DAB	3051	101	1700			1600
0300	BOS DEN	1841	101	2000			2100
0303	BOS BDL	3051	113	2000		1600	1100 1620 2100
0304	BOS HOU	2355	101	1112			1600
0305	BOS HOU	3051	102	1711			1112 1600
0308	BOS JAX	3051	201	1700	1800		1600
0309	BOS MKC	1841	101	2100			2000
0312	BOS SDF	7253	013			1699	1111 1611 2011
0314	BOS MIA	3051	201	1700	1800		1600
0315	BOS MOB	3051	101	1711			1600
0317	BOS BNA	7253	012			1699	1100 1612
0319	BOS NHV	3051	012			1600	1100 1620
0320	BOS MSY	3051	101	1711			1600
0321	BOS NYC	3051	313	1700	2020 2120	1600	1100 1620 1800
0324	BOS OKC	2355	101	2000			1100
0325	BOS ORL	3051	101	1700			1600
0328	BOS PNS	3051	101	1711			1600
0329	BOS PHL	3051	412	1700	1800 2020 2120	1600	1100 1620
0330	BOS PIT	2355	101	1131			2000
0331	BOS PIT	3051	102	2151			1131 2000
0333	BOS PVD	3051	114	1700		1600	1100 1620 1800 2100
0335	BOS RIC	3051	112	1700		1600	1100 1620
0336	BOS PIE	3051	211	1700	1800	1600	1611
0337	BOS SFO	1841	013			1199	1111 2000 2100
0340	BOS SAV	3051	101	1700			1600
0343	BOS TLH	3051	101	1711			1611
0344	BOS TPA	3051	211	1700	1800	1600	1611
0345	BOS TUO	5564	101	2000			1100
0346	BOS TUL	2355	101	2000			1100
0350	BOS DCA	3051	412	1700	1800 2020 2120	1600	1100 1620
0351	BOS PBI	3051	101	1700			1600
0353	BOS ILG	3051	012			1600	1100 1620
0365	BRO CHA	2355	101	1211			1611
0367	BRO BNA	2355	101	1211			1611
0368	BRO NYC	2355	101	1211			1600
0369	BRO DCA	2355	101	1211			1600
0370	SSI HOU	2355	101	1511			1612
0374	BUF CHI	0986	101	1300			1100
0375	BUF YIP	0986	101	1300			1100
0382	BUF NYC	0986	101	1300			1100
0387	BTV JAX	3051	101	1800			1611
0388	BTV MIA	3051	101	1800			1611

Serial (1)	City Names (2)	Docket (3)	Number of Carriers (4)	Carriers' Identifications and Restrictions: New Carriers (5)	Improved Carriers (6)	Original Carriers (7)
0389	BTV PHL	3051	101	1800		1611
0390	BTV PIE	3051	111	1800	1611	1612
0391	BTV TPA	3051	111	1800	1611	1612
0392	BTV DCA	3051	101	1800		1611
0406	CHS HOU	5701	101	1711		1511
0407	CHS PVD	3051	101	1700		1600
0408	CHS PIE	3051	101	1600		1700
0409	CHS TPA	3051	101	1600		1700
0410	CHW BDL	3051	012		1611	1111 1651
0411	CHW NHV	3051	012		1611	1111 1651
0412	CHW PHL	0986	102	1311		1111 1611
0413	CHW PVD	3051	012		1611	1111 1651
0417	CLT CSG	2355	102	1550		1600 4014
0421	CLT HOU	2355	101	1520		1600
0422	CLT HSV	8134	101	1611		1300
0425	CLT MCN	2355	101	1511		1611
0427	CLT MOB	2355	012		1350	1311 1600
0429	CLT MGM	2355	101	1550		1600
0430	CLT MSY	2355	112	1520	1320	1311 1600
0431	CLT NYC	2355	201	1330 1530		1600
0432	CLT PHL	2355	201	1330 1520		1600
0438	CLT DCA	2355	102	1530		1300 1600
0440	CHA CRP	2355	101	1211		1611
0445	CHA HOU	2355	201	1211 1511		1611
0448	CHA MEM	2355	101	1220		1300
0449	CHA BNA	2355	101	1220		1600
0450	CHA NYC	2355	102	1200		1300 1600
0452	CHA PHL	0986	101	1311		1600
0453	CHA PHL	2355	012		1300	1311 1600
0454	CHA SAT	2355	101	1211		1611
0457	CHA DCA	2355	102	1200		1300 1600
0465	CHI DEN	1841	201	1400 2000		2100
0466	CHI YIP	0986	204	1950 2050		1100 1300 2140 3711
0467	CHI BDL	3051	102	2000		1100 2100
0468	CHI MKC	1841	103	1420		1200 2000 3812
0469	CHI LAX	1841	103	1400		1100 2000 2100
0471	CHI NYC	0986	114	1920	1300	1100 1312 2000 2100
0473	CHI PHL	0986	103	1300		1111 2000 2100
0474	CHI PIT	1986	102	2120		1300 2000
0475	CHI PDX	2190	012		2100	1900 2111
0476	CHI ROC	0986	101	1300		1100
0477	CHI SFO	1841	013		1100	1111 2000 2100
0479	CHI SEA	2190	012		2100	1900 2111
0480	CHI GEG	2190	012		2111	1900 2112
0481	CHI TUO	5564	101	2000		1100
0485	CVG BDL	3051	101	2000		1100
0487	CVG OKC	2355	101	2000		1100

Serial (1)	City Names (2)		Docket (3)	Number of Carriers (4)	New Carriers (5)	Improved Carriers (6)	Original Carriers (7)
					Carriers' Identifications and Restrictions		
0488	CVG	PIT	2355	101	1130		2000
0489	CVG	SFO	1841	012		1199	1111 2000
0490	CVG	TUO	5564	101	2000		1100
0491	CVG	TUL	2355	101	2000		1100
0493	CLE	DEN	1841	101	2000		2100
0494	CLE	BDL	3051	102	2011		1100 2100
0495	CLE	MKC	1841	101	2100		2000
0497	CLE	NYC	1789	104	2020		1111 1300 2100 3114
0498	CLE	OKC	2355	101	2000		1100
0500	CLE	PHL	0986	102	1300		2100 3113
0501	CLE	PIT	0986	102	1620		1300 1950
0502	CLE	PIT	1986	103	2150		1300 1620 1950
0503	CLE	PIT	4294	014		1900	1300 1620 1950 2150
0504	CLE	PDX	2190	012		2100	1930 2111
0506	CLE	SEA	2190	012		2100	1930 2111
0507	CLE	GEG	2190	012		2111	1930 2112
0508	CLE	TUO	5564	101	2000		1100
0509	CLE	TUL	2355	101	2000		1100
0515	CAE	HOU	2355	101	1511		1611
0518	CSG	HOU	2355	101	1530		1600
0519	CSG	NYC	2355	101	1530		1600
0520	CSG	PHL	2355	101	1530		1600
0521	CSG	DCA	2355	101	1530		1600
0523	CMH	BDL	3051	101	2000		1111
0526	CMH	NYC	2355	101	1130		2000
0527	CMH	OKC	2355	101	2000		1100
0528	CMH	PIT	2355	102	1130		2000 3511
0530	CMH	TUO	5564	101	2000		1100
0531	CMH	TUL	2355	101	2000		1100
0539	CRP	BNA	2355	101	1211		1611
0540	CRP	NYC	2355	101	1211		1600
0541	CRP	DCA	2355	101	1211		1600
0542	DAL	MEM	2355	014		1200	1100 1211 1511 4212
0543	DAL	BNA	2355	101	1200		1100
0544	DAL	NYC	2355	201	1200 1511		1100
0545	DAL	PHL	2355	101	1511		1100
0547	DAL	DCA	2355	201	1200 1511		1100
0550	DAY	BDL	3051	101	2000		1111
0553	DAY	NYC	2355	012		1131	1112 2000
0554	DAY	OKC	2355	101	2000		1100
0555	DAY	PIT	2355	101	1131		2000
0556	DAY	TUO	5564	101	2000		1100
0557	DAY	TUL	2355	101	2000		1100
0561	DAB	PVD	3051	101	1700		1600
0562	DAB	PIE	3051	101	1600		1700
0563	DAB	TPA	3051	101	1600		1700
0564	DEN	YIP	1841	101	2000		2100

Serial (1)	City Names (2)		Docket (3)	Number of Carriers (4)	Carriers' Identifications and Restrictions: New Carriers (5)	Improved Carriers (6)	Original Carriers (7)
0565	DEN	FWA	1841	101	2011		2100
0566	DEN	FAT	1841	101	2021		2111
0568	DEN	BDL	3051	101	2000		2100
0570	DEN	LGB	1841	101	2211		2111
0571	DEN	LAX	1841	201	1400 2020		2100
0575	DEN	NYC	1841	101	2000		2100
0576	DEN	NYC	2355	102	1211		2000 2100
0578	DEN	PHL	1841	101	2000		2100
0579	DEN	PIT	1841	200	2000 2111		
0581	DEN	RNO	1841	101	2200		2100
0582	DEN	SLC	1841	101	2200		2100
0583	DEN	SFO	1841	201	2020 2200		2100
0586	DEN	SBN	1841	101	2011		2100
0588	DEN	TOL	1841	101	2000		2100
0589	DEN	DCA	1841	101	2000		2100
0590	DEN	DCA	2355	102	1211		2000 2100
0602	YIP	FWA	0986	101	2150		1500
0603	YIP	BDL	3051	101	2011		1100
0604	YIP	MKC	1841	101	2150		2000
0606	YIP	NYC	0986	124	2020	1300 1900	1100 1321 1950 2120
0607	YIP	OKC	2355	101	2000		1111
0609	YIP	PIA	0986	101	2051		1111
0610	YIP	PHL	0986	111	1300	2100	2150
0611	YIP	PIT	0986	102	1620		1300 1950
0612	YIP	PIT	1986	103	2177		1300 1620 1950
0613	YIP	PIT	4294	014		1900	1300 1620 1950 2177
0614	YIP	PDX	2190	012		2130	1930 2131
0615	YIP	ROC	0986	101	1300		1100
0616	YIP	SFO	1841	013		1111	1112 2011 2130
0618	YIP	SEA	2190	012		2130	1930 2131
0619	YIP	GEG	2190	012		2131	1930 2170
0620	YIP	TUO	5564	101	2000		1111
0621	YIP	TUL	2355	101	2000		1111
0691	FWA	BDL	3051	101	2000		2100
0692	FWA	MKC	1841	101	2100		2011
0695	FWA	PIT	1986	101	2150		2000
0700	FWA	TOL	0986	101	2100		1500
0704	FTW	MEM	2355	014		1200	1100 1211 1511 4212
0705	FTW	BNA	2355	101	1200		1100
0706	FTW	NYC	2355	201	1200 1511		1100
0707	FTW	PHL	2355	101	1511		1100
0709	FTW	DCA	2355	201	1200 1511		1100
0710	FAT	BDL	3051	101	2000		2111
0711	FAT	MKC	1841	101	2111		2000
0714	FAT	PIT	1986	101	2112		2000
0735	GSO	HSV	8134	101	1611		1300
0736	GSO	MOB	2355	012		1350	1311 1600

Serial (1)	City Names (2)		Docket (3)	Number of Carriers (4)	Carriers' Identifications and Restrictions: New Carriers (5)			Improved Carriers (6)		Original Carriers (7)		
0737	GSO	MSY	2355	012				1320		1311	1600	
0738	GSO	NYC	2355	101	1330					1600		
0739	GSO	PHL	2355	101	1330					1600		
0746	HAR	PHL	0986	102	1300					2000	3170	
0749	BDL	HOU	2355	101	1112					1600		
0752	BDL	IND	3051	101	2000					1111		
0753	BDL	JAX	3051	101	1800					1600		
0755	BDL	MKC	3051	101	2000					2100		
0756	BDL	LAS	3051	101	2000					2100		
0757	BDL	LAX	3051	102	2000					1100	2100	
0758	BDL	SDF	7253	012				1699		1112	1611	
0759	BDL	SDF	3051	102	2000					1112	1611	
0760	BDL	MIA	3051	101	1800					1600		
0762	BDL	BNA	7253	012				1699		1100	1612	
0763	BDL	NHV	3051	012				1600		1100	1650	
0764	BDL	NYC	3051	223	2020	2120		1600	1885	1100	1650	1820
0765	BDL	OKC	3051	101	2000					1100		
0767	BDL	PIA	3051	101	2011					1111		
0768	BDL	PHL	3051	312	1800	2020	2120	1600		1100	1650	
0769	BDL	PHX	3051	101	2000					1100		
0771	BDL	PIT	3051	201	2000	2151				1131		
0773	BDL	PVD	3051	013				1600		1100	1650	2100
0775	BDL	RIC	3051	012				1600		1100	1650	
0776	BDL	STL	3051	102	2000					1100	1611	
0777	BDL	PIE	3051	111	1800			1600		1611		
0778	BDL	SFO	1841	012				1199		1111	2100	
0779	BDL	SFO	3051	102	2000					1111	2100	
0783	BDL	SBN	3051	101	2011					2100		
0785	BDL	TPA	3051	111	1800			1600		1611		
0787	BDL	TOL	3051	101	2012					2100		
0789	BDL	TUO	3051	101	2000					1100		
0790	BDL	TUL	3051	101	2000					1100		
0793	BDL	DCA	3051	312	1800	2020	2120	1600		1100	1650	
0796	BDL	ILG	3051	012				1600		1100	1650	
0808	HOU	JAX	5701	101	1700					1611		
0812	HOU	LEX	2355	101	1511					1612		
0813	HOU	SDF	2355	101	1131					1611		
0814	HOU	MCN	2355	101	1511					1611		
0819	HOU	MOB	5701	101	1700					1600		
0820	HOU	MGM	2355	101	1530					1600		
0821	HOU	BNA	2355	101	1130					1611		
0823	HOU	NHV	2355	101	1112			8		1600		
0824	HOU	MSY	2355	101	1530					1600		
0825	HOU	MSY	5701	102	1700					1600	1530	
0826	HOU	NYC	2355	301	1111	1211	1500			1600		
0829	HOU	ORL	5701	101	1711					1611		
0831	HOU	PNS	5701	101	1700					1600		

Serial (1)	City Names (2)	Docket (3)	Number of Carriers (4)	Carriers' Identifications and Restrictions: New Carriers (5)		Improved Carriers (6)	Original Carriers (7)		
0832	HOU PHL	2355	101	1500			1600		
0833	HOU PIT	2355	101	1100			1611		
0834	HOU PVD	2355	101	1112			1600		
0835	HOU PVD	3051	102	1711			1112	1600	
0838	HOU SAV	2355	101	1511			1612		
0839	HOU SAV	5701	102	1711			1511	1612	
0842	HOU TLH	5701	101	1700			1611		
0845	HOU DCA	2355	101	1500			1600		
0854	HSV NYC	7253	012			1611	1311	1612	
0855	HSV NYC	2355	012			1330	1311	1611	
0856	HSV PHL	0986	101	1312			1611		
0858	HSV PHL	8134	101	1611			1330		
0861	HSV RDU	8134	101	1611			1300		
0862	HSV RDG	8134	012			1699	1331	1612	
0863	HSV RIC	8134	101	1611			1300		
0868	HSV DCA	8134	101	1611			1300		
0879	IND SFO	1841	012			1111	1112	2000	
0880	IND TUO	5564	101	2000			1111		
0900	JAX MIA	3051	103	1800			1520	1600	1700
0905	JAX NYC	3051	102	1800			1600	1700	
0908	JAX PHL	3051	102	1800			1600	1700	
0912	JAX PVD	3051	201	1700	1800		1600		
0914	JAX PIE	3051	201	1600	1800		1700		
0915	JAX TPA	3051	201	1600	1800		1700		
0916	JAX DCA	3051	102	1800			1600	1700	
0921	MKC LAS	1841	101	2100			2000		
0923	MKC LAX	1841	201	1400	2100		2000		
0928	MKC MLI	1841	101	2100			1200		
0930	MKC NYC	1841	101	2100			2000		
0934	MKC PHL	1841	101	2100			2000		
0935	MKC PIT	1986	101	2121			2000		
0944	MKC SFO	1841	101	2100			2000		
0948	MKC SBN	1841	101	2100			2011		
0951	MKC TOL	1841	101	2100			2000		
0956	MKC DCA	1841	101	2100			2000		
0967	TYS PHL	0986	101	1311			1100		
0968	TYS PHL	2355	012			1300	1100	1311	
0975	LAS PIT	1986	101	2111			2000		
0998	LIT BNA	2355	101	1221			1100		
0999	LIT NYC	2355	101	1211			1100		
1001	LIT DCA	2355	101	1211			1100		
1008	LAX MRY	6503	101	2100			4170		
1009	LAX OKC	2355	101	2000			1100		
1010	LAX PIT	1986	101	2111			2000		
1011	LAX PIT	2355	102	1111			2000	2111	
1012	LAX SBA	6503	101	2100			4170		
1013	LAX TUO	5564	101	2000			1100		

Serial (1)	City Names (2)		Docket (3)	Number of Carriers (4)	Carriers' Identifications and Restrictions: New Carriers (5)	Improved Carriers (6)	Original Carriers (7)
1014	LAX	TUL	2355	101	2000		1100
1015	SDF	NHV	7253	012		1699	1112 1611
1016	SDF	NYC	7253	033		1100 1600 2000	1111 1611 2011
1017	SDF	OKC	2355	101	2000		1100
1018	SDF	PIT	2355	101	1130		2000
1019	SDF	PVD	7253	012		1699	1112 1611
1020	SDF	TUO	5564	101	2000		1100
1021	SDF	TUL	2355	101	2000		1100
1026	MCN	NYC	2355	101	1511		1611
1027	MCN	PHL	2355	101	1511		1611
1028	MCN	DCA	2355	101	1511		1611
1049	MEM	BNA	2355	101	1220		1100
1050	MEM	NYC	2355	113	1200	1300	1100 1311 1611
1051	MEM	PHL	0986	102	1312		1100 1611
1052	MEM	PHL	2355	013		1300	1100 1312 1611
1053	MEM	PIT	2355	101	1120		1311
1054	MEM	SAT	2355	101	1211		1131
1056	MEM	DCA	2355	103	1200		1100 1300 1611
1068	MIA	NYC	3051	102	1800		1600 1700
1071	MIA	PHL	3051	102	1800		1600 1700
1075	MIA	PVD	3051	201	1700 1800		1600
1077	MIA	PIE	3051	112	1800	1600	1620 1700
1078	MIA	TPA	3051	112	1800	1600	1620 1700
1079	MIA	DCA	3051	102	1800		1600 1700
1086	MKE	PHL	0986	101	1300		2120
1087	MKE	PDX	2190	012		2120	1900 2121
1090	MKE	SEA	2190	012		2120	1900 2121
1091	MKE	GEG	2190	012		2121	1900 2122
1098	MOB	PHL	2355	012		1330	1311 1600
1099	MOB	PIT	2355	101	1611		1300
1100	MOB	PVD	3051	101	1711		1600
1101	MOB	RDU	2355	012		1350	1311 1600
1102	MOB	RIC	2355	012		1350	1311 1600
1104	MOB	DCA	2355	012		1300	1311 1600
1105	MOB	INT	2355	012		1350	1311 1600
1136	MRY	SFO	6503	101	2100		4170
1137	MRY	SBA	6503	101	2100		4160
1149	MGM	NYC	2355	101	1530		1600
1150	MGM	PHL	2355	101	1530		1600
1151	MGM	DCA	2355	101	1530		1600
1163	BNA	NHV	7253	012		1699	1100 1612
1164	BNA	NYC	7253	012		1611	1100 1612
1165	BNA	NYC	2355	102	1200		1100 1611
1166	BNA	OKC	2355	101	1200		1100
1168	BNA	PVD	7253	012		1699	1100 1612
1169	BNA	SAT	2355	102	1211		1131 1611
1170	BNA	TUL	2355	101	1200		1100

Serial (1)	City Names (2)	Docket (3)	Number of Carriers (4)	New Carriers (5)	Improved Carriers (6)	Original Carriers (7)
1172	BNA DCA	2355	102	1200		1100 1611
1181	NHV NYC	3051	012		1600	1100 1650
1182	NHV PHL	3051	012		1600	1100 1650
1184	NHV PVD	3051	012		1600	1100 1650
1185	NHV RIC	3051	012		1600	1100 1650
1188	NHV DCA	3051	012		1600	1100 1650
1189	NHV ILG	3051	012		1600	1100 1650
1194	MSY NYC	2355	103	1500		1300 1600 1711
1197	MSY PHL	0986	101	1311		1600
1198	MSY PHL	2355	112	1500	1300	1311 1600
1199	MSY PIT	2355	101	1611		1300
1200	MSY PVD	3051	101	1711		1600
1201	MSY RDU	2355	012		1320	1311 1600
1202	MSY RIC	2355	012		1320	1311 1600
1204	MSY DCA	2355	112	1500	1300	1311 1600
1205	MSY INT	2355	012		1320	1311 1600
1206	NYC PHF	2355	101	1331		1700
1207	NYC PHF	3051	012		1300	1331 1700
1208	NYC ORF	2355	101	1331		1700
1209	NYC ORF	3051	012		1300	1331 1700
1210	NYC OKC	2355	201	1200 2000		1100
1213	NYC PHL	0986	105	1300		1100 1600 2000 2100 3130
1214	NYC PHL	2355	106	1530		1100 1300 1600 2000 2100 3130
1215	NYC PHL	3051	207	1700 1800		1100 1300 1530 1600 2000 2100 3130
1216	NYC PIT	0986	013		1300	1320 2000 3113
1217	NYC PIT	1986	103	2150		1300 2000 3113
1218	NYC PIT	2355	104	1130		1300 2000 2150 3113
1219	NYC PDX	2190	012		2100	1900 2111
1220	NYC PVD	3051	213	1700 2121	1600	1100 1650 1800
1221	NYC RDU	2355	101	1330		1600
1222	NYC RIC	2355	103	1330		1100 1600 1720
1223	NYC RIC	3051	014		1700	1100 1330 1600 1720
1224	NYC ROC	0986	101	1300		1100
1226	NYC STL	7253	013		1699	1111 1611 2000
1227	NYC PIE	3051	112	1800	1600	1611 1700
1228	NYC SAT	2355	102	1211		1131 1600
1229	NYC SFO	1841	013		1199	1111 2000 2100
1231	NYC SEA	2190	012		2100	1900 2111
1233	NYC SHV	2355	200	1212 1511		
1234	NYC GEG	2190	012		2111	1900 2112
1235	NYC TPA	3051	112	1800	1600	1611 1700
1237	NYC TOL	0986	012		1300	1311 2100
1238	NYC TUO	5564	101	2000		1100
1239	NYC TUL	2355	201	1200 2000		1100
1244	NYC DCA	2355	404	1230 1330 1530 2030		1100 1600 1720 3113
1245	NYC DCA	3051	238	1800 2120	1398 1700 2020	1100 1230 1330 1530 1600 1720

Serial (1)	City Names (2)		Docket (3)	Number of Carriers (4)		New Carriers (5)		Improved Carriers (6)			Original Carriers (7)					
											2030	3113				
1246	NYC	HLG	2355	102	2031						1300	3114				
1247	NYC	HLG	3051	013				2021			1300	2031	3114			
1249	NYC	INT	2355	101	1330						1600					
1250	PHF	PHL	2355	101	1331						1700					
1251	PHF	PHL	3051	012				1300			1331	1700				
1253	PHF	DCA	3051	101	1700						1300					
1255	ORF	PHL	2355	101	1331						1700					
1256	ORF	PHL	3051	012				1300			1331	1700				
1258	ORF	DCA	3051	101	1700						1300					
1269	OKC	PHL	2355	101	2000						1100					
1270	OKC	PHX	2355	101	2000						1100					
1271	OKC	PIT	2355	200	1100	2000										
1273	OKC	STL	2355	101	2000						1100					
1274	OKC	SFO	2355	101	2000						1100					
1276	OKC	AVP	2355	101	2000						1111					
1279	OKC	TUO	5564	101	2000						1100					
1280	OKC	TUL	2355	102	2000						1100	1400				
1281	OKC	DCA	2355	201	1200	2000					1100					
1296	ORL	PVD	3051	101	1700						1600					
1297	ORL	PIE	3051	101	1600						1700					
1298	ORL	TPA	3051	101	1600						1700					
1314	PNS	PVD	3051	101	1711						1600					
1315	PIA	TUO	5564	101	2000						1100					
1316	PHL	PIT	1986	102	2150						2000	3132				
1317	PHL	PIT	2355	103	1300						2000	2150	3132			
1322	PHL	PVD	3051	312	1700	1800	2121	1600			1100	1650				
1323	PHL	RDU	2355	101	1330						1600					
1324	PHL	RIC	2355	103	1330						1100	1600	1720			
1325	PHL	RIC	3051	014				1700			1100	1600	1330	1720		
1329	PHL	PIE	3051	112	1800			1600			1611	1700				
1336	PHL	TPA	3051	112	1800			1600			1611	1700				
1337	PHL	TOL	0986	101	1300						2100					
1339	PHL	TUO	5564	101	2000						1100					
1340	PHL	TUL	2355	101	2000						1100					
1344	PHL	DCA	2355	303	1330	1530	2030				1100	1600	1720			
1345	PHL	DCA	3051	236	1800	2120		1398	1700	2020	1100	1330	1530	1600	1720	2030
1347	PHL	HLG	0986	101	1311						3113					
1348	PHL	HLG	2355	102	2031						1311	3113				
1349	PHL	HLG	3051	013				2021			1311	2031	3113			
1351	PHL	INT	2355	101	1330						1600					
1353	PHL	YNG	0986	101	1300						2100					
1354	PHX	PIT	2355	101	1111						2000					
1355	PHX	TUO	5564	102	2000						1100	3400				
1356	PHX	TUL	2355	101	2000						1100					
1357	PIT	PDX	1986	101	2111						1930					
1359	PIT	PVD	3051	101	2152						1131					

Serial (1)	City Names (2)		Docket (3)	Number of Carriers (4)	New Carriers (5)			Improved Carriers (6)	Original Carriers (7)			
					Carriers' Identifications and Restrictions							
1366	PIT	SAN	2355	101	1111				2112			
1367	PIT	SFO	1986	101	2111				2000			
1368	PIT	SFO	2355	102	1111				2000	2111		
1371	PIT	SEA	1986	101	2111				1930			
1372	PIT	SBN	1986	101	2150				2000			
1373	PIT	GEG	1986	101	2112				1930			
1375	PIT	TOL	1986	101	2150				1300			
1377	PIT	TUO	5564	101	2000				1111			
1378	PIT	TUL	2355	200	1100	2000						
1382	PIT	YNG	1986	101	2150				1300			
1396	PDX	DCA	2190	012				2100	1900	2111		
1403	PVD	RIC	3051	112	1700			1600	1100	1650		
1404	PVD	PIE	3051	211	1700	1800		1600	1611			
1407	PVD	SAV	3051	101	1700				1600			
1410	PVD	TLH	3051	101	1711				1611			
1411	PVD	TPA	3051	211	1700	1800		1600	1611			
1415	PVD	DCA	3051	312	1700	1800	2121	1600	1100	1650		
1416	PVD	PBI	3051	101	1700				1600			
1417	PVD	ILG	3051	012				1600	1100	1650		
1426	RNO	SLC	1841	101	2200				2100			
1427	RNO	SFO	1841	101	2200				2100			
1429	RIC	PIE	3051	012				1600	1611	1700		
1430	RIC	TPA	3051	012				1600	1611	1700		
1431	RIC	DCA	3051	014				1700	1100	1300	1600	172
1445	STL	TUO	5564	101	2000				1100			
1446	STL	TUL	2355	101	2000				1100			
1448	PIE	SAV	3051	101	1600				1700			
1451	PIE	TPA	3051	102	1800				1600	1700		
1453	PIE	DCA	3051	112	1800			1600	1611	1700		
1456	PIE	PBI	3051	101	1600				1700			
1463	SLC	SFO	1841	101	2200				2100			
1465	SAT	DCA	2355	102	1211				1131	1600		
1467	SFO	SBA	6503	101	2100				4170			
1468	SFO	AVP	1841	012				1111	1112	2000		
1470	SFO	TUO	5564	101	2000				1100			
1471	SFO	TUL	2355	101	2000				1100			
1472	SFO	DCA	1841	013				1199	1111	2000	2100	
1488	SAV	TPA	3051	101	1600				1700			
1494	AVP	TUO	5564	101	2000				1111			
1495	AVP	TUL	2355	101	2000				1111			
1498	SEA	DCA	2190	012				2100	1900	2111		
1507	GEG	DCA	2190	012				2111	1900	2112		
1511	TPA	DCA	3051	112	1800			1600	1611	1700		
1514	TPA	PBI	3051	101	1600				1700			
1527	TUO	TUL	5564	101	2000				1100			
1528	TUO	DCA	5564	101	2000				1100			
1532	TUL	DCA	2355	201	1200	2000			1100			

APPENDIX TWO: *559 Competitive Docket City Pairs Certification Data and Origin and Destination Passenger Traffic, 1954-1957*

SOURCES AND CODES

Column

(1) City pairs are numbered serially in alphabetical order. Numbers are not consecutive because these are the *competitive* pairs.
(2) Standard three-letter codes for airline stations.
(3) Docket number for the decision affecting competition. The deferred portion of Docket 986 is shown as 1986.
(4) Number of carriers
First digit: number of *new* carriers authorized in the instant decision (Docket number).
Second digit: number of carriers with authorization *improved* in the instant decision.
Third digit: number of carriers authorized before the instant decision (the *original* carriers).
(5) Intent of the Board
1. purposive-specific
2. purposive-group
3. noted-specific
4. noted-group
5. corrective-specific
6. corrective-group
7. mentioned
0. not mentioned in the published opinion

(6) to (9) *Airline Traffic Surveys* expanded to annual totals. See Chapter VIII.

Serial (1)	*City Names* (2)		*Docket* (3)	*Number of Carriers* (4)	*Intent of Board* (5)	*Origin and Destination Passengers* *1954* (6)	*1955* (7)	*1956* (8)	*1957* (9)
0003	CAK	BOS	3051	101	0	1898	2002	2340	3172
0004	CAK	BDL	3051	101	0	806	689	793	1625
0008	CAK	PHL	0986	101	0	3562	4160	5473	5785
0009	CAK	PIT	0986	101	7	3250	3393	2743	3640
0010	CAK	PIT	1986	102	0	3250	3393	2743	3640
0012	CAK	PVD	3051	101	0	351	286	325	650
0021	ALB	OKC	2355	101	0	104	195	117	234
0023	ALB	SFO	1841	012	0	1417	2704	3367	3133
0025	ALB	TUO	5564	101	3	78	182	208	143
0026	ALB	TUL	2355	101	0	65	65	130	299
0028	ABQ	OKC	2355	101	3	1001	1287	1833	2626
0029	ABQ	TUL	2355	101	3	832	949	1287	1287
0037	ABE	BOS	3051	200	0	598	949	650	1196
0038	ABE	DEN	1841	101	0	169	260	169	260
0039	ABE	B.DL	3051	200	0	221	65	91	156
0041	ABE	MKC	1841	101	0	208	260	351	247
0045	ABE	PIT	1986	101	0	4771	6539	8398	8489
0060	AMA	NYC	2355	101	0	3276	4784	3406	4108
0061	AMA	OKC	2355	101	0	4667	5213	4784	5876
0063	AMA	TUL	2355	101	0	2366	3354	2938	3289
0064	AMA	DCA	2355	101	0	1118	1196	1235	1586
0072	ATL	BAL	2355	112	1	2522	3952	5070	5148
0073	ATL	BHM	2355	102	3	41834	39949	44759	48672
0074	ATL	CLT	2355	113	1	32032	37570	46124	48906
0076	ATL	GSO	2355	012	2	8593	10920	12090	13481
0077	ATL	HOU	2355	101	0	9776	8710	12987	12532
0079	ATL	MOB	2355	101	3	8203	10543	11232	13442

Serial (1)	City Names (2)		Docket (3)	Number of Carriers (4)	Intent of Board (5)	Origin and Destination Passengers 1954 (6)	1955 (7)	1956 (8)	1957 (9)
0080	ATL	MSY	2355	102	1	21567	23517	30589	31876
0081	ATL	NYC	2355	102	1	85852	95316	109330	111943
0083	ATL	PHL	0986	101	1	9542	11908	14664	20696
0084	ATL	PHL	2355	112	1	9542	11908	14664	20696
0085	ATL	PIT	2355	101	3	5460	5798	9958	11687
0086	ATL	RDU	2355	012	2	10387	13689	15925	18499
0087	ATL	RIC	2355	012	2	6188	7358	10192	10751
0089	ATL	DCA	2355	112	1	28028	33007	38207	45214
0090	ATL	INT	2355	012	2	2210	3146	4121	4875
0118	BAL	BTR	2355	101	0	117	234	208	286
0120	BAL	BHM	2355	112	1	819	1456	1456	1430
0122	BAL	BOS	3051	412	2	14092	16705	20020	21736
0123	BAL	BTV	3051	101	0	91	39	130	208
0124	BAL	CLT	2355	112	2	2834	2743	3380	2756
0125	BAL	CHA	2355	012	2	247	455	494	767
0126	BAL	CSG	2355	101	0	208	351	390	520
0128	BAL	DAL	2355	101	7	845	1118	1456	1872
0129	BAL	DEN	1841	101	0	858	1261	2262	2626
0132	BAL	FTW	2355	101	7	572	767	468	871
0133	BAL	GSO	2355	012	2	1417	1625	1599	1755
0135	BAL	BDL	3051	312	0	2392	3380	5096	5525
0138	BAL	HOU	2355	101	1	1599	2028	1872	1612
0140	BAL	HSV	8134	101	0	143	468	728	637
0143	BAL	JAX	3051	102	1	1092	2444	1989	2626
0144	BAL	MKC	1841	101	0	1573	2288	2353	2756
0146	BAL	TYS	2355	012	2	858	806	988	1014
0150	BAL	MCN	2355	101	0	234	923	1027	923
0153	BAL	MEM	2355	013	2	1261	1131	1118	1053
0155	BAL	MIA	3051	102	1	8567	9633	19266	26208
0156	BAL	MOB	2355	012	2	624	1183	663	1066
0159	BAL	MGM	2355	101	0	169	455	325	559
0164	BAL	NHV	3051	012	0	221	260	299	481
0166	BAL	MSY	2355	112	1	1937	1768	2106	2795
0167	BAL	NYC	2355	304	3	45435	58630	69602	73099
0168	BAL	NYC	3051	237	3	45435	58630	69602	73099
0169	BAL	PHF	3051	101	1	1274	1534	1599	3705
0170	BAL	ORF	3051	101	1	6643	9425	8255	9659
0171	BAL	OKC	2355	101	2	728	559	390	611
0175	BAL	PHL	2355	303	3	572	468	468	741
0176	BAL	PHL	3051	236	3	572	468	468	741
0181	BAL	PVD	3051	312	2	1976	1950	2782	2535
0182	BAL	RDU	2355	012	2	1742	2587	2340	3211
0183	BAL	RIC	2355	014	2	3848	3965	3432	3419
0184	BAL	RIC	3051	014	0	3848	3965	3432	3419
0187	BAL	PIE	3051	112	2	104	39	156	338
0193	BAL	TPA	3051	112	2	1222	1950	2340	2106
0194	BAL	TUO	5564	101	3	117	208	195	286
0195	BAL	TUL	2355	101	2	208	377	234	273
0199	BAL	DCA	2355	108	3	9750	11440	12220	11011
0200	BAL	DCA	3051	118	3	9750	11440	12220	11011
0203	BAL	INT	2355	012	2	1092	871	1313	884
0211	BTR	CLT	2355	101	0	312	156	117	468
0212	BTR	NYC	2355	101	0	5070	5499	6487	8411
0213	BTR	PHL	2355	101	0	455	234	481	715
0214	BTR	DCA	2355	101	0	1495	1391	1196	1794
0253	BHM	CLT	2355	113	1	3887	4680	4758	5252
0255	BHM	GSO	2355	012	2	637	1079	1300	1365
0256	BHM	HOU	2355	101	4	4979	5707	6305	5928
0257	BHM	NYC	2355	102	4	24440	29354	38974	32760
0260	BHM	PHL	0986	101	0	2275	3588	4290	5733
0261	BHM	PHL	2355	112	1	2275	3588	4290	5733
0262	BHM	PIT	2355	101	3	7943	8086	7995	8216
0263	BHM	RDU	2355	012	2	1157	858	1469	1755
0264	BHM	RIC	2355	012	2	1105	1222	1339	1339
0266	BHM	DCA	2355	112	1	7943	9906	11076	11323
0267	BHM	INT	2355	012	2	442	351	351	533
0296	BOS	CHS	3051	101	2	1235	1612	1781	2080
0297	BOS	CHW	3051	012	0	1976	2106	1859	1859
0298	BOS	CLE	3051	102	0	29068	29237	40521	43693
0299	BOS	DAB	3051	101	2	806	1833	2093	2847

Serial (1)	City Names (2)	Docket (3)	Number of Carriers (4)	Intent of Board (5)	Origin and Destination Passengers 1954 (6)	1955 (7)	1956 (8)	1957 (9)
0300	BOS DEN	1841	101	0	3705	6513	7644	8775
0303	BOS BDL	3051	113	0	15327	23569	27105	26325
0304	BOS HOU	2355	101	0	4199	5317	6565	7436
0305	BOS HOU	3051	102	0	4199	5317	6565	7436
0308	BOS JAX	3051	201	2	4810	5356	5837	11206
0309	BOS MKC	1841	101	0	4459	6292	6370	7046
0312	BOS SDF	7253	013	0	6851	6188	7566	8229
0314	BOS MIA	3051	201	1	50154	79885	114439	116259
0315	BOS MOB	3051	101	0	1482	1716	2041	1898
0317	BOS BNA	7253	012	0	2457	3211	3341	3250
0319	BOS NHV	3051	012	0	1547	1495	1560	1820
0320	BOS MSY	3051	101	0	4498	5993	6968	8489
0321	BOS NYC	3051	313	1	535197	580216	666419	740909
0324	BOS OKC	2355	101	0	1053	1469	2145	2028
0325	BOS ORL	3051	101	2	1352	2769	4095	4524
0328	BOS PNS	3051	101	0	975	1274	1534	2444
0329	BOS PHL	3051	412	2	55133	67873	78611	95654
0330	BOS PIT	2355	101	3	18707	25636	33241	34879
0331	BOS PIT	3051	102	3	18707	25636	33241	34879
0333	BOS PVD	3051	114	3	1690	2301	2691	2366
0335	BOS RIC	3051	112	2	4407	4212	5772	6682
0336	BOS PIE	3051	211	2	351	494	312	2015
0337	BOS SFO	1841	013	1	20384	27872	35464	35828
0340	BOS SAV	3051	101	2	390	793	858	663
0343	BOS TLH	3051	101	0	221	416	442	585
0344	BOS TPA	3051	211	1	8177	13156	20098	27781
0345	BOS TUO	5564	101	3	819	1482	1495	2067
0346	BOS TUL	2355	101	0	1105	1404	1521	1599
0350	BOS DCA	3051	412	1	67769	84734	99736	118508
0351	BOS PBI	3051	101	2	3835	6136	8411	10842
0353	BOS ILG	3051	012	0	2041	2782	4030	4771
0365	BRO CHA	2355	101	0	13	26		78
0367	BRO BNA	2355	101	0			26	130
0368	BRO NYC	2355	101	0	1261	1339	1404	1989
0369	BRO DCA	2355	101	0	559	611	611	416
0370	SSI HOU	2355	101	0	65	52	26	
0374	BUF CHI	0986	101	0	29289	37609	41275	42120
0375	BUF YIP	0986	101	1	31629	36868	40443	43862
0382	BUF NYC	0986	101	1	170170	190294	248183	281073
0387	BTV JAX	3051	101	0	13	39	52	52
0388	BTV MIA	3051	101	0	182	273	364	5161
0389	BTV PHL	3051	101	0	65	208	338	1482
0390	BTV PIE	3051	111	0	39		39	104
0391	BTV TPA	3051	111	0	65	104	52	429
0392	BTV DCA	3051	101	0	702	910	1079	1430
0406	CHS HOU	5701	101	0	624	728	676	1027
0407	CHS PVD	3051	101	2	247	286	468	247
0408	CHS PIE	3051	101	2	156	117	104	65
0409	CHS TPA	3051	101	2	559	858	1378	1196
0410	CHW BDL	3051	012	0	247	468	715	806
0411	CHW NHV	3051	012	0	91	13		52
0412	CHW PHL	0986	102	0	3055	2808	4771	5161
0413	CHW PVD	3051	012	0	338	494	338	611
0417	CLT CSG	2355	102	0	988	1456	1586	1781
0421	CLT HOU	2355	101	4	910	1183	1846	1989
0422	CLT HSV	8134	101	0	221	585	741	546
0425	CLT MCN	2355	101	0	390	689	624	936
0427	CLT MOB	2355	012	2	858	1027	1014	1326
0429	CLT MGM	2355	101	0	507	715	975	871
0430	CLT MSY	2355	112	1	3380	3679	2496	4082
0431	CLT NYC	2355	201	1	27066	35035	44629	48555
0432	CLT PHL	2355	201	1	6903	7397	9919	12220
0438	CLT DCA	2355	102	4	11856	14274	15652	18993
0440	CHA CRP	2355	101	0		78	39	78
0445	CHA HOU	2355	201	0	338	1118	962	1274
0448	CHA MEM	2355	101	0	3549	4602	6448	6240
0449	CHA BNA	2355	101	0	8489	18434	13338	15665
0450	CHA NYC	2355	102	1	7462	14001	17641	14742
0452	CHA PHL	0986	101	0	1287	2340	2548	2535
0453	CHA PHL	2355	012	2	1287	2340	2548	2535

Serial (1)	City Names (2)		Docket (3)	Number of Carriers (4)	Intent of Board (5)	Origin and Destination Passengers 1954 (6)	1955 (7)	1956 (8)	1957 (9)
0454	CHA	SAT	2355	101	0	260	338	286	468
0457	CHA	DCA	2355	102	1	2769	7007	5993	8021
0465	CHI	DEN	1841	201	1	34086	39910	47138	50726
0466	CHI	YIP	0986	204	3	219089	260663	273780	262964
0467	CHI	BDL	3051	102	0	25168	32669	35451	35828
0468	CHI	MKC	1841	103	3	79157	90961	99073	104065
0469	CHI	LAX	1841	103	3	146081	163397	192634	199771
0471	CHI	NYC	0986	114	3	551044	643409	739479	720343
0473	CHI	PHL	0986	103	0	90376	101634	121511	123422
0474	CHI	PIT	1986	102	3	66001	88322	104273	100334
0475	CHI	PDX	2190	012	1	11115	9607	13988	13585
0476	CHI	ROC	0986	101	0	12701	14625	19513	18122
0477	CHI	SFO	1841	013	1	92001	107484	115284	121056
0479	CHI	SEA	2190	012	1	27950	29081	37453	39676
0480	CHI	GEG	2190	012	0	3770	4017	3991	3549
0481	CHI	TUO	5564	101	3	12857	12038	15353	17342
0485	CVG	BDL	3051	101	6	4667	3601	4602	5980
0487	CVG	OKC	2355	101	6	1495	1365	1352	1703
0488	CVG	PIT	2355	101	0	15938	18005	20800	24167
0489	CVG	SFO	1841	012	0	4498	6578	6734	8268
0490	CVG	TUO	5564	101	3	312	1092	1079	637
0491	CVG	TUL	2355	101	6	845	1118	2600	1222
0493	CLE	DEN	1841	101	0	4511	4576	6565	5980
0494	CLE	BDL	3051	102	0	13637	17771	18642	18460
0495	CLE	MKC	1841	101	1	7735	7124	10270	12636
0497	CLE	NYC	1789	104	3	188981	206453	281983	274677
0498	CLE	OKC	2355	101	5	1430	1456	1937	2314
0500	CLE	PHL	0986	102	1	43862	36829	48633	60476
0501	CLE	PIT	0986	102	7	37518	31070	35230	30758
0502	CLE	PIT	1986	103	0	37518	31070	35230	30758
0503	CLE	PIT	4294	014	1	37518	31070	35230	30758
0504	CLE	PDX	2190	012	1	1235	1508	1092	1820
0506	CLE	SEA	2190	012	1	3926	4693	5174	5317
0507	CLE	GEG	2190	012	0	390	338	377	364
0508	CLE	TUO	5564	101	3	1404	2002	1794	2418
0509	CLE	TUL	2355	101	5	2327	1729	2444	2561
0515	CAE	HOU	2355	101	0	273	247	468	416
0518	CSG	HOU	2355	101	0	130	273	247	299
0519	CSG	NYC	2355	101	0	4043	6162	6955	11947
0520	CSG	PHL	2355	101	0	624	1378	1352	2119
0521	CSG	DCA	2355	101	0	1612	3679	2587	3640
0523	CMH	BDL	3051	101	6	1534	2756	2626	3536
0526	CMH	NYC	2355	101	1	49998	60320	70070	73749
0527	CMH	OKC	2355	101	6	585	637	845	676
0528	CMH	PIT	2355	102	7	22763	25389	28821	30979
0530	CMH	TUO	5564	101	3	546	429	1170	845
0531	CMH	TUL	2355	101	6	715	1092	1430	1274
0539	CRP	BNA	2355	101	0	221	91	221	338
0540	CRP	NYC	2355	101	0	3328	4576	4719	5837
0541	CRP	DCA	2355	101	0	1469	1469	1274	2080
0542	DAL	MEM	2355	014	1	10712	12506	12740	13884
0543	DAL	BNA	2355	101	1	3133	4160	4836	5746
0544	DAL	NYC	2355	201	1	58201	68744	84487	92092
0545	DAL	PHL	2355	101	7	4836	6786	9087	10465
0547	DAL	DCA	2355	201	1	16627	19890	26156	29406
0550	DAY	BDL	3051	101	6	3640	3003	3731	5668
0553	DAY	NYC	2355	012	3	45955	62114	69316	72722
0554	DAY	OKC	2355	101	6	3393	2522	3770	2132
0555	DAY	PIT	2355	101	0	9997	13026	13520	14677
0556	DAY	TUO	5564	101	3	533	520	884	884
0557	DAY	TUL	2355	101	6	715	871	962	1326
0561	DAB	PVD	3051	101	2	130	117	273	169
0562	DAB	PIE	3051	101	0	195	546	611	468
0563	DAB	TPA	3051	101	2	2119	2327	2977	2028
0564	DEN	YIP	1841	101	0	6136	9711	10946	12636
0565	DEN	FWA	1841	101	0	247	624	429	728
0566	DEN	FAT	1841	101	0	351	533	559	741
0568	DEN	BDL	3051	101	0	1287	2366	2561	2678
0570	DEN	LGB	1841	101	0	468	195	104	104
0571	DEN	LAX	1841	201	1	41613	54574	67821	78429
0575	DEN	NYC	1841	101	1	35906	44629	52403	59293

Serial (1)	City Names (2)		Docket (3)	Number of Carriers (4)	Intent of Board (5)	Origin and Destination Passengers 1954 (6)	1955 (7)	1956 (8)	1957 (9)
0576	DEN	NYC	2355	102	0	35906	44616	52403	59293
0578	DEN	PHL	1841	101	0	3965	5382	6786	7215
0579	DEN	PIT	1841	200	3	2015	2990	4251	5213
0581	DEN	RNO	1841	101	3	1443	1352	1404	1976
0582	DEN	SLC	1841	101	1	22685	26741	31720	33735
0583	DEN	SFO	1841	201	1	30732	37817	44655	46605
0586	DEN	SBN	1841	101	0	169	676	897	1118
0588	DEN	TOL	1841	101	0	546	1131	1300	1001
0589	DEN	DCA	1841	101	1	13767	17212	19435	23868
0590	DEN	DCA	2355	102	0	13767	17212	19435	23868
0602	YIP	FWA	0986	101	3	3588	4420	5707	5499
0603	YIP	BDL	3051	101	0	9204	13013	14716	15067
0604	YIP	MKC	1841	101	1	11778	14534	19591	20124
0606	YIP	NYC	0986	124	1	230386	275548	315328	337311
0607	YIP	OKC	2355	101	5	2847	2015	3315	3718
0609	YIP	PIA	0986	101	0	1664	2535	2574	3939
0610	YIP	PHL	0986	111	1	59969	73242	68159	77714
0611	YIP	PIT	0986	102	7	45357	49374	47177	57928
0612	YIP	PIT	1986	103	0	45357	49374	47177	57928
0613	YIP	PIT	4294	014	1	45357	49374	47177	57928
0614	YIP	PDX	2190	012	1	2743	2951	2600	3744
0615	YIP	ROC	0986	101	3	10712	13182	14885	15535
0616	YIP	SFO	1841	013	1	20423	25701	30849	31967
0618	YIP	SEA	2190	012	1	8411	9880	10153	13403
0619	YIP	GEG	2190	012	0	1703	1755	1183	1222
0620	YIP	TUO	5564	101	3	3146	3692	4875	4758
0621	YIP	TUL	2355	101	5	2327	2925	2678	2522
0691	FWA	BDL	3051	101	0	572	507	728	871
0692	FWA	MKC	1841	101	0	468	702	741	1014
0695	FWA	PIT	1986	101	0	1313	1378	2080	1950
0700	FWA	TOL	0986	101	3	858	949	1846	1391
0704	FTW	MEM	2355	014	1	1209	3185	3770	2795
0705	FTW	BNA	2355	101	1	650	962	1690	663
0706	FTW	NYC	2355	201	1	11518	11154	14209	11869
0707	FTW	PHL	2355	101	7	2561	1924	2561	3042
0709	FTW	DCA	2355	201	1	7358	7592	8229	7631
0710	FAT	BDL	3051	101	0	104	104	169	143
0711	FAT	MKC	1841	101	0	273	429	403	806
0714	FAT	PIT	1986	101	0	208	104	312	247
0735	GSO	HSV	8134	101	0	234	247	364	481
0736	GSO	MOB	2355	012	2	182	299	429	195
0737	GSO	MSY	2355	012	2	871	754	988	1417
0738	GSO	NYC	2355	101	2	13728	19448	19669	28899
0739	GSO	PHL	2355	101	2	2938	3224	3003	3575
0746	HAR	PHL	0986	102	0	1183	1261	2691	1391
0749	BDL	HOU	2355	101	0	1326	1950	1495	1612
0752	BDL	IND	3051	101	0	1703	2028	3094	3107
0753	BDL	JAX	3051	101	2	1040	1365	1261	1872
0755	BDL	MKC	3051	101	0	1768	2223	2561	2808
0756	BDL	LAS	3051	101	0	143	143	156	78
0757	BDL	LAX	3051	102	0	6396	8528	9464	10270
0758	BDL	SDF	7253	012	6	1742	2197	2522	1690
0759	BDL	SDF	3051	102	6	1742	2197	2522	1690
0760	BDL	MIA	3051	101	2	8268	9906	19682	27534
0762	BDL	BNA	7253	012	0	715	520	624	923
0763	BDL	NHV	3051	012	0	52	26	39	39
0764	BDL	NYC	3051	223	0	49049	58760	62803	82498
0765	BDL	OKC	3051	101	0	910	1131	897	1040
0767	BDL	PIA	3051	101	0	65	377	286	572
0768	BDL	PHL	3051	312	0	9256	8723	10088	12714
0769	BDL	PHX	3051	101	0	455	442	689	975
0771	BDL	PIT	3051	201	6	4680	6799	8463	11921
0773	BDL	PVD	3051	013	0	507	1040	884	650
0775	BDL	RIC	3051	012	0	1547	1235	1430	2197
0776	BDL	STL	3051	102	0	2652	3354	3991	4043
0777	BDL	PIE	3051	111	2	195	52	169	1768
0778	BDL	SFO	1841	012	1	4186	5876	5434	6006
0779	BDL	SFO	3051	102	0	4186	5876	5434	6006
0783	BDL	SBN	3051	101	0	520	819	650	1144
0785	BDL	TPA	3051	111	2	2041	2132	3627	4238

Serial (1)	City Names (2)		Docket (3)	Number of Carriers (4)	Intent of Board (5)	Origin and Destination Passengers 1954 (6)	1955 (7)	1956 (8)	1957 (9)
0787	BDL	TOL	3051	101	0	741	780	1131	1755
0789	BDL	TUO	3051	101	0	650	299	325	260
0790	BDL	TUL	3051	101	0	559	598	754	429
0793	BDL	DCA	3051	312	0	15509	18850	20410	23686
0796	BDL	ILG	3051	012	0	195	273	416	559
0808	HOU	JAX	5701	101	0	1326	1287	1651	1950
0812	HOU	LEX	2355	101	0	403	234	390	468
0813	HOU	SDF	2355	101	0	1846	1599	2483	2457
0814	HOU	MCN	2355	101	0	247	143	377	91
0819	HOU	MOB	5701	101	0	2340	3497	3393	4199
0820	HOU	MGM	2355	101	0	546	663	806	858
0821	HOU	BNA	2355	101	0	1833	1170	3822	2886
0823	HOU	NHV	2355	101	0	13	52		52
0824	HOU	MSY	2355	101	0	57798	79950	88218	90441
0825	HOU	MSY	5701	102	0	57798	79950	88218	90441
0826	HOU	NYC	2355	301	1	60918	75179	89700	91052
0829	HOU	ORL	5701	101	0	299	442	507	858
0831	HOU	PNS	5701	101	0	754	1027	1066	1625
0832	HOU	PHL	2355	101	2	4537	5863	7176	8775
0833	HOU	PIT	2355	101	7	3653	4537	10478	8489
0834	HOU	PVD	2355	101	0	676	819	585	793
0835	HOU	PVD	3051	102	0	676	819	585	793
0838	HOU	SAV	2355	101	0	273	624	338	442
0839	HOU	SAV	5701	102	0	273	624	338	442
0842	HOU	TLH	5701	101	0	286	377	260	533
0845	HOU	DCA	2355	101	2	15678	19578	21294	22165
0854	HSV	NYC	7253	012	0	1703	3536	6851	8359
0855	HSV	NYC	2355	012	2	1703	3536	6851	8359
0856	HSV	PHL	0986	101	0	494	806	1027	1118
0858	HSV	PHL	8134	101	0	494	806	1027	1118
0861	HSV	RDU	8134	101	0	104	169	78	169
0862	HSV	RDG	8134	012	0				
0863	HSV	RIC	8134	101	0	117	143	91	143
0868	HSV	DCA	8134	101	0	2548	5135	8437	8151
0879	IND	SFO	1841	012	0	5954	5486	6500	7137
0880	IND	TUO	5564	101	3	481	1365	1014	923
0900	JAX	MIA	3051	103	3	42458	54171	57070	60151
0905	JAX	NYC	3051	102	1	41613	51675	51558	59423
0908	JAX	PHL	3051	102	1	4641	6032	7592	8242
0912	JAX	PVD	3051	201	2	650	728	1105	1300
0914	JAX	PIE	3051	201	2	572	858	897	1274
0915	JAX	TPA	3051	201	2	16926	18187	19643	22581
0916	JAX	DCA	3051	102	1	11635	12649	13715	15873
0921	MKC	LAS	1841	101	0	1027	1170	2119	1547
0923	MKC	LAX	1841	201	1	22412	26247	30381	35646
0928	MKC	MLI	1841	101	0	1950	2600	2834	3926
0930	MKC	NYC	1841	101	1	51610	51948	66144	65455
0934	MKC	PHL	1841	101	0	12194	8632	10777	11791
0935	MKC	PIT	1986	101	1	6136	6045	7163	9295
0944	MKC	SFO	1841	101	1	13845	14768	19240	18954
0948	MKC	SBN	1841	101	0	806	1209	1521	1794
0951	MKC	TOL	1841	101	0	1729	2184	2314	2197
0956	MKC	DCA	1841	101	1	15756	16783	19253	23205
0967	TYS	PHL	0986	101	0	3549	2405	3848	5837
0968	TYS	PHL	2355	012	2	3549	2405	3848	5837
0975	LAS	PIT	1986	101	0	507	949	1495	1469
0998	LIT	BNA	2355	101	0	2782	2457	2847	2821
0999	LIT	NYC	2355	101	0	6656	8125	9880	9672
1001	LIT	DCA	2355	101	0	3328	5057	4368	5980
1008	LAX	MRY	6503	101	3	12649	13897	25389	45682
1009	LAX	OKC	2355	101	2	7774	9516	13468	15535
1010	LAX	PIT	1986	101	1	16016	19786	26715	33358
1011	LAX	PIT	2355	102	2	16016	19786	26715	33358
1012	LAX	SBA	6503	101	3	4394	5941	6474	7527
1013	LAX	TUO	5564	101	3	24726	37089	40508	41951
1014	LAX	TUL	2355	101	2	8619	8710	12233	13715
1015	SDF	NHV	7253	012	0	78	65	91	39
1016	SDF	NYC	7253	033	1	44343	60190	71539	57811
1017	SDF	OKC	2355	101	6	520	1105	1027	949
1018	SDF	PIT	2355	101	0	8008	11609	9009	14664

Serial (1)	City Names (2)	Docket (3)	Number of Carriers (4)	Intent of Board (5)	Origin and Destination Passengers 1954 (6)	1955 (7)	1956 (8)	1957 (9)
1019	SDF PVD	7253	012	0	481	832	1105	1131
1020	SDF TUO	5564	101	3	156	208	221	364
1021	SDF TUL	2355	101	6	1040	845	1300	1170
1026	MCN NYC	2355	101	0	2886	4433	4602	4667
1027	MCN PHL	2355	101	0	611	650	1196	1313
1028	MCN DCA	2355	101	0	1274	1456	1885	2964
1049	MEM BNA	2355	101	0	24570	25753	27105	28015
1050	MEM NYC	2355	113	1	22100	23907	31226	29536
1051	MEM PHL	0986	102	0	3055	3874	4316	5044
1052	MEM PHL	2355	013	2	3055	3874	4316	5044
1053	MEM PIT	2355	101	0	1937	2574	2678	2561
1054	MEM SAT	2355	101	0	2210	2925	3107	3133
1056	MEM DCA	2355	103	1	10296	11544	12402	13065
1068	MIA NYC	3051	102	1	651170	818701	958607	984126
1071	MIA PHL	3051	102	1	59293	88660	118261	116649
1075	MIA PVD	3051	201	2	4719	7696	7423	9646
1077	MIA PIE	3051	112	3	4134	5668	8736	13286
1078	MIA TPA	3051	112	1	60580	78819	93379	108095
1079	MIA DCA	3051	102	1	66768	79859	89349	105261
1086	MKE PHL	0986	101	0	6916	7982	9087	15275
1087	MKE PDX	2190	012	0	715	1274	923	1612
1090	MKE SEA	2190	012	0	2548	4108	2600	3458
1091	MKE GEG	2190	012	0	520	728	1274	767
1098	MOB PHL	2355	012	2	1235	2678	3575	4056
1099	MOB PIT	2355	101	3	2717	3276	3081	2392
1100	MOB PVD	3051	101	0	195	247	455	234
1101	MOB RDU	2355	012	2	195	312	390	312
1102	MOB RIC	2355	012	2	182	169	312	377
1104	MOB DCA	2355	012	2	4004	7332	5694	5213
1105	MOB INT	2355	012	2	13	78	117	156
1136	MRY SFO	6503	101	3	9919	10816	14716	16406
1137	MRY SBA	6503	101	3	637	1105	1599	2223
1149	MGM NYC	2355	101	0	3744	5668	6773	7865
1150	MGM PHL	2355	101	0	286	715	923	1274
1151	MGM DCA	2355	101	0	3822	3640	5772	5187
1163	BNA NHV	7253	012	0	13	26	39	26
1164	BNA NYC	7253	012	0	22191	27456	32513	33800
1165	BNA NYC	2355	102	1	22191	27456	32513	33800
1166	BNA OKC	2355	101	0	1157	1092	1612	1534
1168	BNA PVD	7253	012	0	299	299	299	559
1169	BNA SAT	2355	102	0	884	1118	1131	1313
1170	BNA TUL	2355	101	0	975	1456	1599	1911
1172	BNA DCA	2355	102	1	13156	14586	16263	18382
1181	NHV NYC	3051	012	0	1430	897	1560	1573
1182	NHV PHL	3051	012	0	52	195	52	169
1184	NHV PVD	3051	012	0	52	13	26	
1185	NHV RIC	3051	012	0	91	91	130	338
1188	NHV DCA	3051	012	0	1170	780	1677	1534
1189	NHV ILG	3051	012	0				13
1194	MSY NYC	2355	103	1	57356	68536	77363	93834
1197	MSY PHL	0986	101	0	5044	6292	8203	11453
1198	MSY PHL	2355	112	1	5044	6292	8203	11453
1199	MSY PIT	2355	101	3	3679	5798	4888	7735
1200	MSY PVD	3051	101	0	702	936	897	1027
1201	MSY RDU	2355	012	2	1235	1495	1443	1339
1202	MSY RIC	2355	012	2	962	1144	1183	1677
1204	MSY DCA	2355	112	1	17719	17966	19539	26819
1205	MSY INT	2355	012	2	312	65	143	234
1206	NYC PHF	2355	101	0	6006	10595	25870	17160
1207	NYC PHF	3051	012	1	6006	10595	25870	17160
1208	NYC ORF	2355	101	3	70772	73463	78455	80249
1209	NYC ORF	3051	012	1	70772	73463	78455	80249
1210	NYC OKC	2355	201	2	9113	13156	15821	17862
1213	NYC PHL	0986	105	7	30966	34918	45045	54041
1214	NYC PHL	2355	106	3	30966	34918	45045	54041
1215	NYC PHL	3051	207	3	30966	34918	45045	54041
1216	NYC PIT	0986	013	3	196820	241449	282711	295828
1217	NYC PIT	1986	103	3	196820	241449	282711	295828
1218	NYC PIT	2355	104	7	196820	241449	282711	295828
1219	NYC PDX	2190	012	1	11479	13754	17420	18668

Serial (1)	City Names (2)		Docket (3)	Number of Carriers (4)	Intent of Board (5)	Origin and Destination Passengers: 1954 (6)	1955 (7)	1956 (8)	1957 (9)
1220	NYC	PVD	3051	213	2	78273	88387	103532	122837
1221	NYC	RDU	2355	101	0	20852	27313	30784	33267
1222	NYC	RIC	2355	103	0	44161	51077	51103	54938
1223	NYC	RIC	3051	014	1	44161	51077	51103	54938
1224	NYC	ROC	0986	101	3	84981	101855	124670	146666
1226	NYC	STL	7253	013	0	90311	108303	117975	130143
1227	NYC	PIE	3051	112	1	4160	9555	5265	10660
1228	NYC	SAT	2355	102	1	36647	40365	46137	47775
1229	NYC	SFO	1841	013	1	172783	223405	240136	257933
1231	NYC	SEA	2190	012	1	38610	45188	54444	67028
1233	NYC	SHV	2355	200	0	4173	5330	7020	7748
1234	NYC	GEG	2190	012	0	4797	6305	6591	6435
1235	NYC	TPA	3051	112	1	62049	77545	93184	100126
1237	NYC	TOL	0986	012	3	17524	28795	30108	30875
1238	NYC	TUO	5564	101	3	8931	11778	13169	14248
1239	NYC	TUL	2355	201	2	16263	18135	23283	22724
1244	NYC	DCA	2355	404	3	493116	568776	629473	659334
1245	NYC	DCA	3051	238	1	493116	568776	629473	659334
1246	NYC	HLG	2355	102	0	3471	5265	6799	8047
1247	NYC	HLG	3051	013	0	3471	5265	6799	8047
1249	NYC	INT	2355	101	0	5967	8892	9919	12493
1250	PHF	PHL	2355	101	0	1118	2496	6929	6682
1251	PHF	PHL	3051	012	1	1118	2496	6929	6682
1253	PHF	DCA	3051	101	1	14456	15145	18876	21021
1255	ORF	PHL	2355	101	0	21346	18148	18694	17381
1256	ORF	PHL	3051	012	1	21346	18148	18694	17381
1258	ORF	DCA	3051	101	1	51493	61399	71045	76648
1269	OKC	PHL	2355	101	2	1287	1664	2353	2262
1270	OKC	PHX	2355	101	0	1170	1157	2535	1768
1271	OKC	PIT	2355	200	2	923	1092	1326	3367
1273	OKC	STL	2355	101	0	7111	7059	9087	10114
1274	OKC	SFO	2355	101	2	5486	3861	5928	5382
1276	OKC	AVP	2355	101	0	130	65	78	208
1279	OKC	TUO	5564	101	0	559	1027	806	689
1280	OKC	TUL	2355	102	3	6604	6227	7072	5083
1281	OKC	DCA	2355	201	2	5876	6214	8203	9230
1296	ORL	PVD	3051	101	2	390	546	416	572
1297	ORL	PIE	3051	101	2	299	416	780	325
1298	ORL	TPA	3051	101	2	4212	5980	7046	6188
1314	PNS	PVD	3051	101	0	78	221	377	390
1315	PIA	TUO	5564	101	0		52	169	130
1316	PHL	PIT	1986	102	3	69849	84968	92131	136786
1317	PHL	PIT	2355	103	1	69849	84968	92131	136786
1322	PHL	PVD	3051	312	2	4212	4290	6474	6669
1323	PHL	RDU	2355	101	0	5369	4953	6890	7475
1324	PHL	RIC	2355	103	0	9958	10933	13013	14274
1325	PHL	RIC	3051	014	0	9958	10933	13013	14274
1329	PHL	PIE	3051	112	1	1196	481	2652	845
1336	PHL	TPA	3051	112	1	6084	9321	10400	15405
1337	PHL	TOL	0986	101	0	6084	8593	8476	13195
1339	PHL	TUO	5564	101	3	689	1261	2002	1963
1340	PHL	TUL	2355	101	2	1703	2041	2808	2873
1344	PHL	DCA	2355	303	3	36634	41041	51233	66846
1345	PHL	DCA	3051	236	3	36634	41041	51233	66846
1347	PHL	HLG	0986	101	0	780	1235	910	897
1348	PHL	HLG	2355	102	0	780	1235	910	897
1349	PHL	HLG	3051	013	0	780	1235	910	897
1351	PHL	INT	2355	101	0	988	1183	1560	2418
1353	PHL	YNG	0986	101	0	3393	3991	4602	4862
1354	PHX	PIT	2355	101	0	1157	2093	2457	2444
1355	PHX	TUO	5564	102	3	13143	15548	15288	14625
1356	PHX	TUL	2355	101	0	845	936	1469	1352
1357	PIT	PDX	1986	101	1	806	1105	1053	1612
1359	PIT	PVD	3051	101	0	2366	2808	5096	4017
1366	PIT	SAN	2355	101	0	1794	1729	2002	3302
1367	PIT	SFO	1986	101	1	9490	12142	15821	15964
1368	PIT	SFO	2355	102	2	9490	12142	15821	15964
1371	PIT	SEA	1986	101	1	3562	4459	5135	4953
1372	PIT	SBN	1986	101	0	1625	1287	2639	2392
1373	PIT	GEG	1986	101	0	546	494	741	806

Serial (1)	City Names (2)		Docket (3)	Number of Carriers (4)	Intent of Board (5)	Origin and Destination Passengers 1954 (6)	1955 (7)	1956 (8)	1957 (9)
1375	PIT	TOL	1986	101	0	4589	6617	5525	5174
1377	PIT	TUO	5564	101	0	663	845	1430	1495
1378	PIT	TUL	2355	200	2	1833	2691	2743	5252
1382	PIT	YNG	1986	101	0	2834	2652	10569	3068
1396	PDX	DCA	2190	012	1	5213	5226	6929	7735
1403	PVD	RIC	3051	112	2	676	676	923	897
1404	PVD	PIE	3051	211	2	78	104	247	403
1407	PVD	SAV	3051	101	2	143	26	104	
1410	PVD	TLH	3051	101	0		39	91	
1411	PVD	TPA	3051	211	2	1287	1521	2548	1729
1415	PVD	DCA	3051	312	2	8502	9867	13624	15652
1416	PVD	PBI	3051	101	2	754	884	793	1469
1417	PVD	ILG	3051	012	0	390	559	260	728
1426	RNO	SLC	1841	101	3	3263	2691	3016	3965
1427	RNO	SFO	1841	101	1	93574	102401	116792	117234
1429	RIC	PIE	3051	012	2		26	39	117
1430	RIC	TPA	3051	012	2	572	520	845	1183
1431	RIC	DCA	3051	014	0	22048	22438	26793	27963
1445	STL	TUO	5564	101	3	1430	975	1222	1872
1446	STL	TUL	2355	101	0	10790	11271	13104	14872
1448	PIE	SAV	3051	101	2	39	52	78	26
1451	PIE	TPA	3051	102	0	26	182		39
1453	PIE	DCA	3051	112	1	1313	299	1937	1027
1456	PIE	PBI	3051	101	2	429	793	299	1287
1463	SLC	SFO	1841	101	3	34853	36998	43693	47801
1465	SAT	DCA	2355	102	1	13234	13611	17069	16380
1467	SFO	SBA	6503	101	3	7280	8645	12493	15678
1468	SFO	AVP	1841	012	0	767	962	949	767
1470	SFO	TUO	5564	101	3	5707	7020	7904	8528
1471	SFO	TUL	2355	101	2	4407	4524	4914	4719
1472	SFO	DCA	1841	013	1	43966	54249	59306	69186
1488	SAV	TPA	3051	101	2	962	1131	767	1222
1494	AVP	TUO	5564	101	3	26	26	91	117
1495	AVP	TUL	2355	101	0	143	78	26	104
1498	SEA	DCA	2190	012	1	12298	15782	17550	23803
1507	GEG	DCA	2190	012	0	1703	1859	2444	2431
1511	TPA	DCA	3051	112	1	12844	16237	17550	23114
1514	TPA	PBI	3051	101	2	3328	4576	4979	6474
1527	TUO	TUL	5564	101	0	1014	1027	559	845
1528	TUO	DCA	5564	101	3	1352	2366	2236	3341
1532	TUL	DCA	2355	201	2	5499	6409	7826	7761

APPENDIX THREE: *559 Competitive Docket City Pairs Origin and Destination Passenger-Miles, 1954-1957*

SOURCES AND CODES

Column

(1) City pairs are numbered serially in alphabetical order. Numbers are not consecutive because these are the *competitive* pairs.
(2) Standard three-letter codes for airline stations.
(3) Docket number for the decision affecting competition. The deferred portion of Docket 986 is shown as 1986.
(4) Distance in miles between the city pair. Source: *Airline Distances Between Cities in the United States, U.S. Department of Commerce, Coast and Geodetic Survey, Special Publication No. 238, 1947.*
(5) to (8) Passenger-miles in thousands from column (4) and Appendix Two.

Serial (1)	*City Names* (2)	*Docket* (3)	*Distance* (4)	*Origin and Destination Passenger-Miles* 1954 (5)	1955 (6)	1956 (7)	1957 (8)
0003	CAK BOS	3051	547	1038	1095	1279	1735
0004	CAK BDL	3051	461	371	317	365	749
0008	CAK PHL	0986	344	1225	1431	1882	1990
0009	CAK PIT	0986	91	295	308	249	331
0010	CAK PIT	1986	91	295	308	249	331
0012	CAK PVD	3051	527	184	150	171	342
0021	ALB OKC	2355	1365	141	266	159	319
0023	ALB SFO	1841	2560	3627	6922	8619	8020
0025	ALB TUO	5564	2149	167	391	446	307
0026	ALB TUL	2355	1267	82	82	164	378
0028	ABQ OKC	2355	517	517	665	947	1357
0029	ABQ TUL	2355	604	502	573	777	777
0037	ABE BOS	3051	259	154	245	168	309
0038	ABE DEN	1841	1556	262	404	262	404
0039	ABE BDL	3051	166	36	10	15	25
0041	ABE MKC	1841	1020	212	265	358	251
0045	ABE PIT	1986	239	1140	1562	2007	2028
0060	AMA NYC	2355	1560	5110	7463	5313	6408
0061	AMA OKC	2355	245	1143	1277	1172	1439
0063	AMA TUL	2355	335	792	1123	984	1101
0064	AMA DCA	2355	1391	1555	1663	1717	2206
0072	ATL BAL	2355	577	1455	2280	2925	2970
0073	ATL BHM	2355	140	5856	5592	6266	6814
0074	ATL CLT	2355	227	7271	8528	10470	11101
0076	ATL GSO	2355	306	2629	3341	3699	4125
0077	ATL HOU	2355	701	6852	6105	9103	8784
0079	ATL MOB	2355	300	2460	3162	3369	4032
0080	ATL MSY	2355	424	9144	9971	12969	13515
0081	ATL NYC	2355	748	64217	71296	81778	83733
0083	ATL PHL	0986	666	6354	7930	9766	13783
0084	ATL PHL	2355	666	6354	7930	9766	13783
0085	ATL PIT	2355	521	2844	3020	5188	6088
0086	ATL RDU	2355	356	3697	4873	5669	6585
0087	ATL RIC	2355	470	2908	3458	4790	5052
0089	ATL DCA	2355	543	15219	17922	20746	24551
0090	ATL INT	2355	286	632	899	1178	1394
0118	BAL BTR	2355	1026	120	240	213	293
0120	BAL BHM	2355	693	567	1009	1009	990
0122	BAL BOS	3051	360	5073	6013	7207	7824
0123	BAL BTV	3051	398	36	15	51	82
0124	BAL CLT	2355	365	1034	1001	1233	1005
0125	BAL CHA	2355	562	138	255	277	431
0126	BAL CSG	2355	664	138	233	258	345
0128	BAL DAL	2355	1212	1024	1355	1764	2268
0129	BAL DEN	1841	1510	1295	1904	3415	3965

Serial (1)	City Names (2)	Docket (3)	Distance (4)	Origin and Destination Passenger-Miles 1954 (5)	1955 (6)	1956 (7)	1957 (8)
0132	BAL FTW	2355	1241	709	951	580	1080
0133	BAL GSO	2355	282	399	458	450	494
0135	BAL BDL	3051	268	641	905	1365	1480
0138	BAL HOU	2355	1251	2000	2537	2341	2016
0140	BAL HSV	8134	634	90	296	461	403
0143	BAL JAX	3051	681	743	1664	1354	1788
0144	BAL MKC	1841	963	1514	2203	2265	2654
0146	BAL TYS	2355	462	396	372	456	468
0150	BAL MCN	2355	593	138	547	609	547
0153	BAL MEM	2355	793	999	896	886	835
0155	BAL MIA	3051	954	8172	9189	18379	25002
0156	BAL MOB	2355	877	547	1037	581	934
0159	BAL MGM	2355	723	122	328	234	404
0164	BAL NHV	3051	239	52	62	71	114
0166	BAL MSY	2355	999	1935	1766	2103	2792
0167	BAL NYC	2355	172	7814	10084	11971	12573
0168	BAL NYC	3051	172	7814	10084	11971	12573
0169	BAL PHF	3051	160	203	245	255	592
0170	BAL ORF	3051	169	1122	1592	1395	1632
0171	BAL OKC	2355	1177	856	657	459	719
0175	BAL PHL	2355	90	51	42	42	66
0176	BAL PHL	3051	90	51	42	42	66
0181	BAL PVD	3051	325	642	633	904	823
0182	BAL RDU	2355	267	465	690	624	857
0183	BAL RIC	2355	129	496	511	442	441
0184	BAL RIC	3051	129	496	511	442	441
0187	BAL PIE	3051	866	90	33	135	292
0193	BAL TPA	3051	851	1039	1659	1991	1792
0194	BAL TUO	5564	1978	231	411	385	565
0195	BAL TUL	2355	1081	224	407	252	295
0199	BAL DCA	2355	35	341	400	427	385
0200	BAL DCA	3051	35	341	400	427	385
0203	BAL INT	2355	297	324	258	389	262
0211	BTR CLT	2355	685	213	106	80	320
0212	BTR NYC	2355	1197	6068	6582	7764	10067
0213	BTR PHL	2355	1116	507	261	536	797
0214	BTR DCA	2355	993	1484	1381	1187	1781
0253	BHM CLT	2355	361	1403	1689	1717	1895
0255	BHM GSO	2355	436	277	470	566	595
0256	BHM HOU	2355	567	2823	3235	3574	3361
0257	BHM NYC	2355	864	21116	25361	33673	28304
0260	BHM PHL	0986	783	1781	2809	3359	4488
0261	BHM PHL	2355	783	1781	2809	3359	4488
0262	BHM PIT	2355	608	4829	4916	4860	4995
0263	BHM RDU	2355	491	568	421	721	861
0264	BHM RIC	2355	596	658	728	798	798
0266	BHM DCA	2355	661	5250	6547	7321	7484
0267	BHM INT	2355	413	182	144	144	220
0296	BOS CHS	3051	820	1012	1321	1460	1705
0297	BOS CHW	3051	622	1229	1309	1156	1156
0298	BOS CLE	3051	551	16016	16109	22327	24074
0299	BOS DAB	3051	1063	856	1948	2224	3026
0300	BOS DEN	1841	1769	6554	11521	13522	15522
0303	BOS BDL	3051	93	1425	2191	2520	2448
0304	BOS HOU	2355	1605	6739	8533	10536	11934
0305	BOS HOU	3051	1605	6739	8533	10536	11934
0308	BOS JAX	3051	1017	4891	5447	5936	11396
0309	BOS MKC	1841	1251	5578	7871	7968	8814
0312	BOS SDF	7253	826	5658	5111	6249	6797
0314	BOS MIA	3051	1255	62943	100255	143620	145905
0315	BOS MOB	3051	1237	1833	2122	2524	2347
0317	BOS BNA	7253	943	2316	3027	3150	3064
0319	BOS NHV	3051	121	187	180	188	220
0320	BOS MSY	3051	1359	6112	8144	9469	11536
0321	BOS NYC	3051	188	100617	109080	125286	139290
0324	BOS OKC	2355	1495	1574	2196	3206	3031
0325	BOS ORL	3051	1114	1506	3084	4561	5039
0328	BOS PNS	3051	1216	1185	1549	1865	2971
0329	BOS PHL	3051	271	14941	18393	21303	25922
0330	BOS PIT	2355	483	9035	12382	16055	16846

Serial (1)	*City Names* (2)		*Docket* (3)	*Distance* (4)	*Origin and Destination Passenger-Miles* 1954 (5)	1955 (6)	1956 (7)	1957 (8)
0331	BOS	PIT	3051	483	9035	12382	16055	16846
0333	BOS	PVD	3051	41	69	94	110	97
0335	BOS	RIC	3051	474	2088	1996	2735	3167
0336	BOS	PIE	3051	1198	420	591	373	2413
0337	BOS	SFO	1841	2699	55016	75226	95717	96699
0340	BOS	SAV	3051	898	350	712	770	595
0343	BOS	TLH	3051	1101	243	458	486	644
0344	BOS	TPA	3051	1182	9665	15550	23755	32837
0345	BOS	TUO	5564	2284	1870	3384	3414	4721
0346	BOS	TUL	2355	1398	1544	1962	2126	2235
0350	BOS	DCA	3051	393	26633	33300	39196	46573
0351	BOS	PBI	3051	1192	4571	7314	10025	12923
0353	BOS	ILG	3051	296	604	823	1192	1412
0365	BRO	CHA	2355	961	12	24		74
0367	BRO	BNA	2355	949			24	123
0368	BRO	NYC	2355	1693	2134	2266	2376	3367
0369	BRO	DCA	2355	1489	832	909	909	619
0370	SSI	HOU	2355	833	54	43	21	
0374	BUF	CHI	0986	454	13297	17074	18738	19122
0375	BUF	YIP	0986	216	6831	7963	8735	9474
0382	BUF	NYC	0986	292	49689	55565	72469	82073
0387	BTV	JAX	3051	1079	14	42	56	56
0388	BTV	MIA	3051	1347	245	367	490	6951
0389	BTV	PHL	3051	328	21	68	110	486
0390	BTV	PIE	3051	1264	49		49	131
0391	BTV	TPA	3051	1249	81	129	64	535
0392	BTV	DCA	3051	432	303	393	466	617
0406	CHS	HOU	5701	936	584	681	632	961
0407	CHS	PVD	3051	780	192	223	365	192
0408	CHS	PIE	3051	381	59	44	39	24
0409	CHS	TPA	3051	365	204	313	502	436
0410	CHW	BDL	3051	530	130	248	378	427
0411	CHW	NHV	3051	506	46	6		26
0412	CHW	PHL	0986	365	1115	1024	1741	1883
0413	CHW	PVD	3051	592	200	292	200	361
0417	CLT	CSG	2355	305	301	444	483	543
0421	CLT	HOU	2355	927	843	1096	1711	1843
0422	CLT	HSV	8134	328	72	191	243	179
0425	CLT	MCN	2355	229	89	157	142	214
0427	CLT	MOB	2355	522	447	536	529	692
0429	CLT	MGM	2355	371	188	265	361	323
0430	CLT	MSY	2355	649	2193	2387	1619	2649
0431	CLT	NYC	2355	533	14426	18673	23787	25879
0432	CLT	PHL	2355	451	3113	3336	4473	5511
0438	CLT	DCA	2355	330	3912	4710	5165	6267
0440	CHA	CRP	2355	870		67	33	67
0445	CHA	HOU	2355	691	233	772	664	880
0448	CHA	MEM	2355	269	954	1237	1734	1678
0449	CHA	BNA	2355	113	959	2083	1507	1770
0450	CHA	NYC	2355	732	5462	10248	12913	10791
0452	CHA	PHL	0986	652	839	1525	1661	1652
0453	CHA	PHL	2355	652	839	1525	1661	1652
0454	CHA	SAT	2355	862	224	291	246	403
0457	CHA	DCA	2355	530	1467	3713	3176	4251
0465	CHI	DEN	1841	920	31359	36717	43366	46667
0466	CHI	YIP	0986	238	52143	62037	65159	62585
0467	CHI	BDL	3051	771	19404	25187	27332	27623
0468	CHI	MKC	1841	414	32770	37657	41016	43082
0469	CHI	LAX	1841	1745	254911	285127	336146	348600
0471	CHI	NYC	0986	713	392894	458750	527248	513604
0473	CHI	PHL	0986	666	60190	67688	80926	82199
0474	CHI	PIT	1986	410	27060	36212	42751	41136
0475	CHI	PDX	2190	1758	19540	16889	24590	23882
0476	CHI	ROC	0986	520	6604	7605	10146	9423
0477	CHI	SFO	1841	1858	170937	199705	214197	224922
0479	CHI	SEA	2190	1737	48549	50513	65055	68917
0480	CHI	GEG	2190	1508	5685	6057	6018	5351
0481	CHI	TUO	5564	1444	18565	17382	22169	25041
0485	CVG	BDL	3051	650	3033	2340	2991	3887
0487	CVG	OKC	2355	758	1133	1034	1024	1290

Serial (*1*)	*City Names* (*2*)	*Docket* (*3*)	*Distance* (*4*)	*Origin and Destination Passenger-Miles* *1954* (*5*)	*1955* (*6*)	*1956* (*7*)	*1957* (*8*)
0488	CVG PIT	2355	257	4096	4627	5345	6210
0489	CVG SFO	1841	2043	9189	13438	13757	16891
0490	CVG TUO	5564	1556	485	1699	1678	991
0491	CVG TUL	2355	661	558	738	1718	807
0493	CLE DEN	1841	1227	5534	5614	8055	7337
0494	CLE BDL	3051	467	6368	8299	8705	8620
0495	CLE MKC	1841	700	5414	4986	7189	8845
0497	CLE NYC	1789	405	76537	83613	114203	111244
0498	CLE OKC	2355	951	1359	1384	1842	2200
0500	CLE PHL	0986	360	15790	13258	17507	21771
0501	CLE PIT	0986	115	4314	3573	4051	3537
0502	CLE PIT	1986	115	4314	3573	4051	3537
0503	CLE PIT	4294	115	4314	3573	4051	3537
0504	CLE PDX	2190	2055	2537	3098	2244	3740
0506	CLE SEA	2190	2026	7954	9508	10482	10772
0507	CLE GEG	2190	1796	700	607	677	653
0508	CLE TUO	5564	1733	2433	3469	3109	4190
0509	CLE TUL	2355	853	1984	1474	2084	2184
0515	CAE HOU	2355	891	243	220	416	370
0518	CSG HOU	2355	642	83	175	158	191
0519	CSG NYC	2355	835	3375	5145	5807	9975
0520	CSG PHL	2355	753	469	1037	1018	1595
0521	CSG DCA	2355	630	1015	2317	1629	2293
0523	CMH BDL	3051	555	851	1529	1457	1962
0526	CMH NYC	2355	478	23899	28832	33493	35252
0527	CMH OKC	2355	852	498	542	719	575
0528	CMH PIT	2355	162	3687	4113	4669	5018
0530	CMH TUO	5564	1645	898	705	1924	1390
0531	CMH TUL	2355	755	539	824	1079	961
0539	CRP BNA	2355	848	187	77	187	286
0540	CRP NYC	2355	1601	5328	7326	7555	9345
0541	CRP DCA	2355	1400	2056	2056	1783	2912
0542	DAL MEM	2355	420	4499	5252	5350	5831
0543	DAL BNA	2355	617	1933	2566	2983	3545
0544	DAL NYC	2355	1374	79968	94454	116085	126534
0545	DAL PHL	2355	1299	6281	8815	11804	13594
0547	DAL DCA	2355	1185	19702	23569	30994	34846
0550	DAY BDL	3051	619	2253	1858	2309	3508
0553	DAY NYC	2355	543	24953	33727	37638	39488
0554	DAY OKC	2355	787	2670	1984	2966	1677
0555	DAY PIT	2355	227	2269	2956	3069	3331
0556	DAY TUO	5564	1581	842	822	1397	1397
0557	DAY TUL	2355	690	493	600	663	914
0561	DAB PVD	3051	1023	132	119	279	172
0562	DAB PIE	3051	140	27	76	85	65
0563	DAB TPA	3051	123	260	286	366	249
0564	DEN YIP	1841	1156	7093	11225	12653	14607
0565	DEN FWA	1841	1048	258	653	449	762
0566	DEN FAT	1841	830	291	442	463	615
0568	DEN BDL	3051	1690	2175	3998	4328	4525
0570	DEN LGB	1841	839	392	163	87	87
0571	DEN LAX	1841	831	34580	45350	56359	65174
0575	DEN NYC	1841	1631	58562	72789	85469	96706
0576	DEN NYC	2355	1631	58562	72768	85469	96706
0578	DEN PHL	1841	1579	6260	8498	10715	11392
0579	DEN PIT	1841	1320	2659	3946	5611	6881
0581	DEN RNO	1841	790	1139	1068	1109	1561
0582	DEN SLC	1841	371	8416	9920	11768	12515
0583	DEN SFO	1841	949	29164	35888	42377	44228
0586	DEN SBN	1841	991	167	669	888	1107
0588	DEN TOL	1841	1131	617	1279	1470	1132
0589	DEN DCA	1841	1494	20567	25714	29035	35658
0590	DEN DCA	2355	1494	20567	25714	29035	35658
0602	YIP FWA	0986	139	498	614	793	764
0603	YIP BDL	3051	534	4914	6948	7858	8045
0604	YIP MKC	1841	645	7596	9374	12636	12979
0606	YIP NYC	0986	482	111046	132814	151988	162583
0607	YIP OKC	2355	910	2590	1833	3016	3383
0609	YIP PIA	0986	358	595	907	921	1410
0610	YIP PHL	0986	443	26566	32446	30194	34427

Serial (1)	City Names (2)		Docket (3)	Distance (4)	Origin and Destination Passenger-Miles 1954 (5)	1955 (6)	1956 (7)	1957 (8)
0611	YIP	PIT	0986	205	9298	10121	9671	11875
0612	YIP	PIT	1986	205	9298	10121	9671	11875
0613	YIP	PIT	4294	205	9298	10121	9671	11875
0614	YIP	PDX	2190	1969	5400	5810	5119	7371
0615	YIP	ROC	0986	283	3031	3730	4212	4396
0616	YIP	SFO	1841	2091	42704	53740	64505	66842
0618	YIP	SEA	2190	1938	16300	19147	19676	25975
0619	YIP	GEG	2190	1709	2910	2999	2021	2088
0620	YIP	TUO	5564	1679	5282	6198	8185	7988
0621	YIP	TUL	2355	813	1891	2378	2177	2050
0691	FWA	BDL	3051	648	370	328	471	564
0692	FWA	MKC	1841	519	242	364	384	526
0695	FWA	PIT	1986	273	358	376	567	532
0700	FWA	TOL	0986	92	78	87	169	127
0704	FTW	MEM	2355	449	542	1430	1692	1254
0705	FTW	BNA	2355	646	419	621	1091	428
0706	FTW	NYC	2355	1402	16148	15637	19921	16640
0707	FTW	PHL	2355	1328	3401	2555	3401	4039
0709	FTW	DCA	2355	1214	8932	9216	9990	9264
0710	FAT	BDL	3051	2518	261	261	425	360
0711	FAT	MKC	1841	1382	377	592	556	1113
0714	FAT	PIT	1986	2150	447	223	670	531
0735	GSO	HSV	8134	394	92	97	143	189
0736	GSO	MOB	2355	604	109	180	259	117
0737	GSO	MSY	2355	730	635	550	721	1034
0738	GSO	NYC	2355	450	6177	8751	8851	13004
0739	GSO	PHL	2355	368	1081	1186	1105	1315
0746	HAR	PHL	0986	94	111	118	252	130
0749	BDL	HOU	2355	1513	2006	2950	2261	2438
0752	BDL	IND	3051	720	1226	1460	2227	2237
0753	BDL	JAX	3051	934	971	1274	1177	1748
0755	BDL	MKC	3051	1166	2061	2592	2986	3274
0756	BDL	LAS	3051	2295	328	328	358	179
0757	BDL	LAX	3051	2515	16085	21447	23801	25829
0758	BDL	SDF	7253	734	1278	1612	1851	1240
0759	BDL	SDF	3051	734	1278	1612	1851	1240
0760	BDL	MIA	3051	1183	9781	11718	23283	32572
0762	BDL	BNA	7253	851	608	442	531	785
0763	BDL	NHV	3051	34	1		1	1
0764	BDL	NYC	3051	98	4806	5758	6154	8084
0765	BDL	OKC	3051	1406	1279	1590	1261	1462
0767	BDL	PIA	3051	883	57	332	252	505
0768	BDL	PHL	3051	180	1666	1570	1815	2288
0769	BDL	PHX	3051	2215	1007	979	1526	2159
0771	BDL	PIT	3051	393	1839	2672	3325	4684
0773	BDL	PVD	3051	66	33	68	58	42
0775	BDL	RIC	3051	387	598	477	553	850
0776	BDL	STL	3051	950	2519	3186	3791	3840
0777	BDL	PIE	3051	1117	217	58	188	1974
0778	BDL	SFO	1841	2625	10988	15424	14264	15765
0779	BDL	SFO	3051	2625	10988	15424	14264	15765
0783	BDL	SBN	3051	701	364	574	455	801
0785	BDL	TPA	3051	1101	2247	2347	3993	4666
0787	BDL	TOL	3051	561	415	437	634	984
0789	BDL	TUO	3051	2197	1428	656	714	571
0790	BDL	TUL	3051	1309	731	782	986	561
0793	BDL	DCA	3051	302	4683	5692	6163	7153
0796	BDL	ILG	3051	205	39	55	85	114
0808	HOU	JAX	5701	821	1088	1056	1355	1600
0812	HOU	LEX	2355	845	340	197	329	395
0813	HOU	SDF	2355	803	1482	1283	1993	1972
0814	HOU	MCN	2355	725	179	103	273	65
0819	HOU	MOB	5701	442	1034	1545	1499	1855
0820	HOU	MGM	2355	566	309	375	456	485
0821	HOU	BNA	2355	665	1218	778	2541	1919
0823	HOU	NHV	2355	1847	24	96		96
0824	HOU	MSY	2355	318	18379	25424	28053	28760
0825	HOU	MSY	5701	318	18379	25424	28053	28760
0826	HOU	NYC	2355	1420	86503	106754	127374	129293
0829	HOU	ORL	5701	849	253	375	430	728

Serial (1)	City Names (2)		Docket (3)	Distance (4)	Origin and Destination Passenger-Miles 1954 (5)	1955 (6)	1956 (7)	1957 (8)
0831	HOU	PNS	5701	490	369	503	522	796
0832	HOU	PHL	2355	1341	6084	7862	9623	11767
0833	HOU	PIT	2355	1137	4153	5158	11913	9651
0834	HOU	PVD	2355	1573	1063	1288	920	1247
0835	HOU	PVD	3051	1573	1063	1288	920	1247
0838	HOU	SAV	2355	862	235	537	291	381
0839	HOU	SAV	5701	862	235	537	291	381
0842	HOU	TLH	5701	665	190	250	172	354
0845	HOU	DCA	2355	1220	19127	23885	25978	27041
0854	HSV	NYC	7253	804	1369	2842	5508	6720
0855	HSV	NYC	2355	804	1369	2842	5508	6720
0856	HSV	PHL	0986	724	357	583	743	809
0858	HSV	PHL	8134	724	357	583	743	809
0861	HSV	RDU	8134	455	47	76	35	76
0862	HSV	RDG	8134	700				
0863	HSV	RIC	8134	547	63	78	49	78
0868	HSV	DCA	8134	603	1536	3096	5087	4915
0879	IND	SFO	1841	1949	11604	10692	12668	13910
0880	IND	TUO	5564	1478	710	2017	1498	1364
0900	JAX	MIA	3051	326	13841	17659	18604	19609
0905	JAX	NYC	3051	838	34871	43303	43205	49796
0908	JAX	PHL	3051	758	3517	4572	5754	6247
0912	JAX	PVD	3051	977	635	711	1079	1270
0914	JAX	PIE	3051	186	106	159	166	236
0915	JAX	TPA	3051	171	2894	3109	3358	3861
0916	JAX	DCA	3051	647	7527	8183	8873	10269
0921	MKC	LAS	1841	1143	1173	1337	2422	1768
0923	MKC	LAX	1841	1356	30390	35590	41196	48335
0928	MKC	MLI	1841	273	532	709	773	1071
0930	MKC	NYC	1841	1097	56616	56986	72559	71804
0934	MKC	PHL	1841	1038	12657	8960	11186	12239
0935	MKC	PIT	1986	781	4792	4721	5594	7259
0944	MKC	SFO	1841	1506	20850	22240	28975	28544
0948	MKC	SBN	1841	475	382	574	722	852
0951	MKC	TOL	1841	609	1052	1330	1409	1337
0956	MKC	DCA	1841	945	14889	15859	18194	21928
0967	TYS	PHL	0986	552	1959	1327	2124	3222
0968	TYS	PHL	2355	552	1959	1327	2124	3222
0975	LAS	PIT	1986	1919	972	1821	2868	2819
0998	LIT	BNA	2355	325	904	798	925	916
0999	LIT	NYC	2355	1081	7195	8783	10680	10455
1001	LIT	DCA	2355	892	2968	4510	3896	5334
1008	LAX	MRY	6503	271	3427	3766	6880	12379
1009	LAX	OKC	2355	1181	9181	11238	15905	18346
1010	LAX	PIT	1986	2136	34210	42262	57063	71252
1011	LAX	PIT	2355	2136	34210	42262	57063	71252
1012	LAX	SBA	6503	87	382	516	563	654
1013	LAX	TUO	5564	440	10879	16319	17823	18458
1014	LAX	TUL	2355	1266	10911	11026	15486	17363
1015	SDF	NHV	7253	714	55	46	64	27
1016	SDF	NYC	7253	652	28911	39243	46643	37692
1017	SDF	OKC	2355	678	352	749	696	643
1018	SDF	PIT	2355	344	2754	3993	3099	5044
1019	SDF	PVD	7253	799	384	664	882	903
1020	SDF	TUO	5564	1480	230	307	327	538
1021	SDF	TUL	2355	582	605	491	756	680
1026	MCN	NYC	2355	763	2202	3382	3511	3560
1027	MCN	PHL	2355	680	415	442	813	892
1028	MCN	DCA	2355	559	712	813	1053	1656
1049	MEM	BNA	2355	197	4840	5073	5339	5518
1050	MEM	NYC	2355	957	21149	22878	29883	28265
1051	MEM	PHL	0986	881	2691	3412	3802	4443
1052	MEM	PHL	2355	881	2691	3412	3802	4443
1053	MEM	PIT	2355	660	1278	1698	1767	1690
1054	MEM	SAT	2355	631	1394	1845	1960	1976
1056	MEM	DCA	2355	765	7876	8831	9487	9994
1068	MIA	NYC	3051	1092	711077	894021	9487	9994
1071	MIA	PHL	3051	1019	60419	90344	46798	74665
1075	MIA	PVD	3051	1214	5728	9342	120507	118865
1077	MIA	PIE	3051	204	843	1156	1782	2710

Serial (1)	City Names (2)		Docket (3)	Distance (4)	*Origin and Destination Passenger-Miles* 1954 (5)	1955 (6)	1956 (7)	1957 (8)
1078	MIA	TPA	3051	205	12418	16157	19142	22159
1079	MIA	DCA	3051	923	61626	73709	82469	97155
1086	MKE	PHL	0986	694	4799	5539	6306	10600
1087	MKE	PDX	2190	1719	1229	2190	1586	2771
1090	MKE	SEA	2190	1692	4311	6950	4399	5850
1091	MKE	GEG	2190	1463	760	1065	1863	1122
1098	MOB	PHL	2355	966	1193	2586	3453	3918
1099	MOB	PIT	2355	810	2200	2653	2495	1937
1100	MOB	PVD	3051	1201	234	296	546	281
1101	MOB	RDU	2355	647	126	201	252	201
1102	MOB	RIC	2355	769	139	129	239	289
1104	MOB	DCA	2355	843	3375	6180	4800	4394
1105	MOB	INT	2355	584	7	45	68	91
1136	MRY	SFO	6503	86	853	930	1265	1410
1137	MRY	SBA	6503	194	123	214	310	431
1149	MGM	NYC	2355	894	3347	5067	6055	7031
1150	MGM	PHL	2355	812	232	580	749	1034
1151	MGM	DCA	2355	689	2633	2507	3976	3573
1163	BNA	NHV	7253	827	10	21	32	21
1164	BNA	NYC	7253	761	16887	20894	24742	25721
1165	BNA	NYC	2355	761	16887	20894	24742	25721
1166	BNA	OKC	2355	605	699	660	975	928
1168	BNA	PVD	7253	913	272	272	272	510
1169	BNA	SAT	2355	823	727	920	930	1080
1170	BNA	TUL	2355	515	502	749	823	984
1172	BNA	DCA	2355	569	7485	8299	9253	10459
1181	NHV	NYC	3051	68	97	60	106	106
1182	NHV	PHL	3051	150	7	29	7	25
1184	NHV	PVD	3051	86	4	1	2	
1185	NHV	RIC	3051	355	32	32	46	119
1188	NHV	DCA	3051	273	319	212	457	418
1189	NHV	ILG	3051	175				2
1194	MSY	NYC	2355	1171	67163	80255	90592	109879
1197	MSY	PHL	0986	1089	5492	6851	8933	12472
1198	MSY	PHL	2355	1089	5492	6851	8933	12472
1199	MSY	PIT	2355	919	3381	5328	4492	7108
1200	MSY	PVD	3051	1324	929	1239	1187	1359
1201	MSY	RDU	2355	776	958	1160	1119	1039
1202	MSY	RIC	2355	895	860	1023	1058	1500
1204	MSY	DCA	2355	966	17116	17355	18874	25907
1205	MSY	INT	2355	710	221	46	101	166
1206	NYC	PHF	2355	292	1753	3093	7554	5010
1207	NYC	PHF	3051	292	1753	3093	7554	5010
1208	NYC	ORF	2355	296	20948	21745	23222	23753
1209	NYC	ORF	3051	296	20948	21745	23222	23753
1210	NYC	OKC	2355	1328	12102	17471	21010	23720
1213	NYC	PHL	0986	83	2570	2898	3738	4485
1214	NYC	PHL	2355	83	2570	2898	3738	4485
1215	NYC	PHL	3051	83	2570	2898	3738	4485
1216	NYC	PIT	0986	317	62391	76539	89619	93777
1217	NYC	PIT	1986	317	62391	76539	89619	93777
1218	NYC	PIT	2355	317	62391	76539	89619	93777
1219	NYC	PDX	2190	2445	28066	33628	42591	45643
1220	NYC	PVD	3051	154	12054	13611	15943	18916
1221	NYC	RDU	2355	426	8882	11635	13113	14171
1222	NYC	RIC	2355	289	12762	14761	14768	15877
1223	NYC	RIC	3051	289	12762	14761	14768	15877
1224	NYC	ROC	0986	250	21245	25463	31167	36666
1226	NYC	STL	7253	875	79022	94765	103228	113875
1227	NYC	PIE	3051	1021	4247	9755	5375	10883
1228	NYC	SAT	2355	1584	58048	63938	73081	75675
1229	NYC	SFO	1841	2571	444225	574374	617389	663145
1231	NYC	SEA	2190	2408	92972	108812	131101	161403
1233	NYC	SHV	2355	1232	5141	6566	8648	9545
1234	NYC	GEG	2190	2179	10452	13738	14361	14021
1235	NYC	TPA	3051	1005	62359	77932	93649	100626
1237	NYC	TOL	0986	501	8779	14426	15084	15468
1238	NYC	TUO	5564	2124	18969	25016	27970	30262
1239	NYC	TUL	2355	1231	20019	22324	28661	27973
1244	NYC	DCA	2355	205	101088	116599	129041	135163

Serial (1)	City Names (2)		Docket (3)	Distance (4)	Origin and Destination Passenger-Miles 1954 (5)	1955 (6)	1956 (7)	1957 (8)
1245	NYC	DCA	3051	205	101088	116599	129041	135163
1246	NYC	HLG	2355	358	1242	1884	2434	2880
1247	NYC	HLG	3051	358	1242	1884	2434	2880
1249	NYC	INT	2355	467	2786	4152	4632	5834
1250	PHF	PHL	2355	219	244	546	1517	1463
1251	PHF	PHL	3051	219	244	546	1517	1463
1253	PHF	DCA	3051	136	1966	2059	2567	2858
1255	ORF	PHL	2355	222	4738	4028	4150	3858
1256	ORF	PHL	3051	222	4738	4028	4150	3858
1258	ORF	DCA	3051	146	7517	8964	10372	11190
1269	OKC	PHL	2355	1260	1621	2096	2964	2850
1270	OKC	PHX	2355	842	985	974	2134	1488
1271	OKC	PIT	2355	1014	935	1107	1344	3414
1273	OKC	STL	2355	459	3263	3240	4170	4642
1274	OKC	SFO	2355	1388	7614	5359	8228	7470
1276	OKC	AVP	2355	1250	162	81	97	260
1279	OKC	TUO	5564	805	449	826	648	554
1280	OKC	TUL	2355	98	647	610	693	498
1281	OKC	DCA	2355	1153	6775	7164	9458	10642
1296	ORL	PVD	3051	1074	418	586	446	614
1297	ORL	PIE	3051	94	28	39	73	30
1298	ORL	TPA	3051	77	324	460	542	476
1314	PNS	PVD	3051	1180	92	260	444	460
1315	PIA	TUO	5564	1322		68	223	171
1316	PHL	PIT	1986	259	18090	22006	23861	35427
1317	PHL	PIT	2355	259	18090	22006	23861	35427
1322	PHL	PVD	3051	235	989	1008	1521	1567
1323	PHL	RDU	2355	345	1852	1708	2377	2578
1324	PHL	RIC	2355	207	2061	2263	2693	2954
1325	PHL	RIC	3051	207	2061	2263	2693	2954
1329	PHL	PIE	3051	942	1126	453	2498	795
1336	PHL	TPA	3051	926	5633	8631	9630	14265
1337	PHL	TOL	0986	455	2768	3909	3856	6003
1339	PHL	TUO	5564	2059	1418	2596	4122	4041
1340	PHL	TUL	2355	1163	1980	2373	3265	3341
1344	PHL	DCA	2355	123	4505	5048	6301	8222
1345	PHL	DCA	3051	123	4505	5048	6301	8222
1347	PHL	HLG	0986	295	230	364	268	264
1348	PHL	HLG	2355	295	230	364	268	264
1349	PHL	HLG	3051	295	230	364	268	264
1351	PHL	INT	2355	384	379	454	599	928
1353	PHL	YNG	0986	300	1017	1197	1380	1458
1354	PHX	PIT	2355	1828	2114	3826	4491	4467
1355	PHX	TUO	5564	106	1393	1648	1620	1550
1356	PHX	TUL	2355	932	787	872	1369	1260
1357	PIT	PDX	1986	2165	1744	2392	2279	3489
1359	PIT	PVD	3051	458	1083	1286	2333	1839
1366	PIT	SAN	2355	2117	3797	3660	4238	6990
1367	PIT	SFO	1986	2264	21485	27489	35818	36142
1368	PIT	SFO	2355	2264	21485	27489	35818	36142
1371	PIT	SEA	1986	2138	7615	9533	10978	10589
1372	PIT	SBN	1986	337	547	433	889	806
1373	PIT	GEG	1986	1908	1041	942	1413	1537
1375	PIT	TOL	1986	203	931	1343	1121	1050
1377	PIT	TUO	5564	1807	1198	1526	2584	2701
1378	PIT	TUL	2355	917	1680	2467	·2515	4816
1382	PIT	YNG	1986	57	161	151	602	174
1396	PDX	DCA	2190	2354	12271	12302	16310	18208
1403	PVD	RIC	3051	436	294	294	402	391
1404	PVD	PIE	3051	1158	90	120	286	466
1407	PVD	SAV	3051	858	122	22	89	
1410	PVD	TLH	3051	1063		41	96	
1411	PVD	TPA	3051	1142	1469	1736	2909	1974
1415	PVD	DCA	3051	358	3043	3532	4877	5603
1416	PVD	PBI	3051	1152	868	1018	913	1692
1417	PVD	ILG	3051	260	101	145	67	189
1426	RNO	SLC	1841	428	1396	1151	1290	1697
1427	RNO	SFO	1841	185	17311	18944	21606	21688
1429	RIC	PIE	3051	738		19	28	86
1430	RIC	TPA	3051	722	412	375	610	854

Serial (1)	City Names (2)		Docket (3)	Distance (4)	Origin and Destination Passenger-Miles 1954 (5)	1955 (6)	1956 (7)	1957 (8)
1431	RIC	DCA	3051	97	2138	2176	2598	2712
1445	STL	TUO	5564	1249	1786	1217	1526	2338
1446	STL	TUL	2355	361	3895	4068	4730	5368
1448	PIE	SAV	3051	311	12	16	24	8
1451	PIE	TPA	3051	17		3		
1453	PIE	DCA	3051	832	1092	248	1611	854
1456	PIE	PBI	3051	175	75	138	52	225
1463	SLC	SFO	1841	600	20911	22198	26215	28680
1465	SAT	DCA	2355	1388	18368	18892	23691	22735
1467	SFO	SBA	6503	277	2016	2394	3460	4342
1468	SFO	AVP	1841	2477	1899	2382	2350	1899
1470	SFO	TUO	5564	753	4297	5286	5951	6421
1471	SFO	TUL	2355	1461	6438	6609	7179	6894
1472	SFO	DCA	1841	2442	107364	132476	144825	168952
1488	SAV	TPA	3051	296	284	334	227	361
1494	AVP	TUO	5564	2041	53	53	185	238
1495	AVP	TUL	2355	1153	164	89	29	119
1498	SEA	DCA	2190	2329	28642	36756	40873	55437
1507	GEG	DCA	2190	2100	3576	3903	5132	5105
1511	TPA	DCA	3051	817	10493	13265	14338	18864
1514	TPA	PBI	3051	171	569	782	851	1107
1527	TUO	TUL	5564	898	910	922	501	758
1528	TUO	DCA	5564	1956	2644	4627	4373	6534
1532	TUL	DCA	355	1058	5817	6780	8279	8211

Index

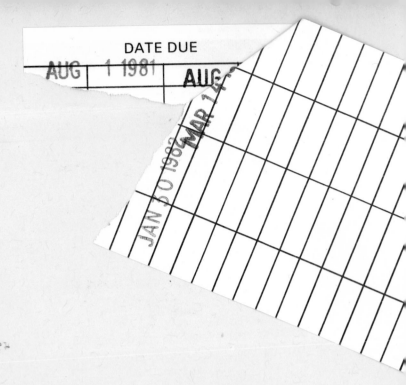